EFFECTIVE EXECUTIVE'S GUIDE TO

The Eight Steps for Designing, Building and Managing Dreamweaver 3 Web Sites

DREAMWEAVER WEB SITES

EFFECTIVE EXECUTIVE'S GUIDE TO

The Eight Steps for Designing, Building and Managing Dreamweaver 3 Web Sites

DREAMWEAVER WEB SITES

Stephen L. Nelson
Jason Gerend

REDMOND
TECHNOLOGY
PRESS

Effective Executive's Guide to Dreamweaver Web Sites:
The Eight Steps for Designing, Building and Managing Dreamweaver3 Web Sites

Copyright © 2000 Stephen L. Nelson and Jason Gerend

All rights reserved. No part of this book may be reproduced in any form or by any method or any means without the prior written permission of the publisher.

Published by
Redmond Technology Press
8581 154th Avenue NE
Redmond, WA 98052
www.redtechpress.com

Library of Congress Catalog Card No: applied for

ISBN 0-9672981-9-9

Printed and bound in the United States of America.

9 8 7 6 5 4 3 2 1

Distributed by
Independent Publishers Group
814 N. Franklin St.
Chicago, IL 60610
www.ipgbook.com

Product and company names mentioned herein may be the trademarks of their respective owners.

In the preparation of this book, both the author and the publisher have made every effort to provide current, correct, and comprehensible information. Nevertheless, inadvertent errors can occur and software and the principles and regulations concerning business often change. Furthermore, the application and impact of principles, rules, and laws can vary widely from case to case because of the unique facts involved. For these reasons, the author and publisher specifically disclaim any liability or loss that is incurred as a consequence of the use and application, directly or indirectly, of any information presented in this book. If legal or other expert assistance is needed, the services of a professional should be sought.

Contents at a Glance

	Introduction	xvii
Step 1	Learn the Logic	1
Step 2	Develop a Content Strategy	25
Step 3	Lay a Foundation	47
Step 4	Collect and Organize Your Content	71
Step 5	Set Up Your Site	101
Step 6	Create Your Pages	127
Step 7	Polish Your Pages	169
Step 8	Deploy Your Web Site	211

Appendix A	**Setting Up Your Web Site on a Local Server**	**237**
Appendix B	**Creating Web Stores**	**241**
Appendix C	**Using Frames**	**253**
	Glossary	**263**
	Index	**273**

Contents

Introduction   xvii

What This Book Assumes About You xvii
How This Book Is Organized xviii
    Step 1: Learn the Logic xviii
    Step 2: Develop a Content Strategy xviii
    Step 3: Lay a Foundation xviii
    Step 4: Collect and Organize Your Content xix
    Step 5: Set Up Your Site xix
    Step 6: Create Your Pages xix
    Step 7: Polish Your Pages xix
    Step 8: Deploy Your Web Site xix
    Appendix A: Setting Up Your Web Site on a Local Server xx
    Appendix B: Creating Web Stores xx
    Appendix C: Using Frames xx
Conventions Used in This Book xx

Step 1 Learn the Logic 1

Why Use Dreamweaver? 2
What Is the Internet? 3
    Connecting to the Internet 3
    Methods of Communication Over the Internet 6
How Do Web Pages Work? 10
Introducing HTML Code 11
    Common HTML Tags 13
    Hyperlink Addresses 15
    New Web Page Technologies 18
Why It Makes Sense to Have a Web Site 19
    Advertising 19
    Publishing 19
    Information Collection 19
    Transaction Processing 20
What Makes a Good Web Site? 21
    Useful Content 21
    Easy Navigation 22
    Visual Appeal 23
Summary 23

Step 2 ## Develop a Content Strategy   **25**

- Common Web Site Goals 26
  - Advertising Your Company or Organization 26
  - Selling or Advertising a Product or Service 29
  - Disseminating Information 31
  - Generating Online Advertising Revenue 33
  - Selling Digital Content 35
  - Supporting a Product 37
  - Complementing a Curriculum 41
- Determining Your Web Site's Goals 43
- Determining Your Technology Requirements 44
- Methodologies for Developing Your Content 45
- Summary 46

Step 3 ## Lay a Foundation   **47**

- Domain Name Background 48
  - IP Address 48
  - DNS 48
  - Domain Hierarchy 49
- Why You Need Your Own Domain Name 50

Choosing a Domain Name 51
    Picking a Host Name 51
    Picking a Top-Level Domain 52
    Valid Domain Names 53
    Domain Name Disputes 54
Choosing a Registrar 55
Choosing a Web Hosting Service 55
    Comparing Host Features 56
    Local vs. National Web Hosting 62
    Finding a Web Hosting Company 62
Signing Up for Service 64
Summary 69

Step 4 Collect and Organize Your Content   71

Determining What Needs to Be Done 72
Creating a Central Location for Content 73
Establishing a File Naming Convention 76
Collecting Existing Digital Content 77
    Types of Digital Content to Look For 77
    Locating Existing Digital Content 78
    Converting Existing Data to an Appropriate Format 83

Creating New Digital Content 88
    Digital Images 88
    Documents 95
Organizing Your Content and Planning Your Web Site 97
    Organizing Your Content 97
    Creating Your Site Plan 98
Summary 99

Step 5   Set Up Your Site   101

Defining a New Local Site 102
Configuring Dreamweaver to Work with a Firewall 105
    Opening Local Sites 107
Overview of the Site Window 108
Creating the Initial Structure 110
    Adding New Pages and Folders 110
    Site Map Overview 113
    Working with Links in the Site Map 114
    Moving and Copying Files 118
    Renaming Files 119
    Deleting Files and Folders 119
    Adding Design Notes to Files 120
Checking Files In and Out 122
Summary 125

Step 6 **Create Your Pages** — **127**

- Overview of the Dreamweaver Interface 127
    - Introducing the Document Window 128
    - The Tag Selector 129
    - The Rest of the Status Bar 130
    - Floating Palettes 132
    - Introducing Dreamweaver's Menus 138
- Opening, Creating, and Saving Pages 139
    - Opening and Closing Web Pages 139
    - Creating New Pages 140
    - Saving Web Pages 140
    - Previewing Web Pages 141
- Working with Text and Hyperlinks 141
    - Importing Text 142
    - Entering and Formatting Text 149
    - Creating Hyperlinks 151
- Working with Images 155
    - Inserting Images 155
    - Resizing Images 158
    - Adjusting Image Layout 160
    - Setting Alternative Image Representations 162
    - Creating Image Maps 163
- Adjusting Page Properties 165
- Summary 167

Step 7	**Polish Your Pages**	**169**

Creating an Effective Home Page 170
    Choosing the Best Content for Your Home Page 170
    Working with Navigation Bars 171
    Making Your Home Page Visually Appealing 176
    Preparing Your Home Page for Search Engines 177

Making Your Pages Look Consistent 179
    Creating Templates for Pages 179
    Using the Library 182

Advanced Web Page Layout 184
    Using Layers 184
    How Dreamweaver Positions Layers 188
    Working with Tables 191

Ensuring Proper Display of Your Pages 196
    Making Your Pages Compatible with Multiple Browsers 196
    Making Your Home Page Resolution-Independent 206

Summary 209

Step 8	**Deploy Your Web Site**	**211**

Testing Your Web Site 212
    Testing and Fixing Hyperlinks 212
    Testing Your Site in Different Browsers 217
    Usability Testing 222

Contents   **xiii**

Publishing Your Web Site 223
Publicizing Your Web Site 225
    Submitting Your Site to Search Engines 226
    Online Advertising 229
    Using Newsgroups to Gain Exposure 232
    Creating a Mailing List 232
    Offline Publicizing 234
Monitoring Your Web Site 234
Summary 236

Appendix A Setting Up Your Web Site on a Local Server — 237

Appendix B Creating Web Stores — 241

How Web Stores Work 242
    What the Shopper Sees 242
    What the Web Server Does 244
E-Commerce Options for Your Company 244
    Creating a Non-Interactive Catalog 245
    Using a Secure Form to Collect Orders 245
    Using a Shopping Cart System 248

Appendix C	**Using Frames**	**253**
	Creating Frames	254
	Saving Frames	259
	Splitting and Deleting Frames	259
	Hyperlinks and Frames	259
	Creating a NoFrames Page	261

Glossary 263

Index 273

INTRODUCTION

Effective Executive's Guide to Dreamweaver Web Sites focuses on the process of creating a Web site by breaking down the work into eight distinct steps. Using this approach, we pick a single construction method for building a Web site and then follow that method through from start to finish. Such an approach means we give you the information you need to prepare a Web site for your business or organization, but we don't provide encyclopedic coverage of the Dreamweaver program.

We think breaking the process of creating a Web site into steps works better for the typical Dreamweaver user—and especially for the business professional who never aspires to become a Dreamweaver expert or professional Web site creator. Breaking the process into steps forces us (the authors and the reader) to focus on the final product—a polished professional Web site. And breaking the process into steps also lets us create a book that filters everything we *could* say about Dreamweaver into just what the executive user *should* know.

What This Book Assumes About You

This book makes two assumptions about you. First, the book assumes that you're not and don't want to become a Dreamweaver expert. Rather, we assume you're a professional working in business, a nonprofit organization, or perhaps public service. We assume that you want to use Dreamweaver to build and enhance the Web sites you make.

The book also assumes that you're familiar working with the Microsoft Windows operating system. In the pages that follow, as a result, you won't get detailed information about how to choose menu commands or select dialog box buttons and boxes. If you don't already possess this knowledge, you'll need to acquire it either by using the online help available in Windows, by getting a quick tutorial from someone such as a co-worker, or by reading a good introductory book.

> **NOTE** *While Dreamweaver is available for the Macintosh, this book covers the Windows version. If you have the Macintosh version, you can still use this book; however, Dreamweaver will look and act slightly differently than shown here. The difference is slight though—in almost every aspect, the two versions are identical.*

How This Book Is Organized

This book breaks the process of building a Dreamweaver Web site into the following eight steps:

Step 1: Learn the Logic

The best place to start a discussion of building a Web site with Dreamweaver is with information about how the Internet and Web work, why it makes sense to have a Web site, and what makes Web sites effective. In Step 1, we provide this information.

Step 2: Develop a Content Strategy

Probably the single most important step for you, the executive user, is determining the purpose of the Web site, and what kind of content is required to fulfill this purpose. Step 2 gives you some common goals for Web sites, makes suggestions to help you determine the goals for your Web site, and offers some methodologies for developing your content.

Step 3: Lay a Foundation

Once you understand how Web sites work and have a content strategy, your next step is to prepare the foundation of your Web site by obtaining a domain name and locating a company to host your site.

Step 4: Collect and Organize Your Content

After deciding on the purpose and content for your Web site, it's time to actually gather content and organize it for use on your site. Besides simply collecting existing content, this also involves creating or digitizing new content, creating a central location to store content, establishing a file naming convention to use on your Web site, organizing your content, and drawing up a plan for your Web site.

Step 5: Set Up Your Site

The actual process of creating a Web site page by page begins with Step 5, and in this step we walk you through setting up your Web site in Dreamweaver, understanding the Dreamweaver Site window interface, managing files in Dreamweaver, and coordinating the work of multiple users when creating the site.

Step 6: Create Your Pages

After setting up your Web site in Dreamweaver, you need to create pages for your Web site. Step 6 shows you how to do this by introducing you to Dreamweaver's Document window, where all page editing is done, and by showing you how to create basic Web pages. This includes working with text, hyperlinks, and images, and adjusting the properties of Web pages.

Step 7: Polish Your Pages

Once you've created your Web site, you can then refine your Web pages to make them more effective and professional. In Step 7, we cover a number of special tasks that you should perform to polish your home page, ways of making the pages in your Web site more consistent and effective, and how to create advanced layouts using layers and tables.

Step 8: Deploy Your Web Site

The last step in the Web site creation process is the actual deployment of your site. This includes testing the site for errors, publishing it to the Internet, submitting your site to search engines, and publicizing your site elsewhere—both on and off the Internet. These tasks are all covered in Step 8, along with monitoring your site for errors after it is posted and tracking the amount and kinds of visitors that your site receives.

Appendix A: Setting Up Your Web Site on a Local Server

Appendix A shows you how to set up a Windows 2000 computer to act as a Web server, in case you want to create a remote site on your local network that multiple users can use to coordinate their work on your Web site using Dreamweaver's Check In/Out feature.

Appendix B: Creating Web Stores

Web stores aren't as easily created using Dreamweaver; however, in Appendix B we discuss the various methods you can use to create a Web store and how to choose a method that's suitable for your company.

Appendix C: Using Frames

Frames can be tricky to implement properly, and they are a disaster when implemented poorly. Fortunately, Dreamweaver makes it easy to create frames and modify them to suit your needs. This appendix shows you the essentials you need in order to properly create a Web site with frames.

NOTE Effective Executive's Guide to Dreamweaver Web Sites *also includes a glossary of Dreamweaver and Web site terms.*

Conventions Used in This Book

This book uses three conventions worth mentioning here. The first is this. We view this book as a conversation among professionals. That means the pronoun *we* refers to us, the authors. And that means the pronoun *you* refers to you, the reader. In this case, this conversation style means you will frequently see the pronoun *we*, because two of us, Gerend and Nelson, wrote the book. Although *we* has sometimes been used as a stilted self-reference by writers, please don't take it that way. Think of us as workshop presenters or discussion group facilitators, with jackets off and ties loosened. Think of us, in other words, as colleagues. Think of this book as a conversation.

Another convention is that we call the main chapters of the book *steps*. The benefit of doing this is that it lets us focus on and emphasize the process of creating a Web site. But, unfortunately, there's a slight problem with this convention. We also want to provide numbered step-by-step instructions in the chapters, or steps, of the book. Whenever some task can't be described in a sentence or two, in fact, we'll use numbered steps to make sure you can follow the discussion. So this "chapters-called-steps" convention may confuse matters. If we say that "in the preceding step, we described how to do such-and-such," are we referring to the preceding chapter? Or a preceding numbered step? You see the difficulty.

Here's what we've come up with. Whenever we use the term *step* to refer to a chapter, we'll give you the entire step name. For example, if we say that in "Step 2: Develop a Content Strategy" we describe how to do such-and-such, you'll know what we mean. If we don't give you the step or section name, you'll know we're talking about the preceding numbered step.

A third convention concerns references to the buttons and boxes in Dreamweaver windows and dialog boxes. Even though they don't appear that way onscreen, this book capitalizes the initial letter of the words that label buttons and boxes. For example, the box that is actually labeled "Save as type" gets referenced in these pages as the Save As Type box. The initial caps, then, will be a signal to you that we're referring to a label.

Introduction **xxi**

Step 1

LEARN THE LOGIC

Featuring:
- Why Use Dreamweaver?
- What Is the Internet?
- How Do Web Pages Work?
- Introducing HTML Code
- Why It Makes Sense to Have a Web Site
- What Makes a Good Web Site?

The Web is a land of opportunity for many companies and organizations—a whole new way of reaching customers and providing information, products, and services to your clientele. To take advantage of this vast new resource, you need to create a Web site for your company or organization, and Macromedia Dreamweaver provides an excellent tool for accomplishing this task.

Before we launch into the reasons for setting up a Web site, it's important to gain an understanding of the Internet, its many methods of communication, and how Dreamweaver figures into the equation. In this step, you'll find out how Web pages work, determine what makes Web sites effective, and learn why it makes sense to have one. When you're finished with this step, you'll have all the background knowledge necessary to start the process of building a Web site for your company or organization.

Why Use Dreamweaver?

Dreamweaver is an extremely powerful Web-site-creation tool. You can use it to make all your Web pages, modify existing pages, and manage you entire Web site. Creating basic pages with Dreamweaver is easy, but this program really excels when it comes to developing complex pages and streamlining the entire process. You can lay out pages using advanced positioning tools such as those used in desktop publishing, convert these to tables for backwards compatibility with older browsers, create animated rollover buttons, and animate page effects. You can also use Dreamweaver's Library, Templates, HTML Styles, and CSS Styles features to give your Web site a consistent look and vastly reduce the amount of work involved in making sitewide changes. Dreamweaver also provides a powerful History feature so that you can record and replay Web-page-creation tasks.

With this said, Dreamweaver isn't the most intuitive Web page editor on the market. Users of Microsoft Office programs may find themselves a little lost when looking for a nonexistent toolbar button or navigating menus that are different from the ones in Office. If you plan to never use any of Dreamweaver's advanced functions and don't like learning new programs, you might be better off picking a simpler program, such as Microsoft FrontPage. However, if you're willing to accept a slightly larger learning curve, you'll find that Dreamweaver is a great program to grow into. In most aspects, it is more powerful and more efficient than other Web-page-creation programs.

> **TIP** *If you need to collect information from visitors using forms on your Web site, you might want to use FrontPage to supplement the work you do with Dreamweaver. FrontPage, when paired with FrontPage Server Extensions support from your Internet service provider, can easily make forms work—something that is a bit tricky with Dreamweaver.*

In keeping with the goal of this book—to provide you with the information you need to quickly create your Web site and manage it effectively—we don't delve into all of Dreamweaver's features. We show you how to get your site created and polished up, along with describing how to use a few of Dreamweaver's more powerful features.

What Is the Internet?

The Internet is a worldwide amalgamation of computers that are capable of "talking" to each other over some form of network connection. As such, the Internet is very similar to the telephone network; in fact, a large amount of Internet traffic is carried over the same physical cables as our telephone systems.

To use the Internet, you must connect to it. Once connected, there are a number of ways of communicating over it, such as by sending e-mail messages, browsing Web pages, or by using newsgroups, chat, or Internet telephones.

Connecting to the Internet

There are several ways of connecting to the Internet. If you are a home or small business user, you probably connect to the Internet using a modem. To connect, you dial your Internet service provider (ISP) with your modem, which is connected to a normal telephone line. A server at the ISP answers the phone, and then connects you to the Internet. This method is available anywhere there are phone lines, and it is relatively inexpensive (typically $10 to $20 per month). However, it is somewhat slow. A 56-kilobit modem can reach a maximum download speed of 53 kilobits per second (Kbps)—taking about two and a half to three minutes to download a 1 megabyte (MB) file, which is roughly the amount of text in this book and approximately two-thirds of the space on a 1.44MB floppy disk.

> **NOTE** *Connection speeds are discussed in terms of kilo**bits** per second (Kbps), while the size of files is discussed in kilo**bytes** (KB) or mega**bytes** (MB). They measure the same thing, except that there are eight bits in a byte, or eight kilobits in a kilobyte, making the numbers different by a factor of eight.*

Digital Subscriber Line (DSL) service is a high-speed form of Internet access that is becoming increasingly popular for both home users and small businesses. DSL also uses a normal telephone line, but requires that the telephone company have special digital equipment installed nearby in order to provide service. Thus, DSL isn't available in all areas.

When available, the service provides constant Internet connectivity (there's no need in most DSL services to dial the ISP—you're always connected) that is much faster than a standard analog modem. DSL speeds range from 192Kbps to around 1.5Mbps, with typical speeds starting at around 300 to 600Kbps (faster speeds are usually available for more money). At 300Kbps, a 1MB file takes about 30 seconds to download. DSL typically costs about $50 per month for the lowest-speed service up to around $200 per month for the highest-speed service available.

DSL requires a DSL router or a DSL bridge—usually (but incorrectly) referred to as modems (technically a modem is a device that modulates and demodulates analog signals, and DSL is all digital). These devices may be included for free when you sign up for service or may cost several hundred dollars. Many can be plugged directly into the uplink port on your network hub to allow computers to easily share the Internet connection.

Cable modems are another increasingly popular form of high-speed Internet access, but they are generally not available for businesses. When available, they are always-on digital connections that work over cable TV lines. Cable modems provide speeds that vary between 300Kbps and 1.5Mbps. Cable modem service usually costs around $40 per month.

Integrated Services Digital Network (ISDN) is a somewhat older high-speed Internet connection that works over (mostly) normal telephone lines (a special ISDN digital connection needs to be configured by the telephone company). ISDN is popular with small businesses because of its wider service coverage (you can often get ISDN where you can't get DSL) and its ability to provide high-speed access. ISDN speeds typically start at 128Kbps and can be increased in increments of 64Kbps up to a maximum of roughly 1Mbps. ISDN costs roughly $40 per month per 64Kbps of bandwidth (data transfer speed). ISDN, like an analog modem, isn't on all the time, but the connection time is so fast that it appears almost instantaneous.

Medium-size companies that need to share an Internet connection with more than about a couple dozen users will need to use a more sophisticated connection option, such as Frame relay. Frame relay and other so-called leased lines generally guarantee a certain amount of bandwidth, provide a lot of it, and charge you amply for it. Frame relay service typically is available with 128Kbps of throughput for around $200 per month, or up to 1.5Mbps of throughput for $600 per month.

> **NOTE** *Wireless solutions are available, but until recently they have been used exclusively for mobile users owing to their very low speeds (9.6Kbps–28.8Kbps) and high per-minute costs. However, speeds are rising, with mobile wireless achieving 128Kbps and fixed wireless service (with roof-mounted antennas) reaching up to 10Mbps. As competition heats up, wireless costs will fall, as will the costs of other forms of Internet connections.*

The different throughput speeds can be challenging to interpret. Table 1-1 summarizes the transmission times to move the photograph shown in Figure 1-1. Note that the photograph—one of medium quality such as you might use as a full-page image in a Web page—is roughly 100 kilobytes in size.

CONNECTION	THROUGHPUT	TIME TO TRANSMIT
Modem	56.6Kbps	14 seconds
ISDN	128Kbps	6 seconds
Cable modem	300Kbps	2.5 seconds
DSL	600Kbps	1.2 seconds
Frame relay	1.5Mbps	Half a second

Table 1-1 Examples of transmission times for a simple photograph.

Figure 1-1 A photograph in an image editor such as you might use on a Web page.

Methods of Communication Over the Internet

Computers that have an Internet connection can communicate with other computers on the Internet in a number of ways. The most common ways to communicate are via e-mail and the World Wide Web (WWW, or just "the Web" for short). Other methods that can be useful as a way of promoting your Web site or company include newsgroups, chat rooms, and Internet telephone applications.

E-Mail

E-mail works like a virtual U.S. Postal Service. You write an e-mail message in an e-mail program—just like you might write a letter using a word processor or a pad of paper and a pen. Figure 1-2 shows an example of the Microsoft Outlook Express e-mail message window.

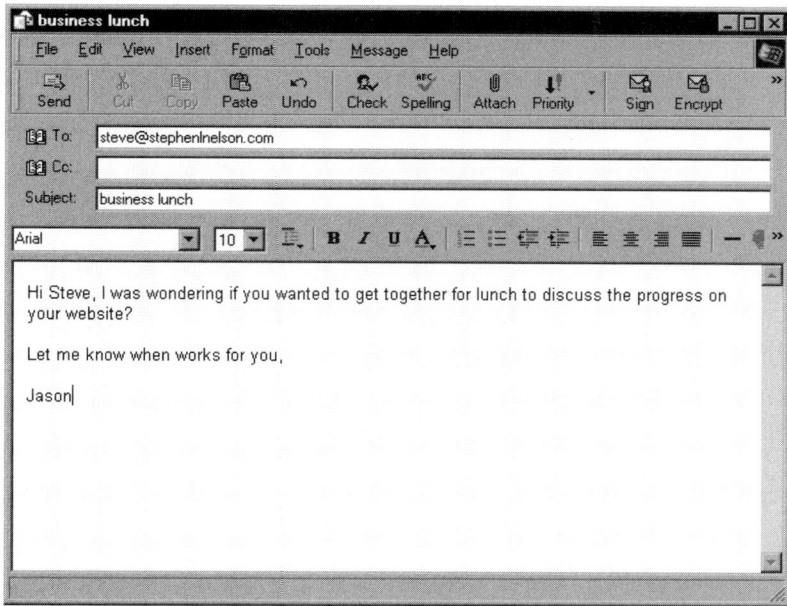

Figure 1-2   An e-mail message.

To send the message, you connect to the Internet and click the Send/Receive button in your mail software to deliver the message to your e-mail "post office" (mail server). This is analogous to getting in your car and driving to the post office to drop off a letter. At both the virtual and real post offices, the next step is to sort the message and deliver it to the post office nearest to the recipient. The recipient then has to connect to the Internet and download his or her new message—like driving to a post office to pick up mail at a post office box.

The Web

The Web works quite a bit differently from e-mail. A Web site consists of a number of specially formatted documents called Web pages that are linked to each other by hyperlinks and that are sitting on a server connected to the Internet. To view a Web site, you use your Web browser program to request a specific Web page from the server storing the Web site. You do this by either clicking a hyperlink or entering the address (known as a uniform resource locator, or URL) of the specific Web site. The Web server responds by sending the requested page across the Internet to your Web browser, which then reads the document, formats it appropriately, and displays it on the screen. Figure 1-3 shows an example Web page.

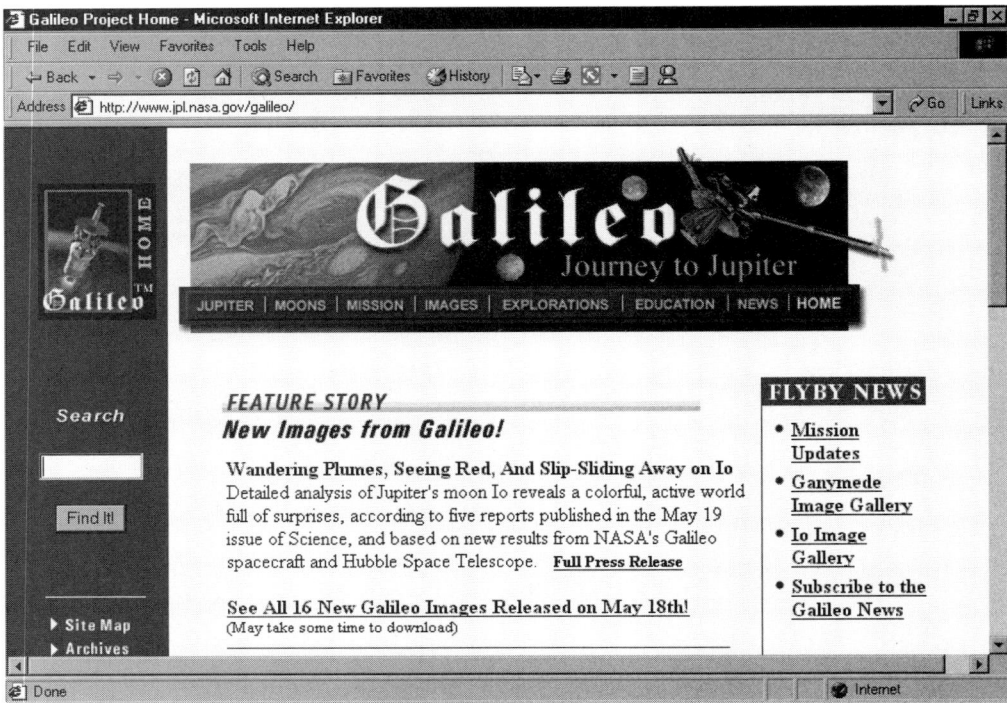

Figure 1-3   A Web page.

The Web has quickly become the most popular part of the Internet for three reasons. The first is the flexibility of the medium. Just about anything can be done in a Web page with a little ingenuity—from online shopping to online gaming. The second is how easy it is to use. Web browsers are fairly self-explanatory, and navigation consists of pointing at links and clicking a mouse button. The third reason is that companies and advertising are welcome on the Web—something that can't really be said of other parts of the Internet. (Although as described in "Step 8: Deploy Your Web Site," there are acceptable ways to use these other parts to draw visitors to your Web site.)

Newsgroups and Chat Groups

Newsgroups are very much like virtual bulletin boards. Anyone can post a message on the newsgroup for anyone else to see. All messages are stored on the news server, and you download only those messages you want to read. Figure 1-4 shows an example of a message in a newsgroup. Newsgroups are organized on different topics and subjects of interest, providing a fairly dynamic medium for communication.

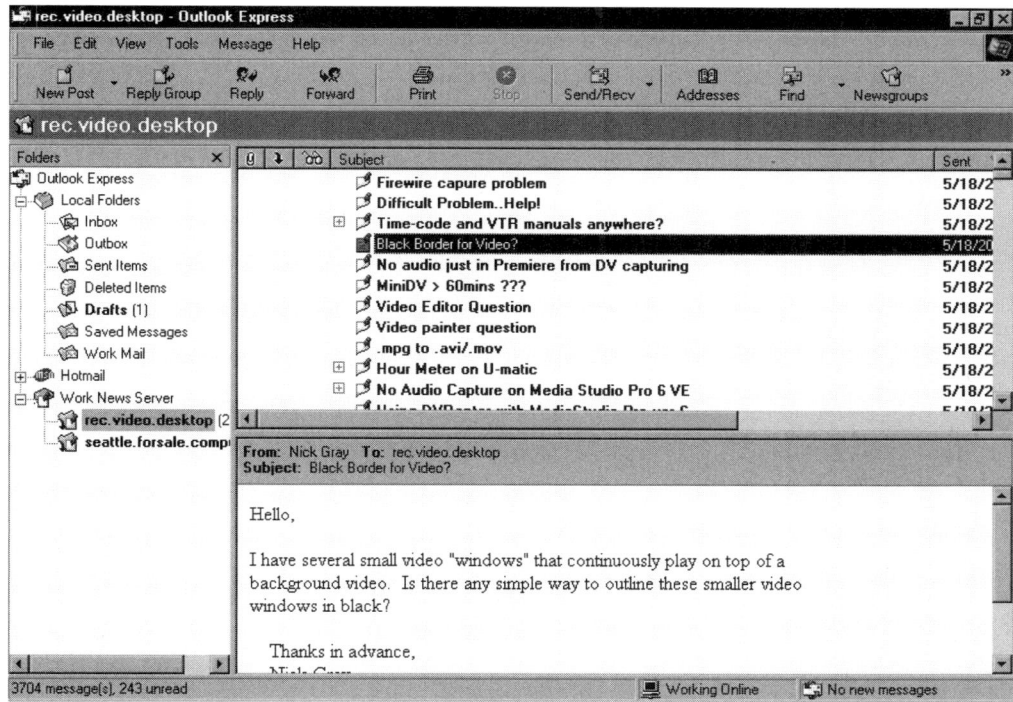

Figure 1-4 A message in a newsgroup.

Chat provides a way to have a real-time, text-based conversation with other users across the Internet. You chat with other people in a so-called chat room, which is basically a chat server that facilitates computer connections. You communicate by typing your message, which then appears instantly on your chat partner's screen.

Instant Messaging

A similar type of real-time, text-based Internet communication method is instant messaging—as provided by applications such as AOL Instant Messenger, ICQ, and MSN Messenger. These programs act as a sort of Internet-based text telephone. When you go online, you can determine which of your friends are online, and then contact them via the software and conduct a one-to-one text-based chat. This is similar to normal chat software, except that conversations are usually private and you can easily find your friends or colleagues when they're online. Figure 1-5 shows an example of a conversation using an instant messaging program.

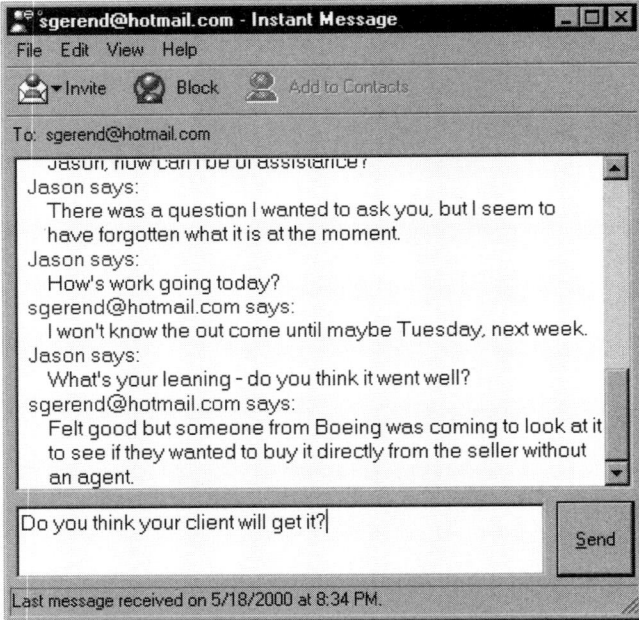

Figure 1-5   A real-time conversation using MSN Messenger.

Internet Telephone Services

Internet telephone software packages take the chat concept a step further. These software programs, such as CU-SeeMe, Net2Phone, or Microsoft NetMeeting, provide real-time voice (and occasionally video) communication with other users who are connected to the Internet and running the same software. Some programs even provide the ability to call normal telephones through the Internet. The chief reasons to use Internet telephone programs are to take advantage of enhanced communication features, such as video teleconferencing (videophone), have the ability to view another user's computer screen while talking, or save on long-distance telephone costs.

How Do Web Pages Work?

A Web page is simply a text document with special codes in it that tell a Web browser how to format and display the contents of the page. In addition to the special formatting, Web pages can also contain embedded images (that show up in the page onscreen but are stored separately on the server) and links (hyperlinks) to other pages.

In the old days, all Web pages were created manually in Hypertext Markup Language (HTML), which is discussed briefly in the next section. Although some people still create Web pages this way, it is far easier and faster to use a program such as Dreamweaver to create Web pages graphically—without having to write any code. However, if you know a little bit about how HTML pages are created and can recognize some common HTML tags, you'll be able to use Dreamweaver's highly effective Tag selector tool to select quickly and accurately exactly which parts of a Web page you want to edit.

Introducing HTML Code

It's highly probable that you'll never want to write a Web page from scratch in HTML, but it is useful to know what HTML looks like, especially if you want to use Dreamweaver's Tag selector tool. Although Dreamweaver allows you to easily work without touching a line of code, it helps to see how your pages are actually built and know that you could possibly add code yourself if need be. You'll also have a better idea about what someone you hire to perform HTML editing and coding is actually doing.

To begin, let's look at a simple sentence in HTML code. For example, every programmer's first assignment is to create code that displays the phrase "hello world," so let's do that in HTML.

```
<html>
<p>hello world</p>
</html>
```

This is a complete Web page. It's made up of two tags, which are the basic building blocks of an HMTL document. The first tag, *<html>*, states that the document is an HTML document and marks the beginning of the Web page. The second half of this tag, *</html>*, comes at the end of the document and signifies the end of the page. The next tag, *<p>*, signifies a new paragraph. The actual paragraph in this case is simply "hello world," and the paragraph ends with the second half of the paragraph tag, *</p>*.

> **TIP** *All HTML tags begin with a left angle bracket (<) and end with a right angle bracket (>). They usually begin and end similarly to the <html> and <p> tags—with the end of the tag the same as the beginning, except for the addition of a slash (/). For example, </p> closes the <p> tag, ending it.*

Now let's try to decipher something a little more complex. The next page includes an image and a hyperlink. Figure 1-6 shows what this page looks like in a Web browser. Here's the code for it:

```
<html>
<p><img src="images/un.gif"></p>
<p>hello <a href="http://www.un.org">world</a></p>
</html>
```

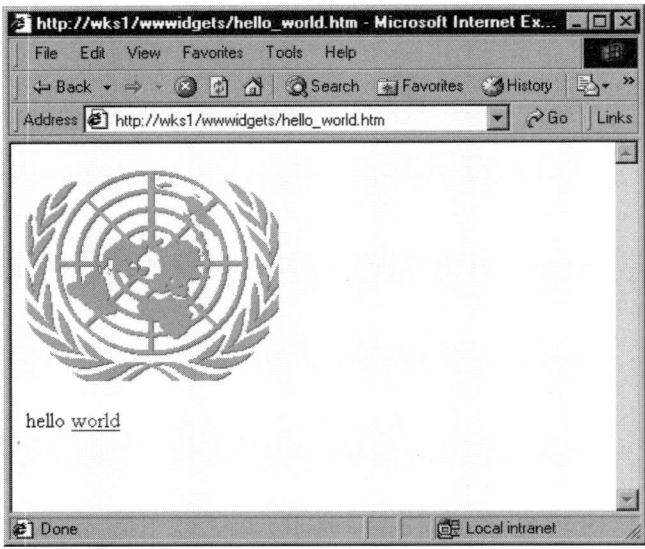

Figure 1-6   A simple Web page displayed in a Web browser.

Notice that the code includes an additional paragraph, which contains the *<img>* tag. This is the inline image tag (which means it is an image displayed in a Web page instead of an image that you can download), and it works like this. The tag starts with *<img* to indicate that it's an inline image, and then it contains one or more attributes. The only attribute used here is the *src* attribute, which contains the URL (address) of the image to be displayed. In this case, the image is the *images/un.gif* image. The tag ends with a right angle bracket (>).

NOTE *The acronym URL stands for uniform resource locator. Essentially, URLs identify files by name and give their precise location.*

Notice also that in the middle of the "hello world" paragraph there is now a hyperlink. The hyperlink tag starts with <*a* and ends with </*a*>, and in between are the attributes of the hyperlink and the text to which the hyperlink is attached. In this case, the only attribute is the *href* attribute (which is the URL of the hyperlink). You can use the *href* attribute by typing *href=* and then entering the URL to use, enclosed in quotes. The tag is partially closed by the right angle bracket (>) following the *href* attribute, but don't let this fool you. This is so that the text to which the hyperlink is actually attached, *world*, isn't thought of as another attribute. The hyperlink tag actually ends after this text with the </*a*> tag.

One final comment concerning HTML: If you create this same simple page using Dreamweaver, you will see some additional HTML codes, or tags. Dreamweaver sets up a more complex page, including header information that isn't displayed (using the <head> tag) and the title of the Web page (using the <title> tag). Dreamweaver also delineates the body of the page (using the <body> tag) and provides some additional information about the page's contents using meta tags (<meta>). Meta tags, among other things, can provide information to search engines using the <meta name="keywords"> tag so that search engines can more easily and accurately index the contents of a Web site.

Common HTML Tags

As mentioned previously, Dreamweaver includes a very useful tool called the Tag selector, as shown in Figure 1-7, that permits you to select parts of a Web page quickly and accurately. You'll find that learning to use this tool will save you a lot of time and frustration when creating Web pages in Dreamweaver.

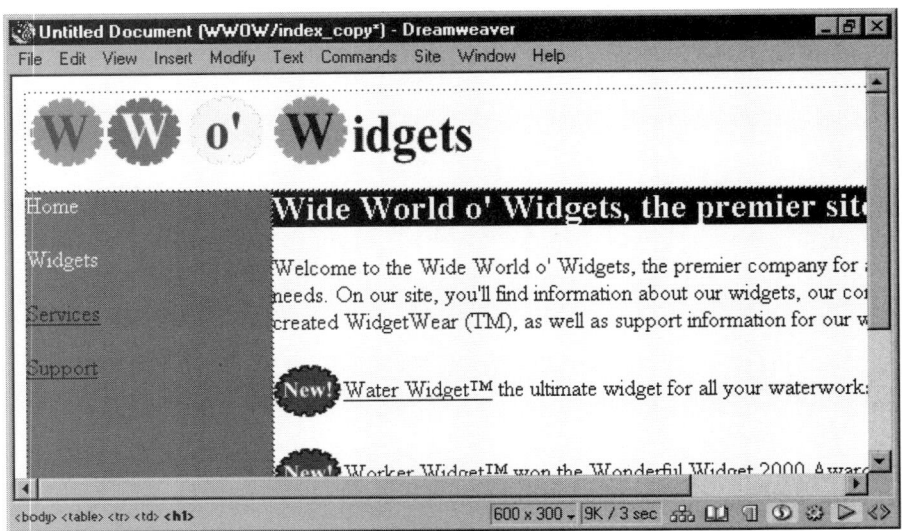

Figure 1-7 A Web page in Dreamweaver with the Tag selector in the bottom left of the window.

To use this tool effectively, it helps to be able to recognize the most common HTML tags. Table 1-2 lists the more common tags you might run across in the Web pages you create.

TAG	COMMON NAME	DESCRIPTION
<a>	Anchor	A hyperlink of any sort.
<b>	Bold text	Text formatted as bold.
<body>	Document body	The main, visible, section of a Web page.
 	Line break	A forced new line in a single paragraph.
<button>	Button	A button in a form.
<col>	Table column	A column of a table.
<dd>	Definition description	The description of a definition term.
<div>	Layer	A CSS layer.
<dl>	Definition list	A list consisting of definition terms and descriptions.
<dt>	Definition term	A term that will be defined.
<font>	Font change	Text with a font specified.

TAG	COMMON NAME	DESCRIPTION
<form>	Interactive form	A form for visitor input.
<frame>	Frame	A frame or Web page displayed within another page.
<frameset>	Frameset	The container for multiple frames.
<h1>	Level-one heading	The highest-level heading on a page.
<head>	Document head	The hidden place where Web page information is kept.
<hr>	Horizontal rule	A horizontal line on a page.
<i>	Italic text	Text formatted as italics.
<img>	Inline image	An image displayed on a Web page.
<label>	Form field label	The label for a form field.
<li>	List item	A bulleted item in an unordered (bulleted) list.
<meta>	Meta data	Hidden information about a Web page's content.
<ol>	Ordered list	A numbered list.
<p>	Paragraph	A paragraph of text.
<table>	Table	A table.
<td>	Table cell	A cell, or box, in a table.
<tr>	Table row	A row in a table.
<ul>	Unordered list	A bulleted list.

Table 1-2   Some common HTML tags you'll encounter.

Hyperlink Addresses

There are three types of hyperlink addresses you might want to use when creating your Web pages: absolute addresses, document relative addresses, and site-root relative addresses. In general, Dreamweaver deals with these addressing schemes for you, but it's useful to understand the difference so that you're not caught off guard with broken hyperlinks.

To use a different addressing scheme when creating a hyperlink in Dreamweaver, either enter the absolute address in the URL box or choose the relative addressing method you want to use from the Relative To drop-down list box, as shown in Figure 1-8. See "Step 5: (Set Up Your Site" for more information on creating hyperlinks.)

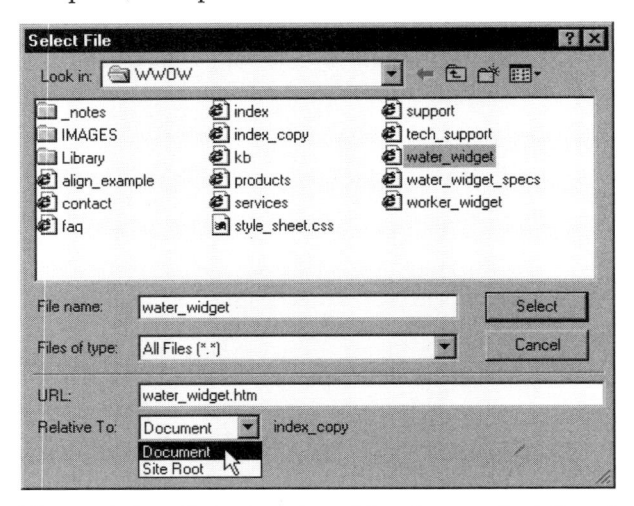

Figure 1-8   Selecting the addressing method for a hyperlink.

Absolute Addresses

You're probably used to seeing Web page addresses that are in the following form: *http://www.somecompany.com/index.htm*. These kinds of addresses are called absolute addresses because they point to an absolute and unchanging location. No matter where you or the referring Web page are, on (or off) the Web, the address points to the same location.

Document Relative Addresses

Another form of hyperlink addressing is relative addressing. Relative addressing describes the location of a file relative to either the referring Web page (document-relative addressing) or the root folder of the Web site (site-root relative addressing).

Document relative addresses describe an address relative to the Web page containing the link. For example, to link to a Web page in the same directory as the referring Web page, simply enter the name of the page you want to link to, for example, *products.htm*. To refer to a page in a subdirectory, enter only the subdirectory and filename, not the complete path. For example the *images/logo.gif* address points to a logo.gif file in the images subdirectory.

Document relative addresses are the most commonly used addresses when creating Web pages because the links continue to work even if you move your entire site to a different location—perhaps from your local hard drive to a Web server or to a new domain name. As long as the internal structure of the Web site doesn't change, all links work fine because the relative address of each file hasn't changed.

For the most part, Dreamweaver uses document relative addresses automatically, and we feel that this is the most appropriate method for most users. You don't need to perform any special actions to use document relative addressing.

Site-Root Relative Addresses

Site-root relative addressing is similar, but instead of describing an address relative to the document containing the hyperlink, the address is relative to the root directory of the Web site. To link to the logo.gif file in the images subdirectory, you'd enter the path to this directory *relative to the root of your Web site*, as shown in Table 1-3.

ADDRESSING METHOD	PATH
Absolute	*http://www.mycompany.com/manuals/images/logo.gif*
Document relative	*images/logo.gif*
Site-root relative	*/manuals/images/logo.gif*

Table 1-3 An absolute address and relative addresses from a Web page located in the manuals directory.

Site-root relative addressing works well if you often need to move files from one directory to another within the Web site. If you want to use site-root relative addressing, choose Site-Root from the Relative To drop-down list box when creating a hyperlink (see Figure 1-8).

TIP *If you move Web pages around in your Web site using Dreamweaver's Site window, Dreamweaver can automatically update your hyperlinks. This makes document relative addressing more desirable than it would be otherwise, making it a better choice than site-root relative addressing in most instances.*

NOTE *You can only use hyperlinks that use site-root relative addressing when they are published to your Web server or when previewed using Dreamweaver's Preview In Web Browser feature. If you open the Web page containing the link directly in your Web browser while still on your local hard drive, the link won't work.*

New Web Page Technologies

In addition to HTML pages, a number of new technologies have been developed for Web pages. Even if these technologies don't apply to your Web site initially, it's good to know that if you need something more sophisticated than that provided by Dreamweaver, the capability exists. The following list describes relevant Web page technologies and what they do.

- Dynamic HTML introduces movement and the ability to react to a user's actions to Web pages. For example, text may highlight when a user moves the mouse over it. Mainly useful for adding visual flair to a Web site, DHTML can be created directly within Dreamweaver, which makes it fairly easy to use.

- Cascading Style Sheets (CSS) are a supplement to HTML that allow much greater control over text style and position. CSS also permits Webmasters to link all Web pages in a site to a single external CSS file containing information on how text should be formatted. You can then implement sitewide formatting changes by modifying one CSS file.

- Macromedia Flash and Shockwave allow professional Web developers to create fancy effects and interactivity on a Web page—like DHTML, except more powerful and flexible. Web browsers don't natively support Flash or Shockwave, so a browser plug-in must be downloaded before users can view the effects.

- Javascript, Java, and ActiveX provide a way of performing complex tasks within a Web page and can even function as full-featured programs. You can accomplish some simple tasks in Dreamweaver if you have a bit of patience, but these technologies are complicated—and using them is best left to professional Web developers.

- CGI scripts are used on some Web servers to provide server-based features such as forms, visitor counters, and discussion groups. CGI scripts are tricky to set up; you should get outside help if you need to use them to handle forms on your Web site.

- XML stands for Extended Markup Language. XML provides a way of giving detailed content information about a Web page, allowing for more meaningful searching and information gathering.

Why It Makes Sense to Have a Web Site

Although a great deal of exuberance surrounds the Internet and especially the Web, it's fairly easy to identify and describe the handful of reasons why it makes good business sense for your organization to have a Web site.

Advertising

The Web let's you create powerful advertisements and publicity for a very modest cost. The quickest way to visualize this is to think of your Web site and its Web pages as substitutes for enhanced versions of any telephone directory advertising you do now.

It's not an exaggeration to say that anything you can do in a directory listing or advertisement, you can do better and more cheaply using a Web page. You can also more frequently change and update your information.

> **TIP** *The Web really levels the playing field for small businesses. A small business can create a Web site as good or better in many ways than a larger company's Web site without a tremendous amount of expense or time, giving small businesses an unprecedented ability to compete.*

Publishing

Many organizations are de facto publishers. For example, if your company or organization creates and distributes brochures, newsletters, product or service literature, or similar items, you actually are publishing. The Web provides a convenient way to complement or even replace this paper-based publishing.

Developing material for publication on the Web doesn't cost any more than developing equivalent material for paper publishing. But with the Web, you don't have the costs of printing or mailing. Furthermore, with the Web, you can more quickly update your information.

Information Collection

In addition to the advertising and publishing advantages that the Web offers to organizations, the Web also offers the ability to collect information from the people for whom you advertise and publish. You can put forms right on a Web page to collect information from the visitors to your site. For example, you might gather names for a mailing list, get feedback from customers, or take in sales orders.

> **NOTE** *Although creating forms in Dreamweaver is relatively easy, they require the use of CGI scripts or Active Server Pages to actually process the information submitted using the form. Both of these technologies are complex, so hire a professional if you need to use forms on your Web site.*

Transaction Processing

One further advantage of the Web that's of great value is the opportunity for transaction processing. As an extension of the Web's information collection ability, transaction processing lets you use the Web as a virtual store, salesperson, or distribution facility.

Using the Web for transaction processing is considerably trickier than using it for advertising or publishing. Obviously, your Web pages need to list and describe the products you sell. But practically speaking, you need to do more than simply list products or services. Good Web stores have the following features:

- Information about product availability and about the lead times for ordering items that aren't immediately available.

- A variety of ways to track down your products and services so that they are easy to find and buy.

- A shopping cart feature that lets customers build a list of the items they want.

- A checkout feature that lets customers easily order all the items in their shopping cart. (It's during this checkout process, of course, that customers provide their credit card numbers and shipping instructions.)

- A non-Web way for resolving problems the Web store can't handle, such as lost or damaged goods.

This book doesn't spend much time on setting up a transaction-processing Web site. This process is beyond the skill set of most business professionals—principally because you need to be able to search and then show your product inventory database on your Web pages. "Appendix B: Creating Web Stores" describes in specific terms how to set up simple transaction-processing capabilities and then in more general terms how to use a third-party Web store hosting service if transaction processing is what you need or want.

> **NOTE** *Regardless of what you think about Amazon.com, you should visit their Web site (www.amazon.com)—even if you compete with them (perhaps especially if you compete with them). They've done an impressive job of providing numerous paths to find their products and different ways to search through their inventory. For example, they have several different bestseller lists for Microsoft Excel books, each listing books in a different order for a different group of Excel readers. We strongly suspect that having multiple lists, each really an alternative path to the same products, boosts their sales of Excel books because they make it more likely someone will find them.*

What Makes a Good Web Site?

No matter what you choose to use your Web site for—advertising, publishing, information collection, or transaction processing—three main features differentiate effective sites: useful content, easy navigation, and aesthetic appeal. The following sections briefly identify how to spot an effective Web site, and by extension, how to create one.

Useful Content

More than anything else, useful content is the single most important feature of an effective Web site. It doesn't matter how well designed a site is, if it doesn't have useful content, the site is worthless.

Besides having worthwhile content, good Web sites also bring visitors back repeatedly. Generally, visitors return to sites to view new or changed information or to view information that remains useful, perhaps as a reference source. Having both consistently useful content *and* frequently changing or new information is ideal, but both approaches are also effective by themselves.

Dynamic Content

Web sites that make use of dynamic content to keep visitors coming back require more work than Web sites that remain largely unchanged, but also tend to result in people coming to the site more frequently.

There are many ways that effective Web sites make use of dynamic content to entice visitors back to their Web sites. A company or organization may choose to post updated schedules and event listings or information on special sales. Other potential sources for updated content include press releases, reports, or news about the company or organization.

Content doesn't have to be limited to strictly company information either. A Web site that provides freshly updated news, a regular column, tips, or advice on a subject of interest to its visitors will get return visitors. Even if people weren't explicitly coming to the site to buy something or to get information about the company or organization, once they're at the site, many will investigate further.

Another approach that may work for some Web sites is to dole out new information about something to build suspense and interest—and keep visitors coming back. Usually this approach is taken when releasing a major new product or event. However, wise Webmasters use this trick sparingly so as not to annoy visitors.

Static Content

Consistently useful information is always good to have in a Web site. A site for a nonprofit organization might have a reference library of documents it has prepared, or simply directions to its place of business. Companies selling products may post their product catalogs, manuals, or support information. The goal of a Web site is to provide visitors with the information they seek, and if that information doesn't change, that's fine.

Easy Navigation

Although good content is the most important feature of a good Web site, it can be seriously hampered by poor site layout. Not only should visitors be able to easily find what they're looking for but the organization of Web pages and hyperlinks should also give visitors a good idea of the site's contents at a glance from the home page. Creating an effective organization for your Web site is covered extensively in "Step 4: Collect and Organize Your Content" and implementing it on your home page is discussed specifically in "Step 5: Set Up Your Site."

Visual Appeal

Aesthetics is very important for Web sites, but it is also the part of Web site creation that is most overemphasized by many companies. Professional artists and programmers are hired to create custom interfaces using trendy technologies, such as Macromedia's Flash, and altogether too much time, money, and resources are spent making Web sites look sophisticated instead of filling them with good content.

A flashy site may grab the attention of visitors, but a clean and simple site can be just as effective (or more so), and much less expensive to create and maintain. Complex effects and graphics can also make a site slow to download and confusing to use. Not to mention that sophisticated Web page programming can be incompatible with older browsers, along with some handheld devices and stand-alone Internet appliances.

Summary

This step introduced the Internet, Web sites, and how Web pages work. Now that you know about the most popular methods of communication on the Internet—e-mail, the Web, and newsgroups—have seen some HTML code, and have learned about the three most important features of effective Web sites—content, layout, and visual appeal—it's time to start developing your Web site.

Step 2

DEVELOP A CONTENT STRATEGY

Featuring:
- Common Web Site Goals
- Determining Your Web Site's Goals
- Determining Your Technology Requirements
- Methodologies for Developing Your Content

Once you understand the Internet and the Web in a general way—you're ready to decide what you want to do with your own Web site. You can easily start by looking at what's out there, as discussed in the pages that follow. Then answer some questions that allow you to begin developing a content strategy for your Web site. Finally, we think you can use an iterative development methodology that lets you get started now and get smarter about your content later on, as discussed at the end of this step.

NOTE *We're using the phrase "content strategy" to describe the information you want to share and maintain using your Web site.*

Common Web Site Goals

A good place to start your own work on a content strategy is by looking at what other organizations—both organizations like your own and those completely different from yours—have done with their Web sites. Even though the popularity of the Internet and the World Wide Web are relatively recent, there are many examples available of what you should and shouldn't do with your own site. The following sections present some common goals for Web sites to give you a better idea about how to form your own content strategy.

Advertising Your Company or Organization

Advertising a company or organization represents one of the most common reasons for creating a Web site. This kind of institutional advertising falls into at least five categories: general information, current activities information, location and direction information, financial information, and contact information.

General Information

General information describes what your firm or organization does, what distinguishes it from other similar organizations, and in short, what makes the organization noteworthy. Nonprofit organizations, for example, may want to discuss the organization's purpose and mission. Businesses may want to discuss not only their services and products but also their history and any special credentials.

Oftentimes, you'll already have this content in the form of a brochure or print publication that can be adapted for a Web site. (We'll talk about this recycling of content in more detail in "Step 4: Collect and Organize Your Content.") But the general rule is that someone visiting your site should come away with the impression that your organization is unique.

> **NOTE** *As you gather general information, remember the bookmark rule. Web browsers like Microsoft Internet Explorer and Netscape Navigator let a visitor add a Web page address to a list of remembered pages. Internet Explorer calls these pages "favorites"; Netscape Navigator calls these pages "bookmarks." We suggest that any information you can include that might increase the chances that someone will add your Web site to their list of bookmarks or favorites is worth considering.*

Current Activities Information

If your organization regularly sponsors events, your visitors should usually be able to learn about these events by looking at a calendar or schedule on your Web site.

Consider, too, the possibility of including an archive or history of past activities. In some situations, information about successful past events works well for promoting upcoming events or activities. This archival information might include transcripts of meetings or seminars, pictures from past events, reports on completed projects, and quotations from event participants.

Location and Direction Information

If clients or customers will need to visit your physical location besides visiting your Web site, you may want to include maps and directions on your site—especially if they already exist in the form of printed material that can be adapted for use on your site. This is particularly true for nonprofit institutions, retail businesses, and professional service firms. In all of these cases, your organization may regularly be providing location and direction information over the phone or via mail.

> **NOTE** *Many smaller organizations may be able to identify useful content simply by consulting the receptionist. The questions that callers ask most often should probably be answered on your Web site. For example, if people call asking for directions, location information really does belong on your site.*

Financial Information

Many organizations are required by law to provide financial information to the public. Still others, either by tradition or to foster a policy of openness and transparency, provide financial information voluntarily. If your organization wants to provide this information, a Web site is another way to distribute this data, as shown in Figure 2-1.

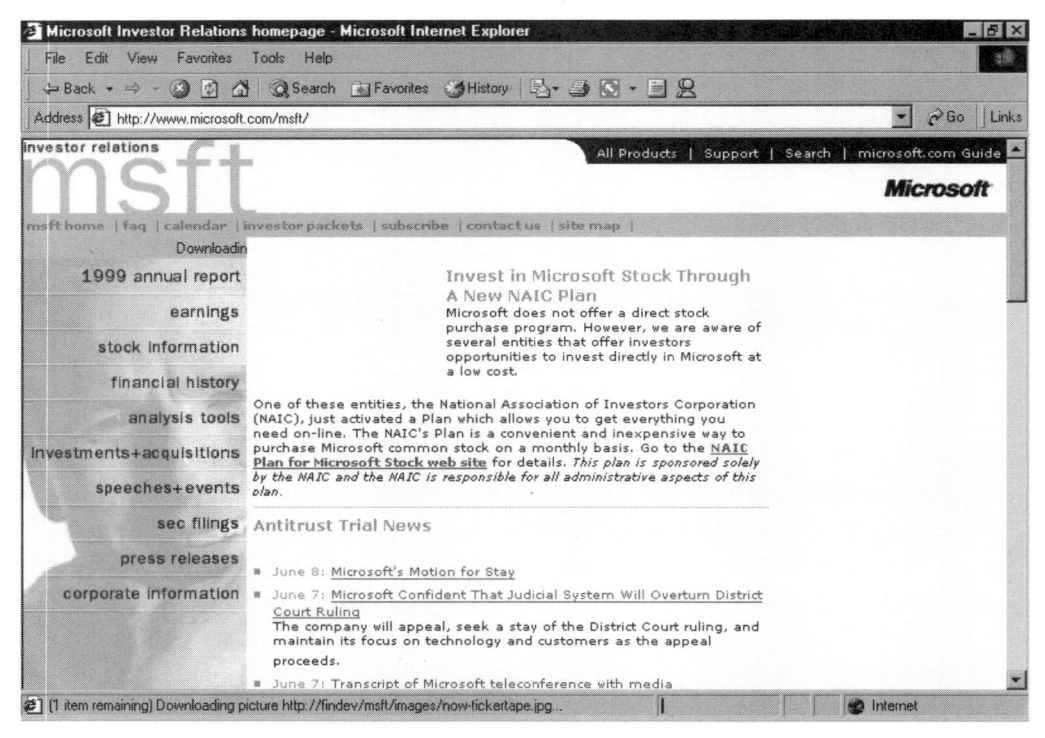

Figure 2-1   The Investor Relations page at Microsoft's Web site.

Contact Information

Your Web site should provide appropriate content information so that if visitors have questions or want to contact someone for more information, they'll be able to do so. Typically, firms provide an e-mail address in addition to mailing and street address information and telephone and fax numbers.

> **NOTE**   *While a Web site is one of the best ways to advertise, usually you need to put a little effort into advertising the site before it can be truly effective. This is because Web sites often act as second-stage advertising. Once people realize that they want more information (either because they're looking for something or because you've attracted their attention through some other form of advertising), they can go to your Web site and find all the information they want. That's powerful. But before your site can be effective, you need visitors. "Step 8: Deploy Your Web Site" describes tactics to employ for performing this first-stage advertising for your firm's Web site.*

Selling or Advertising a Product or Service

A Web site designed to advertise or sell a product or service differs somewhat in its content and focus as compared to a Web site designed to primarily advertise the firm or organization itself. Product advertising Web sites focus on presenting product information, pictures, and ordering information, while Web sites focusing on advertising a firm or organization tend to emphasize the purpose, activities, and future of the company over its products or services. However, there is some overlap between the two, and most sites advertising a product or service will also have some emphasis on the company itself.

Product or Service Information

An online catalog of products or services arguably is the meat of any Web site attempting to advertise a product or service. You'll probably find that it's most effective to summarize each product so that visitors can quickly get a feel for the product or service and what's good about it, similar to the way a print catalog is usually created.

With the practically unlimited space available on a Web site, however, it's often desirable to have detailed information available for those visitors who are looking for more specifics. Ideally, all the information available on a given product or service should be accessible from your Web site, including third-party reviews, technical documents, and support information.

Asus's Web site *(www.asus.com.tw)* is a good example of a site that includes just about every bit of information a customer might want about a product, as shown in Figure 2-2.

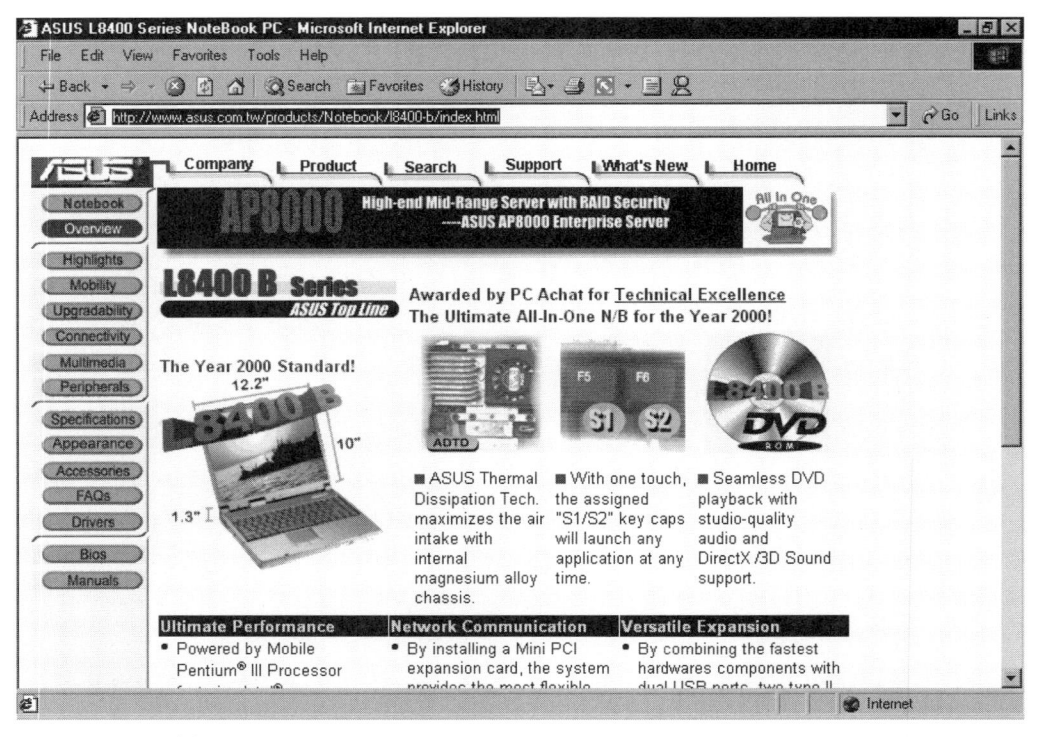

Figure 2-2   The product information page for an Asus laptop.

Pictures of Products or Services

Although pictures may not always be worth a thousand words on the Web, they can be extremely useful when trying to advertise a product or service. Usually one or two good pictures per product is adequate, though certain products or services may lend themselves to having a small photo gallery available (in a separate page) for curious visitors.

Ordering Information

Your Web site may not be a full e-commerce site—a site that allows for online orders—but it's still a good idea to present potential customers with easy ways to buy your products or services. This can include the locations where your products or services are available, price lists, a phone number for placing orders, a form that visitors can use to place an order that will be processed via e-mail, or full online ordering ability with a shopping cart and credit card processing.

NOTE   *Setting up an e-commerce site can be very involved. See "Appendix B: Creating Web Stores" to learn more about it.*

Support Links or Information

Depending on your product or service, it may be highly desirable to feature links to online product support information or customer support. Many potential customers check specifically on the quality of support for a given product before making a purchase, so having a helpful product support section on your site could help convince visitors to become patrons.

Disseminating Information

Perhaps the greatest strength of the Web is how well it's suited to passing on information. No printing costs are involved; information can be changed as frequently as necessary; pictures, audio, and even video can be included with text; and there are no real limits on how much information can be posted on a Web site. There are many different reasons that your organization may find it valuable to create a Web site designed to share information with your visitors.

One reason is the need to streamline the day-to-day operations of a company. The Web site of the U.S. Internal Revenue Service (IRS) is a good example of streamlining, as shown in Figure 2-3. By making just about every bit of tax information available online, the IRS reduces the burden on its phone staff, reduces the number of taxpayer errors on the tax returns it reviews, and presumably builds goodwill toward the organization. UPS and Federal Express are two other examples of companies that streamline their businesses by providing valuable information to their visitors (they post sending and tracking information).

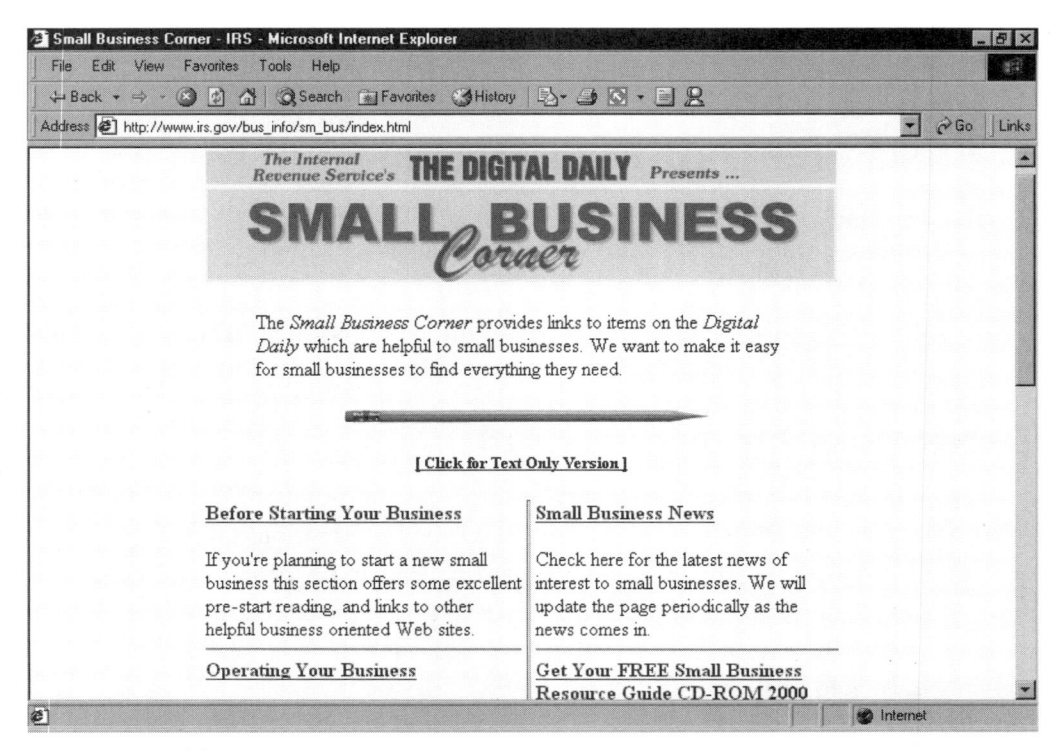

Figure 2-3 The Small Business Corner page of the IRS Web site.

A nonprofit organization may use its Web site to educate the public about issues in which the organization is involved, helping to make progress on the issues while at the same time increasing public awareness of them and the organization.

Firms and organizations can also disseminate information as a way to entice visitors to their sites, acting as a great form of advertising. When valuable information is shared (and appropriately advertised, as described in "Step 8: Deploy Your Web Site"), people will be drawn to your site, which increases the exposure of your site. If you then strategically place links to your product or company information, you can generate increased traffic to the parts of your site that directly benefit your organization. This is a powerful advertising technique because it actually offers something of value to visitors while at the same time exposing them to your Web site.

Chances are good that if your company or organization is creating a Web site primarily aimed at disseminating information, you probably already know exactly what content you'll use. However, if you're using an online newsletter or information source as a way to draw visitors to your site, you might be able to use some help. Here are some suggestions:

- Create a Web site that people will find a valuable source of information by drawing upon your company or organization's unique knowledge or perspective. This offers visitors something of value that they can't get elsewhere.

- If your company manufactures or sells a product, create some tutorials or product tips on your site to help customers make better use of the product.

- Create a newsletter related to your business's occupation. This newsletter can contain industry news, opinion articles, case studies, and product reviews.

- Provide information on activities or tasks that are slightly outside the scope of your company's products. This can help to make your company's Web site a central hub, which visitors can use to find related information of interest to them.

Generating Online Advertising Revenue

Many firms and organizations can help support the cost of a Web site (or even make it a profit source) by allowing other companies to advertise on their site or by earning commissions from referring visitors to online stores. Just as magazines are largely advertiser supported, it's possible to run a profitable online magazine or newsletter supported largely or exclusively by banner ads and affiliation programs on your site.

Yahoo! *(www.yahoo.com)* is an example of such a Web site, as shown in Figure 2-4. Even though the ads placed on the site aren't as obtrusive as some, because of the volume of visitors to the site, Yahoo! makes money from those visitors who click on the ads. Advertisers typically pay a small amount for each user who clicks on an ad. And a large number of visitors means a reasonable amount of income.

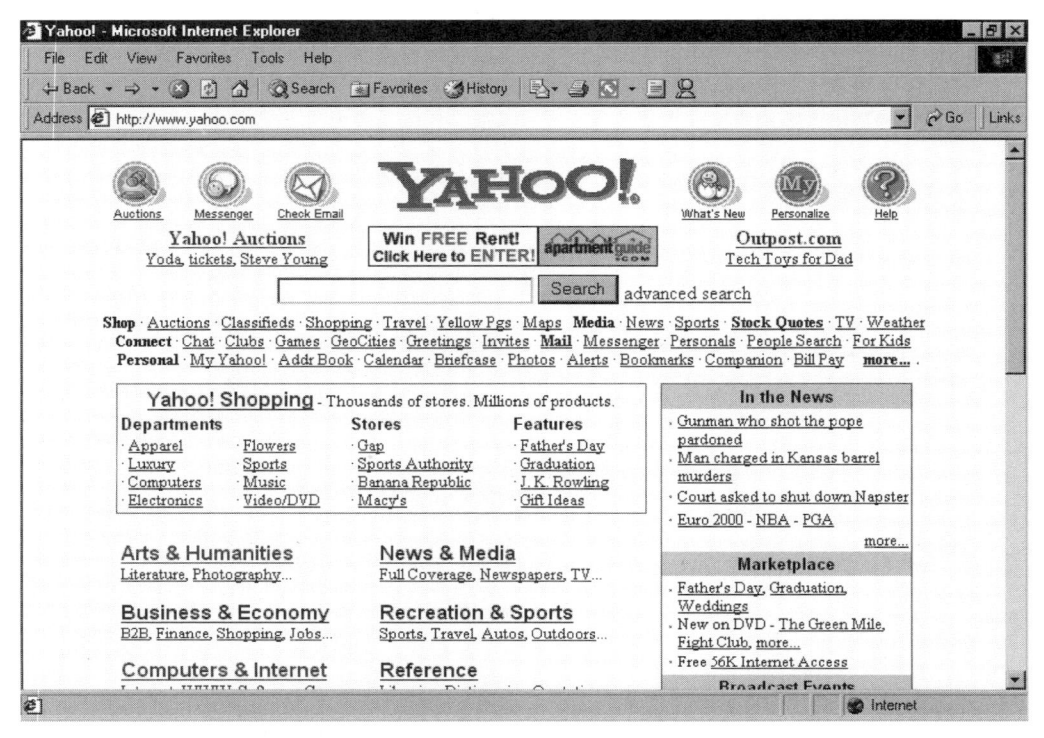

Figure 2-4   Yahoo!'s Web site.

The key to making money from advertisements on your Web site is getting enough visitors to your site to generate a large number of click-throughs (instances where a visitor clicks on an ad). To do this, you'll probably need some enticing content—possibly an online newsletter, tutorials, or free downloads relating to your products or industry. Because of this need for a large number of visitors, you might want to hold off on placing ads on your Web site until your site is established and generating a significant amount of traffic, and then choose the ads that are most appropriate to your visitors.

> TIP   *If your Web site presents reviews or recommendations on products that can be purchased over the Web, consider becoming an affiliate with an online store that sells these products. You can then place special hyperlinks on your site that link to the products at the online store you're affiliated with. This way, your organization earns referral commissions for each visitor who uses your links to make a purchase at the online store.*

Selling Digital Content

If your company or organization provides unusually valuable content, you may be able to charge Web site visitors to access or use the information. This approach requires additional development effort, however, and you'll probably need to hire outside help to set this up.

> **NOTE** *Nobody likes to pay for information. If you can make your Web site work without charging for access, do so—your site will have more visitors, fewer irritated visitors, and eliminate the added expense and hassle involved with setting up and maintaining a restricted access site. However, if your information really is valuable, charging for its access may be the only way to go. (If it's* too *valuable, you may not want to entrust it to a Web site, since it's not difficult for disgruntled or unethical subscribers to share their usernames and passwords with others.)*

Although most content isn't very amenable to selling over the Internet, some types of content can be sold online. For example, data your company or organization has collected that is unique and valuable can be very saleable. A fairly sky-high example of this is Space Imaging *(www.spaceimaging.com)*, as shown in Figure 2-5, which sells spy satellite photos.

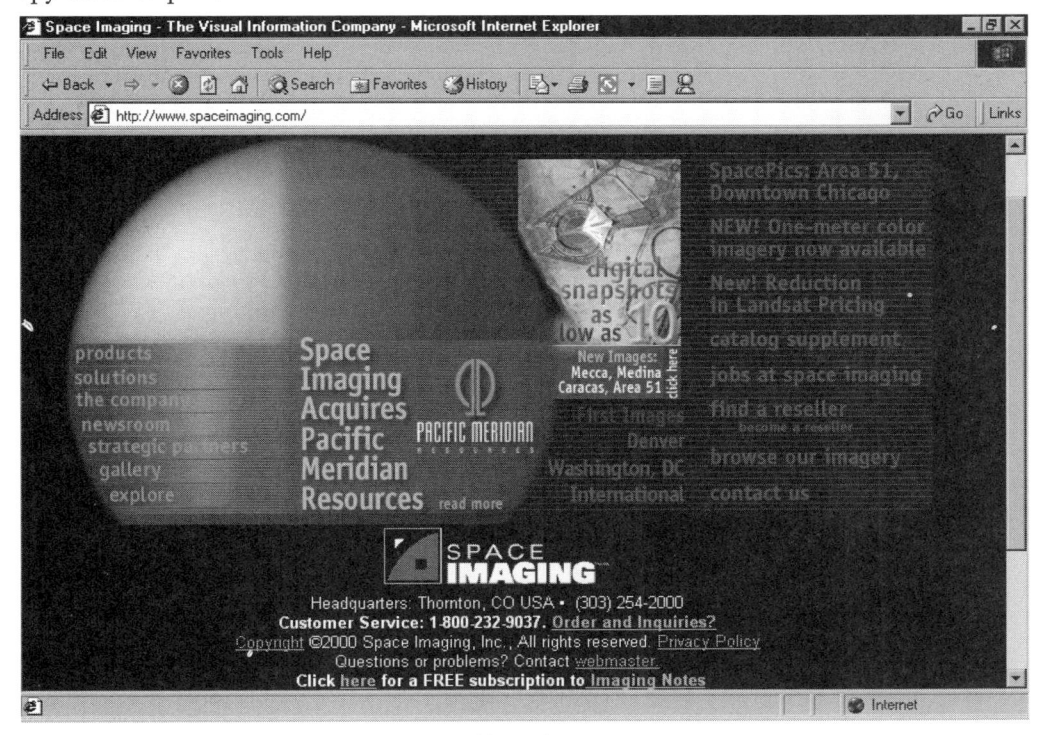

Figure 2-5   A Web site selling spy satellite photos.

High-quality information that your company or organization used to charge for can also often be sold via a Web site. An example site is World Book Online (www.worldbookonline.com), as shown in Figure 2-6, which sells access to its World Book Encyclopedia.

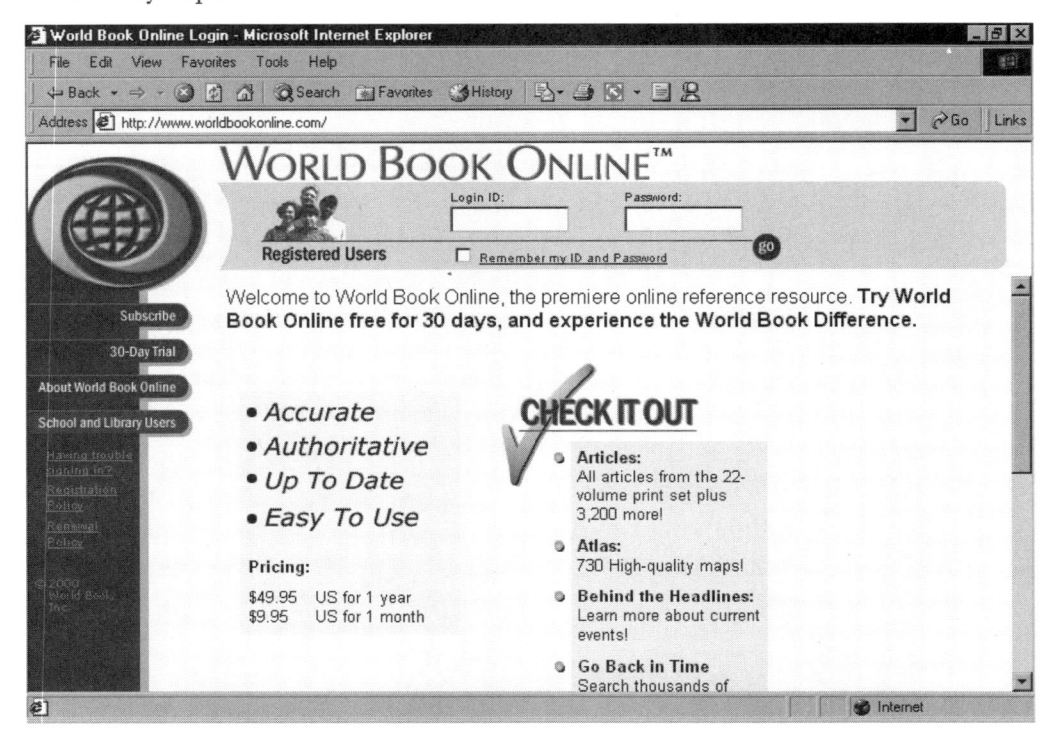

Figure 2-6   The World Book Online Web site.

Professionally created content of interest to visitors, such as high-resolution photos, artwork, sounds, or music, can often be sold online. Instead of treating your content as products to sell, you can instead treat it as a service to which visitors can subscribe. An example of this kind of site is ArtToday *(www.arttoday.com)*, as shown in Figure 2-7, which sells access to its images and clip art.

Figure 2-7   The ArtToday Web site.

Supporting a Product

Customer and technical support are two business activities that can significantly eat into profits. It's expensive to maintain a staff to handle customer and technical support (or divert resources from employees with other job functions), pay the expense of a toll-free number, and deal with unsatisfied and disappointed customers.

Creating a Web site or a portion of a site dedicated to customer or technical support won't eliminate the need for it, but it can help reduce the need for traditional offline (usually phone-based) support by empowering customers to solve the most common problems themselves. At the very least, it could help to streamline the support process. As with everything relating to Web site construction, each company will have its own unique content requirements, but here are some of our suggestions.

A List of Frequently Asked Questions (FAQ)

Creating a list of answers to the most commonly asked questions may lower the number of customer support calls you receive, or at least make some customers happier because the availability of instant help eliminated a phone call—and a wait on hold.

A Knowledge Base of Support Articles

Another way to reduce your support costs is to create a knowledge base of articles addressing potential problems your customers might encounter. One way to build up a knowledge base is to encourage your support staff to write up an article for every problem they encounter (this is what Microsoft Corporation does). The articles can then be placed on the site along with a form that allows users to search for a specific article, as shown in Figure 2-8.

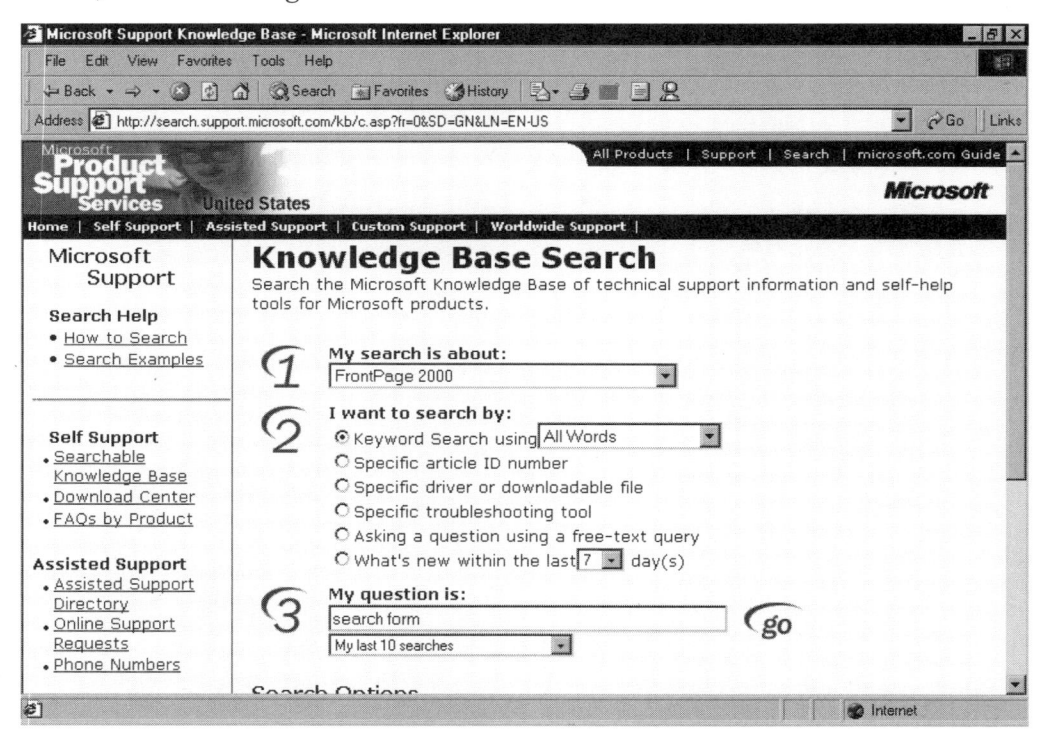

Figure 2-8   The Knowledge Base Search section of Microsoft's Product Support Services Web site.

NOTE *Microsoft's Product Support Services Web site at* http://support.microsoft.com *is perhaps the best product support Web site in existence. It provides FAQs for each of the company's products, along with information on how to get phone support as well as online support. It also provides users with the ability to search the same database of articles the product support staff uses, enabling users to essentially be their own support technicians. Take a look at this site if your company needs more product support.*

Contact Information

A product support Web site won't eliminate the need for traditional means of support, so you need to consider providing customers with the contact information for your customer and technical support staff. Although this usually means a telephone number, you may want to encourage visitors to preferentially e-mail the support staff, as this eliminates any wait time users might have with phone support, reduces phone bills, and allows your company's support staff to more efficiently respond to requests.

Online Discussion Groups

Web site discussion groups allow visitors and company personnel to post and reply to messages, much like a Web-based newsgroup (see "Step 1: Learn the Logic," for more information on newsgroups).

The advantage of discussion groups is that users can often get help from other users of the discussion group, reducing the load on your company's support staff and also expediting the resolution of the user's problem. More than just a resource for resolving problems, discussion groups are also an excellent way for users to share experiences, tips, and other information related to your product, service, or company.

NOTE *Unfortunately, Dreamweaver provides no easy way of setting up discussion groups. However, if your ISP supports FrontPage Server Extensions, you could potentially use Microsoft FrontPage to create a separate section of your Web site dedicated to discussion groups, since FrontPage provides an easy method of creating them.*

Because discussions aren't conducted in real-time, however, they can't replace more immediate forms of support, such as e-mail, chat, or telephone support. Figure 2-9 shows a discussion group Web site dedicated to Ulead's MediaStudio Pro (although Ulead did not create the site) that provides users with lots of information for which they might otherwise have turned to technical support.

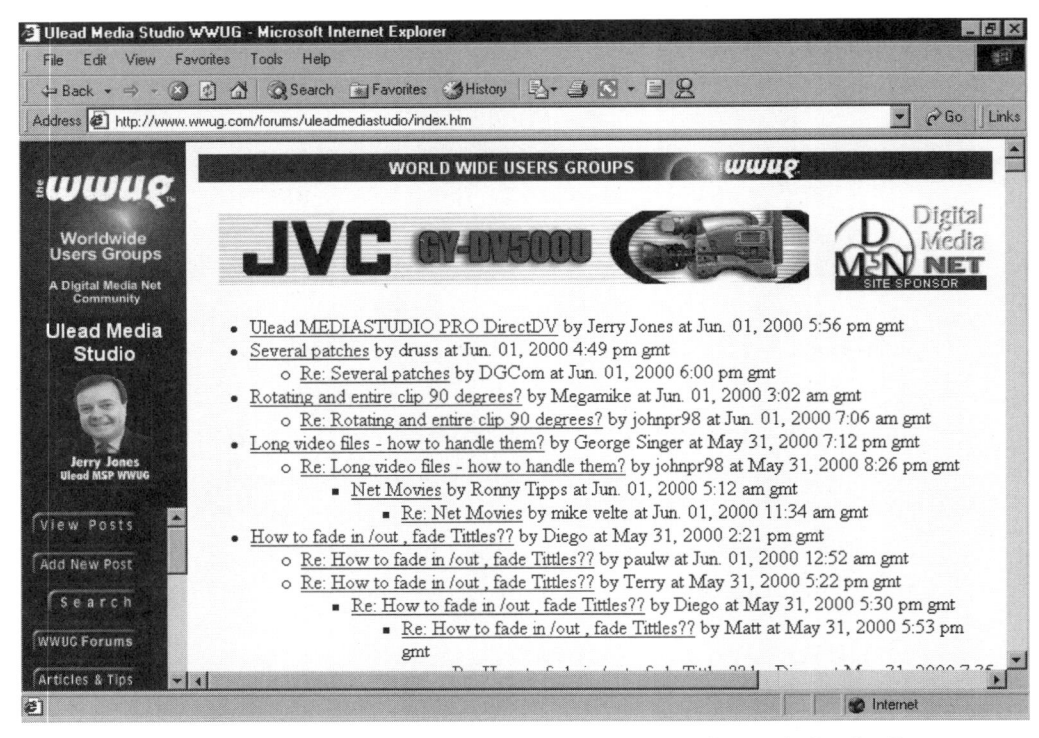

Figure 2-9   A discussion group Web site dedicated to Ulead's MediaStudio Pro.

Chat-Based Online Support

This is a relatively new form of providing customer support, and it's not for every company. A chat-based support system allows users to contact support personnel in a real-time, text-based chat session across the Internet. The advantages of this method are that it's generally cheaper than phone-based support (no telephone costs or need for additional phone lines), more efficient (personnel can often handle multiple users at once), and more convenient for some users (many users prefer to wait online instead of on hold).

While chat-based online support amounts to a fairly effective way of supporting customers, it's not natively supported in Dreamweaver, so you need to turn to third-party solutions if your company needs this functionality. Figure 2-10 shows an example (HumanClick at *www.humanclick.com*).

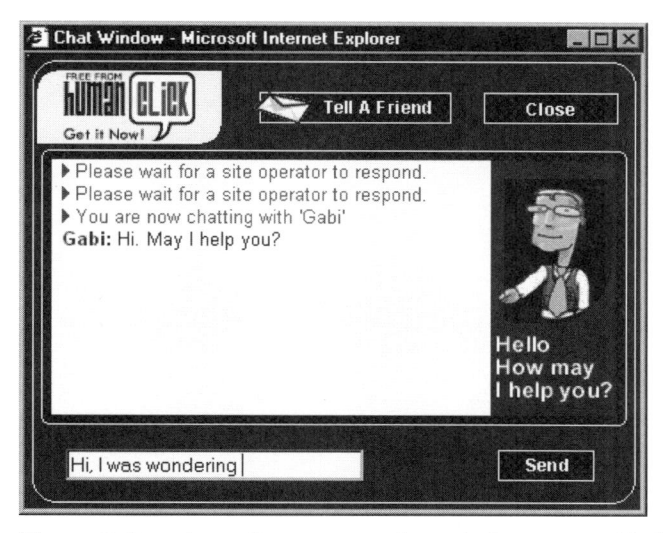

Figure 2-10   An online support chat window as provided by HumanClick's software.

Product Manuals

Placing online versions of product manuals on a Web site makes it easier for users to find information without contacting customer support.

Product Updates

You might want to place product updates on your Web site for users to download or give information on how users can get updated versions of your products.

Complementing a Curriculum

Any parent of a school-aged child knows that most schools make a lot of printouts, and children inevitably lose some of them. Students of professional schools are also familiar with the inconvenience of lost papers.

The Web can help out parents, teachers, and students by serving as a sort of online publication location where just about anything that normally would appear in print can be found, as shown in Figure 2-11. This reduces the amount of paper used for handouts, makes it easier for students to get assignments done, and generally helps students and parents more easily find the information they need.

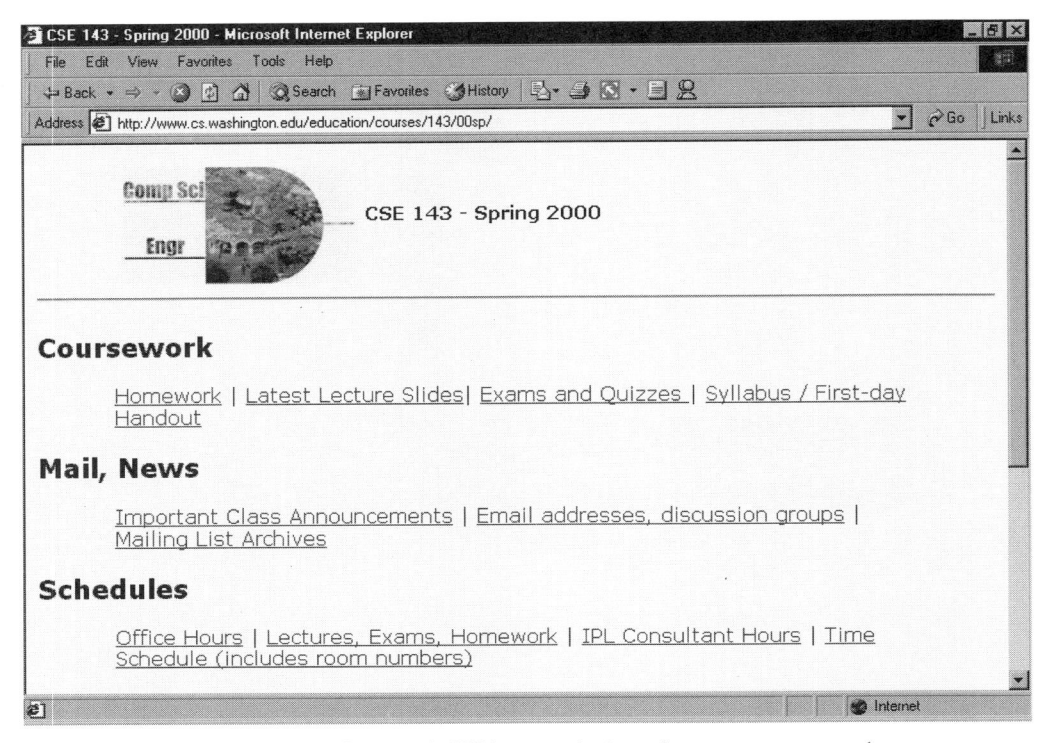

Figure 2-11 An example of a simple Web page designed to accompany a class.

Ideally, a Web site designed to complement a curriculum or school should contain anything that it would ordinarily make hard copies of. Here are some of our suggestions:

- Make current assignments available for convenient access.
- Post the due dates for assignments, test dates, special lectures, and anything else of importance.
- Make copies of lectures available online, if this is appropriate. Making lecture slides available can also increase the perceived value of the class.
- Include information on how grades are calculated and other background information, such as attendance policy and office hours.
- Post current course descriptions, class times, and dates for easy reference.
- List registration information and instructions. Not all schools will want to make online registration available because of the complexity and cost involved (it generally requires hiring an outside contractor to set up online registration systems), but most will want to post information on the proper way to register.

- Post cafeteria menus and prices.
- List the faculty, their credentials, and contact information.
- Post specific information about the school, its history, and its future. (See the "Advertising Your Company or Organization" section earlier in this step for more ideas.)

Determining Your Web Site's Goals

After reviewing the content strategies that other Web publishers have chosen, it's time to determine the goals for your own Web site. Practically speaking, you may choose to mimic some other Web publisher—at least initially. Even when that's the case, however, you'll find it helpful to answer the four questions listed below. Write down your answers so that everyone involved in the project can refer to them as they create the Web site. This document becomes especially important in "Step 4: Collect and Organize Your Content" when we suggest that you use it as an aid to planning your site.

1. What should the site accomplish?

    Are you advertising your company, selling a product or service, acting as an online newsletter, providing customer support, or complementing a teaching curriculum with your Web site? Although more than one purpose for a Web site is generally the norm, clearly defining what your site should accomplish is a vital step in creating an effective site.

2. How is this site going to benefit my company or organization?

    There are many ways a company can benefit from a Web site, including increased sales, decreased customer support costs, improved public image, or a better understanding of the company or organization (especially beneficial to nonprofit organizations).

3. What content should the site contain in order to accomplish the Web site's purpose?

    After determining what you want your Web site to accomplish, identify the content that will help your site live up to your company or organization's expectations. If the site exists to inform the public about a specific issue, it's important to have lots of information regarding that issue and not as important to have pictures of your company picnic. Your content needs to attract users to your site, keep them there, and entice them to return. Keep asking whether any potential content will help further the purpose of the site—if it doesn't, think twice before spending time and resources on it.

4. Is the content appropriate for the target audience?

While it's generally a bad idea to create a Web site that excludes people outside your usual clientele, it is desirable to tailor your site to match your typical visitor. For example, a Web site devoted to industry professionals probably doesn't need to talk in basic terms. It can give visitors just the information they need—not information they already know. (You might include a primer for newcomers.)

> **TIP** *Do some research on your target audience. Identify the types of people who are most likely to view your site, but make sure not to exclude people too quickly. You might find it useful to create personas that embody the different demographics you are trying to appeal to. By posing questions—Will Betty like the site? Will John find the information he's looking for?—the hypothetical users help you keep your focus when designing your site.*

Determining Your Technology Requirements

As you think about Web content, you should also consider the Web tools and technologies available. The tools and technologies you choose affect the type of content you will publish. Table 2-1 summarizes qualities of some of the more popular tools and technologies available. (Internet Explorer is abbreviated as IE.)

TECHNOLOGY	AESTHETICS	EASE OF CREATION	COMPATIBILITY	SPEED
Plain HTML	Low	Very easy	All browsers	Best
Tables	Fair	Moderately easy	All browsers	Very good
Frames	Fair	Easy	IE, Netscape 2+	Good
Layers	High	Easy	IE, Netscape 4+	Good
HTML Styles	Fair	Fair	All browsers	Best
CSS Styles	High	Fair	IE, Netscape 4+	Very good
DHTML	High	Moderately difficult	IE, Netscape 3+	Good
Javascript	High	Difficult	IE, Netscape 3+	Good
Shockwave	Very high	Difficult	Requires a plug-in	Poor
Flash	Very high	Difficult	Requires a plug-in	Fair
Java	Very high	Very difficult	IE, Netscape 3+	Poor

Table 2-1   Web page technologies and their relative merits.

NOTE *Dreamweaver doesn't provide tools for easily creating Web page forms or discussion groups. To collect information, you need to use either CGI scripts or Active Server Pages. (Alternatively, you can create forms in Microsoft FrontPage.) For this reason, creating a Web store with Dreamweaver is challenging, as discussed in "Appendix B: Creating Web Stores."*

We suggest that you choose from the easier technologies. Any tool noted in Table 2-1 as being difficult to use probably requires help from an outside developer or consultant. If you want to maximize the appeal of your site—across browsers, screen resolutions, and Internet connection speeds—stick with plain HTML (the type Dreamweaver creates for most everyday objects), create your complex layouts with tables (as described in "Step 7: Polish Your Pages"), and optionally use HTML Styles to customize your text. Frames can be used for navigation, although creating template pages with your navigation controls already inserted may be a better choice.

If compatibility isn't your primary concern, consider using Layers for your layouts and an external Cascading Style Sheet (CSS) file to centralize the text formatting for all your Web pages. This approach trades ease of use and modification for somewhat poorer browser compatibility; browsers older than Microsoft Internet Explorer 4 and Netscape Navigator 4 do not support these technologies.

TIP *Don't be overly concerned with making all your technology decisions now. Start your site with basic HTML Web pages and then work up to more advanced technologies. When you're ready to implement these technologies, make sure you have a consensus on which to use.*

Methodologies for Developing Your Content

As we wrap up this short discussion of the Web content strategies people usually consider, we'd like to leave you with one last thought. We recommend you more or less take a bulletin-board approach to developing your Web content. By this, we mean that you should develop the content for your Web site in much the way that the content for the bulletin-board in your coffee room or at your local market is developed.

Following a bulletin-board methodology, as you find or create some appropriate Web content, you simply pin the content to the bulletin board—or post the content to your Web site. When content needs to change, you update the content or replace it. If content needs to be removed, you remove, or unpin, it from the bulletin board.

This bulletin-board methodology is somewhat opposite of the strategy taken by larger companies, which is to treat a Web site almost like a software product—something that needs extensive research, development, and testing before it can be rolled out. The advantage of this large-system-development approach is that the Web site usually hits the pavement running strong, which is important for the IPO-focused high-tech companies of today's business world that can get tens of thousands of visitors their first day online.

However, the software product methodology doesn't work as well for smaller businesses and organizations because it delays and may even kill the project if the resources expended in developing the Web site so burden the project that it never gets completed.

Accordingly, we suggest you think about a Web site as something that's constantly under construction, where you post content as it's created or updated, and where you revise as needed, thereby letting your Web site grow and become more polished naturally, almost organically. Since smaller companies probably won't be immediately generating the huge amount of traffic that larger companies can often get as soon as their Web sites go live, they're free to create a Web site that may initially be less-than-perfect, and then slowly expand and refine it. In sum, we suggest you think about your Web site as looking more like an electronic bulletin board than a software product.

Summary

When developing your content strategy, it's helpful to examine common goals for Web sites and then look at the types of content appropriate to accomplish these goals. After seeing what other companies have done, it's easier to determine the goals for your organization's Web site. Once you establish your goals, we believe that you'll be able to rapidly create and make your site available to visitors by taking a sort of bulletin-board approach to your site—placing whatever information you have up rather quickly, and then slowly refining your site.

Step 3

LAY A FOUNDATION

Featuring:
- Domain Name Background
- Why You Need Your Own Domain Name
- Choosing a Domain Name
- Choosing a Registrar
- Choosing a Web Hosting Service
- Signing Up for Service

Before you can begin constructing a Web site, you need to lay a foundation by acquiring a domain name and choosing a company to host your site. Because of how quickly domain names are being registered (and thus eliminated as potential names for your company or organization), it's important to take care of this step as soon as possible.

TIP *This is a good time to assess who will work on your Web site and to assemble everyone involved. If you have any information technology professionals in your company or organization, they could be a big help in laying your Web site's foundation, as well as smoothing out the creation process. Artistic employees can often help determine what works visually for the Web site, or create unique graphics for your site as necessary. Others can prove invaluable for their knowledge of what content is available for use on the Web site or for their ideas on what would be appropriate content to add to the site.*

Domain Name Background

Although it is not absolutely necessary to understand what domain names are and how they work, a little background helps to make the process of acquiring a domain name and setting it up with your Web host easier and more logical. Fortunately, as a business user, there are only three essential pieces of information you'll want to understand: IP addresses, DNS, and domain hierarchy.

NOTE *To follow this discussion, you'll find it helpful to first understand the technical details of how the Internet works. If you don't already possess this information, you may want to quickly review "Step 1: Learn the Logic."*

IP Address

Computers on the Internet use an Internet protocol (IP) address to identify the precise location of a computer. An IP address consists of four sets of three numbers, for example, 169.254.255.254. Without an IP address, a computer can't communicate on the Internet.

DNS

Because of the cumbersome nature of IP addresses, a service was created to allow people to access Internet computers using names instead of long strings of numbers. This service is called the Domain Name Service (DNS). What the DNS service does, essentially, is translate the name you use to identify an Internet resource, such as a Web site, to the IP address that the network actually uses to locate the Internet resource. The DNS service is performed by a computer called a DNS server.

If you type *www.microsoft.com* in the Address box of a Web browser, for example, your computer asks your ISP's DNS server for Microsoft's IP address. The DNS server looks up the IP address and sends it back. Your computer then uses the IP address that it received to retrieve the Web page. This process is illustrated in Figure 3-1.

Effective Executive's Guide to Dreamweaver Web Sites

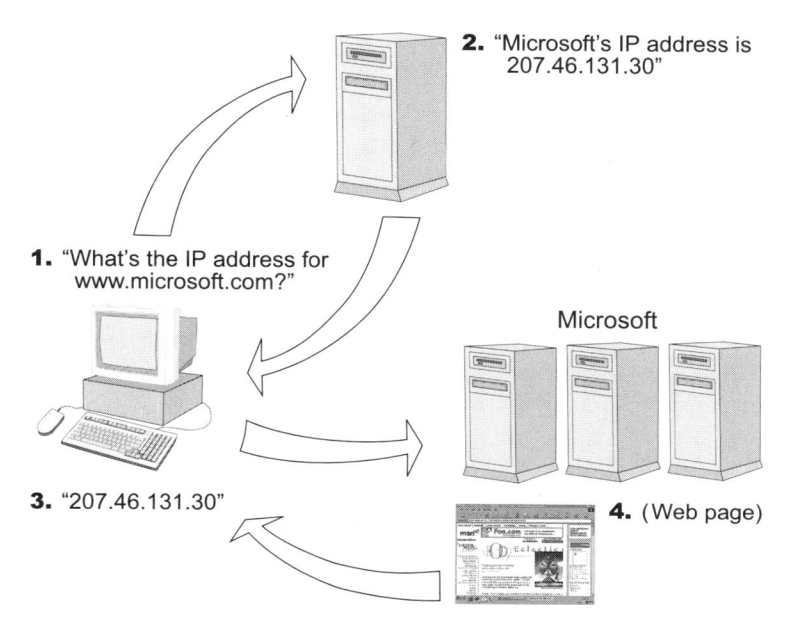

Figure 3-1   The process that takes place when you request a Web page from *www.microsoft.com*.

Domain Hierarchy

Domain names themselves are hierarchical and are read in blocks from right to left, with each dot indicating the next layer of hierarchy. Thus, the three letters at the end (right side) of the domain name make up the top-level domain—in the case of most businesses, *.com*.

Past the top-level domain *(.com)* is the domain name itself, for example *microsoft*. To the left of the domain name is the host name, or subdomain, that is, the name of a specific computer or a child domain. Usually this is the *www* host name, the traditional host name of a Web server. Figure 3-2 shows this hierarchy for Microsoft's domain name.

> **NOTE**   *A company can also have multiple subdomains within its domain. For example, besides* www.microsoft.com, *Microsoft also has* support.microsoft.com *(for product support) and* search.microsoft.com *(for searching Microsoft's Web site) subdomains.*

Step 3   Lay a Foundation   **49**

Top-Level Domain: .net .com .org .gov .edu

Domain Name: microsoft

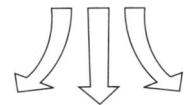

Host Name
or Subdomain: www   support   search

Figure 3-2   The hierarchy of Microsoft's domain name.

NOTE *In reality, a single Web server may host multiple domains (as is typical with Web hosting companies), or multiple Web servers may host the same domain and appear as the same host (as is typical with very high-volume Web sites that would overload a single server—for example,* www.microsoft.com*). While these two exceptions are more the norm on the Internet itself, on corporate intranets (private networks using Web servers and the TCP/IP protocol), each computer has its own host name and normally only one.*

Why You Need Your Own Domain Name

When creating your Web site, you don't *have* to acquire your own domain name. You *can* use the domain name of your Web hosting company to save money, since most ISPs provide free Web hosting under their domain name. Thus your Web site's address would be something like *www.yourisp.com/~yourcompany,* where *yourisp* is the name of your ISP and *yourcompany* is the name of your company.

You typically don't want to do this, however. This approach confuses Web visitors about your firm's identity, usually creates awkward URLs (or addresses), and makes it more difficult to move from one ISP to another.

Getting your own domain name—such as *www.yourcompany.com*—requires only a bit more work, and the extra cost is usually modest. You may pay $15 to $35 a year for the name and perhaps an extra $10 a month for Web hosting.

Your own domain name also gives you insurance in case you need to or want to switch Web hosting companies. If you don't have your own domain name, your Web site address (and most likely your e-mail addresses, too) will change if you change Web hosts. When you have your own domain name, the only thing you need to change are some hidden settings maintained by the registrar from whom you purchased the domain name. Your Web site address and e-mail address continue to work as before.

Choosing a Domain Name

Choosing a domain name is a small step in the creation of a Web site, but in many cases your domain name is at least as important as the name of your organization. Your domain name identifies your Web site, and by extension, your business or organization.

Picking a Host Name

There are several points to consider when picking a domain name. First of all, you want your domain name to be descriptive of your company or organization. Your first choice is your business's name, but in some instances you might choose a domain name that's based on your business's purpose instead. For example, it might be much better for a business named Vladimir Berkowitz Faucets, Inc. to select the *www.greatfaucets.com* domain name instead of *www.vladamirberkowitzfaucets.com*.

Second, your domain name should be easy to remember and spell. While a name like *www.rhythm.com* may be short and easy to remember, some people will have trouble spelling *rhythm*, potentially eliminating a large number of visitors. Perhaps something like *www.beat.com* would be a better choice.

Third, short domain names are far preferable to long ones, although not if the name is difficult to remember. This is particularly important since most of the desirable short domain names have already been taken. It may be tempting to abbreviate your domain name to shorten it, but do this only if the abbreviation doesn't make the name harder to remember.

> **NOTE** *Barnes and Noble provides a good example of abbreviating a domain name. Its abbreviation is only two letters,* www.bn.com, *which for many people is easier to remember than* www.barnesandnoble.com. *However, visitors can use either domain name—*www.bn.com *or* www.barnesandnoble.com*—to access the site.*

Multiple domain names may be something you want to consider, too. They increase the likelihood that people will find you, and cost only $15 to $35 per year more per domain name (although your Web host will probably charge a one-time setup fee of $30 or so). Multiple domain names also prevent others from skimming visitors from your Web site by choosing a similar domain name. Extra domain names to consider purchasing include the following:

- Your company or organization name if you picked a more descriptive domain name to use as your primary domain name.
- Former names of the company or organization.
- Common misspellings of your domain name.
- Longer versions of your domain name, or an abbreviated version of your domain name.
- The same domain name using a different top-level domain. For example, if you registered the *www.mycompany.com* domain name, you might want to also register *www.mycompany.org* or *.net* if you want to prevent others from taking those names.

Picking a Top-Level Domain

Besides the domain name itself, your company or organization also needs to choose which top-level domain to use, such as *.com* or *.net* or *.org*. By far the most popular top-level domain to use is *.com*. Since this is the top-level domain most people will look under first, we recommend that businesses look for a *.com* domain name. The *.net* domain is more appropriate for ISPs, Web hosting companies, and other Internet technologies companies. Nonprofit organizations generally use the *.org* top-level domain, although depending on the nature of the organization, you might also consider registering your domain name with a *.com* top-level domain.

Once your organization has come up with some ideas for domain names, it's time to check for their availability. Because a large number of domain names are registered every day, make a list of alternative domain names in case the domain name you want is already taken. Then either go to any registrar's Web site (Network Solutions is the original, and most expensive, registrar *www.networksolutions.com*) or go to *www.betterwhois.com* and enter your domain name idea in the box provided, as shown in Figure 3-3.

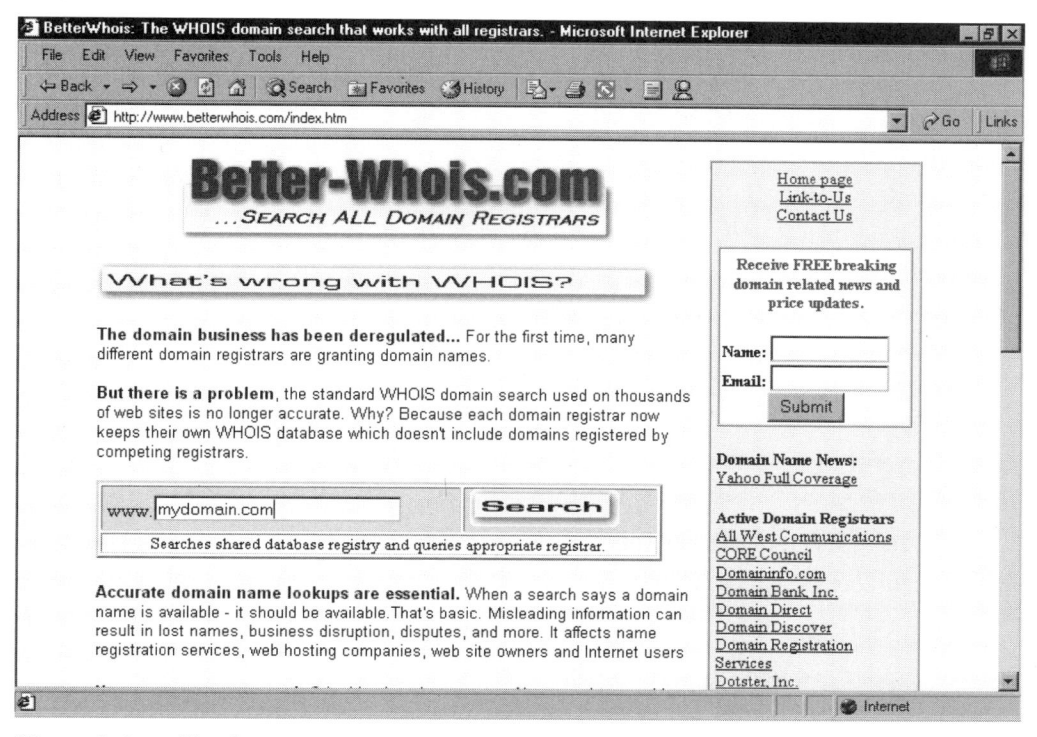

Figure 3-3   Checking out a potential domain name at the *www.betterwhois.com* Web site.

TIP   *If it's absolutely necessary for your company or organization to get a great domain name and all of your top choices are taken, you can look into aftermarket domain names. These are domain names that were already purchased and are now being resold for a usually obnoxious price. A list of aftermarket domain name brokers is available on* www.dnresources.com.

Valid Domain Names

Although it's likely that your company will choose a valid domain name, there are a few restrictions to keep in mind. Domain names are case insensitive, so don't spend time thinking about what letters to capitalize. Also, you can use only letters and the hyphen character, but a hyphen can't start or finish a domain name. Lastly, the domain name can be a maximum of 63 characters long, not including the *www.* and the top-level domain (*.com*, *.net* or *.org*).

TIP *Try to keep your domain names as short as possible. The average adult can remember at most seven or eight "chunks" of information, which can be letters, numbers, or words. If you choose a domain name longer than about five or six words (with maybe a chunk or two used up by the* www *and* .com*), people aren't going to be able to remember your domain name long enough to write it down, let alone remember it the next time they're in front of a computer.*

Domain Name Disputes

In general, if another company or individual takes the domain name you wanted, use one of the alternative domain names your company or organization chose. However, if the other company or individual took the domain name specifically to negatively affect your company, you may be able to dispute their domain name registration.

In order to dispute a domain name registration, your company or organization needs to give evidence that all three of the following conditions were met:

- The domain name in question is identical or confusingly similar to a trademark or service mark to which your company or organization has legal rights.
- The current owner of the domain name has no rights or legitimate interests in the domain name.
- The domain name was registered and used in bad faith (to somehow take advantage of the domain name by either selling it for a profit, preventing the legitimate company or organization from acquiring it and/or disrupting their business, or by using it to take advantage of confused visitors going to the wrong site).

If you feel that your company or organization has a legitimate dispute on a domain name and you want to take action, refer to the Internet Corporation for Assigned Names and Numbers Web site at *www.icann.org*.

When your ideal domain name is already taken, it's often by another company with a similar name but a different business. This typically means that you can't dispute the domain name. However, depending on the domain name you end up choosing and the willingness of the other company, you may be able to arrange a link exchange to help both companies' visitors find the correct site. Usually each company places a small link to the other company's Web site on their home page, enabling lost visitors to find the correct Web site.

Choosing a Registrar

In order to use a domain name, you need to purchase it from an accredited Internet domain name registrar. In the past, this meant Internic—now called Network Solutions *(www.networksolutions.com)*. However, the Network Solutions lock on domain name registrations is over, and a multitude of companies can now sell you domain names.

Generally, the easiest way to set up a domain name is to let your Web hosting company set it up for you. This is usually done when you sign up for Web site hosting, and it saves you the work of transferring your domain name from an independent registrar to your Web hosting company (see the "Signing Up for Service" section later in this step). The only downside is that this service is usually provided through Network Solutions, which is the most expensive registrar.

If you are willing to expend a slightly larger amount of time and effort in acquiring a domain name, you can get one yourself from another registrar. Network Solutions charges $70 for two years, but other registrars are available for lower prices. Some even offer free domain name registration if you use the registrar as your Web hosting company. Besides the additional time required to find a registrar, you'll also need to transfer your new domain to your Web hosting company, which takes a bit more time and effort (see the "Signing Up for Service" section later in this step). For a current listing of available registrars, go to the Domain Name Resources Web site at *www.dnresources.com*.

Choosing a Web Hosting Service

Choosing a company to host your Web site can be a bewildering experience. With thousands of Web hosting companies, each usually offering several different hosting plans, it takes knowledge and a certain amount of patience to choose a Web hosting company.

In general, however, you want to look at two issues. The first issue is what are the features the company is offering for its price. The reliability and quality of the company also need to be established; although this is notoriously difficult to ascertain, we can give you some pointers to look for in the following sections. The second issue is whether to choose a local Web hosting company or a national one.

Comparing Host Features

Web hosting companies offer numerous features—most described with hard-to-decipher technical jargon. Therefore, the following paragraphs provide you with summary descriptions of the features that are often available, along with information you can use to determine which ones are relevant for your company or organization.

Virtual Domains/Domain Hosting

In order to use your own domain name *(www.yourcompany.com)*, the Web hosting company needs to support virtual domains or domain hosting (different companies use different terms). Usually, this capability is a basic feature of "business" hosting plans, but often it isn't a feature of most "personal" hosting plans; hence, the business vs. personal distinction (personal Web sites don't usually need their own domain names).

The bottom line is that the Web hosting company you choose must support virtual domains or domain hosting if you want to be able to use your own domain name (which you do).

Database Support and Active Server Pages

If your firm or organization wants to use a database on your Web site and dynamically create pages based on data from the database, your Web hosting company needs to support both databases and Active Server Pages (ASP). Active Server Pages can also be used to process form results, but as with setting up a database, this isn't a trivial task, and really requires professional help.

If you think that your company may want to set up a database on your Web site for information retrieval, online ordering, or some other purpose, make sure that your hosting plan supports Active Server Pages.

CGI Scripts

Most ISPs offer the ability to use CGI or Perl scripts on your Web site. These scripts are what permit Web page forms and online ordering to work. If you want to create forms with Dreamweaver, your ISP needs to support CGI scripts (or ASP).

FrontPage 2000 Server Extensions

If you plan to use FrontPage to create any parts of your site that Dreamweaver has difficulty with—such as forms or discussion groups—then you want your Web hosting company to support FrontPage Server Extensions.

FrontPage Server Extensions provide server-based tools that make it easy for FrontPage to create Web page components that are normally difficult to create, such as forms, discussion groups, and Web site search capability.

Disk Space Allotment

Many organizations will find that the amount of disk space allotted to their Web site isn't a crucial factor in the decision of which company to use for Web hosting. Most companies and organizations' sites are rather small, and generally don't have trouble fitting comfortably in the 25MB of Web space provided by even the most barebones Web hosting plans you might look at.

If you plan on having a large number of images, audio, or video files on your site, however, disk space allotment becomes an important issue. If this could be the case, you may want to opt for a hosting plan that offers 100MB, 200MB, or unlimited disk space.

E-Mail Accounts and Aliases

Most Web hosting companies will provide your company or organization with e-mail accounts using your domain name for free with your Web hosting. For most organizations this is a pretty important feature.

However, different hosting plans offer different numbers of e-mail accounts (though most offer additional accounts for a charge). So, in general, pick a hosting plan or company that provides the number of e-mail accounts you need included in the price, since adding extra mail accounts can quickly increase the monthly cost of your Web site.

Besides e-mail accounts, most hosting plans also offer e-mail aliases. An e-mail alias works like a sort of virtual e-mail address that forwards received mail to another address. For example, you could set up an info@yourcompany.com alias that forwards all mail received by that e-mail address to an individual's address, such as gerendj@hotmail.com. Most Web hosting plans provide either a very large number of aliases or an unlimited number. This allows you to create as many e-mail addresses using your domain name as you want (even if you have a limited number of real e-mail accounts)—provided the people you're creating addresses for already have at least one e-mail account elsewhere that they can use.

NOTE *E-mail accounts can be accessed in several ways. The most common way is to use a POP server in which all mail is downloaded from the server into your mail program, such as Microsoft Outlook, Outlook Express, or Qualcomm Eudora. A newer method that allows messages to be stored on the mail server (and thus remain accessible from multiple locations) is IMAP, which can also be used with most popular e-mail programs (although Outlook Express can't create message rules for IMAP accounts). Some Web hosting companies also provide Web-based e-mail account access (in addition to POP or IMAP access), allowing you to check your e-mail from any Web browser when away from your own computer. If your company or organization has users who frequently use multiple computers or travel often, consider using IMAP e-mail accounts or a Web hosting company that provides Web-based e-mail account access.*

Subdomains

Some Web hosting companies allow you to create subdomains for your Web site, such as *support.yourcompany.com* or *events.yourcompany.com*. This isn't an important feature for most smaller companies and organizations. In fact, you should avoid needlessly creating subdomains, since the main reason to create a subdomain is to make it easier for people to go directly to a specific part of your Web site—something that is generally better done with a link on your home page.

If your company has separate divisions that want their own Web sites, however, subdomains are a cost-effective solution, since you can have as many subdomains as your Web host allows without having to pay any additional registration fees (because you're still using only one domain name). Subdomains are administered and created separately, which can be highly desirable for divisions of your company that want their own autonomy, but it is an added burden on your Web site staff if this autonomy isn't needed.

Mailing Lists, List Servers, and Majordomo

Depending on your business or organization, you may want to start an e-mail mailing list that you can use to send mass mailings to all people subscribed to the list. This is very useful for sending out information about upcoming events, specials, or tips.

A number of methods exist for creating mailing lists, but if your organization thinks this might be a desirable capability, consider finding a Web hosting company that includes some sort of mailing list capability at little or no extra cost. Some of the more common programs used for mailing lists are the Majordomo programs, Listserv, and Petidomo.

NOTE   *For more information on dealing with mailing lists, see "Step 8: Deploy Your Web Site."*

Data Transfer Limitations

Some Web hosting companies have a limit on how much data can be transferred per month. Every time someone views a page on your Web site or downloads a file, they're transferring data from your Web site. Similarly, when you upload new pages or files to your Web site, you're also transferring data. If your Web site goes above the set limit (because of lots of visitors or large file downloads), you're charged extra.

Although most Web sites don't generate a lot of data transfers even when they're busy, if you anticipate having a popular Web site with lots of images, audio/video, or downloadable files, you may want to opt for a Web hosting service that doesn't have a data transfer limit.

SSL (Security)

Secure Sockets Layer (SSL) is a way of encrypting data that is transferred to and from a Web site, and it is typically used for Web stores that process credit card transactions. As such, it is an important feature if your organization plans to set up an online store. Otherwise, the feature isn't necessary.

Technical Support

All Web hosting companies provide technical support for any problems with publishing your Web site, Web site availability, e-mail, and so forth. However, the type, quality, and availability of this support vary. Not all companies provide toll-free technical support phone numbers; not all companies provide 24-hour, 7-day-a-week (24/7) technical support.

NOTE   *The toll-free number might be important to you, but the always-available technical support might not be if there isn't going to be anyone working on or checking the Web site after hours.*

Another support option that is becoming increasingly popular is Web-based technical support. This allows you to conduct a live chat with a technical support person over your Internet connection, and it is handy for people who don't want to wait on hold. (You might have to wait online, but many people find it easier to get work done while they are waiting this way.)

Web Server Speed

The speed of a Web server is difficult to ascertain from reading promotional material on a company's Web site. This is unfortunate because Web server speed is important.

Reading reviews of hosting companies can be helpful, but they are difficult to find. You can ask companies about their Web hosting speed, but in our experience people often tell you the same thing—they're fast enough. To be thorough, you probably want to ask the following questions:

- How much bandwidth is available? A Web server running off a T1 connection may saturate the connection during busy times or if it is hosting too many Web sites. When the connection is fully utilized, Web site performance suffers. Table 3-1 summarizes the different connection speeds commonly used for Web servers.

CONNECTION TYPE	BANDWIDTH
T1	1.544Mbps
T3	45Mbps
T4	259.4Mbps
DS1	3.088Mbps
DS2	6.176Mbps
DS3	45Mbps
OC1	51.84Mbps
OC2	103.68Mbps
OCn	n*51.84Mbps

Table 3-1   Web server Internet connections and their associated bandwidths.

- How many sites is a Web server hosting? A super-fast Internet connection on an extremely powerful Web server doesn't mean your Web site is going to be fast if too many other sites are hosted by the same Web server. Similarly, if too many users share the Internet connection's bandwidth, performance will suffer. (Many Web hosting companies also act as ISPs and share the available bandwidth with both dial-up and DSL customers as well as their Web servers.)

- How fast is their server? While Web hosting isn't typically a processor-intensive application, hosting many sites or hosting very busy sites can strain a server. Generally, Web servers running powerful, multiple processors and using a RAID (a collection of hard drives treated as one drive by the operating system) for storage provide extra speed and reliability.

Web Server Reliability

Even more important than Web server speed is the reliability of the server. Although people can still view a Web site on an overburdened Web server (at a slower speed), when a server goes down, nobody can view the sites hosted by that server. To assess Web server reliability, most people rely on the uptime percentage, which is something that can easily be measured. Most organizations aim for 99.9 percent uptime (roughly 9 hours of downtime a year).

To attain a good uptime percentage, reliable Web hosts use a variety of hardware and software to decrease the potential for downtime. Web servers should use a hardware RAID for storage, protecting your data in case a hard drive dies. The hosting company should also perform routine tape backups of all data, as well as keep its Web servers on Uninterruptible Power Supply (UPS) devices and possibly even have backup generators for major power trouble.

There's no real consensus on what server software your ISP should run. Most ISPs operate on either Linux with the Apache Web server, Sun's Solaris, or Microsoft Windows NT or Windows 2000. In general, it's not important, although if you plan on using Microsoft FrontPage to create parts of your Web site (such as any forms or discussion groups), you'll probably want to stick with either Windows NT hosting or Windows 2000 Server hosting, since FrontPage Server Extensions are more stable under Windows 2000 than Unix.

NOTE *Many Web hosting companies may still be running their Web servers on Windows NT 4 Server with the latest service pack. While this isn't a bad thing (Windows NT 4 is a very reliable operating system), Windows 2000 Server is even more reliable and easier to keep running. It's not a major issue, but in general, it's preferable for a Web server to be running under Windows 2000 than Windows NT 4.*

Local vs. National Web Hosting

One important decision that can be difficult to make is whether your organization should use a local or out-of-state Web hosting company.

Using a local company can be advantageous if you need consulting work done on your Web site in addition to Web hosting, since most companies also do consulting work. While national companies can also consult or work on your Web site, there's often no substitute for a meeting in person. And when the consultant works for your local company, he or she is often more effective in working on your site (particularly if database integration or electronic commerce is involved).

However, local Web hosting companies usually cost more and provide fewer features than national companies. This is what nationwide competition does for you—it allows you to pick the best mix of price and features for your company from a pool of thousands of Web hosting companies. It's unlikely that the best value will happen to be your local Web hosting firm. Local companies also often lack some of the features that out-of-town companies offer, such as 24/7 technical support, large numbers of e-mail addresses, large amounts of disk space, and the ability to use subdomains.

Finding a Web Hosting Company

Even armed with good selection criteria, you'll still need to locate prospective Web hosting companies. And with the thousands of Web hosting companies that you can choose from, narrowing your list of candidates to a reasonable number can be a time-consuming and difficult process. Several useful resources exist, however, to point you in the right direction.

> **TIP** *Choosing a Web hosting company isn't a permanent decision. You can easily switch companies at almost any time (although you might choose to sign up for a one-year contract to avoid setup fees). So don't spend too much time trying to find "the one"—take a little time, find one you like, and then try it out. If you later locate a better one, switch when your contract is up.*

DN Resources

The *www.dnresources.com* Web site has a special Hosting section, as shown in Figure 3-4, that provides a list of Web sites that have lists of Web hosting companies. It's a little confusing, since each Web site shows a different list of Web hosting companies. However, it can still be a good place to come up with companies to possibly host your site.

Figure 3-4 The Web Site Hosting section of the DN Resources Web site.

Microsoft's Locate A Web Presence Provider Web Site

Located at *www.microsoftwpp.com*, as shown in Figure 3-5, the Microsoft Locate A Web Presence Provider Web site allows you to perform a search for a Web hosting company that is a Microsoft registered host for FrontPage Web sites. This is probably the best place to search for a Web hosting company if you plan to use FrontPage 2000 to create forms or discussion groups for your Web site.

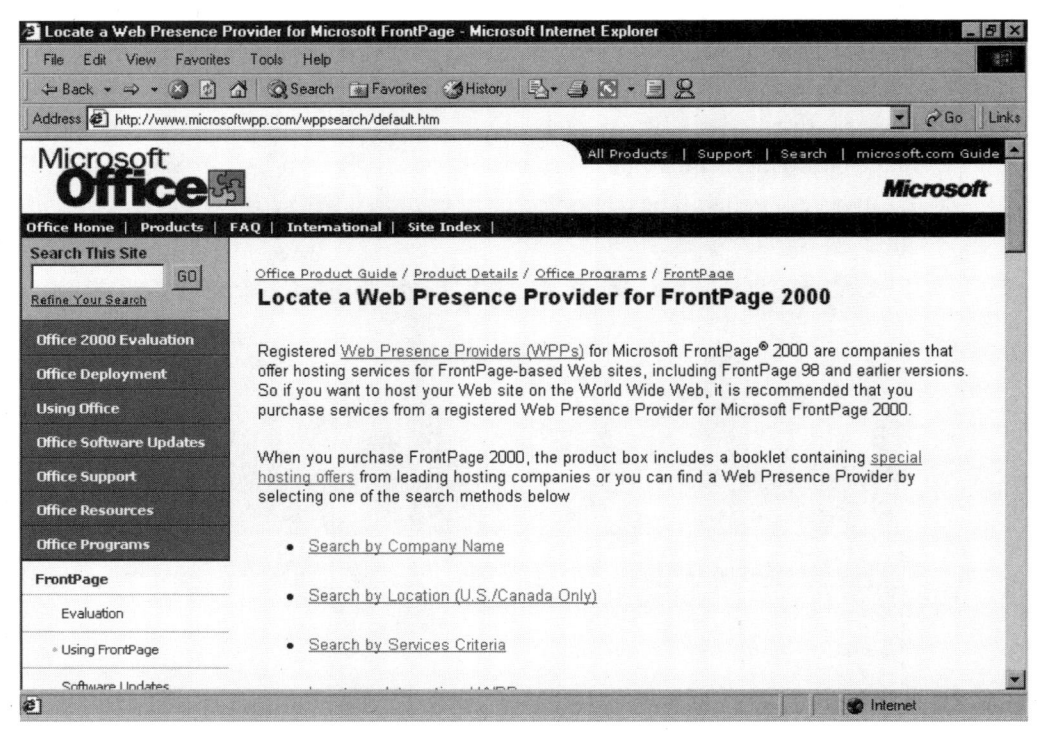

Figure 3-5 Microsoft's Locate A Web Presence Provider Web site.

Local Computer Papers

If you're looking for a local Web hosting company, check out any local computer papers or the technology section of your local paper for ads from local companies. You can also check the Yellow Pages under Internet.

Signing Up for Service

After deciding on a domain name, locating a Web hosting company, and selecting the appropriate hosting plan, you need to sign up for the actual service. Although the details of the sign-up process are different for every company, the basic steps will be nearly identical no matter which company you use.

1. **Locate your Web hosting company.**

    Find the Web hosting company you want to use and go to its Web site. More information on locating Web hosting companies is given in the previous section.

2. **Find the plan you want, and start the sign-up process.**

   Locate the hosting plan that is best suited to your company or organization on the Web hosting company's Web site. This is typically the cheapest one that offers all the features you need. Look for the "business" plans. Once you've found the best plan for your company or organization, click Order Now or a similar link.

   TIP   *If you're uncertain about some of the questions on the sign-up forms or prefer to talk to a person, call the Web hosting company—it's just as easy to sign up for Web hosting service over the phone.*

3. **Get your domain name.**

   This is typically the first step of the hosting company's sign-up process, as shown in Figure 3-6. To allow the Web hosting company to take care of the domain name registration, indicate that this is a new domain and enter the domain name you want in the box provided. If you already have a domain, specify that you already have a domain or that you want to transfer a domain, and then enter the domain name in the box provided. If you want to get your domain name from a registrar other than Network Solutions, go to the registrar's site and purchase the domain name, and then come back and enter it on the Web hosting company's sign-up form.

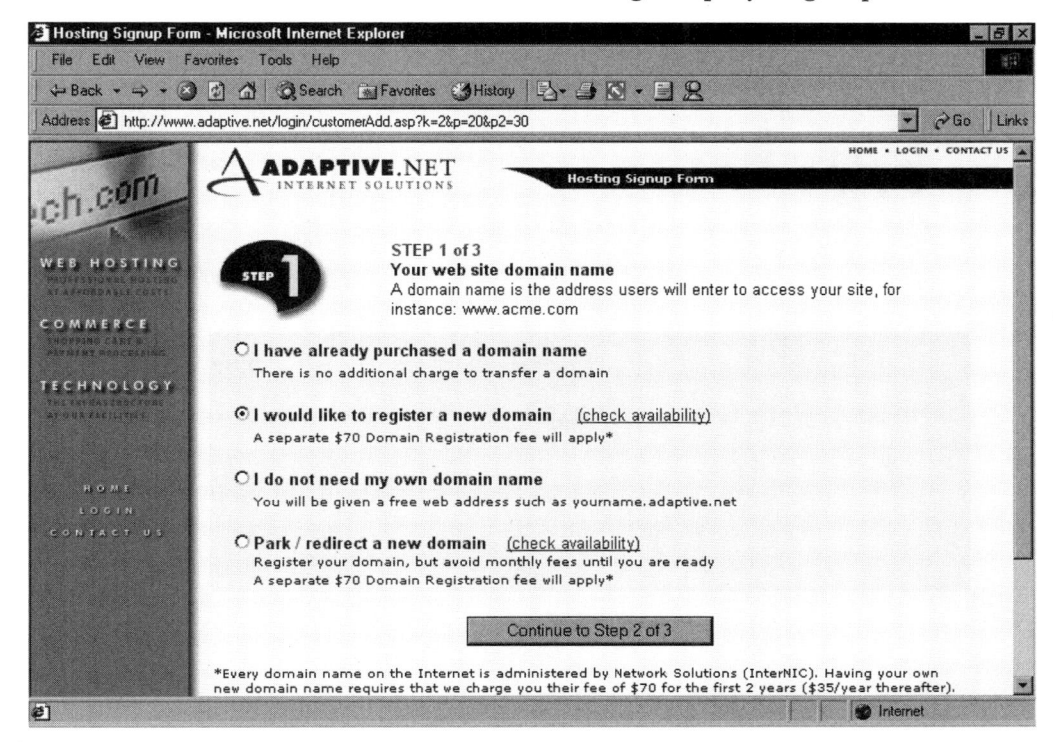

Figure 3-6   Signing up for Web hosting and registering a new domain name.

Step 3 Lay a Foundation

NOTE *Most Web hosting companies use Network Solutions for registering domain names, which charges $70 to register your domain name for two years. If you already have a domain name or want to save money by using a different registrar, make sure to choose Transfer Existing Domain or a similar option.*

4. Provide an e-mail address and password.

Enter the e-mail address that you want to use to receive information about your new Web site, as shown in Figure 3-7. Enter a password for your site also—preferably a long one that only you or your Web site administrator will know.

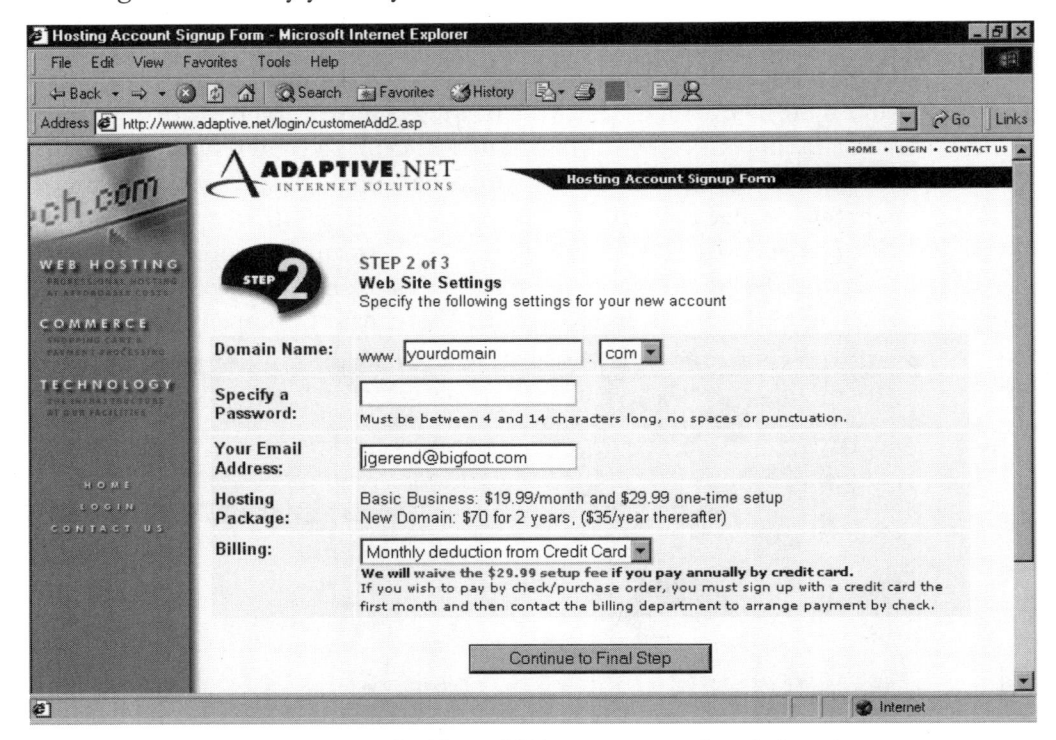

Figure 3-7   Entering an e-mail address, Web site password, and domain name.

TIP *Keep your Web site's password in a secure location and only give it to employees who will administer the Web site. When employees who know the password leave your organization, change the password.*

5. **Fill out user and billing information.**

Verify your domain name and enter your credit card and billing information in the last step (typically) of the Web hosting sign-up form, as shown in Figure 3-8.

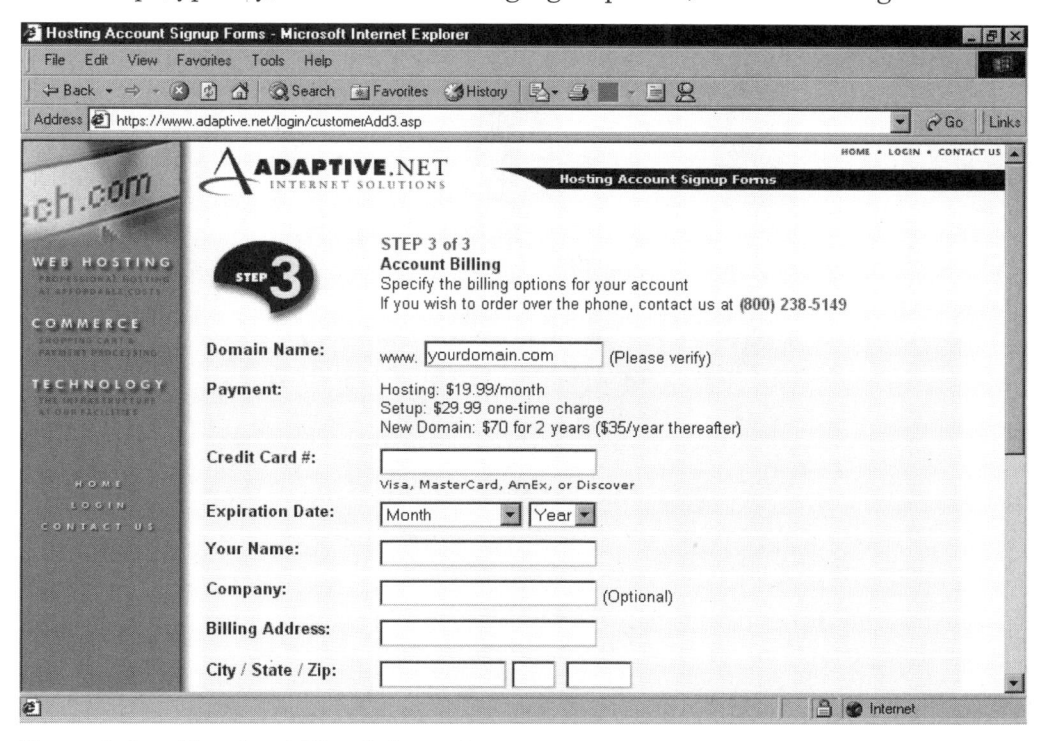

Figure 3-8   Entering billing information.

6. **Transfer your domain name (if registered separately).**

If you are transferring a domain name from another Web hosting company (or if you purchased a domain name from another registrar), go to your registrar's Web site, sign in, and change the name servers to those provided by your new Web hosting company. This typically involves clicking one or more Modify Domains links, as shown in Figure 3-9.

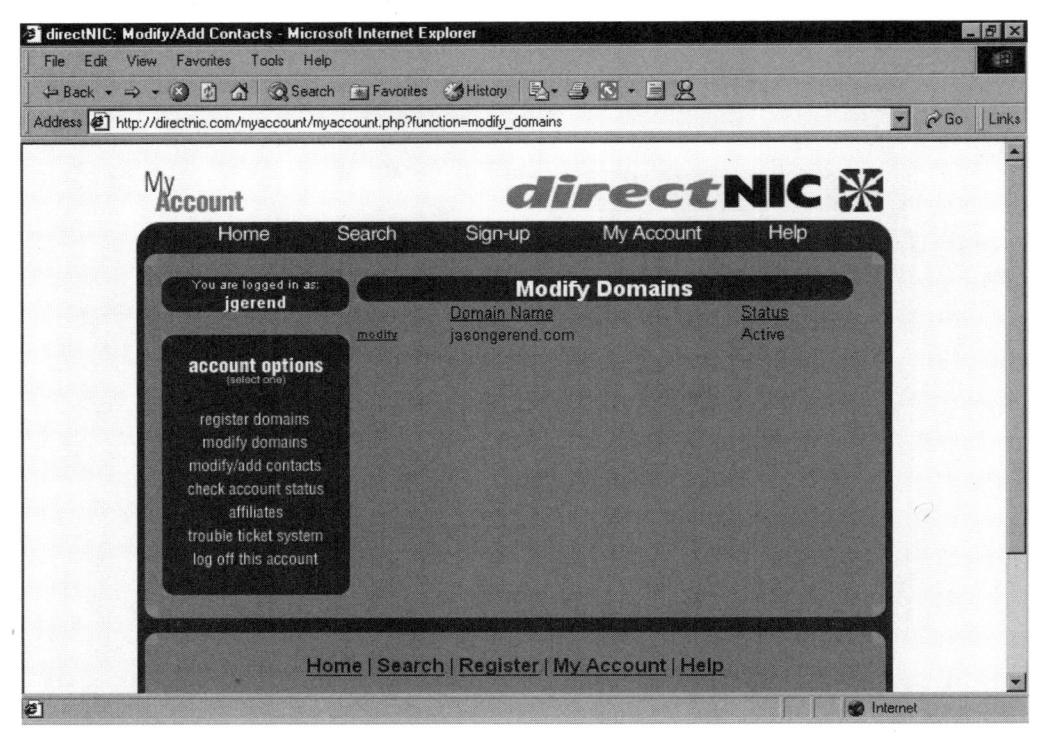

Figure 3-9   The Modify Domains section of a domain name registrar.

7. Provide your name server information.

Enter the primary and secondary name servers' IP addresses and names (your Web hosting company will give you these) in the boxes provided, as shown in Figure 3-10. Doing this instructs the domain name registrar where to send the visitors who are looking for your site.

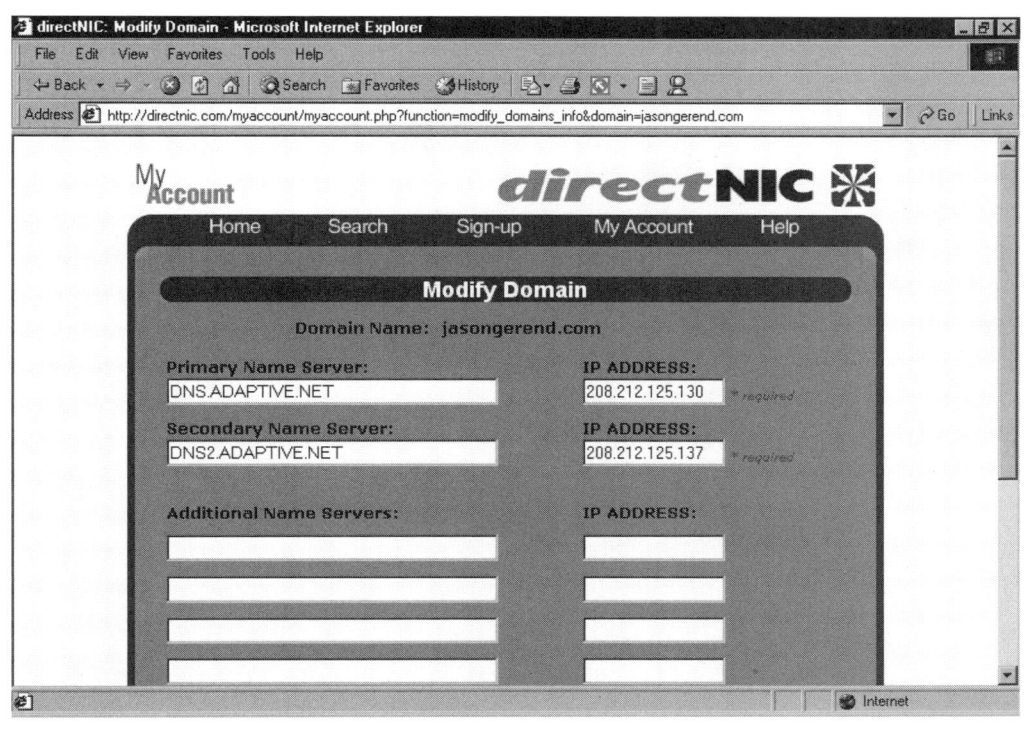

Figure 3-10 Entering your Web hosting company's name servers.

NOTE *Once you've set up your Web hosting account, you'll need to set up any e-mail accounts you want to use in a separate procedure. You should at the very least create info@yourdomain.com and webmaster@yourdomain.com accounts or aliases to handle general information questions and comments or problems with the Web site. This is typically done by logging onto your Web hosting company's site and adding any e-mail accounts and aliases you want. Check with your Web hosting company for more information on the exact procedure. It varies with each company.*

Summary

After selecting a domain name and signing up for Web hosting service, you're ready to assemble your content in preparation for constructing your Web site.

Step 4

COLLECT AND ORGANIZE YOUR CONTENT

Featuring:
- Determining What Needs to Be Done
- Creating a Central Location for Content
- Establishing a File Naming Convention
- Collecting Existing Digital Content
- Creating New Digital Content
- Organizing Your Content and Planning Your Web Site

Once you've completed the initial steps in the process of creating a Web site, it's time to actually round up your content and create the site itself. It pays off in the long run to take some time to collect and create your content first, organize it into a logical structure, and *then* begin creating your Web pages. Doing so will yield a site that makes more sense, conveys the information you want, is easier to use—basically a Web site that is more effective.

The process of organizing and planning a Web site can be as simple or as complex as you desire. Whole businesses exist solely to help companies plan Web sites, and conversely, simple sites can be created with no prior planning or organization. However, the majority of organizations will find that the optimal path lies somewhere in between these two extremes.

TIP *Even though we recommend spending a little time gathering and organizing your content before creating your site, it is appropriate to create a simple Web page (even something as simple as a glorified Yellow Pages listing) and post it to your site in the interim.*

Determining What Needs to Be Done

Now it's time to sit down with everyone involved in creating the Web site and develop a game plan that your organization can use to get started efficiently. Briefly walking through the items in the following list can help you assign tasks and increase the quality of the content that you ultimately collect.

- Where should content be stored? All content should ideally be moved or copied to a central location while the Web site is under construction. Decide on what network disk or computer the content should be stored, and inform everyone involved with the project of this location.

- Do you have existing digital content? What kind of existing content does your company or organization have that's already in digital (computer readable) form and is appropriate to use for your Web site? An exhaustive inventory isn't necessary. Just quickly identify the kinds of content that you already have and determine what needs to be done in order to prepare it for use on your site.

- What new content needs to be created? Briefly identify the kinds of content that needs to be created from scratch or imported into the computer (through scanning, retyping, or importing from a digital camera), and then establish how the content will be created.

- How should the content be structured? Sketch a rough outline of how your Web site should be organized. Creating this preliminary outline may help you find and create content that fits with the purpose and design of your site. Don't stick too firmly to your preliminary design, because as content is created and collected, you'll probably want to make some changes. After you create the site, you'll find even more changes to make.

TIP *As you collect, create, and organize content for your site, it's possible that your idea about the Web site's purpose will change. If need be, flip back to "Step 3: Lay a Foundation" as necessary, and refine your Web site's new purpose.*

Creating a Central Location for Content

Repeatedly searching for content in a number of different locations not only decreases productivity but also increases the chance that important content will get misplaced or duplicated on your Web site.

When you actually create a Web site in Dreamweaver, you first need to create a new folder called the local root folder, or your local site, that Dreamweaver uses to store the Web site. However, because most, if not all, files stored in your local folder will eventually get published to your Web server (and be made available on the Internet), it makes sense to have a completely separate folder in which to store content before it gets added to the Web site, as shown in Figure 4-1. Think of it as a staging area for content—anything that your company considers potential content can be placed in this separate folder to be evaluated and added to the site as appropriate.

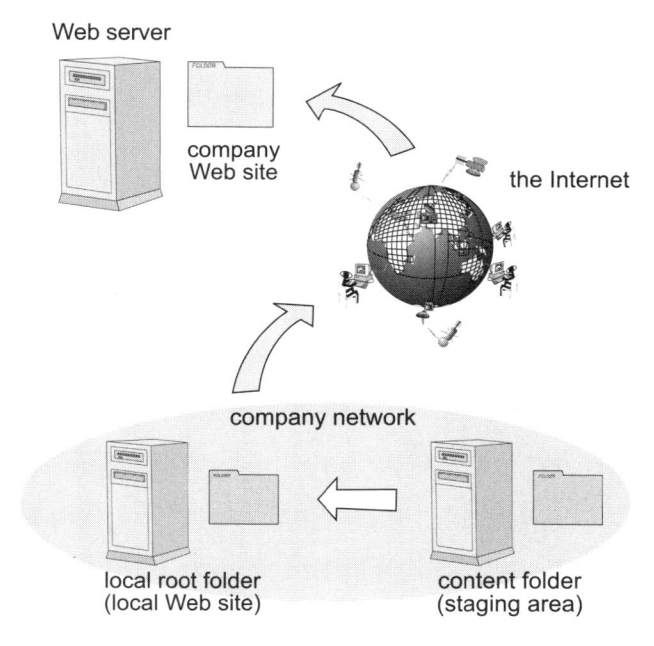

Figure 4-1 Where Web content is stored in the process of creating Web pages.

TIP *You may find that your organization doesn't need a central content folder, perhaps because all your content is quickly integrated into the site or because it is easy to locate without having to centralize it. If this is the case, when we suggest looking in or placing content in your central content folder, just go to the source of your content instead.*

Before you create a folder in which to store your potential Web content, first decide on an appropriate computer or network disk. It's ideal to use a network disk that is both backed up regularly and uses some method of protecting against hard disk failure (such as a Redundant Array of Independent Disks, or RAID). It's also preferable to use a Windows 2000 or Windows NT partition formatted using the NTFS file system, which provides additional security features. However, if your company or organization doesn't have these resources, simply choose the most convenient computer or network disk.

The central content folder could be located on the same computer or network disk as the Dreamweaver local site, or in a completely different location. After you've decided on a location, create the folder by following these steps:

1. **Launch Windows Explorer.**

   Click the Start button, choose Programs, and then click Windows Explorer. (If you're using Windows 2000, click the Start button, choose Programs, choose Accessories, and then click Windows Explorer.)

2. **Navigate to the location where you want to create the folder.**

   In the Folders pane on the left of the Windows Explorer window, click the plus sign next to the location where you want to store the content folder to expand the location's subfolders. For example, click the plus sign next to My Computer to view the local hard drives in your system (and any network disks that are mapped to a drive letter), as shown in Figure 4-2.

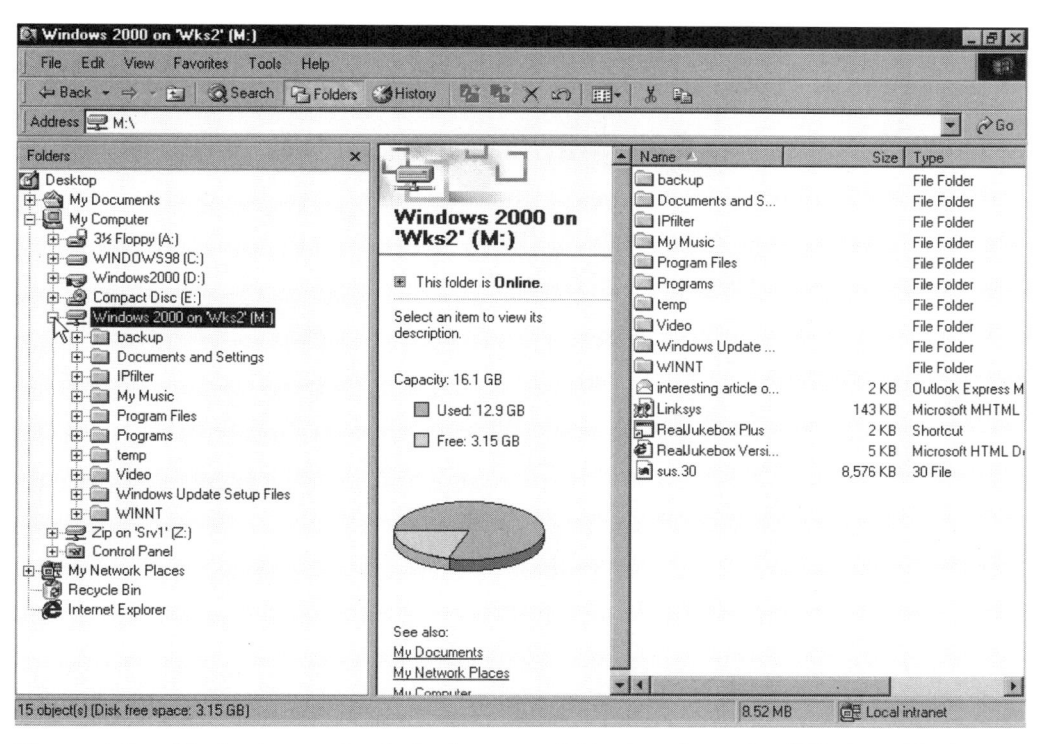

Figure 4-2   Navigating to the desired content folder location using Windows Explorer.

3. Create a new folder.

While viewing the drive or folder where you want to store your content, right-click a blank area of the right pane, choose New from the shortcut menu, and then choose Folder from the submenu, as shown in Figure 4-3.

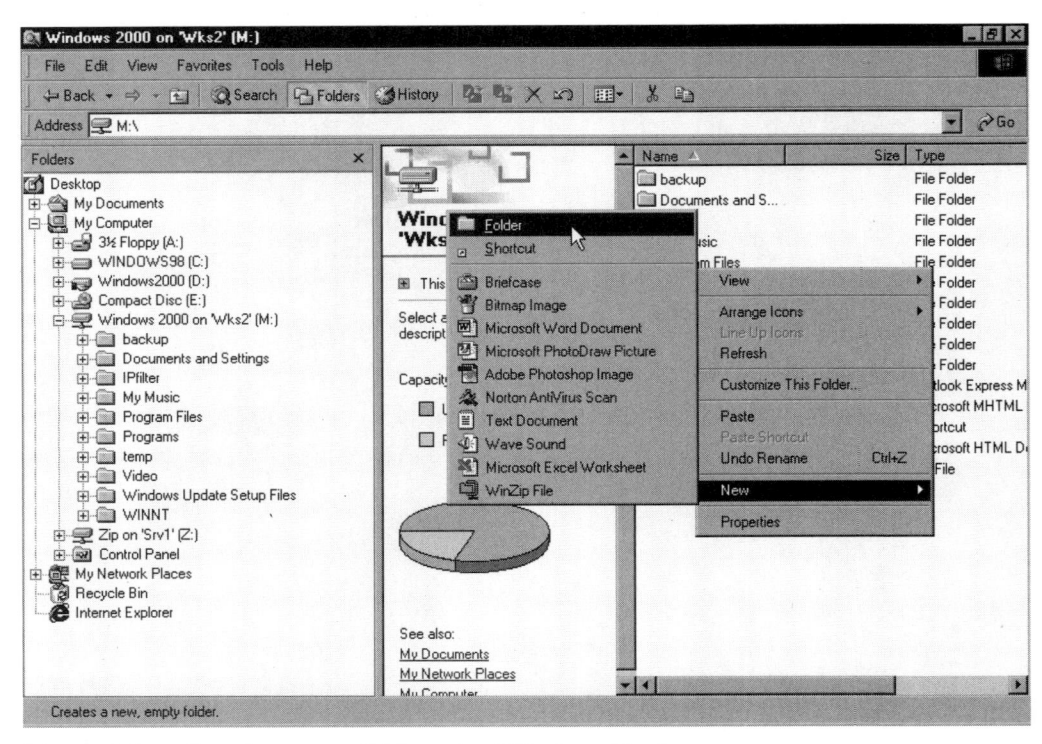

Figure 4-3 Creating a new folder using Windows Explorer.

4. **Enter a name for the folder.**

   When you create a new folder, the folder name is automatically highlighted. Enter the name you want for the folder, and then click anywhere onscreen to save the name. If you make a mistake, right-click the folder and choose Rename from the shortcut menu.

Establishing a File Naming Convention

Before you start collecting or creating content for your company or organization's Web site, it's important to establish a file naming convention. This step makes it easier to identify files and work with them.

There are differing views as to what makes good file naming conventions, but consistency is paramount. Create some rules that work for you, and stick to them. Here are some recommendations:

- Unix Web servers don't like spaces in filenames and handle capitalization differently than do Windows Web servers. To accommodate this, name your files using all lowercase letters, and instead of using spaces, use the underscore character or simply run words together, for example, webpresentation1.htm or web_presentation1.htm. Even if you're using a Windows Web server now, this makes your Web site more flexible if you decide to move to a Unix Web server in the future.

- If your content is time-sensitive, such as newsletter copy, use a date in the filename, either at the beginning of the name or at the end.

- Images often come in large and small sizes (full size and thumbnail). Append some sort of short tag to differentiate large and small images—perhaps small_ or s_ in front of the image name (for example, small_product1.jpg or s_product1.jpg) or at the end (for example, product1_small.jpg or product1_s.jpg).

Collecting Existing Digital Content

When creating a Web site, it can be a bit daunting at first thinking about all the content that needs to be created. Fortunately, most companies and organizations already have a large amount of digital content that can be used on a Web site with only a minimal amount of work.

When we say digital content, what we mean is any content that can be opened in a computer. This includes data on hard drives, your local network, the Internet (though be careful about copyrights), floppy and Zip disks, CD-ROMS, and so forth.

To use existing digital content (which comes in many types), you first need to locate it, and if necessary, convert the content to an appropriate format for importing into Dreamweaver.

Types of Digital Content to Look For

Just about any kind of digital content your company or organization has can be adapted for use on the Web. The following list gives examples of some common types of content that your organization might have that would be suitable for publishing on your Web site. (This list is by no means comprehensive. Other data types can also be used, although depending on your applications, it might take a little work to get them into Web page format.)

- Word processor documents (.doc, .txt, .wpf) include materials such as project reports, manuals, company objectives, newsletters, and notices to customers created with word processing programs, such as Microsoft Word, AppleWorks, or WordPerfect.

- PowerPoint presentations (.ppt), such as presentations, lecture slides, or demos, might be great additions to your Web site.

- Spreadsheet documents (.xls) might also be good content for your Web site, provided the data relates to your site's purpose and target audience. This could include financial information, analyzed data from technical companies, or statistical data from test results.

- Digital images (.jpg, .gif, .png, .fpx) are a staple of any Web site, and any digital images that your company has are potential content for your site. This includes company logos or graphics.

- Flyers, brochures, or other computer-created content stored in some sort of computer format (perhaps created using Microsoft Publisher or Adobe PageMaker) are also excellent sources of content.

- E-mails can often be a rich source of content, although care needs to be taken when using e-mail conversations on a Web site. Special messages sent out to customers can be placed in a Web page for users who didn't receive the e-mail, customer questions and answers can be integrated into a Frequently Asked Questions page, or visitor comments can be placed on a Feedback page (usually with names removed).

- Existing Web pages might seem an obvious choice, but if your company or organization already has Web pages it has created for one reason or another, you should probably evaluate how useful they'd be on your new Web site.

- Sound files and/or video files (.wav, .au, .mp3, .mpg, .avi, .mov) are usually very large and should generally be avoided on Web sites, but you might find audio and/or video files that would be perfect for your site. Use discretion with these files because of their large size and the slow speed of most visitors' Internet connections.

Locating Existing Digital Content

Before you can use any existing digital content on your company or organization's Web site, you need to identify where it is located. This may or may not be so easy, depending on the company and the data.

To locate the data, either look for it manually on your hard drives or use the Search tool built into Windows.

Manually Looking for Content

If you have a good idea where your content is located, look for it manually by following these steps:

1. **Launch Windows Explorer.**

   Click the Start button, choose Programs, and then click Windows Explorer. (If you're using Windows 2000, click the Start button, choose Programs, choose Accessories, and then click Windows Explorer.)

2. **Navigate to the folder containing your content.**

   In the Folders pane on the left of the Windows Explorer window, click the plus sign next to the location where you want to look for subfolders. For example, click the plus sign next to My Documents to look for content stored on your computer, as shown in Figure 4-4.

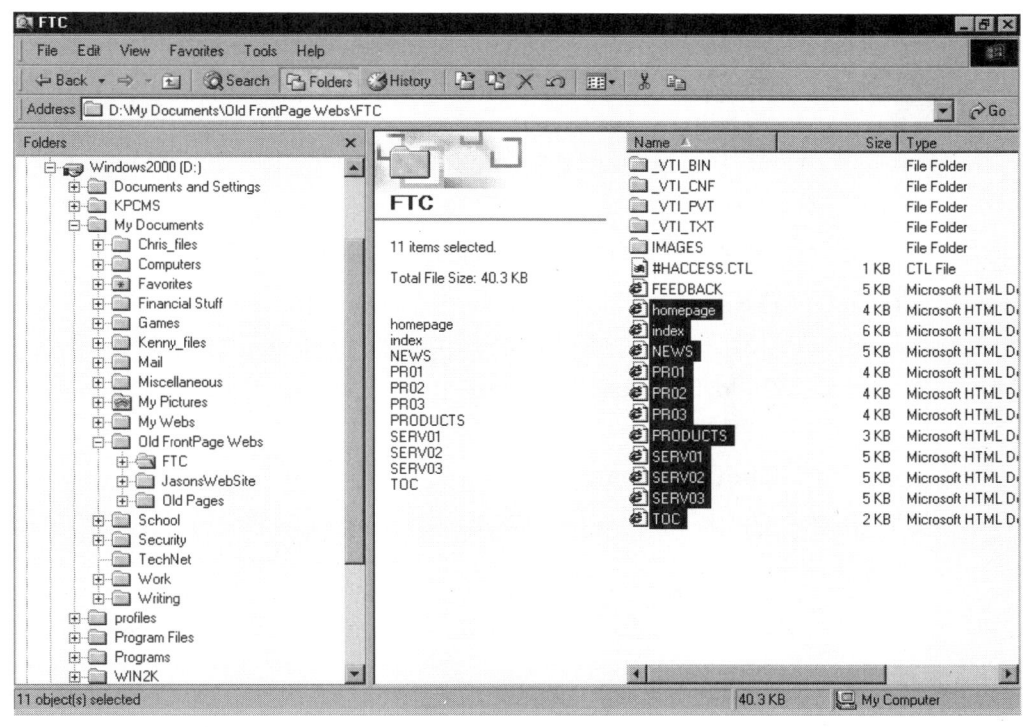

Figure 4-4   Locating content manually using Windows Explorer.

Step 4   Collect and Organize Your Content

3. **Copy the data to your central content folder.**

   To make it easier to find your content again, select the files you want to use and then choose the Edit menu's Copy command. Navigate to your content folder, select the folder or subfolder into which you want to copy the files, and then choose the Edit menu's Paste command.

   TIP *To select multiple contiguous files, select the first file, hold down the Shift key, and then select the last file you want to select. To select multiple files that aren't contiguous, hold down the Ctrl key while selecting each file. To copy selected files, press the Ctrl and C keys simultaneously. To then paste the copied files, press the Ctrl and V keys simultaneously.*

Performing a Search for Content

If you don't know where your content is located or you want to do a thorough job searching for potential content, use the Search tool built into Windows. This tool scours your drives looking for certain types of content. You'll need to specify what to look for, and you'll still need to look through the potentially large amount of content that is located, but this can be a great way to find content that's filed away in less-than-optimal locations.

To perform a search for content, follow these steps:

1. **Open the Search tool.**

   Click the Start button, choose Search, and then click For Files Or Folders. (If you're using Windows 98, click the Start button, choose Find, and then click Files Or Folders.)

2. **Enter the search criteria.**

   To search for all files of a specific file type, in the Search For Files Or Folders Named box, enter an asterisk, and then enter the three-letter extension of the file type you want to search for. For example, to search for Word documents, enter *.doc*, as shown in Figure 4-5. This is usually the most effective way to search for files. A list of the more common file extensions was presented earlier in the section "Types of Digital Content to Look For."

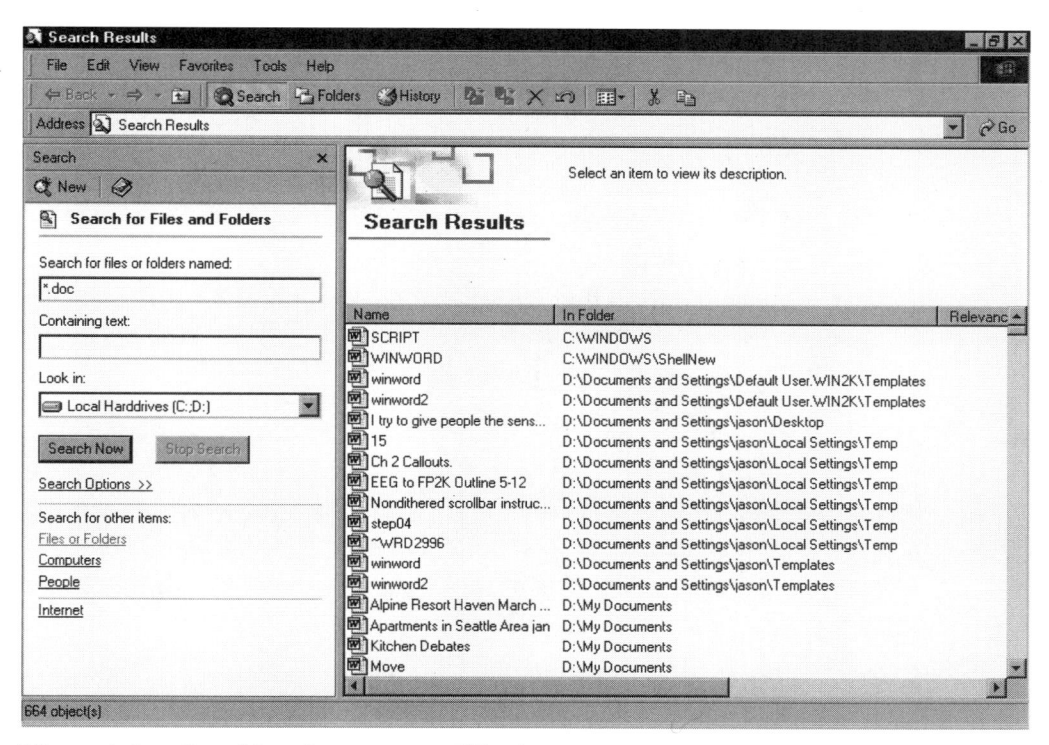

Figure 4-5 Searching for content in Windows 2000.

TIP *You can use asterisks as wildcards when performing a search. The search program ignores the asterisk and returns any files that have the rest of the characters you specify in their filename. For example, *.doc returns all files that have the .doc file extension; report.* returns all files named "report" no matter what their file extension. You can also use asterisks inside filenames. For example, report*.doc returns any Word documents that begin with the characters "report." Wildcards also work within Dreamweaver's own search tool, which is accessible by choosing the Edit menu's Find command.*

3. Specify where to search.

Use the Look In box to specify the drives or network computers in which to look for content. Select a drive from the list, or select Browse from the list to browse for a drive or network location.

4. **Start the search.**

   Click the Search Now button to start searching for files that match the search criteria. If the search is taking too long, click the Stop Search button to discontinue the search.

5. **Examine the search results.**

   Windows displays all the files it found that matched your search criteria in the Search Results pane on the right side of the window (see Figure 4-5). Scroll down the list to locate files that are potentially useful on your Web site. If you want to open a file in the search results, double-click it.

   TIP   *If you uncover content that's stored in a location you haven't manually looked in, select the file in the Search Results window. This displays the file details at the top of the window, including the folder in which it's stored. Click the hyperlink labeled In Folder to look in that folder. Sometimes this uncovers additional files that did not show up in the search results that might be useful on your Web site.*

6. **Copy the data to your central content folder.**

   To make it easier to find your content again, select the files you might want to use, and then choose the Edit menu's Copy command. Navigate to your content folder (as described earlier in the section "Creating a Central Location for Content"), select the folder or subfolder into which you want to copy the files, and then choose the Edit menu's Paste command.

   TIP   *Windows 2000 contains a powerful search feature called the Indexing Service. When turned on (it's off by default), the Indexing Service scans all supported data files (such as Microsoft Office documents) on your hard drives, making an index of information about each file's contents. After this index is created, you can perform searches for documents containing certain words or content. See the Windows 2000 Help system for more information.*

Converting Existing Data to an Appropriate Format

Although you'll be able to import some of the content that you find directly into Dreamweaver, you'll need to convert most content into another file format in order to use it in Dreamweaver.

Deciding how to get content into Dreamweaver usually requires examining the export capabilities of the applications used to create the content, since Dreamweaver has such a limited range of file formats it can open. Table 4-1 lists the most common formats.

EXTENSION	FILE FORMAT
.htm, .html, .htx, .otm, .asp	HTML files (Web pages)
.txt	Plain text files
.shtm, .shtml, .stm	Server-Side Includes (Web pages inserted by the server)
.xml	XML files
.css	Cascading Style Sheet files
.asp	Active Server Pages

Table 4-1   Common document formats Dreamweaver can open.

In the following paragraphs, we offer some general recommendations for importing content.

If the application that created the content is capable of exporting Web pages, this is usually the best way to get text into Dreamweaver. Export the content to a Web page and then open the page in Dreamweaver and see whether you can easily integrate it with your other Web pages and content. ("Step 6: Create Your Pages" gives you the full details on working with Web pages in Dreamweaver.) Some programs, such as Microsoft Office 2000, will actually export enhanced Web pages with a fair amount of interactivity. An example is the PowerPoint presentation exported to a Web page that's shown in Figure 4-6. If you're dealing with a complete presentation, spreadsheet chart, or any sort of content that you want to use in its entirety with little or no changes, using the native program's Save As Web Page feature (or equivalent feature) usually yields the most professional-looking results.

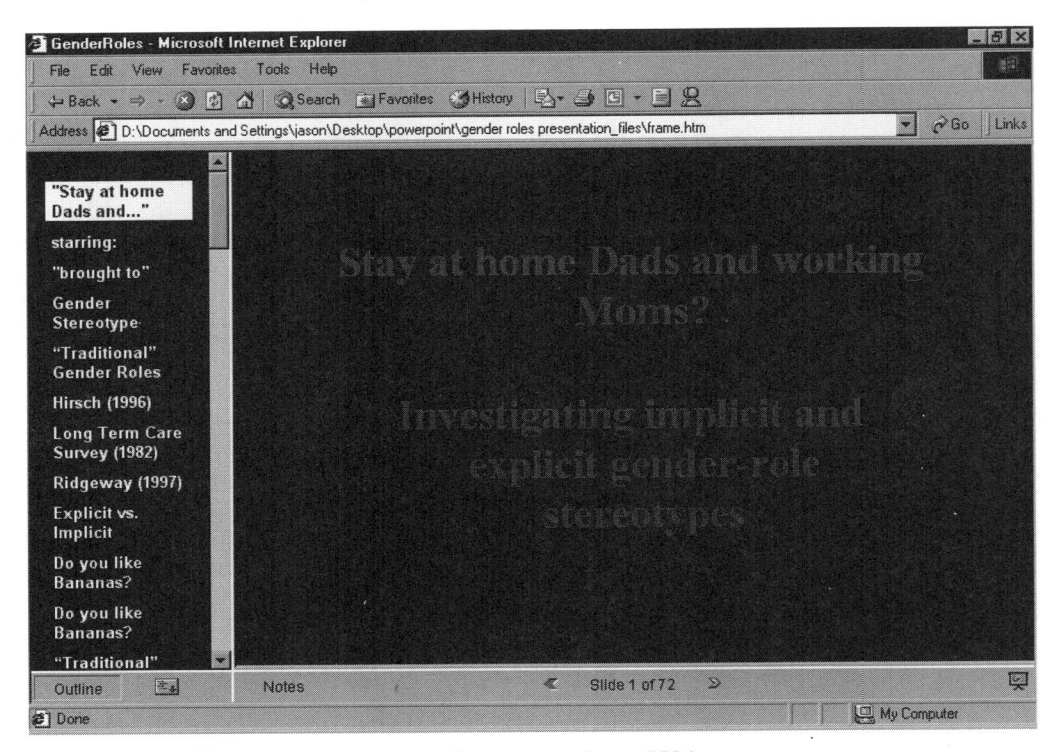

Figure 4-6   A PowerPoint presentation exported to a Web page.

NOTE *In general, if the native application can't export content to HTML format effectively, it's best to copy and paste the text directly into Dreamweaver. However, if the formatting is important, you can sometimes circumvent this limitation of the native application by opening the file in another program that does support saving in HTML format, such as Microsoft Word.*

If you need to merge the content with other content within a single Web page, save the file as an HTML document if possible, open that document in Dreamweaver, and then copy and paste the text into the appropriate Web page. (This process saves all or most of the formatting information.) If you simply cannot export an HTML document, the simplest method is to copy and paste the text from the application that created the content into Dreamweaver, as described in "Step 6: Create Your Pages"; however, be aware that this usually strips out *all* formatting. You could alternatively convert the content to plain text, open this file in Dreamweaver, and then copy the text into the appropriate page. Typically, this is what you'll have to do if you can't open the content on the computer running Dreamweaver because you don't have a program installed that can read the file.

> **TIP** *Dreamweaver has a special command for importing Web pages that were created using Microsoft Word: the File->Import->Import Word HTML command. This command opens the Web page and strips out a large amount of unnecessary code that Word places in the page. See "Step 6: Create Your Pages" for more information.*

If you want to import spreadsheet content, you can either test out the spreadsheet program's Web page export capabilities or you can save the content as a text file (either tab delimited or using comma separated values, .csv). Then use Dreamweaver's Import Table Data command, as discussed in "Step 6: Create Your Pages."

Images present their own set of importing issues. Table 4-2 displays a list of the image formats that Dreamweaver can use. In general, if the image is small, or is a computer-created graphic, such as a company logo, use the GIF image format. If the image is a full-color, photograph-quality image, save it in JPEG format. The newer PNG format is becoming a viable alternative for both formats, since it can be used in low-color mode to keep file size down or in full-color mode for photographs. PNG images maximize cross-platform quality.

EXTENSION	FILE FORMAT
.gif	CompuServe Graphics Interchange Format (GIF) image
.jpg, .jpeg	Joint Photographic Experts Group (JPEG) image
.png	Portable Network Graphic (PNG) image

Table 4-2   Image formats that Dreamweaver can import.

> **WARNING** *PNG images aren't supported by versions of Netscape Navigator or Microsoft Internet Explorer older than 4 without using a plug-in.*

If the quality or size of the image is important, or if you need to do something sophisticated like create an image with transparency, you'll need to modify the file by using either the program that created the image or a stand-alone image editor, such as Macromedia Fireworks, Adobe Photoshop, or Microsoft PhotoDraw. If the program has a Save For Use On The Web function or similar command, consider using it. Figure 4-7 shows a screen from Microsoft PhotoDraw's Save For Use In Wizard. Commands like this usually walk you through saving the image as a GIF or JPEG file, choosing the proper amount of compression (balancing file size with image quality), or making part of the image transparent, which saves some guesswork on your part.

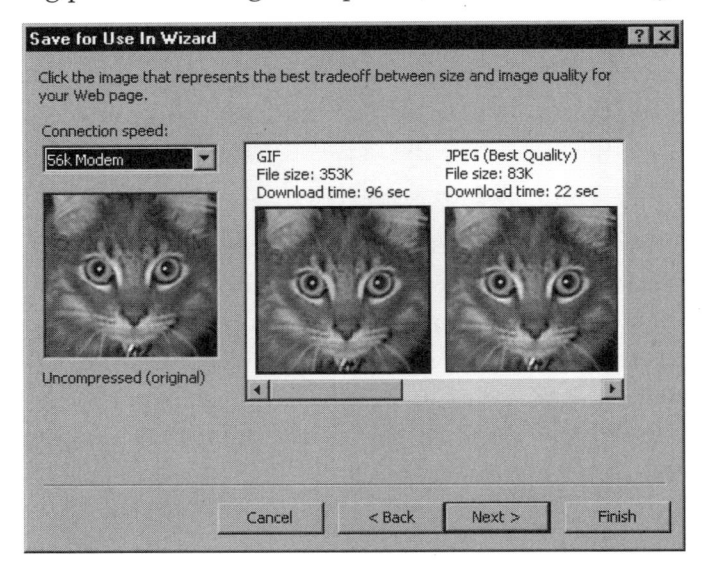

Figure 4-7   Converting an image to an appropriate format using an image editor's wizard.

Using Macromedia Fireworks as your image editor offers some specific benefits when creating Web pages in Dreamweaver, including the ability to quickly optimize an image directly from Dreamweaver, as shown in Figure 4-8. (It also allows you to easily create rollover buttons and perform batch image processing, such as quickly creating a photo album from an image folder.)

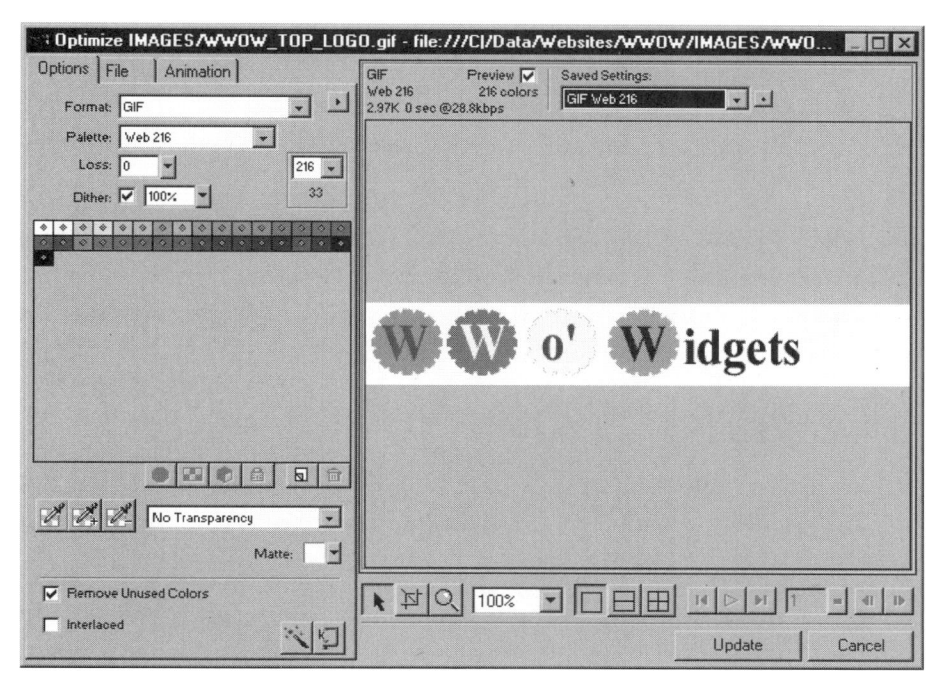

Figure 4-8 Optimizing an image with Dreamweaver's Optimize Image In Fireworks command.

TIP *It's best to avoid using large images to prevent Web pages from taking too long to load. If you want to display a large, high-quality image, create a thumbnail (miniature version) of the image that is linked to the full-size image. This allows the Web page to load quickly, and then if some visitors want to see the high-resolution image, they can click the hyperlink to display the larger image. There is no hard rule about image sizes, but generally, if your page takes longer than 30 seconds to load over a 28.8 connection, make your images smaller or remove some of them. For more information about working with images in Dreamweaver, see "Step 6: Create Your Pages."*

Creating New Digital Content

Not all content for your Web site is going to be available in digital format. Some of it will exist in print form and still more will need to be created from scratch.

In general, the new content falls into two categories: images and documents. Images are usually created using a digital camera, a scanner, or from scratch using an art program. Documents are generally created from scratch using a word processor or spreadsheet program, although you might be tempted to scan printed documents that aren't already available in digital format.

Digital Images

Images are an important type of content for most Web sites. Acquiring and importing images into the computer thus is a fairly important task for most companies with a Web site.

There are several ways to create new digital images for use on a Web site. Photographs can be scanned into the computer using a scanner, imported using a Photo CD picture disk or online image processing service, or they can be taken using a digital camera and imported directly into the computer. Digital images can also be created in the computer using an art program. The following sections give you an overview of how digital image resolution works, help you get images into the computer no matter what method you choose, and also help your company decide which method will work best for future image acquisition.

Dots per Inch and Image Resolution

Two factors determine the size and resolution of an image: dots per inch (dpi) and resolution (pixels). All images on a computer monitor are displayed at 96dpi (or 72dpi), so the only way to increase the quality onscreen is to increase the resolution.

However, when discussing photographs to scan or images to print, the situation gets a little contradictory. When scanning a photograph, size (resolution) can't be changed, so to get a higher-quality image into or out of the computer, you need to increase the dpi. Similarly, when printing an image, if you keep the resolution (size) the same or lower it, but increase the dpi, you end up with a possibly smaller but more richly detailed printout. (Although a 300dpi image and a 96dpi image will look the same onscreen, the 300dpi image will look *much* better when printed out on a high-resolution printer.)

> **NOTE** *Inkjet printers can print upwards of 1440dpi, but you don't need to create 1440dpi images to make the best use of these printers (and please don't—the resulting images would be gigabytes in size). A 300dpi image yields finely detailed printouts on a 1440dpi inkjet printer and increasing the dpi further doesn't provide a large increase in image quality.*

When you scan an image, the dpi you specify controls the resolution (size) of the image. For example, a four-by-six-inch photograph scanned at 150dpi makes a roughly 900x600-pixel image—just a bit bigger than full screen for a computer using the 800x600 screen resolution. You can then crop this image a bit and save it as an 800x600-sized image at 96dpi for use as a large image on the Internet.

Here are some recommendations for resolution, image size, and dpi:

- Scan images at whatever dpi necessary to get the size of image you want (150dpi yields a 900x600 image from a four-by-six-inch photo).
- Save images for use on the Internet or computer screens at 96dpi.
- Save images intended for high-quality printouts at between 150dpi and 300dpi, depending on the resolution of the printer and the importance of quality.

Digital Cameras

The best way to quickly and easily acquire images for use on a Web site is with a digital camera. Digital cameras are here to stay, and they are already replacing standard film cameras for many businesses and organizations—especially those that need to take lots of pictures for use on the Web (such as real estate professionals).

Digital cameras offer numerous advantages. They're the fastest way to get an image into the computer because there is no need to develop prints. Most have a small display screen so that you can instantly view captured photos—and immediately delete any that you don't like. The image quality on most new megapixel digital cameras (cameras that take images at 1024x768 resolution or higher) are more than adequate for any Web site work, and even print work can be accommodated by the highest resolution cameras (though not *quite* as well as standard film).

The biggest drawbacks with digital cameras are cost, battery life, and complexity. They're still pretty expensive, although this is changing, especially for midrange or low-end cameras (which are now usually sufficient for Web site work). A smaller downside to digital cameras is their typically voracious appetite for batteries. (Stock up on rechargeable batteries if your camera doesn't come with them.) Also, digital cameras are more complex to operate than normal film cameras and have a slightly larger learning curve than normal cameras.

TIP *If you're in the market for a digital camera, we strongly urge you to consider getting one that has a USB interface, unless you have or plan to get a memory card reader (preferably USB) for your computer. The USB interface makes transferring images from the camera faster and much easier to configure, and it is now a standard feature on most cameras. Also, consider getting a camera with a zoom lens. Even a moderate two- or three-times magnification zoom provides a lot of flexibility when taking pictures.*

Here are some recommendations for using digital cameras for Web site image acquisition:

- Configure your camera to take pictures at the highest resolution you think your company may require. If you *know* that the images will never be used anywhere other than on the Internet or in a computer, it may be adequate to take pictures at 896x592 or similar resolution. You could even shoot images at 640x480 if the images will never be used full screen or for print work. If it's at all possible that the images will be used for high-quality printouts, take images at 1440x960 resolution or higher.

- Even if you don't require high-resolution images, configure your camera to use the highest or second-highest quality setting available. Some cameras offer an uncompressed image quality setting, which makes images much larger and generally should be avoided unless you are doing high-resolution print work.

- After taking pictures, consider transferring them into a separate subfolder located in your central content folder.

- Give images a short but descriptive name so that it's easy to tell what they are at a glance.

Scanning Photos

One of the most popular ways to get images into the computer is to take pictures using a standard camera, get prints made, and then scan the prints using a scanner.

Scanning photos has a low up-front cost associated with it: standard cameras are relatively inexpensive and of high quality, film isn't very expensive, and excellent flatbed scanners can be purchased for $100 or less. It's also the only way to get existing photos into the computer, and it's still the best way to get extremely high-quality images into the computer.

> **TIP** *Flatbed scanners provide the most flexibility in the types of items that can be scanned, although sheet-fed scanners and photograph-specific scanners are usually less expensive. Also, if all that your company plans to scan is photographs, a photograph scanner may prove easier to use than a flatbed scanner because there's no glass to smudge, and photographs won't slide around as much.*

However, if your company frequently takes pictures for use on its Web site, scanning pictures isn't always the most effective way of getting pictures into the computer. Generally, a whole roll of film must be taken before prints can be made and getting prints made takes both time and money. Once prints are made, scanning them also takes a fair amount of time and patience.

> **TIP** *If you're in the market for a scanner, we recommend picking up a USB scanner that's supported by Windows 2000. USB scanners are easy to set up and fast, and even if your company doesn't have Windows 2000 yet, Windows 2000 will serve as the foundation for Microsoft's future mainstream operating systems, making it a good idea to get devices supported by it.*

Here are some recommendations for scanning images into the computer:

- Scan images to the largest size you might need, and keep these high-resolution images in a separate high-resolution folder. For use on the Web, resize the images down to an appropriate size and save them in a different location or using a different filename.
- Scan to images into the central content folder so that everyone working on the Web site can find them.
- Give images a short but descriptive name so that it's easy to tell what they are at a glance.

Picture CDs and Disks

One way to get photographs into the computer if you don't have a digital camera or scanner is to pay an additional fee to get a Picture CD, Photo CD, or pictures on disk when getting regular print film developed.

This method eliminates the hassle of scanning pictures; however, it isn't very cost-effective for most organizations. Generally, in addition to the cost of developing and creating prints, there is another charge of $3 to $20 per roll of film, depending on the scanning resolution and the company. It doesn't take too many rolls of film at this price before you've matched the price of a new scanner.

However, if there's a pressing need to acquire images and your company or organization doesn't have an alternative means to acquire images, paying to get pictures placed on CD or floppy disk at the time of developing can be an effective way to accomplish the task at hand.

Here are some recommendations for helping you make the most of images from a CD or floppy disk:

- If you regularly use picture CDs or floppies, label the CDs or floppies well and store them somewhere that all people working on your Web site know about.
- The best way to take images from a picture CD or floppy is to browse to the images on the CD or floppy using Windows Explorer and then copy the images directly into your central content folder, as shown in Figure 4-9. Alternatively, you can use the export function of the software included with the images to save the pictures as JPEG images, as shown in Figure 4-10.

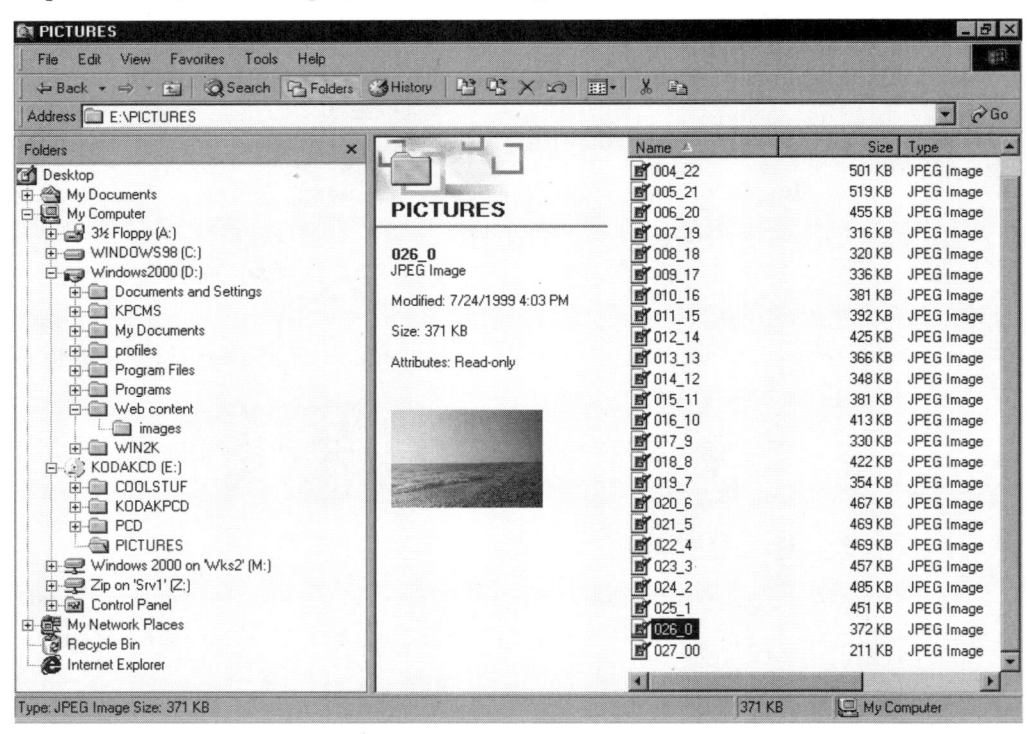

Figure 4-9 Manually taking images off a picture CD using Windows Explorer.

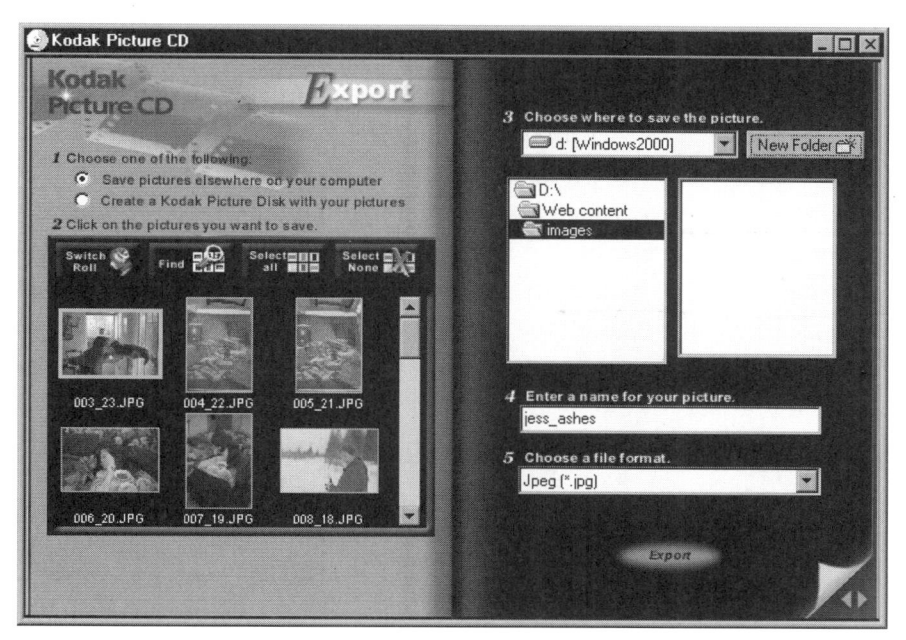

Figure 4-10 Exporting an image from a picture CD.

> **NOTE** *When you export images using the software included with the photos, you will usually lose some image quality and/or resolution. This usually isn't a problem, but if you're finicky about quality, take the original images off the CD using Windows Explorer and manually resize them to the proper size for your Web page using an image editor.*

- Keep a close eye on the resolution and quality of the pictures exported. Typically the highest resolution available is around 1536x1024, which is far too big for use on the Web. However, it's usually preferable to take the high-resolution image and manually resize it to a more appropriate size for your Web site, instead of initially exporting a lower resolution image that might later turn out to be too small.

- Save images into the central content folder so that everyone working on the Web site can find them.

- Give images a short but descriptive name so that it's easy to tell what they are at a glance.

Online Photo Services

Instead of paying to get your prints scanned and placed on a CD or floppy disk, many photo labs and services now offer to scan photos and place them on a secure Web site, from which you can then download them, as shown in Figure 4-11. This can provide somewhat quicker turnaround than picture CDs and disks, but in most respects it is otherwise identical—except that instead of taking pictures off a CD or disk they are downloaded over the Internet. Of course, if your company or organization needs high-resolution images and has a slow-speed Internet connection, this might not be the most effective means of acquiring images. Instead, use picture CDs, or preferably, get a scanner or digital camera.

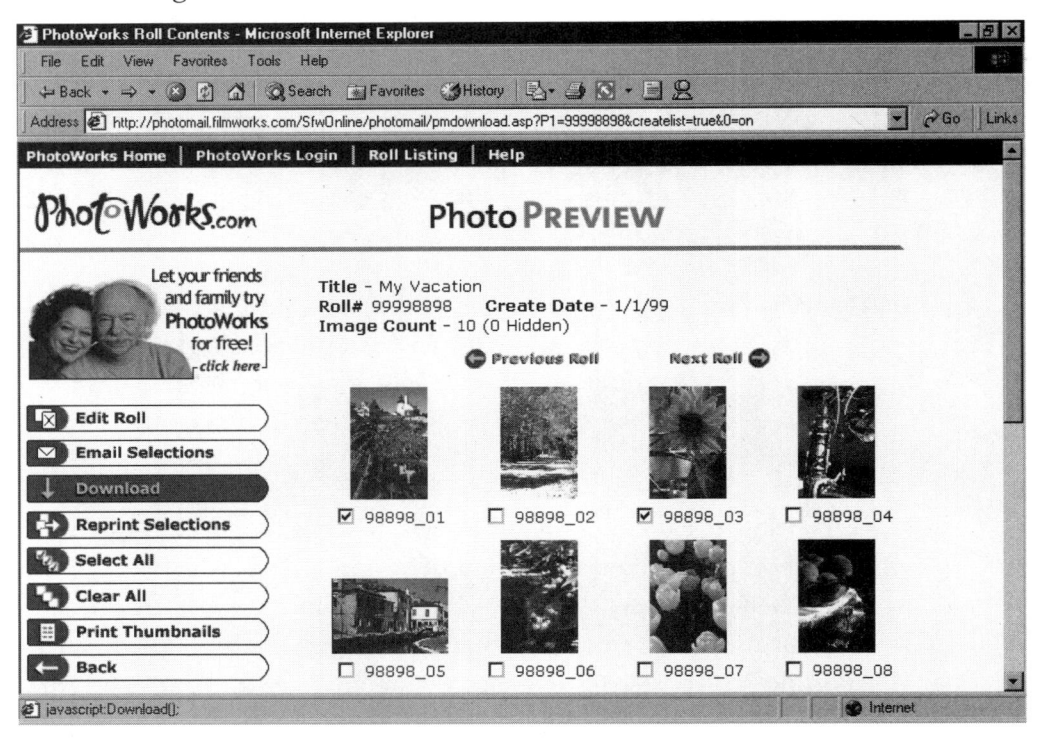

Figure 4-11 A scanned roll of film at an online photo service.

Here are some recommendations for using an online photo service more effectively:

- Download the highest resolution version of the image you might need, since the higher resolution image may not be available later. In general, it's best to download a high-resolution image, make a copy of it, and then resize it for use on your Web site.

- Depending on the processing company, you may need to convert the images you download into JPEG (.jpg) images using their software before you can work with the images on your Web site.

- Make sure to download the images you want to use promptly. Some services keep images posted for only 30 days.

- Save images into the central content folder so that everyone working on the Web site can find them.

- Give images a short but descriptive name so that it's easy to tell what they are at a glance.

Documents

Documents are the other half of the new content equation, and unfortunately, not every document that belongs on your Web site is going to exist, or at least not in digital form.

Working with Print Documents

If you have content that would be good on your Web site, but you can't find a digital version of it, here's a suggested course of action:

1. **Look again.**

    We can't emphasize enough how much easier it is to use content that's already in digital form than it is to bring a print document into the computer.

2. **Retype the document.**

    Unless the document is really long, and even if it is, consider retyping any print documents that you want to use on your site. This is especially true for documents that have small typefaces, complex layouts or graphics, or are in poor condition. It's usually less hassle than scanning and performing Optical Character Recognition (OCR), and many documents won't need to be entirely retyped—just those sections that are needed for your site.

3. **Scan the document and use an OCR program.**

    Although OCR programs have improved and they are now quite useful, unless you have a long document that needs to be placed in its entirety on your Web site, it's usually faster to retype the document than it is to scan it, run it through the OCR program, and then correct the mistakes.

TIP *OCR programs are stand-alone programs that convert a scanned document into text that can be used in a word processing program or Web page editor. They can provide an easy way to digitize existing, typewritten content, but they do produce errors in the scanned documents. We recommend that you carefully evaluate the amount of time involved in correcting scanned documents before relying heavily on OCR programs.*

4. **Save the document to the central content folder.**

   After finding, retyping, or scanning the content, save it to your central content folder with a descriptive filename so that the file can be identified easily.

Creating New Documents

When creating new content for use on a Web site, you can take specific steps to make the content import into Dreamweaver more elegantly:

- Create any large amounts of text you want to use on your Web site using Microsoft Word or another word processing program, and then either copy and past the text into your Web pages, save it as a plain text file for importing into your pages, or save it directly as an HTML document that Dreamweaver can then edit. While Dreamweaver is a passable text editor, it's much easier and more efficient to create content of any substantial length in a dedicated word processor.

- Avoid using complex formatting or graphics in documents. These are best created later using Dreamweaver, since complex formatting generally doesn't export to HTML format accurately and the resulting HTML file may prove difficult to edit in Dreamweaver.

- Before creating a large amount of content with a particular application, test out how well the content can be exported to HTML from the application and then imported into Dreamweaver. Knowing the limitations of the process beforehand can save a lot of time and money in the long run.

- Save new documents in the central content folder with useful filenames so that everyone working on the Web site can identify them.

Organizing Your Content and Planning Your Web Site

The organization and structure of a Web site rarely turns out well unless it is planned beforehand. Failing to plan and organize a Web site generally leads to a site that is confusing and ineffective at the job of presenting information to visitors.

Gathering all or most of your content together in one place is a good first step in planning your Web site's structure because it gives you an understanding of the content the site will contain. After doing this, we recommend that you sit down and organize the content, and then draw up a preliminary site plan.

> **NOTE** *The contrarian position to all this organizing and planning is that although it's true that Web sites created without much thought given to organization generally turn out to be confusing and maybe even ineffectual, it's okay to create one of these sites as a starting point. Just keep in mind that you'll probably want to restructure your site into a more effective form at a later date.*

Organizing Your Content

After you've rounded up the content for your Web site, it makes a lot of sense to organize it before starting work on the site—both physically in the central content folder and logically for the structure of the Web site.

There are a number of different ways to organize content in your central content folder. One method that works well is to place content into folders depending on what action needs to be done with it. For example, a high_priority folder could store important content, or a possible_content folder could store content that you're not yet sure belongs on the Web site. Within these folders you could further organize the data by subject, source, and data type (i.e., documents and images).

In addition to deciding how to physically organize your content, you might want to work on some more abstract content organization. One way to do this is to sit down with a pad of paper and poke around the central content folder, making notes of what you have available and creating some logical groupings. The organization you decide upon may or may not be reflected in the folder structure of your central content folder. It's more important to get an idea of how the content should be logically organized on your site than to actually organize it into separate folders.

We can't tell you exactly how to organize your content, since the content usually dictates this, but here are some general recommendations:

- Look at the Web site's purpose and the content that you identified as important in "Step 2: Develop a Content Strategy" and keep this focus central in your mind.
- Organize content logically and intuitively by subject. For example, a Web site designed to advertise or sell products would do well to organize content into product information, company information, and support information categories. This makes sense and is intuitive for visitors, since they match key topics that visitors will probably look for.
- Try to organize your content in a way that leaves no one category with too much content or too little. If you find this happening, consider splitting or merging the categories, or creating subcategories.

Creating Your Site Plan

At this point you may want to actually sketch out the design for your Web site. Simple as it sounds, this is one of the more important parts of the process, since the way in which you structure the site determines how easy and intuitive it is for visitors to use.

To create a plan for your site, sit down with a pad of paper or create a new Word document in Outline view. Pull out any notes you took on the content available for the site (see the section "Organizing Your Content" earlier in this step). Also take out the document you prepared in "Step 2: Develop a Content Strategy" that lists the purpose of the site and what it should accomplish, how the site will benefit your company or organization, what kind of content should be used, and the target audience for the site. This document gives the direction for your site, so we suggest that you review it thoroughly before creating your site plan.

When actually creating the site plan, you'll probably want to start with the home page—the page that is first displayed when visiting a site. The home page acts as the top of the outline that is your Web site. Briefly list what content should be contained here—perhaps a summary of the site, as well as short leaders on the site's most interesting or frequently accessed content. (For more help with this, see the section "Creating an Effective Home Page" in "Step 7: Polish Your Pages.") Then write down the categories for the next level of your site. Each of these categories will be a page and a navigational link for your site if you make a navigation bar or set of hyperlinks for your site (you'll probably want to). As previously discussed, the categories should be logical and intuitive to visitors. Also, the second-level headings (the first level below the home page) should provide users with an accurate summary of the content in your site.

> **TIP** *Allow room for additional pages and content when creating your site plan, especially when creating your second-level headings (those right under the home page). Redesigning a Web site to accommodate new content can be resource intensive as well as inconvenient to visitors who have learned your site layout or bookmarked individual pages in the site.*

Try to avoid making too many levels in your Web site. From the home page, the most important content should be one click away, and all important content should ideally be no more than three clicks away for most sites. (Larger sites may need to have additional levels, but avoid it if possible.) Keeping information accessible with a low number of clicks makes accessing information faster and easier for visitors. It also increases the chance that visitors will stay rather than get impatient and leave.

Besides watching out for a Web site structure that's too deep, you also need to avoid making the structure too wide (too many pages at the same level). This is especially true for the second level of pages (the first under the home page). Too many second-level pages will overload the site's navigation bars with too many options. Although there are no rules about how many links are too many, navigation bars (and Web pages) lose their effectiveness if there are too many options to choose from. In general, limit your navigation bars to fewer than ten links, and possibly no more than five, depending on your page design.

While not absolutely necessary, we recommend taking at least a quick pass through your entire site at this stage, creating a diagram of what pages should be created and what content belongs on each page. Creating this site plan will not only make your Web site more coherent, intuitive, and effective but also make it easier to delegate work.

Summary

This step walked you through the last phase of Web site planning—collecting, creating, and organizing your company or organization's content—before you actually start creating pages. This step involves preparing a directory to store all content before it's actually added to the site, collecting existing digital content, creating new digital content, organizing the content, and then creating a plan for your Web site's structure.

Step 5

SET UP YOUR SITE

Featuring:
- Defining a New Local Site
- Configuring Dreamweaver to Work with a Firewall
- Overview of the Site Window
- Creating the Initial Structure
- Checking Files In and Out

When you're ready to start construction on your Web site, you begin by using Dreamweaver's Site window. Dreamweaver's interface consists of two windows: the Site window, where you perform all site management tasks, and the Document window, where you edit and create individual Web pages.

This step introduces the Site window and helps you set up your Web site by defining your local Web site in Dreamweaver and then developing your initial site structure—creating new pages and folders to mimic the site design you worked out in "Step 4: Collect and Organize Your Content." You'll also learn the basics of working with remote sites (Web servers).

Defining a New Local Site

The first thing you need to do when actually creating your Web site is to create or open your local Dreamweaver Web site—the local version of your site—which is stored in a folder somewhere on your company network. You perform all your work on the local site, and after testing for errors, you transfer the files to your Web hosting company's Web server, which then makes the site accessible to everyone on the Internet.

Although you can skip using Dreamweaver's Web site management capabilities and use Dreamweaver only to create pages, using Dreamweaver to manage your site saves a lot of time, provides additional functionality, and decreases errors such as broken hyperlinks.

You don't need to spend too much time defining your new site—you can change the information in your site definition anytime after creating it—just choose the Site menu's Define Sites command, select your site, and click the Edit button.

To define a new site, follow these steps:

1. **Start Dreamweaver.**

   Click the Start button, click Programs, click Macromedia Dreamweaver 3, and then click Dreamweaver 3.

2. **Create a new site.**

   To do this, choose the Site menu's New Site command.

3. **Enter the local site information.**

   Enter a descriptive name for your Web site in the Site Name box, as shown in Figure 5-1. In the Local Root Folder box, enter the path to the folder in which you want to store your local Web site, or click the folder icon to locate or create the folder. (You can also open an existing Web site you've created.) In the HTTP Address box, enter the domain name you acquired for your Web site. Leave the Refresh Local File List Automatically and the Cache check boxes selected.

Figure 5-1 Creating a new Web site.

4. **Specify the type of Web server.**

   Click the Web Server Info item in the Category list box in the Site Definition dialog box to enter information about your Web server, as shown in Figure 5-2. In the Server Access box, select FTP. If you're publishing your pages onto a company intranet or a local Web server, select Local/Network from the Server Access box and then enter the path to the remote network folder or Web server in the Remote Folder box that appears after you select the Local/Network option.

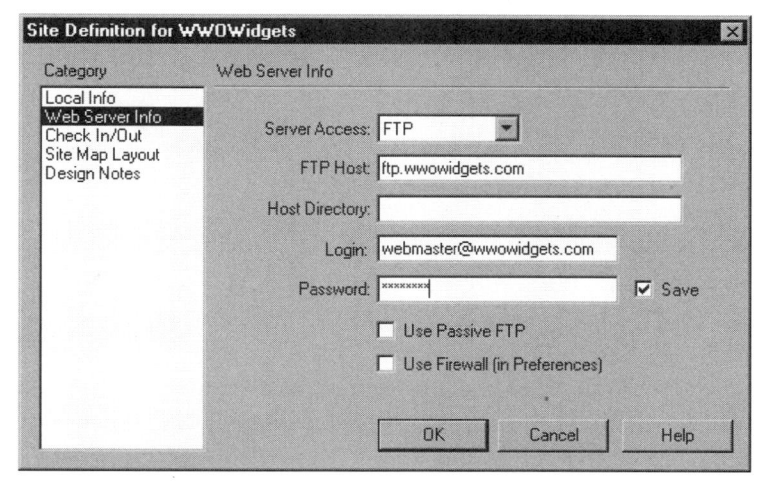

Figure 5-2 Entering the information about your remote Web server.

Step 5 Set Up Your Site

5. **Enter the FTP information.**

    In the FTP Host box, enter the FTP hostname given to you by your ISP, for example, *ftp.mycompany.com* (leave out the ftp://). Enter your Web site username and password in the Login and Password boxes, and select the Save check box to save this information. If your company or organization uses a network firewall, see the next section. Leave the Host Directory box blank, and check with your ISP if you have trouble with publishing to the wrong directory.

6. **Enable File Check In and Check Out.**

    If several people will be working on your Web site from different locations or computers, it's a good idea to enable Dreamweaver's File Check In and Check Out capabilities, which prevents two users from editing the same files at the same time. To do so, select Check In/Out in the Category list box and then select the Enable File Check In And Check Out check box, as shown in Figure 5-3. Leave the Check Out Files When Opening check box selected, and enter the name you want others to see associated with files you check out in the Check Out Name box.

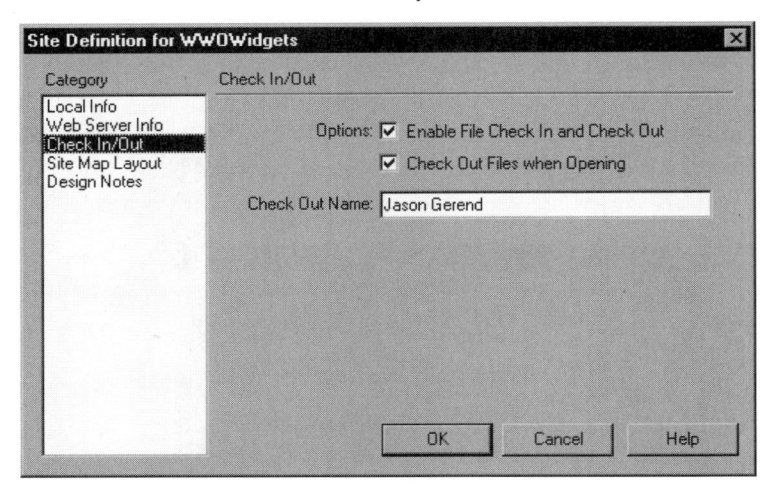

Figure 5-3 Enabling File Check In/Out for multiple users.

7. **Specify a home page.**

    Select Site Map Layout in the Category list box, and then enter a filename for your home page in the Home Page box, as shown in Figure 5-4. We recommend entering *index.htm*. Optionally, select the Page Titles option to display the page titles of pages in your Site Map instead of filenames. Click OK when you're finished. Click OK if Dreamweaver asks whether you'd like to create the index.htm file. Dreamweaver then creates your local site and displays it in the Site window.

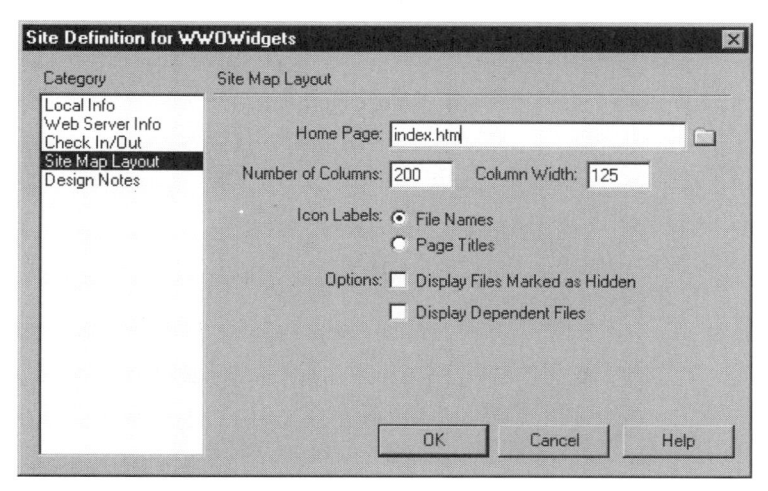

Figure 5-4   Specifying the home page for your Web site.

Configuring Dreamweaver to Work with a Firewall

If your company network is protected by a firewall and you can't access your remote site using Dreamweaver, you'll probably have to configure Dreamweaver to find your firewall host or proxy server.

Make sure that you know your firewall settings before you follow this procedure. If you don't know the address of your firewall host, either ask someone who does or check Microsoft Windows's Internet Options. To do this, click the Internet Options icon in Windows Control Panel, click the Connections tab, click the LAN Settings button, and then look for an address entered in the Proxy Server box.

To configure Dreamweaver to work with a firewall, follow these steps:

1. Open the Preferences dialog box.

Choose the Edit menu's Preferences command, and then select Site FTP in the Category list box, as shown in Figure 5-5.

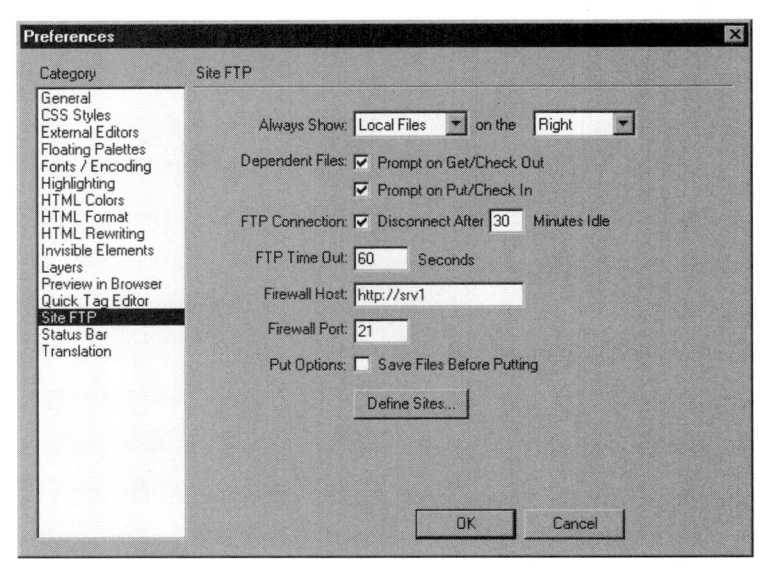

Figure 5-5 Specifying the home page for your Web site.

2. **Specify your firewall or proxy server.**

   In the Firewall Host box, enter the address of your firewall or proxy server. In the Firewall Port box, enter the port FTP on which access is allowed. (This is most likely 21, but check your firewall if this doesn't work.) Click OK.

3. **Configure your site to use a firewall.**

   Choose the Site menu's Define Sites command, select your site from the list, and then click the Edit button. Select Web Server Info in the Category list box, and then select the Use Firewall check box, as shown in Figure 5-6. Click OK.

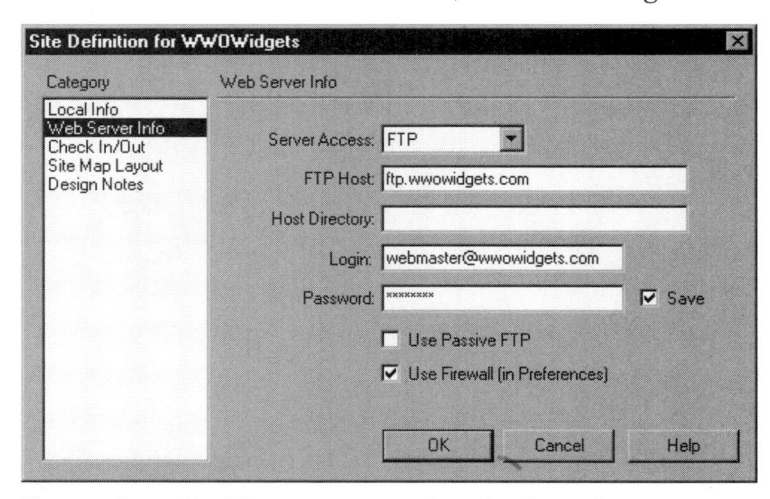

Figure 5-6 Enabling a site to work with a firewall.

TIP *If you have everything configured correctly but you have problems with your FTP connection timing out, increase the number in the FTP Time Out box. Don't increase the timeout duration to more than 120 seconds though, or you'll be forced to wait excessively when the FTP server can't be reached.*

Opening Local Sites

When you launch Dreamweaver, it automatically opens the last site you worked on, allowing you to get started quickly. However, if you have multiple sites, you'll need to be able to switch between these sites.

To open a local site, select the site from the Site window's drop-down list box, as shown in Figure 5-7, or choose the Site menu's Open Site command, and then select the site you want to open from the submenu.

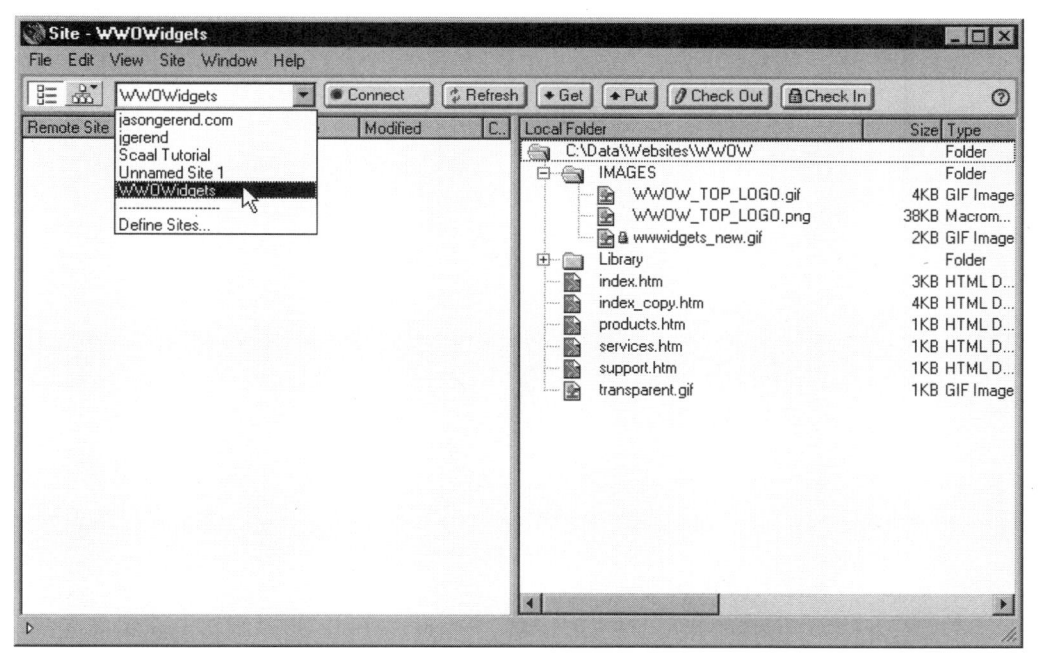

Figure 5-7 Switching sites in the Dreamweaver Site window.

Overview of the Site Window

Before we go much farther, it helps to be more comfortable with the Site window interface. At the top of the window, as shown in Figure 5-8, is a familiar-looking menu bar—where the File, Edit, View, Site, Window, and Help menus are located. Immediately below this is the site management toolbar, where the most frequently accessed site management commands are located.

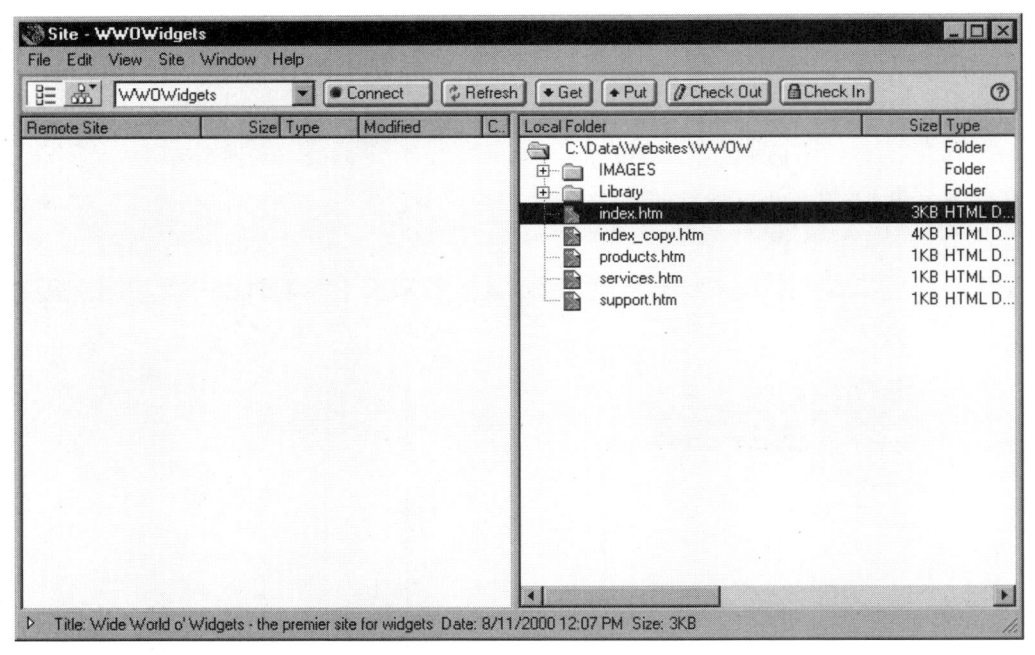

Figure 5-8   The Dreamweaver Site window, displaying the local folder.

Below the menu bar and toolbar is the main portion of the Site window. The default view shows the contents of your local folder (the local copy of your Web site) and displays an empty pane on the left, which shows the contents of your remote site (your actual Internet Web site) when you connect to it. The folder displays look and act almost exactly like Windows Explorer or the Macintosh Finder. At the bottom of the window is the Status Bar, which shows you the status of file transfers or the properties of the currently selected file.

> **TIP**   *You can hide the left pane (which displays either the remote site or the Site Map) by clicking the small triangle on the far left side of the Status Bar. Click it again to restore the pane.*

The following list describes some of the tasks you can do in the Site window:

- To connect to your Internet Web site, click the Connect toolbar button.
- To sort your files by name, click the Local Folder heading.
- To sort files by Size, Type, or some other field, click the corresponding heading in the Local Folder (or Remote Site) pane.
- To open a page, double-click it. (This works in all panes: the Local Folder, Remote Site, and Site Map.)
- To switch between viewing your site files and viewing a visual map of your Web site, as shown in Figure 5-9, use the Site Files and Site Map buttons on the left of the toolbar.

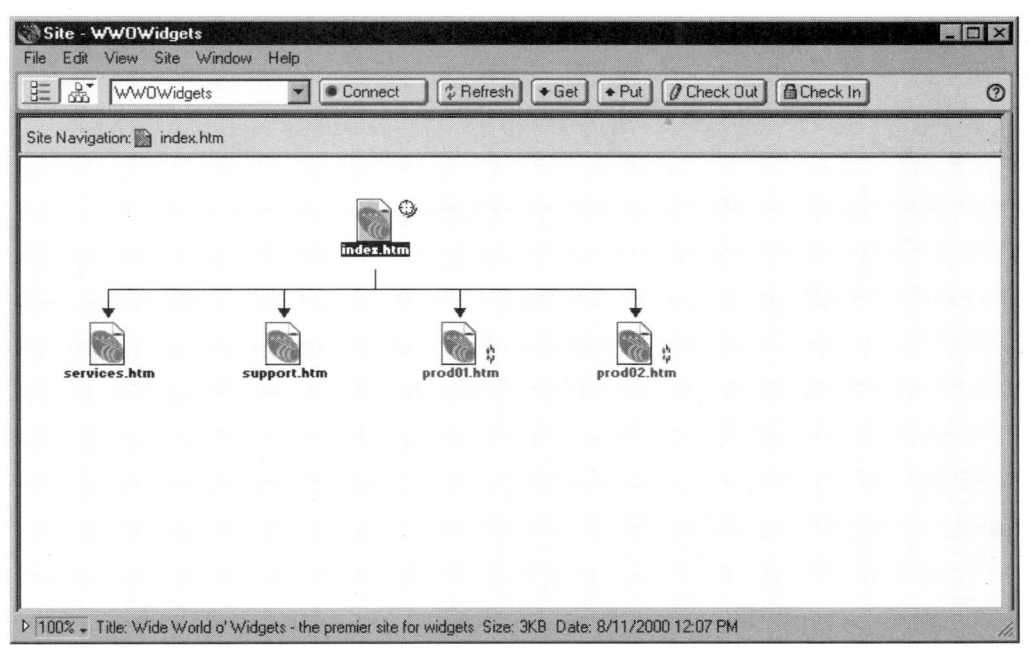

Figure 5-9 The Dreamweaver Site window in Site Map view.

The following sections describe other features of the Site window.

Step 5 Set Up Your Site 109

Creating the Initial Structure

If you're creating a Web site from scratch, it's a good idea to create the site's structure before you do anything else. Since Dreamweaver functions best when you save Web pages before editing them, creating all or most of your pages in the Site window makes the actual editing process work smoother. You can also link the pages together in the Site window to form a coherent Site Map and automatically insert the proper hyperlinks into the empty pages.

Besides just setting up your site structure, you'll also need to perform some file management tasks, such as moving and copying files, renaming files, and deleting files and folders. The following sections explain how to carry out these tasks, which you'll find yourself performing frequently throughout the life of your Web site.

> **TIP** *You'll probably want to move and rename files in Dreamweaver to minimize the chance that hyperlinks are broken. If you move or rename a file using Dreamweaver, hyperlinks to that file are automatically updated.*

Adding New Pages and Folders

To add a new Web page or folder to your site without creating any links, right-click the folder in the Local Folder pane to which you would like to add a page or folder and then choose New File or New Folder from the shortcut menu. This creates a new file or folder in the Local Folder pane, all ready for you to name it. Enter the name you want to assign to the file or folder, and then click anywhere else onscreen to save the name.

To add a new page that is pre-linked to an existing page (a great way to quickly build the structure of your site), follow these steps:

1. **Display the Site Map.**

   Click and hold the Site Map toolbar button, and then select Map And Files from the drop-down menu that appears, as shown in Figure 5-10. This displays a map of your site along with your local folder along the right side of the window.

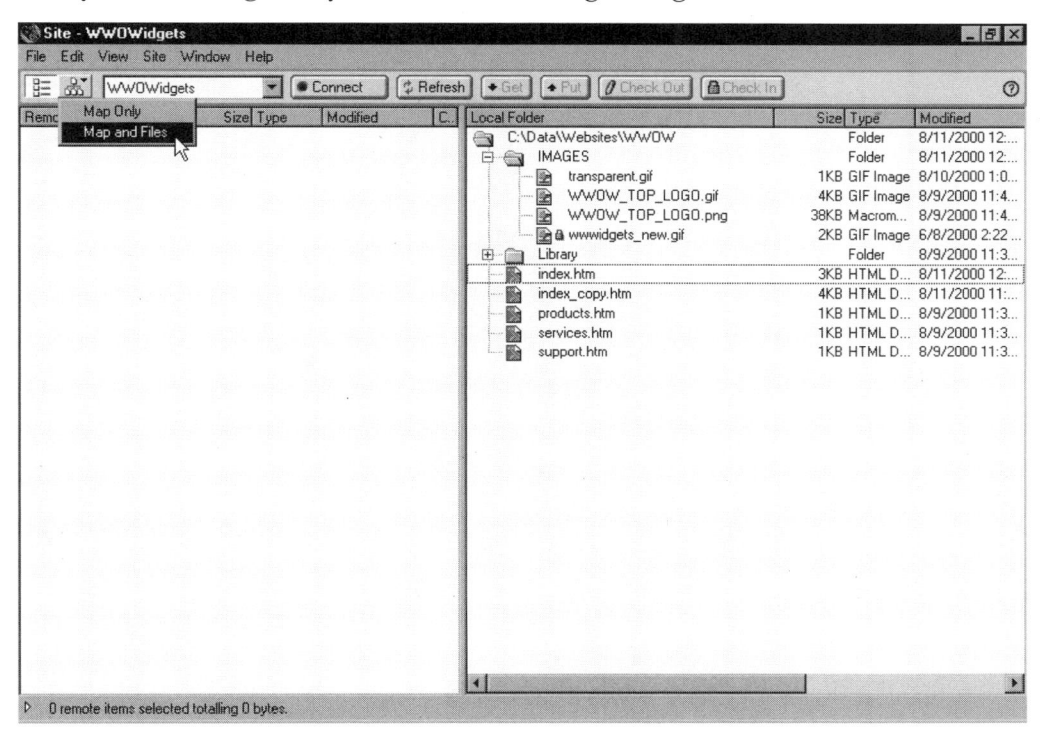

   Figure 5-10 Displaying the Site Map and the Local Folder pane at the same time.

2. **Create the new file.**

   Right-click the page in the Site Map pane that you want to link to a new file, and then choose Link To New File from the shortcut menu, as shown in Figure 5-11.

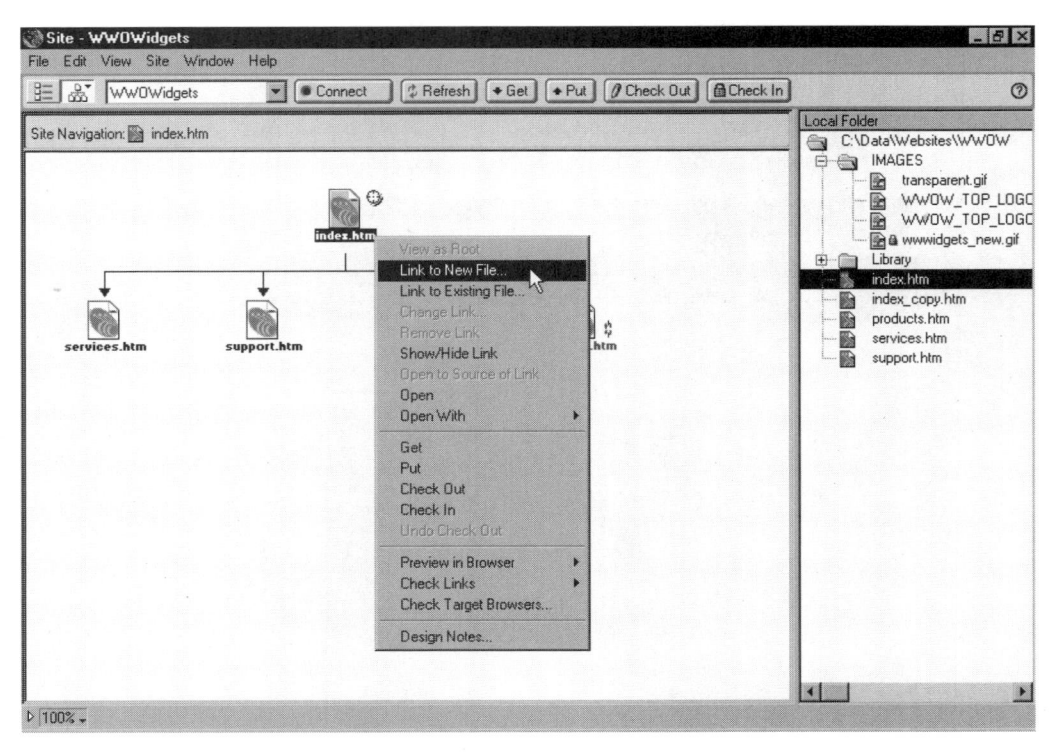

Figure 5-11   Creating a new page already linked to an existing page.

3. Name the file.

In the Link To New File dialog box, as shown in Figure 5-12, enter a filename for the page. In the Title box, enter a title for the page, and in the Text Of Link box, enter the text you want to appear as the hyperlink in the original page (the page that links to the page you're creating). Click OK to create the page.

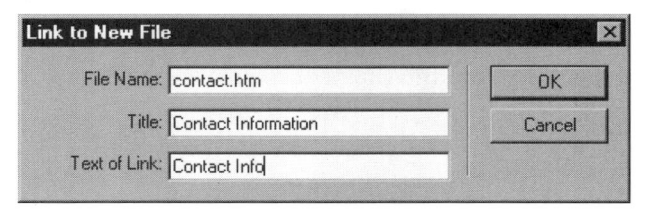

Figure 5-12   Naming the newly created page.

NOTE   *The only page that works as a home page on most Web servers is index.htm or index.html.*

Site Map Overview

In the Site Map display, shown in Figure 5-13, click 100% on the Status Bar to resize the Site Map display. To display your local folder as well as the Site Map, drag the bar at the right side of the window to the left, revealing the Local Folder pane, or click and hold the Site Map button and select Map And Files from the drop-down menu.

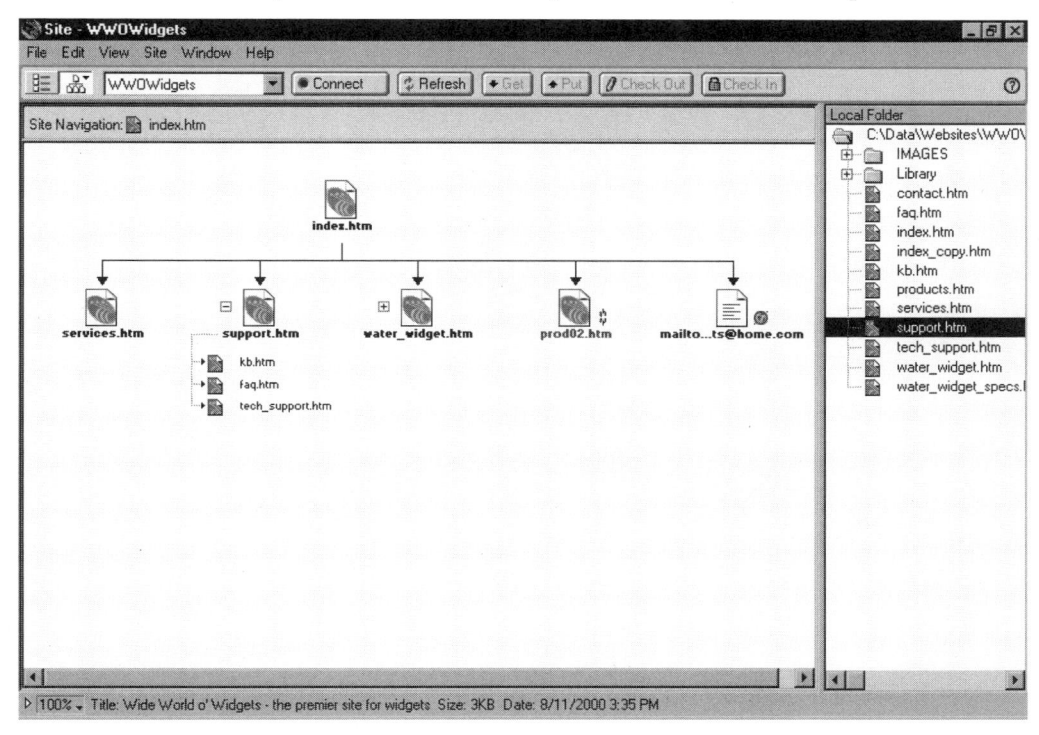

Figure 5-13   The Site Map.

Click a plus sign next to a page to view the pages it links to, or click a minus sign to hide the pages. Pages that are "lost" (the links to them are broken) appear in red, while external links (links to pages outside your local site) appear in blue and have a small globe icon next to them.

To view a page as the root of the Site Map (the topmost page displayed), right-click the page and choose View As Root from the shortcut menu. This hides all pages above the selected page, as shown in Figure 5-14. To get back to the parent page (the page that links to the page you temporarily designated to be the root of the Site Map), click the parent page's name in the Site Navigation pane right underneath the toolbar.

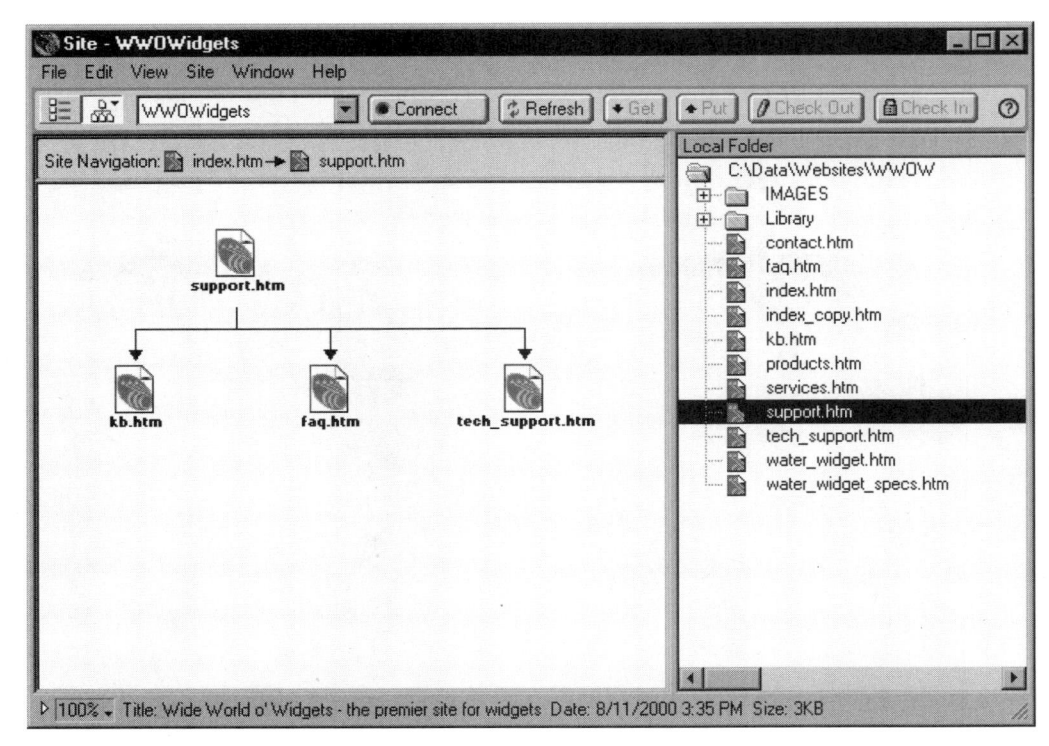

Figure 5-14 A page viewed as the site root.

TIP *To switch the Site Map display from showing filenames to showing page titles, choose the View menu's Show Page Titles command.*

To select multiple pages in the Site Map, click and drag an outline around the pages you want to select, or hold down the Ctrl key and click the pages you want to select. (This method also works in the Local Folder pane.)

Working with Links in the Site Map

The Site Map is your primary location to view and modify links, other than inside pages themselves. You can quickly get a feel for how pages are linked to each other. You can also create new links and modify or remove existing links. You can even use the Site Map to quickly prototype your site layout and then save a picture of the Site Map for later review outside of Dreamweaver (or to print out and review offline).

Creating New Links

There are two ways to create a new link between existing files in the Site window. One way is to right-click a page, choose Link To Existing File from the shortcut menu, select the file you want to link to, and then click Select. Or another way is to create the link with your mouse, as described in the following procedure:

1. Display the Site Map and Local Folder pane.

Click and hold the Site Map button and then select Map And Files from the drop-down menu.

2. Select the file.

Click the file in which you want to create a link.

3. Drag the link icon to another file.

When you drag the round icon that's to the right of the file in the Site Map onto a page or file in the Local Folder pane, an arrow connects the two icons, as shown in Figure 5-15, and a box appears around the selected file. When you release the mouse button, Dreamweaver creates the link.

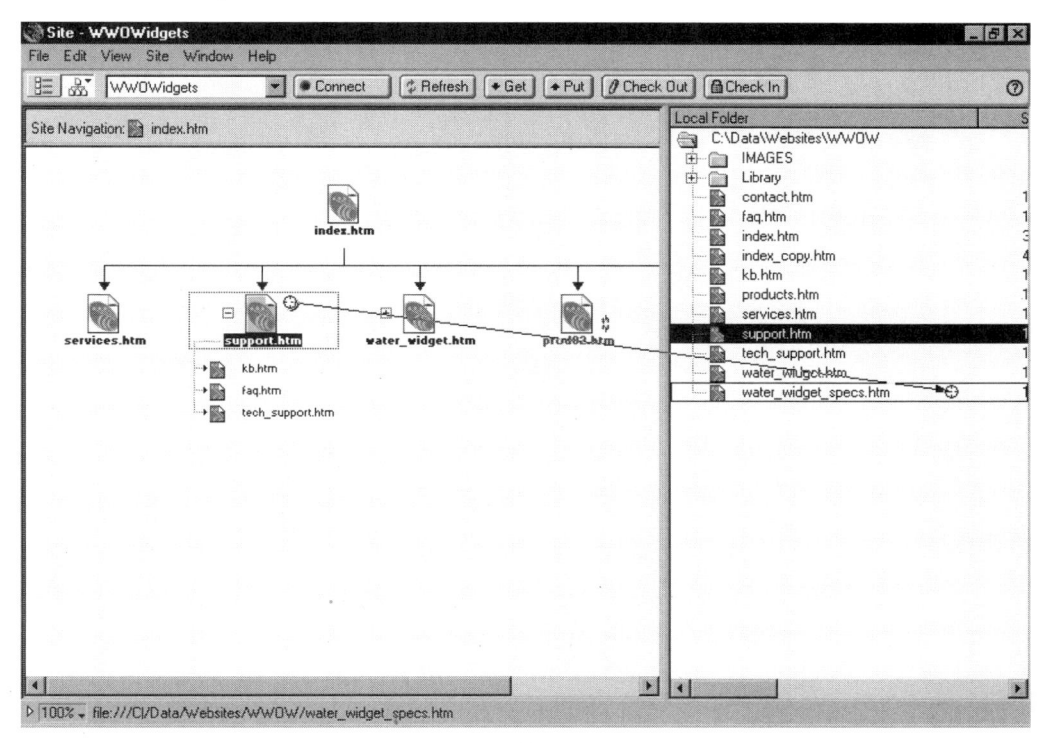

Figure 5-15 Creating a link to an existing file.

NOTE *If you're using Dreamweaver's Check In/Out feature, you'll need to check out a file in order to create a hyperlink in it. In other words, check out the file in which you're creating a link, not the file to which you're linking.*

Changing Existing Links

If you decide that you need to change a link in the Site Map, right-click the target of the link (the page that the link points to). From the shortcut menu, choose Remove Link to remove the link. (Note that the text for the link is left on the page, however.) To change the link, choose Change Link from the shortcut menu and select a different page from the Select HTML File dialog box, as shown in Figure 5-16.

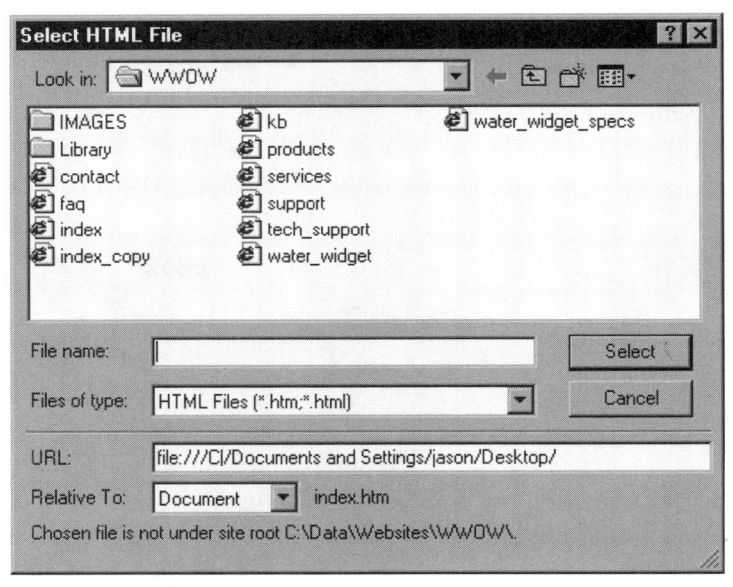

Figure 5-16 Modifying an existing link.

NOTE *The URL listed in the URL box of the Select HTML File dialog box isn't the current link, it's just a generic link that usually connects to your Windows desktop. When you select a page, Dreamweaver fills in the URL box, either in document relative format or as site-root relative format (if you select Site-Root from the Relative To box, which we don't recommend). See "Step 1: Learn the Logic" for more information on relative addressing.*

Sometimes there will be a link that you don't want to see in the Site Map, but that you don't want to delete. The best solution to this problem is to hide the link. To do so, right-click the page or file that you don't want to appear in the Site Map and choose Show/Hide Link from the shortcut menu. If you later want to redisplay the page, choose the View menu's Show Files Marked As Hidden command. (You can also select Show Dependent Files if you want to see images and other dependent files in the Site Map.) Hidden files appear in italics when Show Files Marked As Hidden is selected, as shown in Figure 5-17.

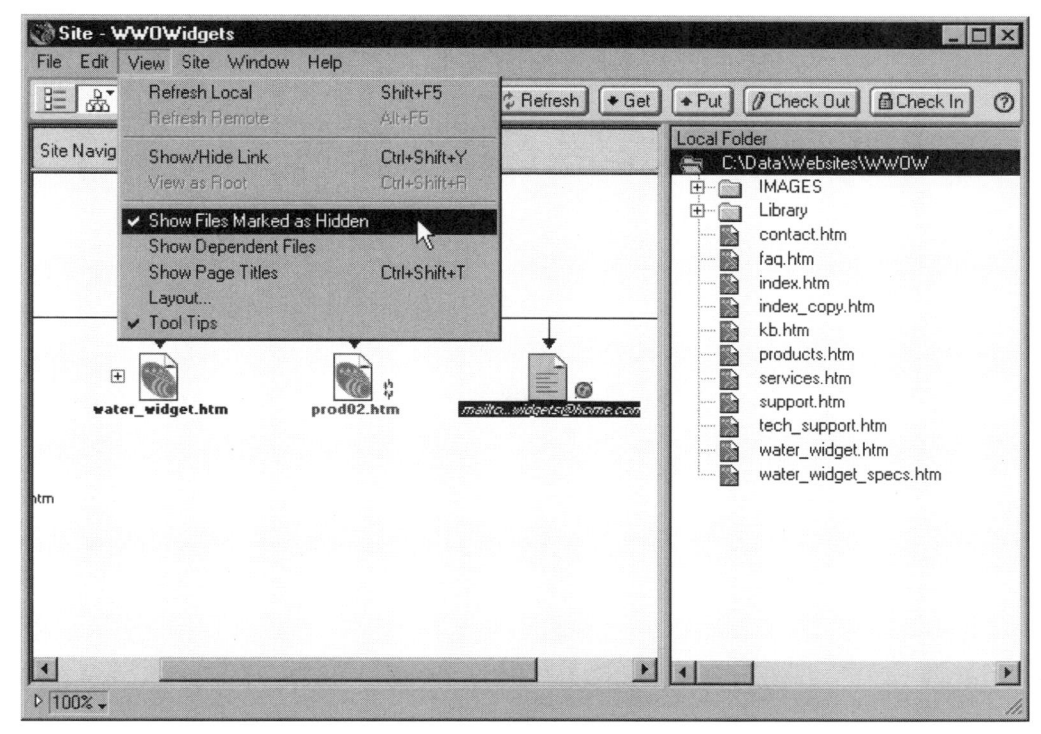

Figure 5-17 Modifying an existing link.

Saving the Site Map as a Graphic

After you've created your basic Web site structure using the Site Map, you might want to save a picture of the Site Map for review on a computer without Dreamweaver, for use in a Web graphic (the Site Map makes a great table of contents image—just create hotspots over each page in the map), or to print out.

To save the Site Map as an image, display the Site Map the way you want it and then choose the File menu's Save Site Map command. In the Save Site Map dialog box, choose where to save the file, enter a name for the image, and choose to save it either as a bitmap file (.bmp) or as a PNG file (.png). Figure 5-18 shows an actual Site Map saved this way and placed directly into this book.

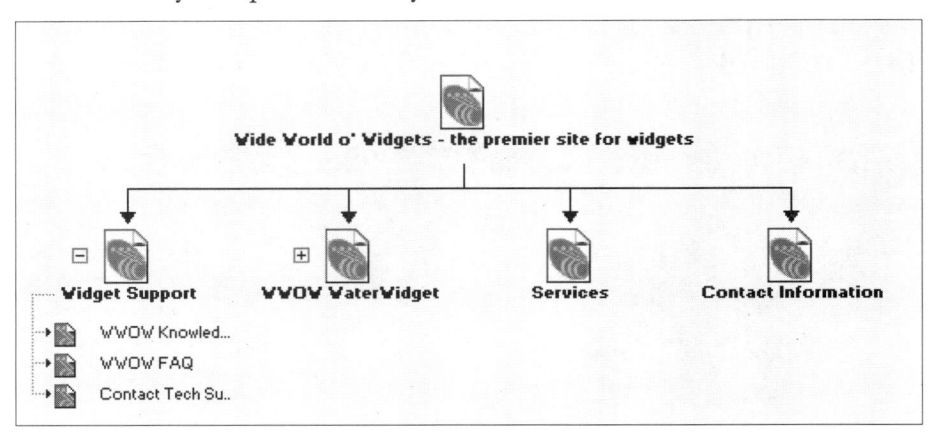

Figure 5-18 A Site Map image.

TIP *Consider selecting the View menu's Show Page Titles command if you're saving the Site Map as an image. This labels each page in the map by the page's title instead of the filename.*

Moving and Copying Files

There are times when you'll need to move or copy files into different folders in your Web site, perhaps to keep all pages or files dealing with a certain part of your Web site in one spot. For example, if your company or organization publishes an online newsletter, you may want to create a separate directory for all the newsletters. Similarly, you'll probably want to place all images in the Images folder.

To move a file to another folder, click the file in the Local Folder pane and drag it to the desired folder.

To copy a file, select the file and press Ctrl-C. Then navigate to the folder in which you want to place a copy and press Ctrl-V.

TIP *These keyboard shortcuts—Ctrl-C for copy and Ctrl-V for paste—work in every part of Windows and any Windows application, so you can use them to copy and paste files, text, or images anywhere.*

118   *Effective Executive's Guide to Dreamweaver Web Sites*

Renaming Files

To rename a file, select a file in the Folder list, wait a moment (maybe a second), and then click it again. The filename is highlighted, and you can then type in a new filename or edit the existing one, as shown in Figure 5-19. Alternatively, choose the File menu's Rename command.

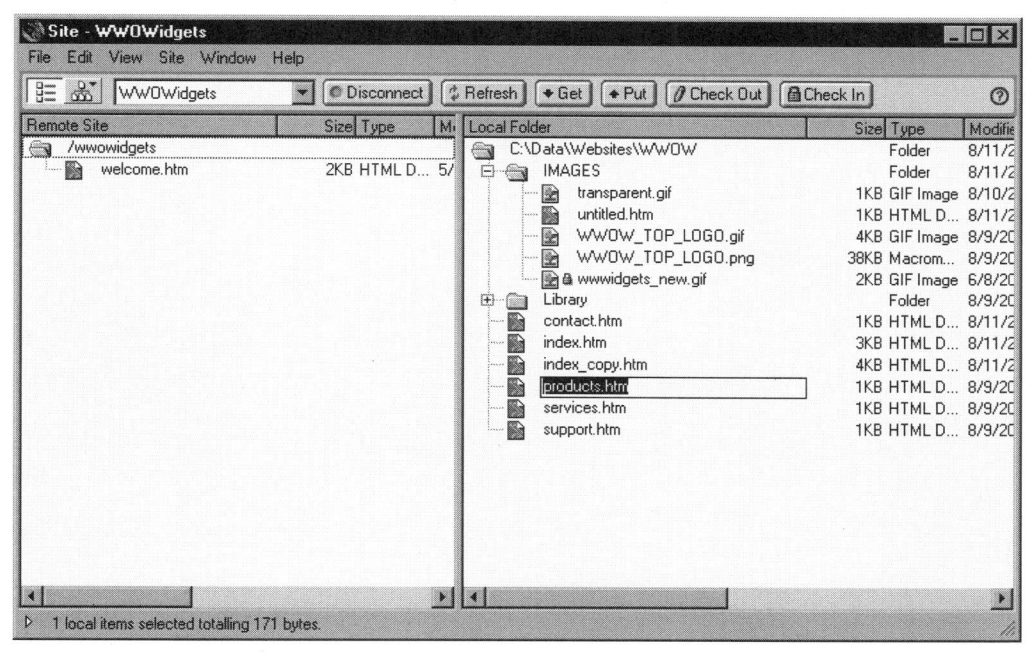

Figure 5-19 Renaming a file.

WARNING *Don't change the file's three-letter extension or you won't be able to view the file or use it properly.*

Deleting Files and Folders

Even though it usually makes sense to leave most files on your Web site indefinitely, there are times when you might need to delete some. You might want to do this if you want to replace a file with a revised version, or if you need more space on your site.

Deleting items is quite easy. Simply right-click the file or folder you want to delete, and choose Delete from the shortcut menu, as shown in Figure 5-20. Alternatively, select the file or folder, and press the Delete key.

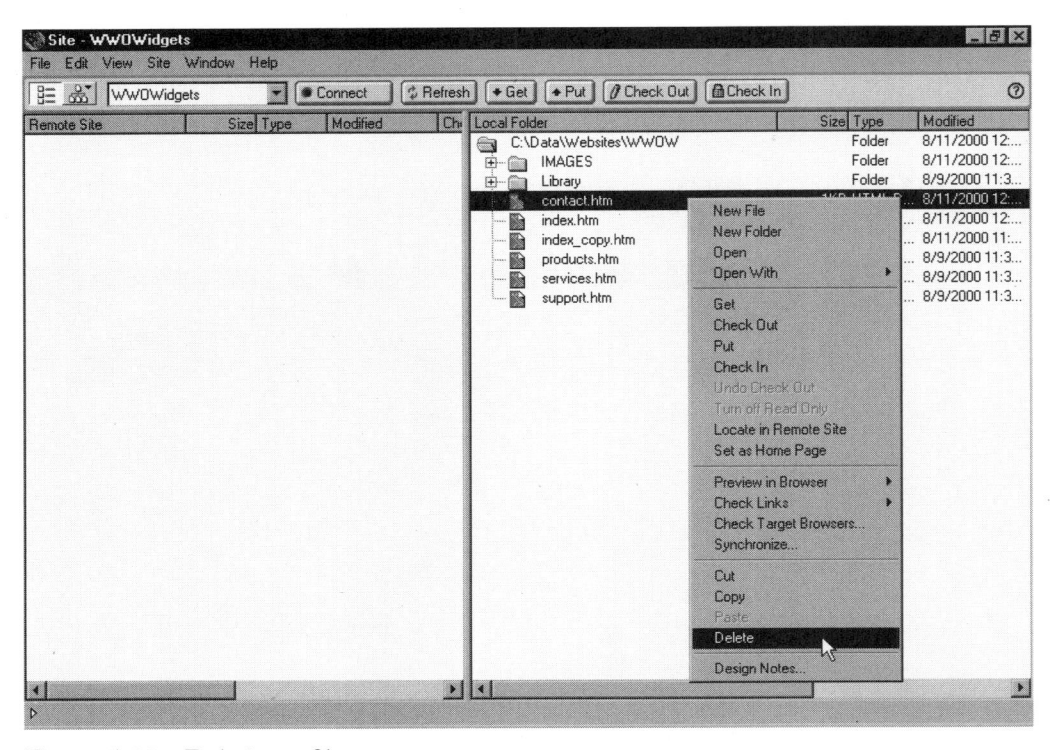

Figure 5-20 Deleting a file.

> **WARNING** *Files that you delete in Dreamweaver do **not** go to the Recycle Bin. After you respond to Dreamweaver's confirmation, the files that you deleted are immediately and permanently removed.*

Adding Design Notes to Files

Design Notes is a useful feature that allows you and your collaborators to store notes about files in Dreamweaver. Using Design Notes, you can share the status of the file and any other notes with all authors of your Web site.

> **TIP** *You can add Design Notes to any kind of file in Dreamweaver. Additionally, Macromedia Fireworks supports Dreamweaver-compatible Design Notes so that users of Fireworks can work seamlessly in both applications, making it easy to share information with any graphic designers you may employ.*

To use Design Notes, follow these steps:

1. **Open the Design Notes dialog box.**

   Right-click the file to which you want to add Design Notes, and then choose Design Notes from the shortcut menu.

2. **Specify the status and enter notes.**

   Choose a status for the file from the Status drop-down list box, and enter any notes about the file in the Notes box, as shown in Figure 5-21.

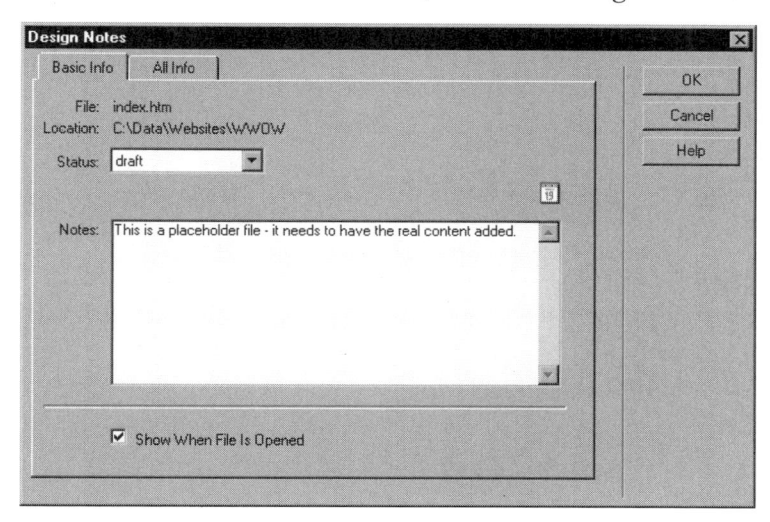

Figure 5-21 Entering Design Notes information.

3. **Specify when to display the Design Notes.**

   Select the Show When File Is Opened check box to automatically display the Design Note when this particular file is opened.

4. **Add optional fields.**

   To add custom fields, click the All Info tab, as shown in Figure 5-22. Click the plus sign button to create a new field, enter a name for the field (such as Author), and then enter a value for the field (such as your name). To remove a field, select it and click the minus sign button. Click OK when you're finished entering information in the Design Note.

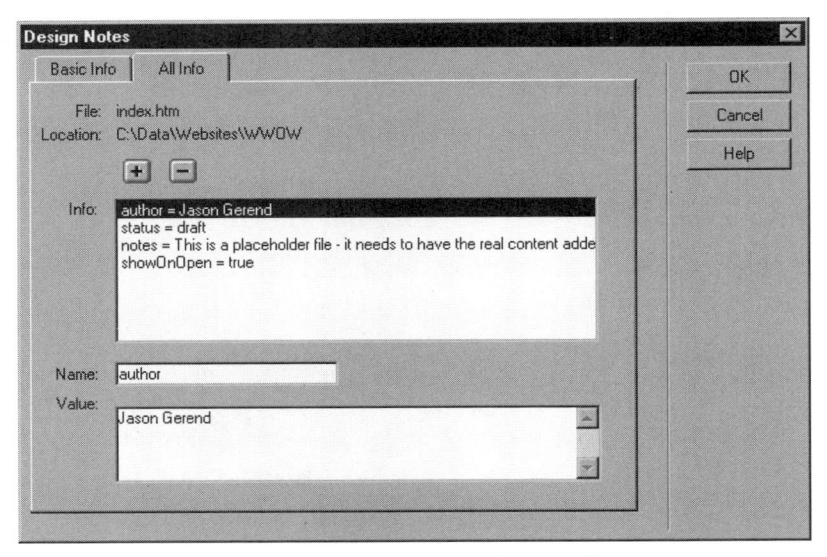

Figure 5-22 Creating a custom field in a Design Note.

> **NOTE** *You should have the Maintain Design Notes and Upload Design Notes For Sharing check boxes selected in the Design Notes category of your site's Site Definition. These are enabled by default.*

Checking Files In and Out

Dreamweaver comes with an editing safeguard feature that lets you check out individual files to a particular user. During the time that the file is checked out, it is unavailable for editing by other users. This feature prevents the loss of data from a situation in which two users try to edit the same file at the same time.

If you enabled the Check In/Out feature when you created your site definition in Dreamweaver (see the section "Defining a New Local Site" earlier in this step), it's simple to check files in and out. The following points will help you to use this handy feature:

- Before you can check out files, you need to publish your local folder to your remote site. See "Step 8: Deploy Your Web Site" for more information on uploading your files.
- To check out a file, right-click the file in the Folder List pane and choose Check Out from the shortcut menu, or open the file by double-clicking it. This prevents other users from editing the file until you check it back in. If you want to prevent other users from modifying embedded files, such as images, while you have the file checked out, click Yes when asked whether you want to check out dependent files.

- Files checked out by you have a green checkmark next to them.
- Files checked out by another person have a red checkmark next to them. Move your mouse over the file to see the name of the user who checked out the file displayed in the Status Bar.
- You can open files checked out by other users, but you can't save them using the same filename.
- If you try to check out a file already checked out by another user, Dreamweaver asks whether you want to override the checkout. Obviously, this is something you do only when absolutely necessary.
- To check in a file, right-click a checked-out file (one with a green checkmark next to it) and choose Check In from the shortcut menu, as shown in Figure 5-23. The check-in step saves your changes and allows others to then edit the file.
- To check in a file *without saving your changes*, right-click a checked-out file and choose Undo Check Out from the shortcut menu.

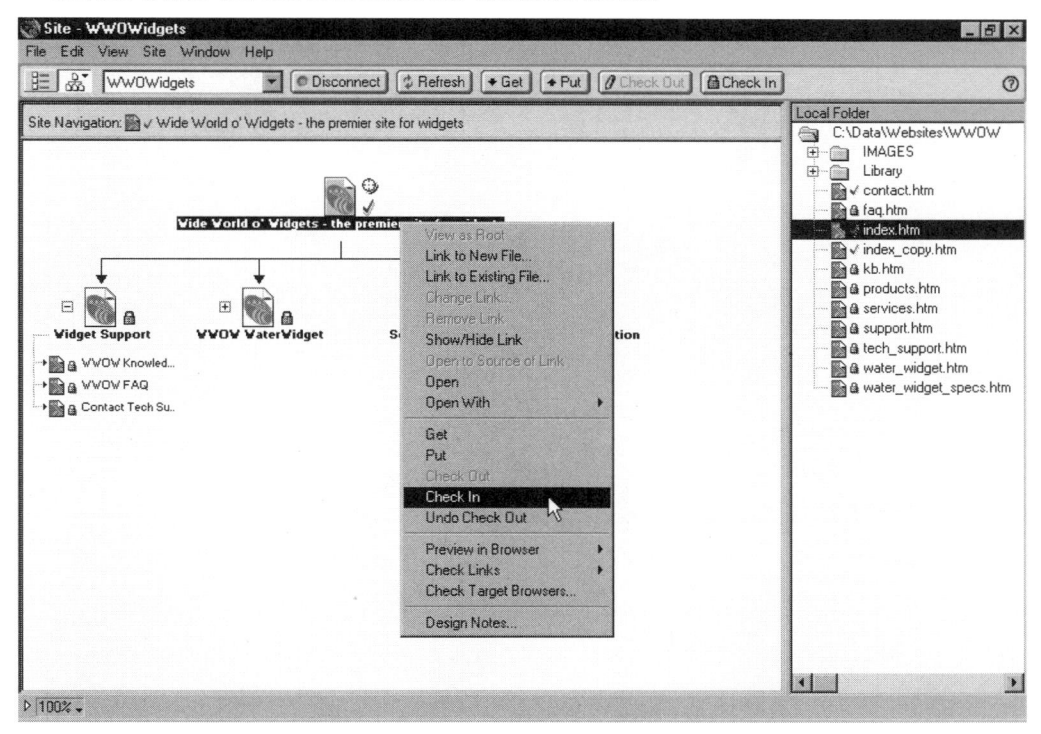

Figure 5-23 Checking in a file.

TIP *You must first connect to the Internet before you can check files in or out.*

Step 5 *Set Up Your Site* **123**

Dreamweaver's Check In/Out feature is valuable, but it only works if each user has his or her own local folder and all changes are synchronized at the remote site. This works fine if your company or organization doesn't mind creating its Web site directly on your Internet Web site (instead of constructing it locally, testing it, and then posting it to the Internet). Unfortunately, if you need to manage the work of multiple people on the site and keep the site private until you're ready, this approach doesn't work.

Fortunately, there is a workaround. You can create a remote site that sits on your local network and have everyone use this site as his or her remote site instead of using your actual Internet Web site.

To do this, first set up all users with their own copy of Dreamweaver and their own local folder (users can't share local folders). Set up each user's site definition so that the Web Server Info part of the Site Definition dialog box is configured to use this remote site on your local network instead of your actual Internet Web site, as shown in Figure 5-24. All users then synchronize their changes with the locally stored remote site, ensuring that it is up-to-date and that no changes are lost.

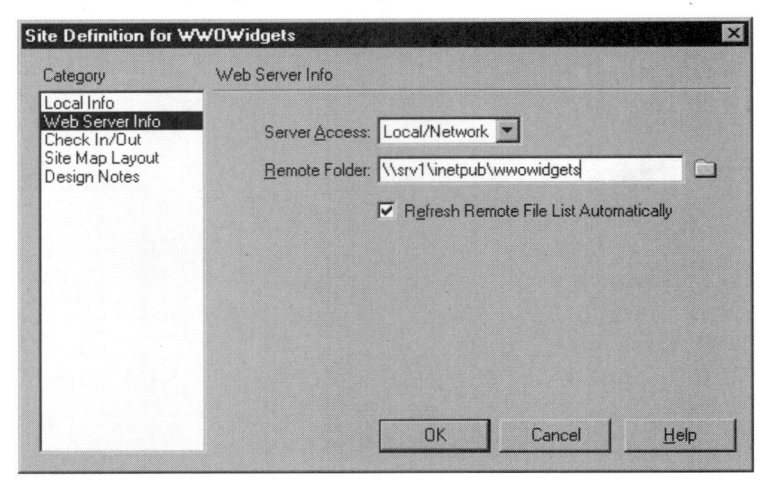

Figure 5-24 Configuring a locally stored remote site.

To publish this locally stored remote site (which acts as your master copy of the Web site) to your Internet Web site, set up a site definition on one computer (most likely on the computer belonging to whomever's in charge of the Web site) with the locally stored remote site *as the local folder*, as shown in Figure 5-25. Configure this site definition to use your actual Internet Web site as the remote site by using the Web Server Info part of the Site Definition dialog box. All publishing to the Internet is done with this site definition, but to do any editing, you should switch back to a site definition configured to do all publishing to the locally stored remote site instead of your Internet Web site.

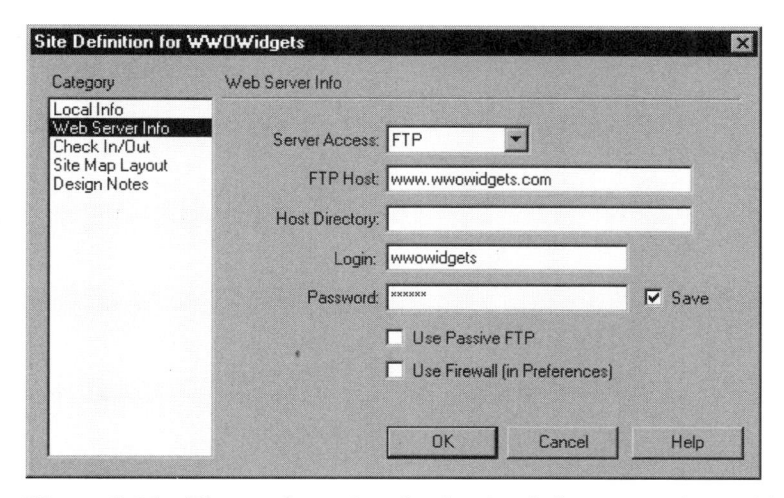

Figure 5-25   The configuration for the site definition used to publish to the Internet.

Although this pseudo remote site can be located anywhere on your local network, if you create it on an actual Web server, you can preview your pages better before publishing them to your Internet Web site. For help in setting up a local Web server, see "Appendix A: Setting Up Your Web Site on a Local Server."

Summary

The first step in creating your Web site is to define the site in Dreamweaver and create an initial site structure. This involves creating new Web pages and linking them together. Dreamweaver makes this easy by providing a Site Map feature that allows you to see the organization of your Web pages. Dreamweaver also lets you control the work of multiple authors on your Web site by using Dreamweaver's file Check In/Out feature.

Step 6

CREATE YOUR PAGES

Featuring:
- Overview of the Dreamweaver Interface
- Opening, Creating, and Saving Pages
- Working with Text and Hyperlinks
- Working with Images
- Adjusting Page Properties

Web sites are made up of individual Web pages, and creating these pages is what comprises the bulk of the Web creation process. The most important thing is to get your basic pages created, and this step helps you accomplish this by familiarizing you with the Dreamweaver interface, showing you how to add text and images to your Web pages, create hyperlinks, and modify the properties of your Web pages.

Overview of the Dreamweaver Interface

Dreamweaver's interface is extremely powerful as well as elegant; however, it is significantly different from most office productivity programs. The first time you launch Dreamweaver can be a bit daunting when you find yourself face to face with a completely blank document, flanked by myriad floating palettes and with no recognizable toolbars. The menus aren't familiar and neither are the shortcut menus that appear when you right-click.

Fortunately, this stage passes quickly, and with the help of this section, you'll soon grow to love Dreamweaver's interface and wonder how features could be any different. The following sections introduce you to key aspects of the interface.

Introducing the Document Window

The Dreamweaver program has two main windows: the Site window and the Document window. "Step 5: Set Up Your Site" introduced the Site window, where you can manage all aspects of your local and remote sites. Now we take a look at the Document window, as shown in Figure 6-1.

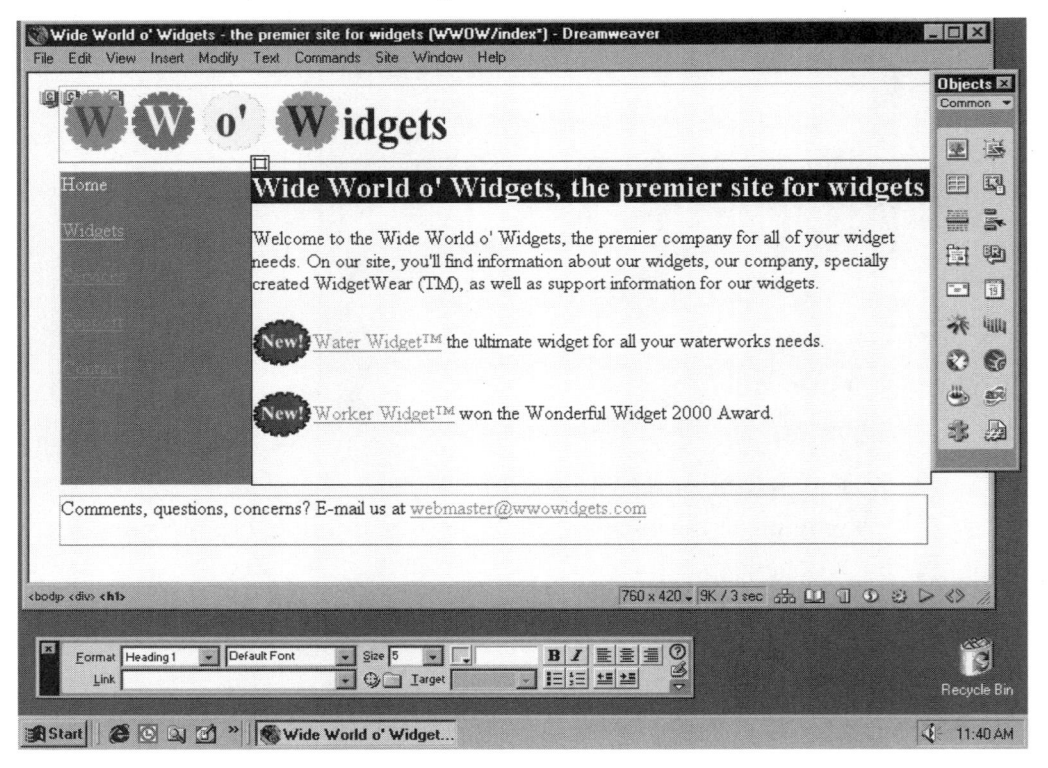

Figure 6-1   The Dreamweaver Document window.

Dreamweaver is a so-called WYSIWYG (What You See Is What You Get) Web page editor. This means that when you create a Web page in Dreamweaver, the way the content appears in the Document window is pretty much what it will look like in a Web browser.

Notice that the Document window has a Status Bar that runs along the bottom edge of the window. In addition to showing the status of your Web page, many useful tools and indicators are located on the Status Bar.

All commands are accessible either through floating palettes (small toolbar windows that you can reposition anywhere onscreen), through Dreamweaver's menus, or through context-sensitive shortcut menus, available when you right-click an item. There are no toolbars of the kind that you've come to expect with Microsoft programs, although Dreamweaver's floating palettes serve as very flexible and adaptable toolbar replacements. With that said, there is a much heavier reliance on menus in Dreamweaver than in most Microsoft programs, which takes some getting used to.

The Tag Selector

The Tag selector, located on the left side of the status bar, as shown in Figure 6-2, is an extremely useful tool for making selections in a Web page quickly and precisely. Simply click a tag to select and highlight all the content within that tag.

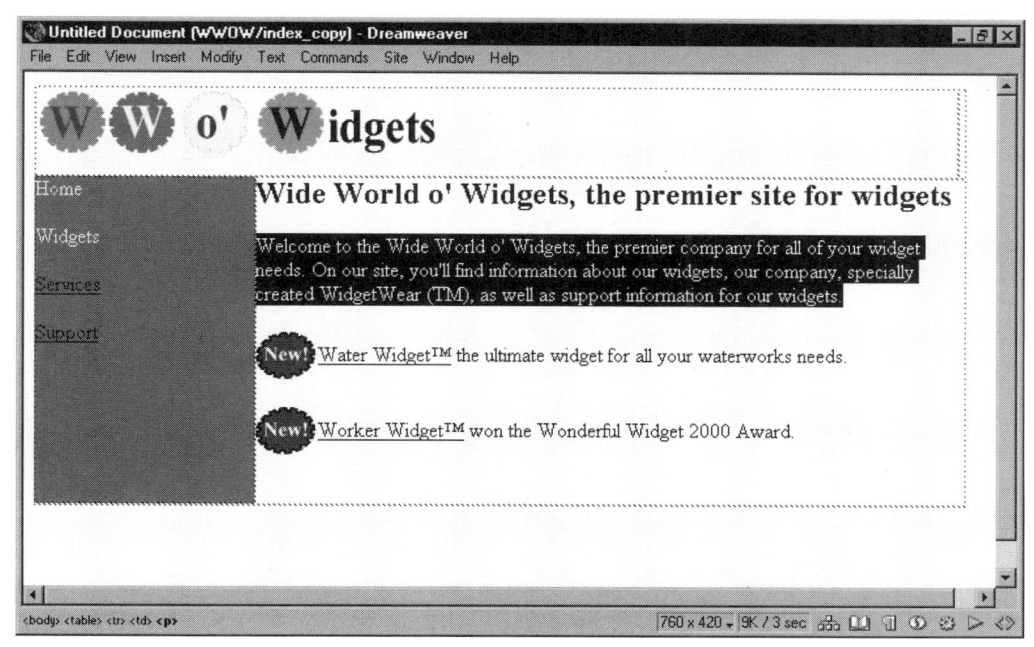

Figure 6-2   A paragraph selected using the Tag selector.

Wherever you place the cursor, the Tag selector displays the HTML tags associated with the current location in the Web page. The tags are displayed left to right, ranging from general to specific.

Step 6   Create Your Pages   **129**

Clicking on a tag immediately selects everything on the page within that particular tag. For example, clicking <body> would select the entire page, while clicking <h1> would select only the particular heading where the cursor is located. Because tags are hierarchical, other headings aren't selected.

The Rest of the Status Bar

To the right of the Tag selector is the Window Size pop-up menu. This menu displays the current size of the Document window in pixels, which is helpful when trying to target your Web pages to visitors using different screen resolutions (see "Step 7: Polish Your Pages").

To select a window size that matches a typical screen resolution, click the Window Size display. From the pop-up menu that appears, choose the screen resolution you want, as shown in Figure 6-3. Dreamweaver resizes your window to match the selected size.

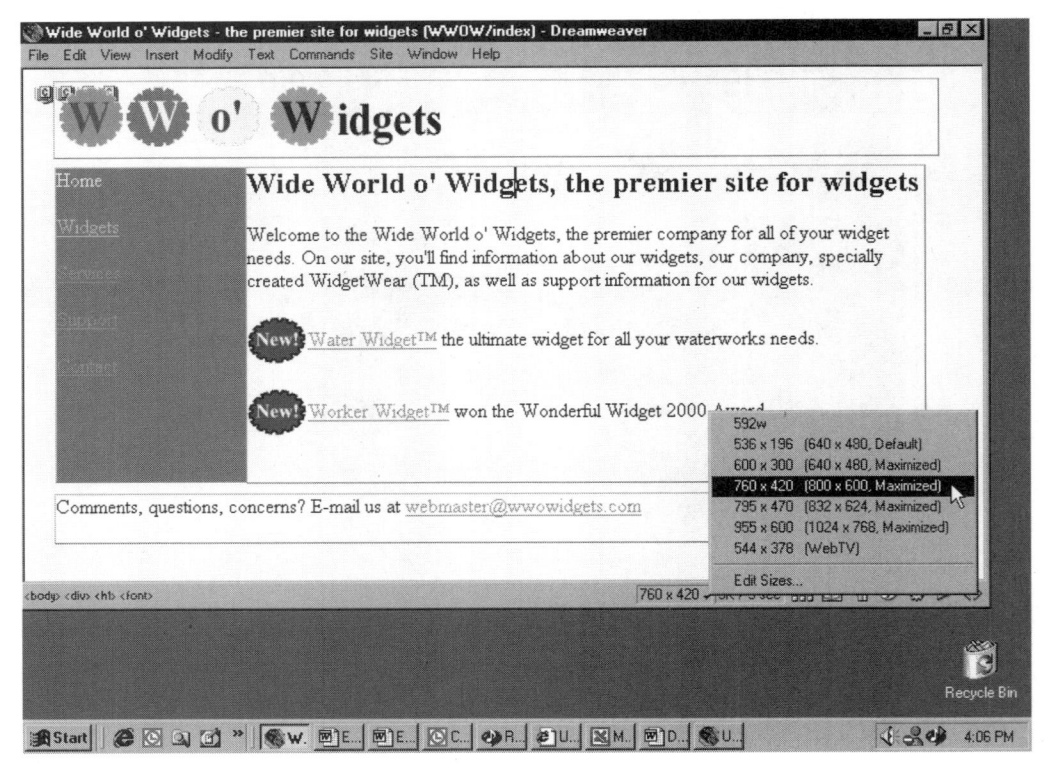

Figure 6-3 Resizing the Document window to better match visitors' screen sizes.

NOTE *Dreamweaver adjusts its window size to match the typical viewable area that visitors will have in their Web browsers when viewing your page. For example, if a visitor has her or his monitor set to 800x600 resolution and the Web browser window is maximized (filling the screen), typically only a 760x420 resolution will be available for viewing pages, after accounting for the Web browser's menu bar, status bar, and toolbars.*

To the right of the Window Size display, the current size of the open Web page is recorded along with the estimated amount of time required to open the page across the Internet when using a 28.8Kbps modem. In general, no Web page you create should take longer than 30 seconds to download over a 28.8Kbps modem. Keep an eye on this indicator while you make your Web pages, and if they get too big, delete some images or reduce their size.

If you want to change the display to show a different connection speed, choose the Edit menu's Preferences command, choose Status Bar from the Category list in the Preferences dialog box, and then select a speed from the Connection Speed box, as shown in Figure 6-4.

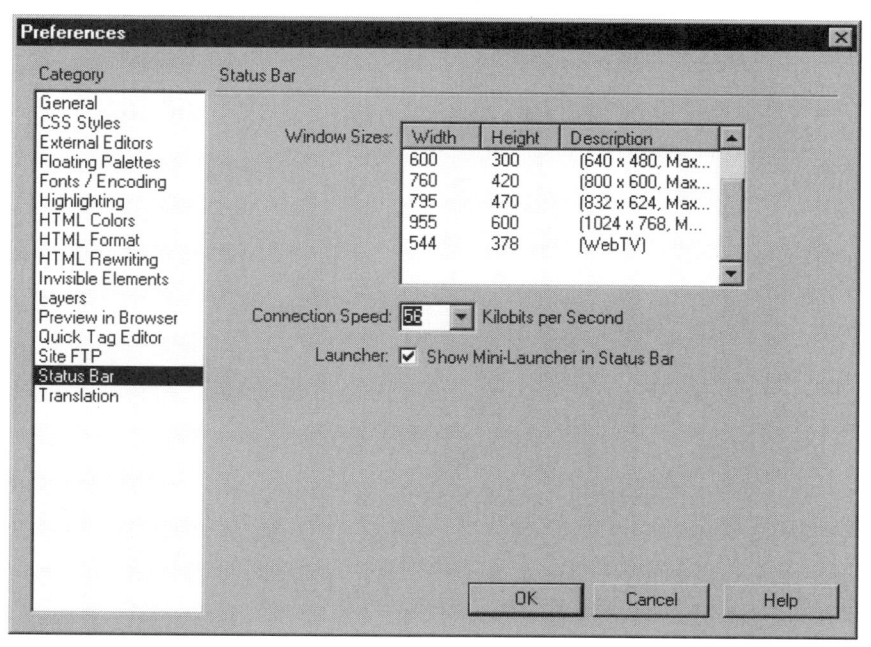

Figure 6-4   Changing the connection speed used for download time estimates.

TIP *To create your own download speed—such as 42Kbps, a typical speed for most 56Kbps modem connections—enter the speed directly in the Connection Speed box.*

On the far right side of the status bar is the Mini-Launcher, a reduced-size version of the Launcher palette that is displayed by default in the upper right corner of your screen. (Close this palette to make more room on your screen.) Table 6-1 shows the buttons as they appear from left to right on the Mini-Launcher and describes which palette or interface element they display. Each palette is discussed in more detail in the following sections.

BUTTON	BUTTON NAME	DESCRIPTION
	Show Site	Opens the Site window.
	Show Library	Displays the Library floating palette.
	Show HTML Styles	Displays the HTML Styles floating palette.
	Show CSS Styles	Displays the CSS Styles floating palette.
	Show Behaviors	Displays the Show Behaviors floating palette.
	Show History	Displays the Show History floating palette.
	Show HTML Source	Displays the HTML source editor.

Table 6-1 The small in size yet potent buttons of the Mini-Launcher.

Floating Palettes

Floating palettes are the heart of the Dreamweaver Document window. You use floating palettes to insert images, position elements using layers or tables, reuse chunks of text or images throughout your Web site, selectively undo or redo actions, and change the properties of items on your pages.

Before we cover the individual palettes, you should know a few things about palettes in general. To display a palette, either click its button on the Mini-Launcher or select it from the Window menu. Once displayed, you can move a palette anywhere on the screen that you find convenient. Simply click the blue title bar of the palette and drag it where you want it. Most palettes can be resized like normal windows. Just move your cursor over an edge until it turns into a dual-sided arrow, and then drag the edge out or in to get the size you want. To close a palette, click the small X in the corner of the palette.

Any palette that uses a tabbed interface to switch between multiple palettes (such as the History and Library palettes) can be combined with any other tabbed palette. To do so, open both palettes and then drag the tab you want into the palette that you want to keep. Click the tab that you want to work with to display it within the single floating palette. Figure 6-5 shows a palette created by adding the Library and Templates tabs and removing the Frames and Behaviors tabs. (To remove tabs from a floating palette, drag them out of the palette and then close the new palette that is created.)

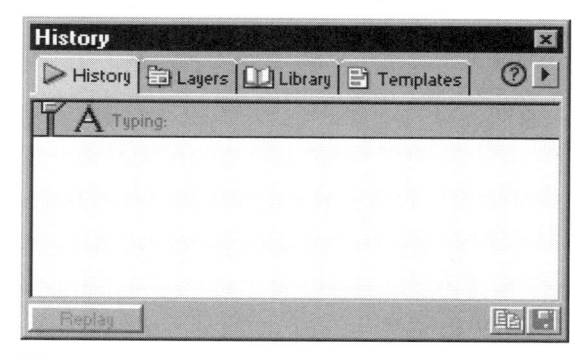

Figure 6-5   Combining floating palettes to suit your work style.

Objects Palette

The Objects palette, shown in Figure 6-6, is one of the most useful palettes in Dreamweaver. You can use its series of buttons to quickly insert objects such as images, positioning layers, tables, special characters, and rollover buttons into your Web pages.

Figure 6-6   The Objects palette.

To insert an object in your Web page by using a button on the Objects palette, either click the button to add the object at the current cursor location or drag the button to the location where you want to insert the object.

The Objects palette has six groupings of buttons, as shown in Table 6-2.

GROUP	PURPOSE
Common	Inserting commonly used objects, such as images and tables.
Characters	Inserting special characters such as ™, ©, or ®.
Form	Inserting Web page forms and form elements.
Frames	Creating Web pages with frames.
Head	Inserting hidden information such as meta tags for search engines.
Invisibles	Inserting hidden tags such as named anchors and nonbreaking spaces.

Table 6-2   The different groups of the Objects palette.

TIP   *Since you probably won't need to insert Plug-ins or ActiveX components or make use of some of the other buttons at the bottom of the Objects palette, you might want to resize the palette to hide these buttons to reduce the amount of space the palette takes up.*

Property Inspector Palette

Unlike most programs that force you to right-click an object and choose Properties from a shortcut menu in order to see an object's properties, Dreamweaver provides the Property inspector palette that you can use to view the properties of any object you select—without having to use menus. This takes a little getting used to, but this method quickly becomes far more efficient than opening separate dialog boxes. To use the Property inspector, simply select an object or piece of text to display its properties in the Property inspector, as shown in Figure 6-7. Use the fields of the Property inspector palette just as you would use any normal dialog box.

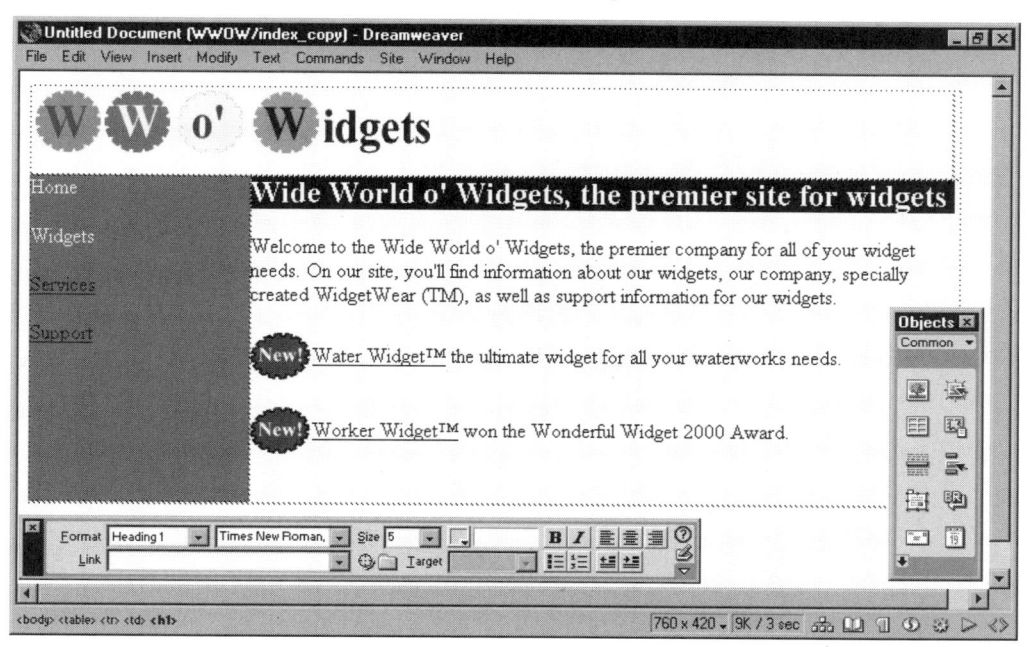

Figure 6-7   The Property inspector displaying the properties of a heading.

TIP   *To display advanced fields for the selected object, click the down arrow in the lower right corner of the Property inspector.*

Library Palette

The Library palette, shown in Figure 6-8, allows you to duplicate content on multiple pages in your Web site. When you place an object in the Library, such as your company logo or a paragraph with legal copyright information, it becomes available for quick insertion into other pages on your Web site. In addition, all changes to Library objects are done centrally—in the Library. This means you can't make changes to a Library object that you've inserted into a page—you have to change it in the Library. However, when you change the object in the Library, *every page using the object is updated automatically*. This is an extremely powerful feature, and one to keep in mind as you construct your Web site.

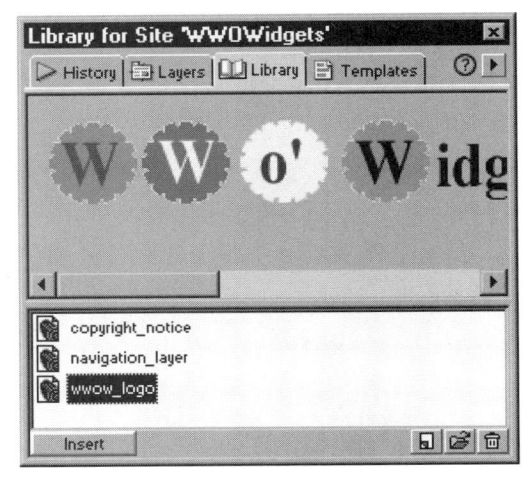

Figure 6-8   The Library palette.

To add an object to the Library, drag it into the Library. To preview a Library object, select it in the Library palette. To add a Library object to your Web page, drag it from the Library into your page. The Library is discussed in more depth in "Step 7: Polish Your Pages."

History Palette

The History palette provides enhanced Undo and Redo functionality, and a little bit more. You can use the History palette to undo recent actions by dragging the small slider on the left side of the window up until all commands you want to undo are grayed out, as shown in Figure 6-9. If you change your mind, just drag the slider back down to redo the functions you undid.

Figure 6-9 Undoing steps using the History palette.

The power of the History palette starts to show when there's a step or series of steps you want to perform again—on a different object. Simply select the new object, select the steps in the History palette you want to repeat, and then click the Replay button in the palette. Click the Save button in the palette to save these steps to a new command that you can then access later from the Command menu. This is a tremendous way to save time on tasks that you perform often.

> **NOTE** *Unfortunately, you can only undo and redo contiguous actions—you can't selectively undo actions.*

Other Palettes

Dreamweaver has a number of other palettes, but we're not going to discuss them here because they deal with advanced Web page tasks such as creating layers, frames, and templates and viewing HTML code. Some of these palettes are discussed later when specific features are covered, for example, the Positioning and Templates palettes, while the rest are beyond the scope of this book.

> **TIP** *Click the Insert Other Characters button on the Objects palette (in the Characters group) to insert a special character not located in the Characters group of the Objects palette.*

Introducing Dreamweaver's Menus

Because Dreamweaver's menus are different from those you generally run across, we briefly describe them here:

- The File and Edit menus are similar to those in any Microsoft Windows program—use them to open and save pages, undo actions, copy and paste objects, and locate text in your pages.

- The View menu controls what kinds of content Dreamweaver displays within the Web pages you work in and other aspects of the Web-page-creation process—for example, you can toggle background grids and rulers here.

- The Insert menu provides a comprehensive list of objects that you can insert on your Web page.

- The Modify menu is similar to other programs' Format menu—use it to alter the properties of any object in your Web page (or use the Property inspector).

- The Text menu is concerned with everything having to do with text on your Web pages (except for hyperlinks, which are best modified using Property inspector).

- The Commands menu contains specially created commands that extend the capabilities of Dreamweaver, such as the Clean Up Word HTML and Optimize Image In Fireworks (which requires Macromedia Fireworks) commands. You can also easily create your own commands using the History palette (as discussed earlier in this section) or download new commands from the Dreamweaver Exchange Web site (choose the Help menu's Dreamweaver Exchange command).

- The Site menu contains commands that you can use to work with your Web site. For more information on managing your Web site, see "Step 5: Set Up Your Site" and "Step 8: Deploy Your Web Site."

- The Window menu differs from most typical Window menus—besides allowing you to switch between open pages, the Window menu is where you turn on or off all floating palettes.

- The Help menu offers access to the Help system and Dreamweaver-related Web sites. Dreamweaver's Help system takes a little getting used to—it's done completely in HTML and works through your Web browser, but it offers lots of good information when you're stuck. Several useful animated tutorials can help you get up to speed with different parts of Dreamweaver.

Opening, Creating, and Saving Pages

The basics of working with files in Dreamweaver's Document window is much the same as working with files in any other Windows program. Opening pages, creating new pages, and saving pages all work as you expect them to, so you might be tempted to skip this section. Don't. At the least, read the information on saving Web pages.

Opening and Closing Web Pages

You open and close Web pages in Dreamweaver in the same way that you open a file in any other Windows program.

To open a Web page, choose the File menu's Open command. When Dreamweaver displays the Open dialog box, as shown in Figure 6-10, select the folder containing the Web page from the Look In drop-down list box. When you find the Web page you want to open, select it and then click Open.

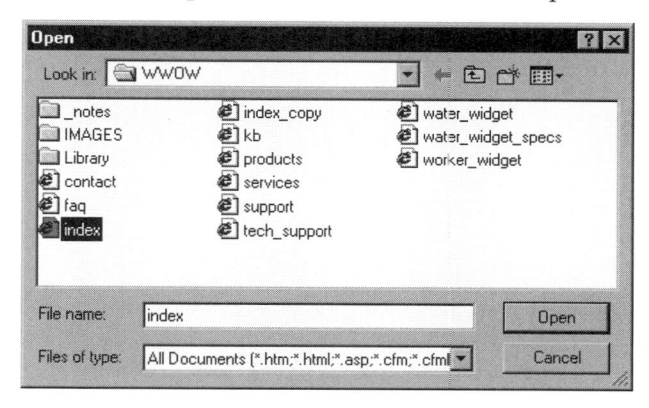

Figure 6-10 Using the File menu's Open command to open a Web page.

TIP   *If you have a Web page open, you can double-click any file in the Site window to open the file in Dreamweaver's Document window.*

To close a Web page, click the Close button on the page's title bar or choose the File menu's Close command.

Creating New Pages

Creating new pages in Dreamweaver is just like creating new documents in any other Windows program. To create a new page, choose the File menu's New command. After creating a new page, it appears open in Dreamweaver ready for you to add your content.

If you've created any template pages (as described in "Step 7: Polish Your Pages"), you can create pages based on your templates. To do so, choose the File menu's New From Template command. In the Select Template dialog box, shown in Figure 6-11, select the local site that contains the template, select the template, and click Select.

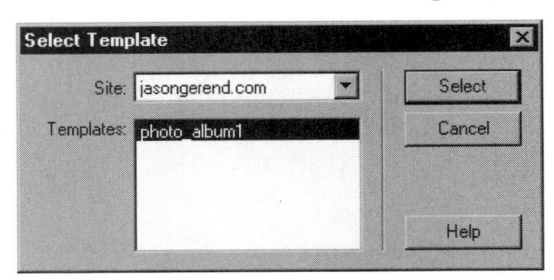

Figure 6-11 Creating a new Web page from a previously created template.

Saving Web Pages

After creating a Web page in Dreamweaver, you need to save it. This is step very important because many Dreamweaver features won't work properly unless you save the page first.

To save your Web page, choose the File menu's Save As command. Choose the folder you want to use, and enter the name of your file in the File Name text box, as shown in Figure 6-12. Click the Save button when you're finished.

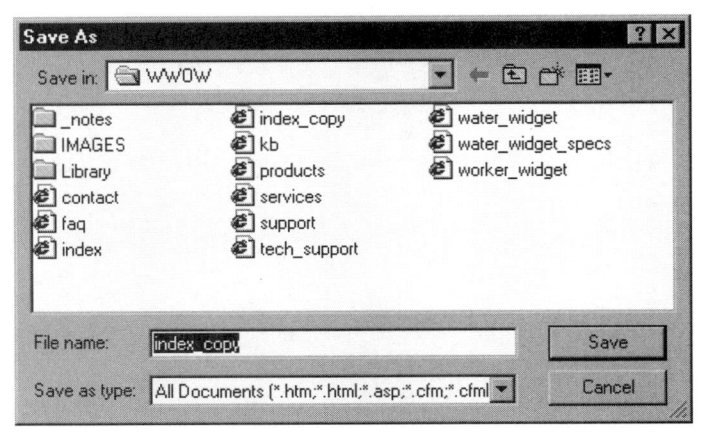

Figure 6-12 Using the Save As dialog box to save your Web pages.

Effective Executive's Guide to Dreamweaver Web Sites

TIP *Even though Dreamweaver will let you create a Web page with spaces or uppercase letters in its filename, don't use them. Filenames with spaces or uppercase letters may never cause problems if you stick with a Web hosting company that uses Windows 2000 or Windows NT Web servers, but if you move to a Unix-based Web server at some point, you could end up in big trouble. Unix deals with spaces and capitalization much differently than does Windows, and this could cause your entire Web site to break.*

Previewing Web Pages

Even though the Web pages you create in Dreamweaver will appear almost identical in a Web browser as they do in Dreamweaver, it is important to frequently double-check this, especially since each Web browser displays pages a bit differently.

To preview a page in a Web browser, choose the File menu's Preview In Browser command and then select a browser from the submenu. This opens a new browser window with your page displayed in it.

TIP *When previewing pages in Internet Explorer 5 or later using Dreamweaver 3, you need to close the browser window each time you want to update the preview—otherwise, an error message will appear. To fix this bug, install the Dreamweaver 3.01 or later update from Macromedia's Web site (choose the Help menu's Dreamweaver Support Center command).*

Working with Text and Hyperlinks

Despite the multimedia emphasis of the Web, text is still the heart of most good Web pages. Besides being a clear and concise means of communicating to your visitors, text also downloads very quickly, can be indexed by search engines, and is usually easier to create than more visual forms of content.

Because text and hyperlinks are the most important content on virtually every Web page, adding them to your pages is a critical task in Web site construction In the following sections, we show you just what to do to place text and create hyperlinks quickly and easily.

Importing Text

If you have text that you can import directly into Dreamweaver rather than having to retype it, this is ideal. Dreamweaver provides support for importing text saved in the HTML file format, as plain text, and also provides special support for importing tables and importing HTML files created using Microsoft Word.

Importing HTML Files

The best way to import text into Dreamweaver is to first save it as an HTML file using whatever program you created it in, and then open this file in Dreamweaver and move the text into the Web page where you want to place it. To do so, follow these steps:

1. **Choose the File menu's Open command.**

    This displays the Open dialog box, as shown in Figure 6-13.

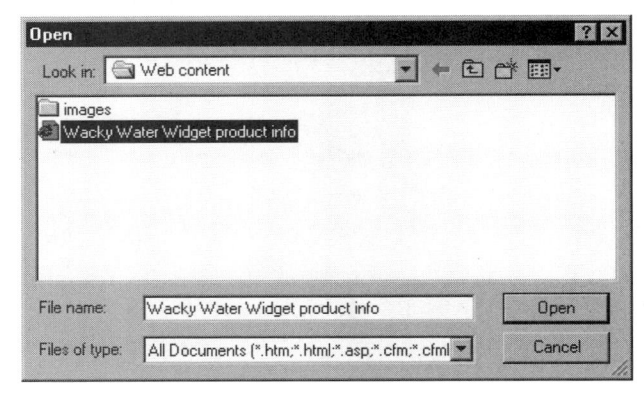

Figure 6-13   Opening a HTML file.

2. **Locate your central content folder**

    Select the drive where your central content folder is located from the Look In drop-down list box (see "Step 4: Collect and Organize Your Content" for more information). Navigate to your central content folder by double-clicking folders to open them. When you find it, double-click it to view the contents of the folder. (If the file is located elsewhere, open the appropriate folder.)

3. **Choose the file type you're looking for.**

    Select the type of file you want to import from the Files Of Type drop-down list box, or select All Documents from this box if you're unsure.

4. **Select the file you want to import, and click Open.**

    Dreamweaver opens the file in a new Document window, as shown in Figure 6-14.

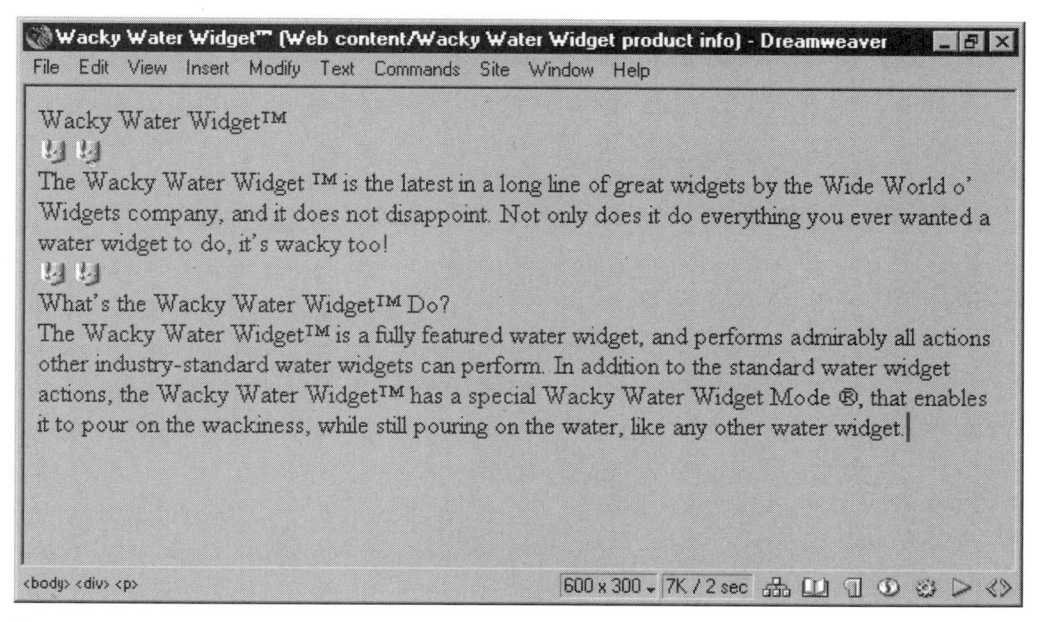

![Dreamweaver screenshot showing Wacky Water Widget page]

Wacky Water Widget™

The Wacky Water Widget ™ is the latest in a long line of great widgets by the Wide World o' Widgets company, and it does not disappoint. Not only does it do everything you ever wanted a water widget to do, it's wacky too!

What's the Wacky Water Widget™ Do?
The Wacky Water Widget™ is a fully featured water widget, and performs admirably all actions other industry-standard water widgets can perform. In addition to the standard water widget actions, the Wacky Water Widget™ has a special Wacky Water Widget Mode ®, that enables it to pour on the wackiness, while still pouring on the water, like any other water widget.

Figure 6-14 The HTML file, opened in Dreamweaver.

5. **Work with the text.**

Edit the page as you would any other Web page. To place the text in a different Web page, press Ctrl-C to copy it, open the page in which you want to insert the text, position the cursor where you want to insert the text, and press Ctrl-V.

Importing HTML Files from Microsoft Word

Dreamweaver has a special command for importing Microsoft Word documents saved in HTML format that opens the HTML document and removes a large amount of unnecessary code that Word places in the page. To use this command, follow these steps.

1. **Use the Import Word HTML command.**

To do so, choose the File menu's Import command and then choose Import Word HTML from the submenu. (Or you could open the file and then clean up the code using the Commands menu's Clean Up Word HTML command.) The Select Word HTML File To Import dialog box is displayed, as shown in Figure 6-15.

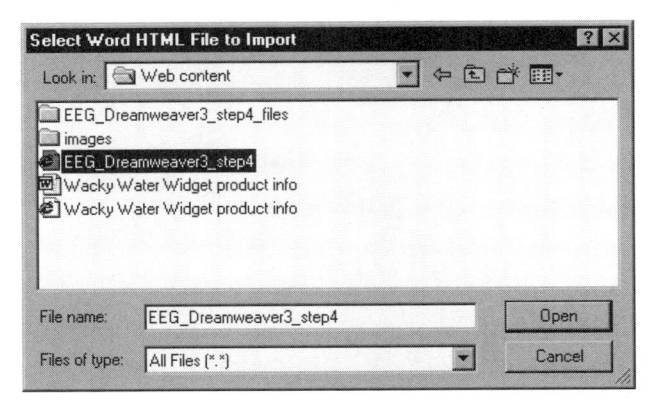

Figure 6-15 Importing an HTML file created with Word.

2. **Locate your central content folder.**

   Select the drive where your central content folder is located from the Look In drop-down list box (see "Step 4: Collect and Organize Your Content" for more information). Navigate to your central content folder by double-clicking folders to open them. When you find it, double-click it to view the contents of the folder. (If the file is located elsewhere, open the appropriate folder.)

3. **Select the file you want to import, and click Open.**

   Dreamweaver displays the Clean Up Word HTML dialog box, as shown in Figure 6-16. Verify that the correct version of Word is selected (Dreamweaver automatically detects the file type), and then click OK.

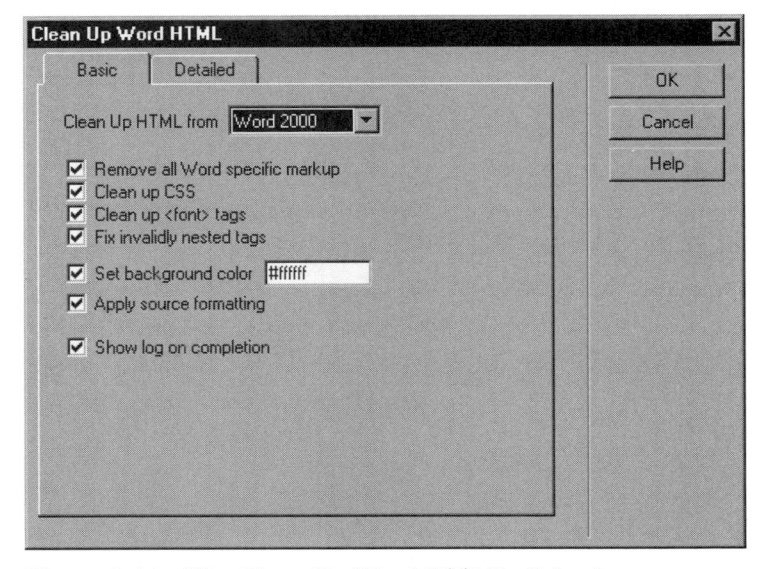

Figure 6-16 The Clean Up Word HTML dialog box.

Effective Executive's Guide to Dreamweaver Web Sites

4. Work with the text.

Dreamweaver opens the file in a new Document window, as shown in Figure 6-17. You can edit the page as you would any other Web page. To place the text in a different Web page, press Ctrl-C to copy it, open the page in which you want to insert the text, position the cursor where you want to insert the text, and press Ctrl-V.

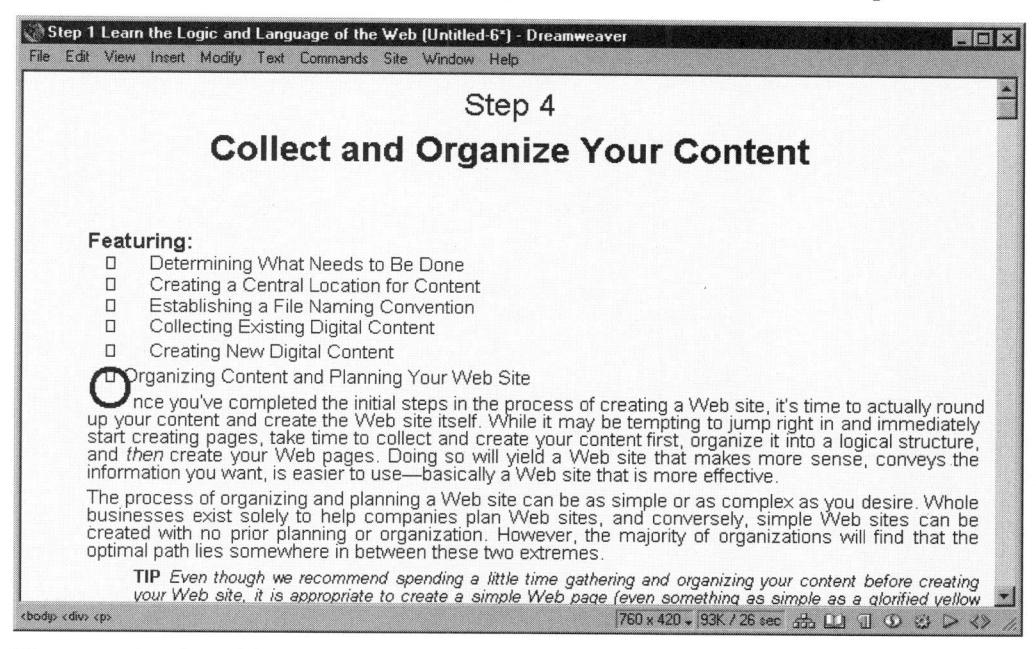

Figure 6-17 An HTML file opened in Dreamweaver.

NOTE *When you move text from a Word-created HTML file into another Web page inside Dreamweaver, Dreamweaver strips out Word's special CSS style information. This allows you to better format the text; however, it also results in the loss of some of the text's original formatting information. If you want to strip out this style information without moving the text, making it easier to format the text, choose the File menu's Convert command, and then choose 3.0 Browser Compatible from the submenu. See "Step 7: Polish Your Pages" for more information.*

Importing Plain Text

If you can't import the text you want as an HTML file, the best way to get the text into Dreamweaver is to open the text in a program that can read the text file and then copy and paste it into your Dreamweaver Web page. To do this, follow these steps:

1. **Open the document in its native application.**

   Open the text in the application that created it or another application that can read it. Figure 6-18 shows an e-mail message opened in Microsoft Outlook.

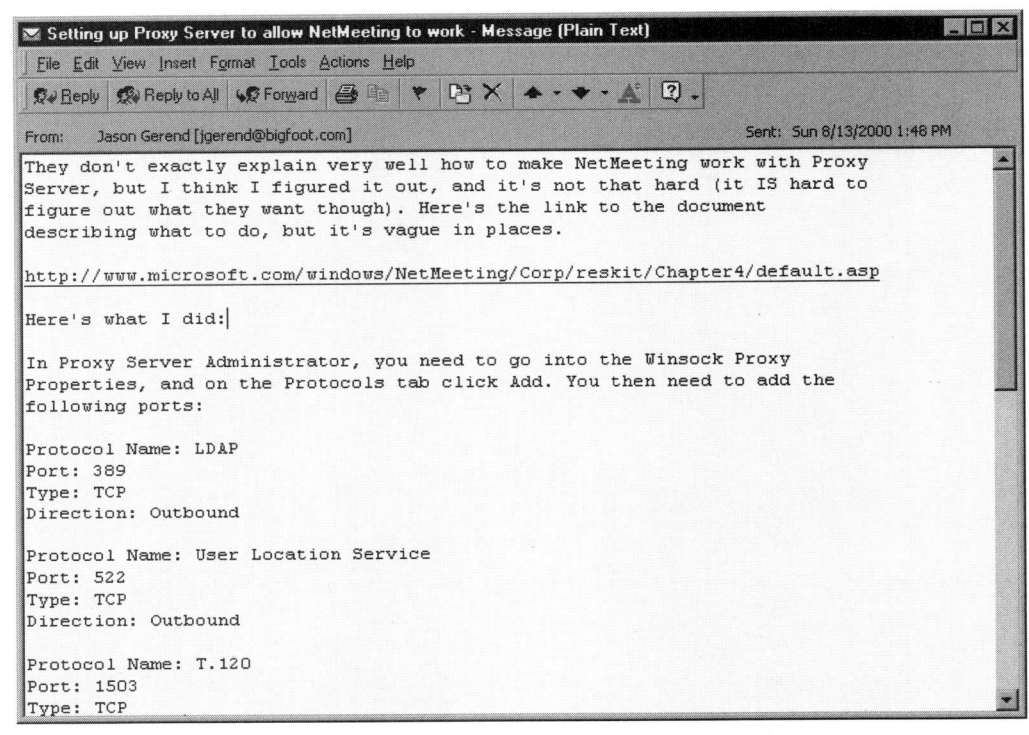

Figure 6-18 Importing text from an e-mail message.

2. **Copy the text.**

   Select the text you want to import, and press Ctrl-C.

3. **Paste the text in your Web page.**

   Open the Web page in Dreamweaver in which you want to place the text, place the cursor where you want to insert the text, and press Ctrl-V. Dreamweaver inserts the text, without any formatting, as shown in Figure 6-19. You'll probably need to go in and format the text as appropriate for your Web page.

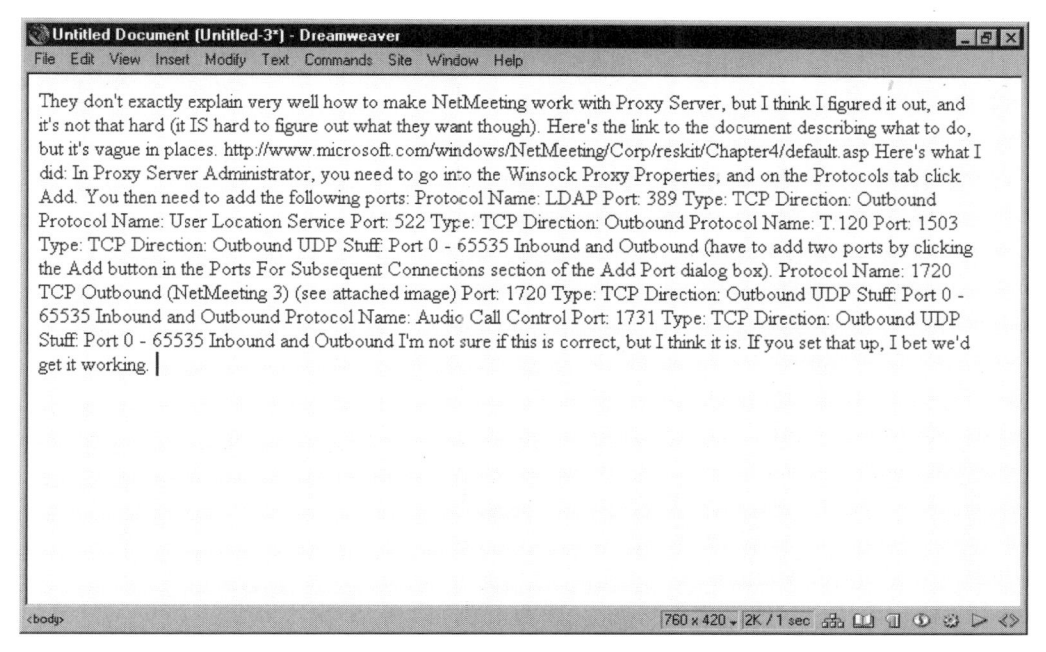

Figure 6-19 An e-mail message converted to plain text and imported into Dreamweaver.

Importing Tables

If you want to import a table from a spreadsheet or other program, you can use the spreadsheet program's Web page export capabilities (if available), and then treat it as any other HTML file you want to import. You can also use Dreamweaver's Import Table Data command to import the data from a text file.

To import spreadsheet data into a table from a text file, follow these steps:

1. **Save the data as a text file.**

    In your spreadsheet program, save the table as a text file, as shown in Figure 6-20, preferably using tab delimiters, although comma-separated values (.csv files) and other delimiters also work.

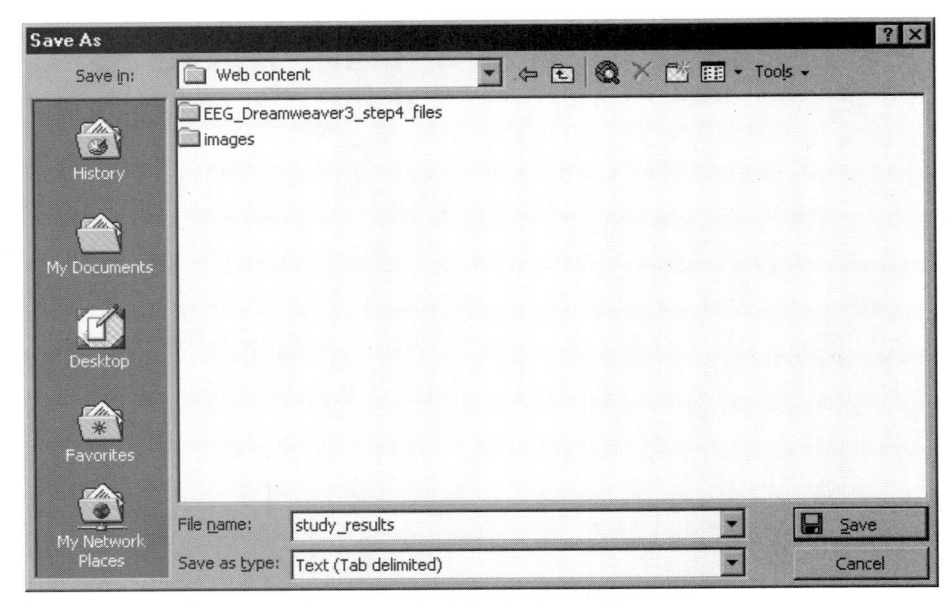

Figure 6-20 Saving a table as a tab-delimited text file.

2. **Import the data into Dreamweaver.**

   In Dreamweaver, position the cursor where you'd like to insert the table, choose the File menu's Import command, and then choose Import Table Data from the submenu.

3. **Select the file to import.**

   In the Import Table Data dialog box, shown in Figure 6-21, click the Browse button to specify the file you want to import. In the Open dialog box, select the file and click Open. Use the Delimiter drop-down list box to specify what character separates columns in the table. Optionally, specify additional table characteristics and then click OK. Dreamweaver inserts the table in your Web page.

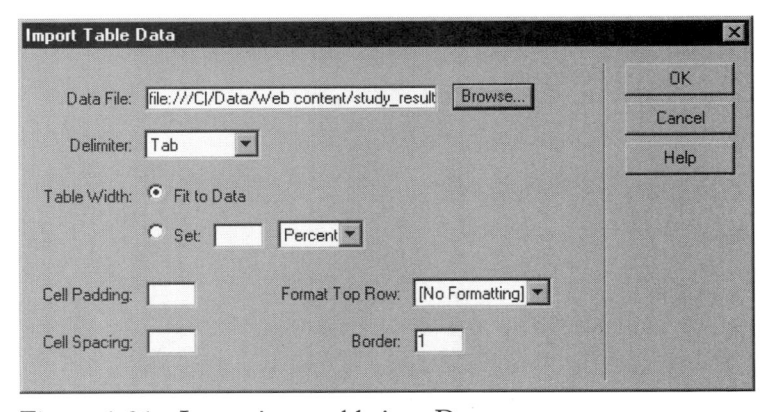

Figure 6-21 Importing a table into Dreamweaver.

Effective Executive's Guide to Dreamweaver Web Sites

Entering and Formatting Text

In Dreamweaver, you enter text exactly as you would in a normal word processor. Click in the location where you want to add text, and type the text. Press the Enter key only at the end of a paragraph. If you press Enter at the end of every line, your Web page will look strange when displayed on a different-size monitor or in a different-size window. If you want to manually create a new line within the same paragraph, press Shift-Enter—this is called a line break, and uses the <br> tag.

Formatting text in Dreamweaver works a little different from most word processors—all formatting is done using the Property inspector floating palette, as shown in Figure 6-22, or using the Text menu. To format text, select it and then use the Property inspector to change the formatting, as described in the list below.

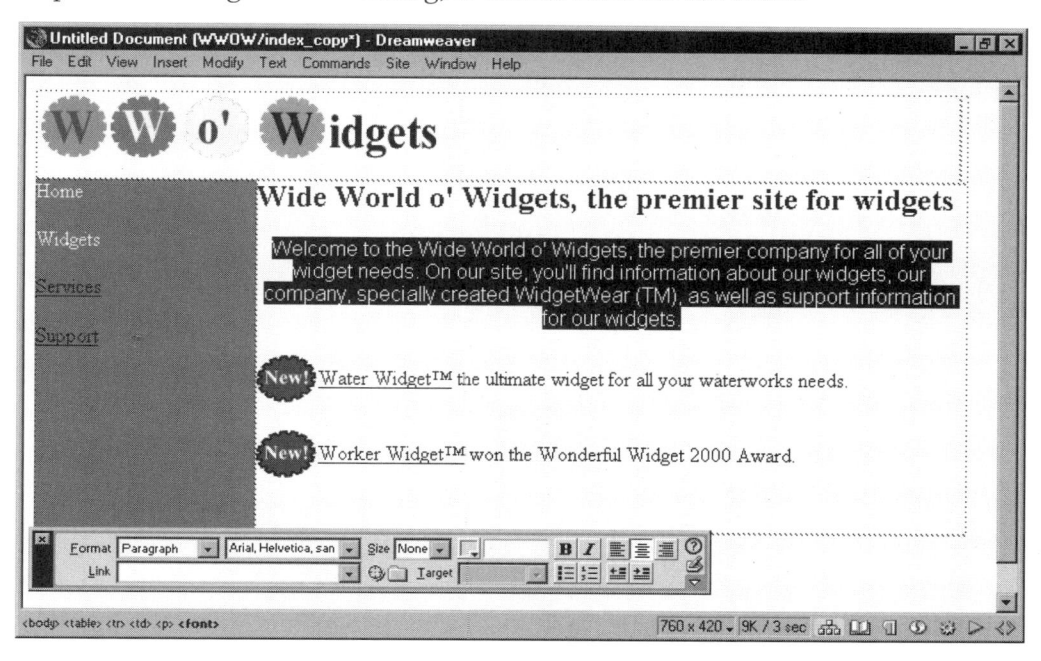

Figure 6-22 Using the Property inspector to format text.

- To change the style of text—for example, to make the text into a heading—select the text and choose the style you want from the Format drop-down list box on the Property inspector.

- Using styles standardizes the look of pages across your site, especially when used in conjunction with CSS or HTML styles. For example, use the Normal style for most text, use Heading 1 for the page or Web site title, and Heading 2, 3, etc. for subsequent headings.

- To change the font, select the text and choose the font you want from the Font drop-down list box. The available fonts are relatively common across different computers and alternative fonts are indicated in case the specified font is unavailable. To specify a different font, choose Edit Font List from the Font drop-down list box and then use the dialog box to create your own list of alternative fonts.

    TIP *Although it's tempting to use a fancy font that you have on your system, it really is best to stick with the fonts available in Dreamweaver. Although this limits the choices, it ensures that your pages will appear as you intend, since your visitors will have the correct fonts.*

- To change the font size, select the text and then choose the font size from the Size drop-down list box. Font sizes in Web pages are relative—unless you use CSS styles, the best you can do is make the font "bigger" or "smaller." There are seven font sizes; the default is size 3. Choosing size 1 or 2 makes the text smaller, anything over 3 makes the text bigger. Numbers with a plus (+) or minus (-) sign are relative to the default size.

- Use the Bold and Italic buttons to boldface or italicize the selected text.

- Use the Align Left, Align Center, and Align Right buttons to change the alignment of the selected paragraph.

- Use the Unordered List and Numbered List buttons to make bulleted or numbered lists.

- To increase or decrease the indentation of the text, click the Text Indent or Text Outdent toolbar buttons.

- To change the color of the selected text, click the Text Color box on the Property inspector, and choose a color from the pop-up menu.

- Choose the Text menu's Check Spelling command to check your Web page for spelling errors. The rest of the typical text-formatting tools are also here, and quite easy to use.

    TIP *Any formatting you specify manually by using the Property inspector overrides settings from any CSS files you're using, so to maintain consistency when using an external CSS style sheet, avoid formatting text using the Property inspector and instead specify all formatting in a CSS file that you link to all the pages in your Web site. Doing so assures that Heading 1, for example, looks the same throughout your site, and also makes it easy to change this look quickly on all pages.*

Creating Hyperlinks

A hyperlink is a piece of text or an image that when clicked takes the visitor to another page, image, or file. Hyperlinks are one of the most useful features of Web pages. They allow visitors to easily access information they're seeking and provide a way for visitors to access related information they might not have otherwise sought.

Although hyperlinks are indispensable tools, they are not without hazard. Hyperlinks leading to other Web sites can quickly take visitors away from your site, something that you need to be careful about. In general, placing a hyperlink in a document is an invitation for visitors to follow the link, so only place links when you want to lead visitors elsewhere.

> **TIP** *If you want to include references to related information but don't want to explicitly send visitors away from the current page, make a related information column or section of the page with links to other pages and sites with more information.*

The following sections show you how to create all types of hyperlinks—links to Web pages, e-mail addresses, links within a Web page, and links that open a Web page in a new window.

Basic Hyperlinks

To create a hyperlink, follow these steps:

1. **Select the text or image.**
2. **Specify what page to link to.**

   To do this, type the file's address in the Link text box on the Property inspector or click the folder icon to display the Select File dialog box, as shown in Figure 6-23. Select the file to which you want to link, and click Select. The most recently created hyperlinks can be quickly reused by selecting them from the Link drop-down list box. (Click the down-arrow button to the right of the Link box.)

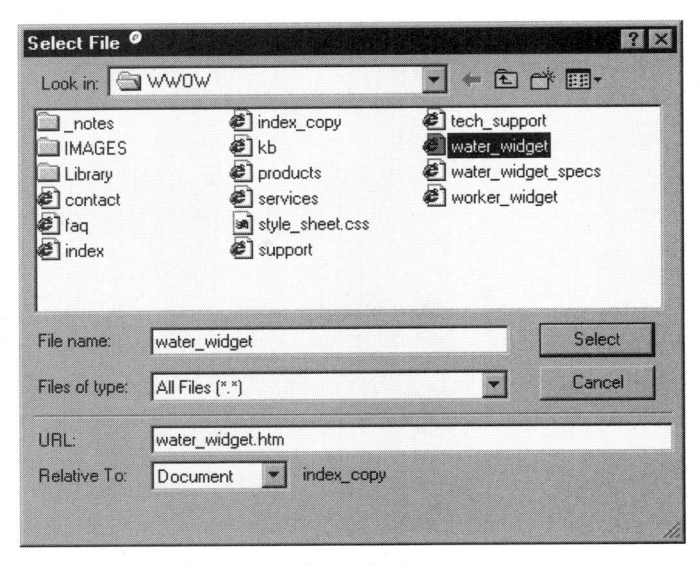

Figure 6-23   Creating a hyperlink.

TIP   *Creating effective text for hyperlinks can be an art unto itself, but in general, all you need to do is make the linking text short and descriptive. There's no need to include the words* click here—*this instruction is implicit. For example, use* <u>widgets</u> *instead of* <u>click here for widgets</u>.

E-Mail Hyperlinks

To make a hyperlink to an e-mail address, click the Insert E-Mail Link button (the envelope icon) on the Objects palette (or choose the Insert menu's E-Mail Link command). In the Insert E-Mail Link dialog box, shown in Figure 6-24, enter the text you'd like to appear in the Web page, and enter the e-mail address in the E-Mail box. Click OK when you're finished.

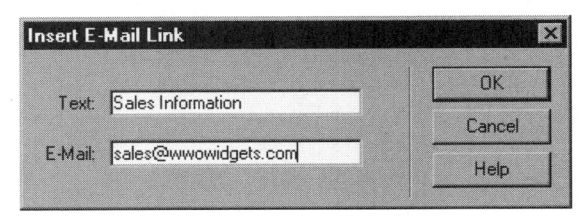

Figure 6-24   Creating a hyperlink to an e-mail address.

Hyperlinks Within a Web Page

Although it's a good idea to keep your Web pages short enough to fit mostly onscreen, sometimes it's appropriate to have longer pages, as is often the case with online articles or product literature. When you create long pages, it is helpful to include hyperlinks to different sections within the same page—to a heading partway down the page or to a link back to the top of the page.

In order to create a hyperlink to a particular location within a Web page, you first need to create one or more invisible objects called named anchors (also called bookmarks). These named anchors serve as the destinations for your in-page hyperlink. Clicking a hyperlink to a named anchor in a Web browser automatically scrolls the page until the named anchor is at the top of the screen.

To create a named anchor, follow these steps:

1. **Locate the appropriate section.**

    Position the cursor at the place where you want visitors to be able to link (such as a heading midway down a long page).

2. **Create the named anchor.**

    Choose the Insert menu's Named Anchor command, or click the Named Anchor button in the Invisibles group of the Objects palette.

3. **Name the anchor.**

    In the Insert Named Anchor dialog box, shown in Figure 6-25, enter a short name for the anchor in the Anchor Name text box, and then click OK. Dreamweaver places a small yellow anchor icon onscreen to represent the named anchor. To delete the anchor, select it and press Delete; to move it, drag it to a new location.

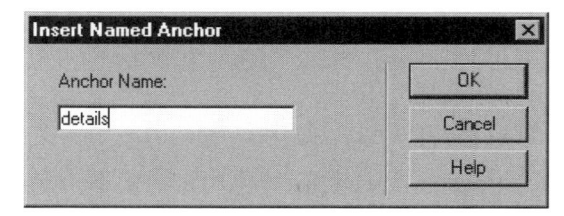

Figure 6-25 Creating a named anchor to permit in-page hyperlinks.

TIP   *Place your named anchors a line above the heading or section to which you want to link. Doing this ensures that the heading won't end up partially offscreen.*

To create a hyperlink within a Web page to a named anchor, follow these steps:

1. **Highlight the text.**

   Highlight the text you want to make into a link (most likely at the top of the page).

2. **Drag the link Point To File icon to the named anchor.**

   Drag the Point To File icon (the small target icon located to the right of the Link box in the Property inspector) until the target pointer is over the named anchor to which you want to link, as shown in Figure 6-26. When you do this, Dreamweaver fills in the Link field with the named anchor's name, preceded by the pound (#) sign (which indicates the link is to a named anchor).

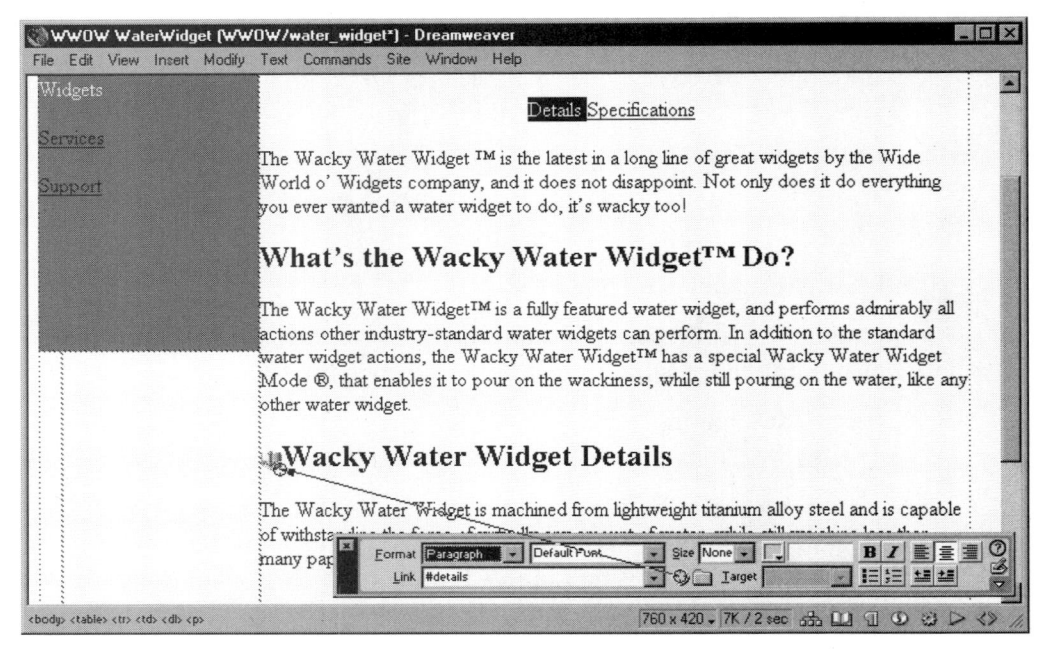

Figure 6-26 Linking to a named anchor by dragging the Point To File icon.

Opening Links in a Different Window

Usually, when a visitor clicks on a hyperlink, you want the link to open in the same browser window. However, if it's a link to another company's Web site or somewhere outside your own Web site, you might want to make the link open in a new browser window so that your site remains open. To do so, follow these steps:

1. **Select the link.**

   Select the hyperlink you want to open in a new window.

2. **Specify the target window.**

   Select the window you want the link to open in from the Target drop-down list in the Property inspector, as shown in Figure 6-27. Choose _blank to open the link in a new window—the other options are primarily for targeting different frames if your site uses them.

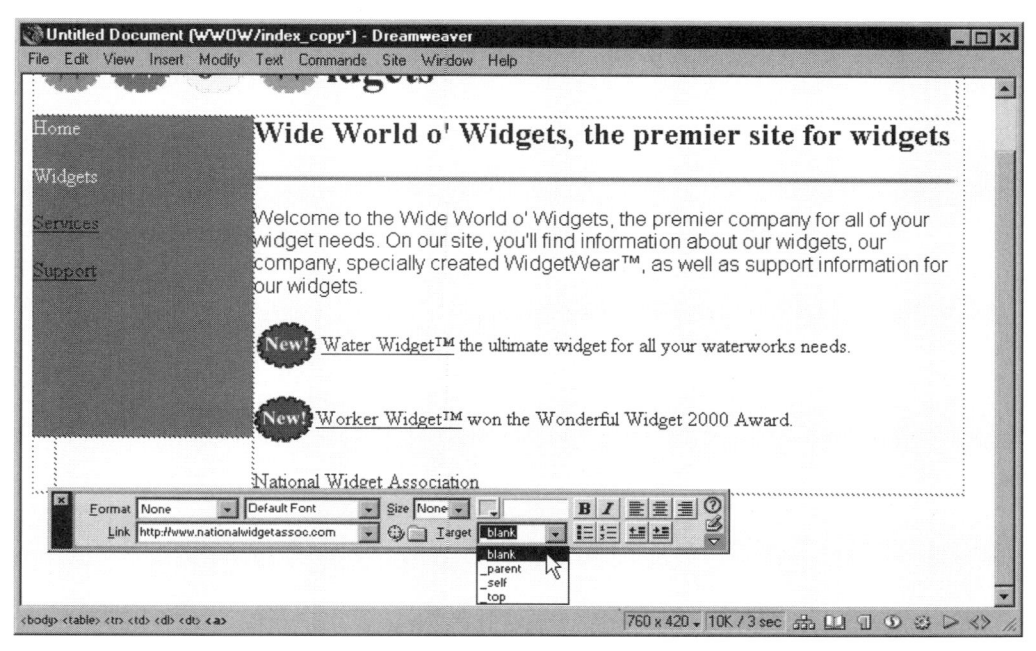

Figure 6-27 Making a hyperlink open in a new browser window.

Working with Images

After text, images are the next most important element in a Web page. The following sections explain how to insert images, modify image properties (including size and spacing), and set alternative representations.

Inserting Images

There are several ways to insert images into a page in Dreamweaver. The following procedures show you each method.

To insert an image by dragging and dropping, follow these steps:

1. **Locate the image.**

   In Dreamweaver's Site window or Windows Explorer, open the folder containing the image you want to insert—either in your local folder if you're using the Site window or perhaps in your central content folder if you're using Windows Explorer.

2. **Drag the image into your page.**

   Drag the image to the position where you want it in your Web page, as shown in Figure 6-28. You might want to resize the Document window so that you can see your current page at the same time you are viewing the Site window or Windows Explorer. If you drag an image from Windows Explorer, Dreamweaver will alert you that the image isn't contained in the root folder for your site (the local folder) and ask if you'd like to copy the image into your local folder. Click Yes to do so.

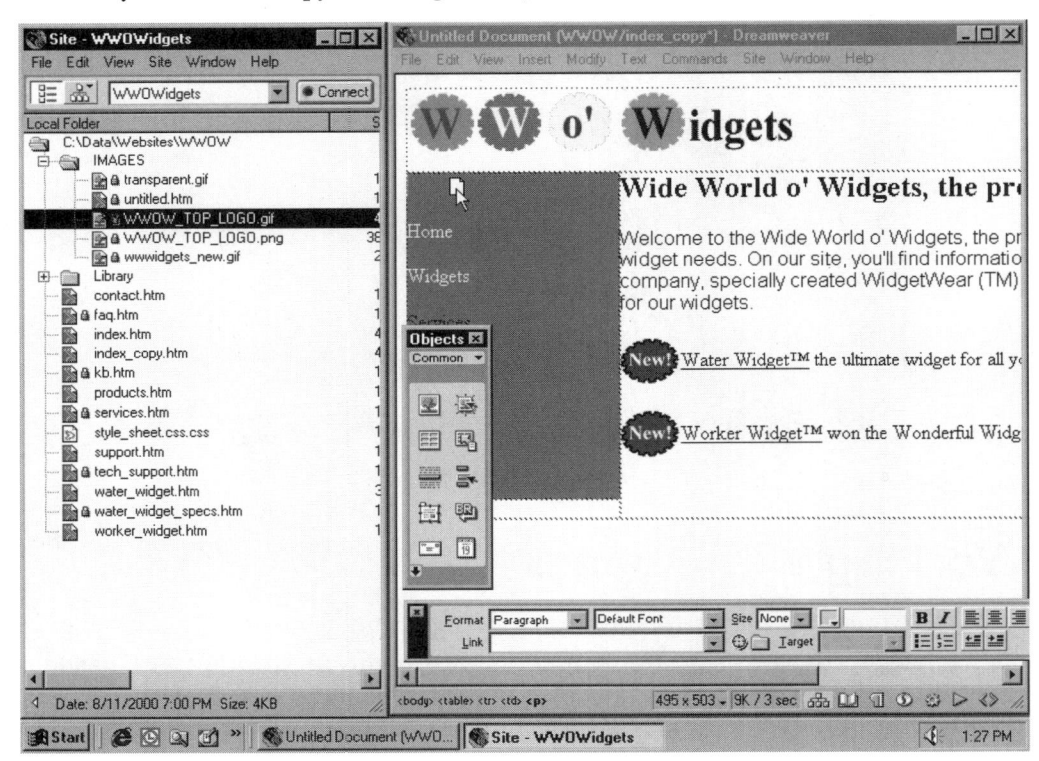

Figure 6-28 Inserting an image by dragging it from the Site window.

Alternatively, you can use the Insert Image object in the Objects palette to insert an image. To do this, follow these steps:

1. **Click or drag the Insert Image object.**

   Either click the Insert Image object on the Objects palette to insert an image at the current cursor location or drag the Insert Image object to the location where you want to insert the image.

2. **Select an image.**

   In the Select Image Source dialog box, shown in Figure 6-29, select the image you'd like to insert, displaying a preview of the image. When you've found the image you want, click the Select button. Dreamweaver inserts the image into your Web page.

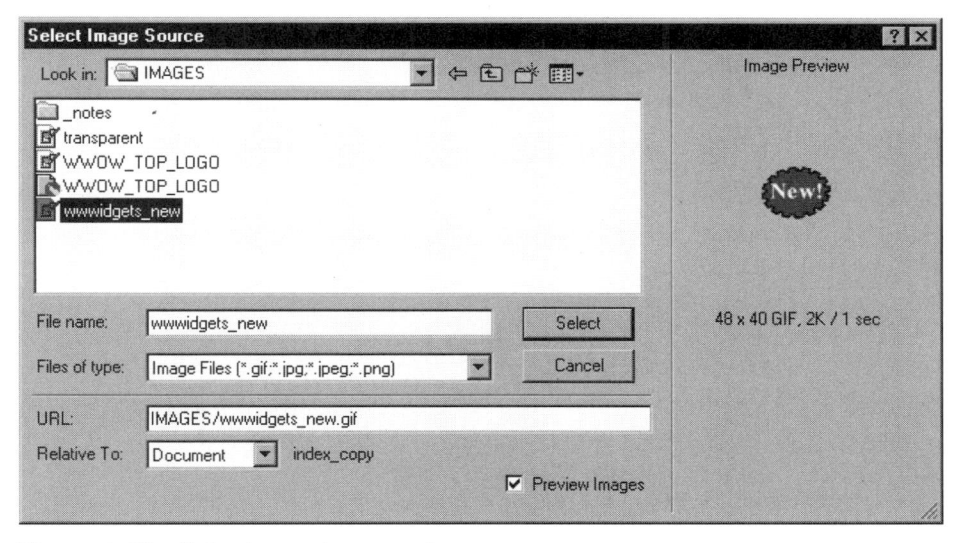

Figure 6-29 Selecting an image to insert.

To insert a horizontal rule—a visual divider used to separate content elements—position the cursor where you want to place the horizontal line and then click the Insert Horizontal Rule object on the Objects palette, or drag the Insert Horizontal Rule object to the desired location. To modify the horizontal line's properties, select it and use the Property inspector to change its size, alignment, or shading, as shown in Figure 6-30.

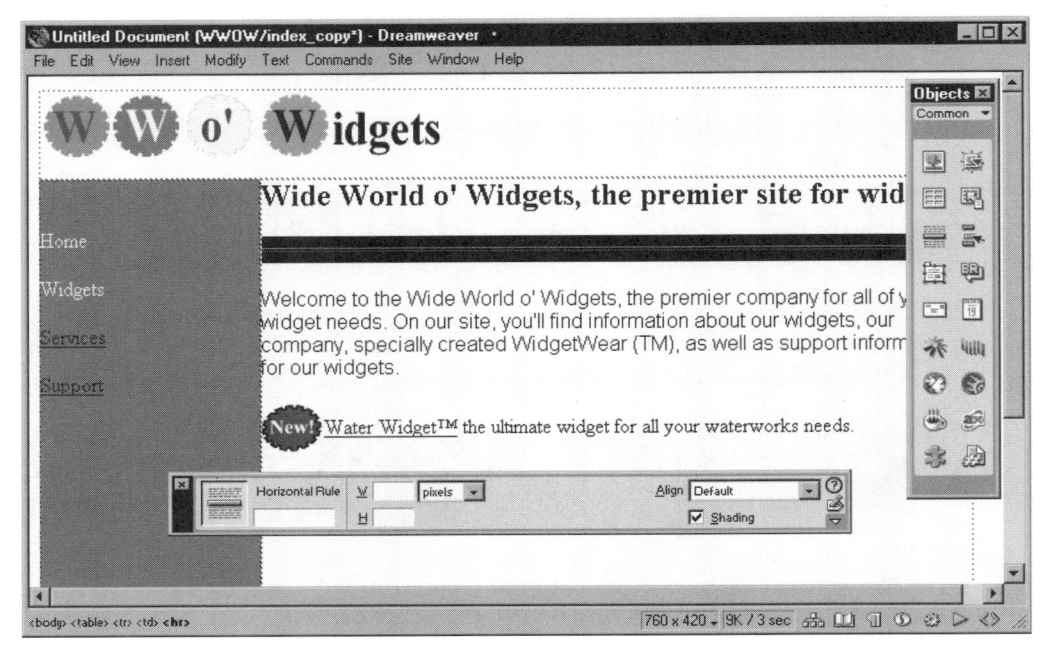

Figure 6-30   Modifying a horizontal rule.

Resizing Images

Some images just won't be the right size for your Web page. In general, if the image doesn't fit properly on your page, you should resize the image in a stand-alone image editor such as Macromedia Fireworks.

You *can* resize images directly in Dreamweaver, but doing so only changes how large the image is displayed in a Web browser—the actual image file remains exactly the same size. This means that even if you reduce the size of an image in Dreamweaver, it will still take the same amount of time to download unless you resize the actual image file in a stand-alone editor.

There are circumstances, though, when it is appropriate to resize an image in Dreamweaver. For example, perhaps you've created an image to serve as a visual divider for the page—maybe a graphical horizontal rule or an image to delimit a column of a table. Instead of resizing the image file itself to fit the page, simply adjust the size in Dreamweaver to expand the image to fit the space you intend. This allows you to use a smaller image to fit a larger space, which lets the page download faster.

TIP   *Keep in mind that you can only discard image information, not gain it; so try to increase the size of images on only one axis—the axis where the image simply repeats. An image that you enlarge too much on the wrong axis looks pixilated and unattractive, something that doesn't reflect well on a Web site. To see this in action, resize some images and look at them.*

To resize an image, follow these steps:

1. Select the image.

2. Resize the image.

Move the mouse over an edge of the image until the cursor turns into a dual-sided arrow, and then drag the outline of the image in or out to make the image smaller or bigger, as shown in Figure 6-31.

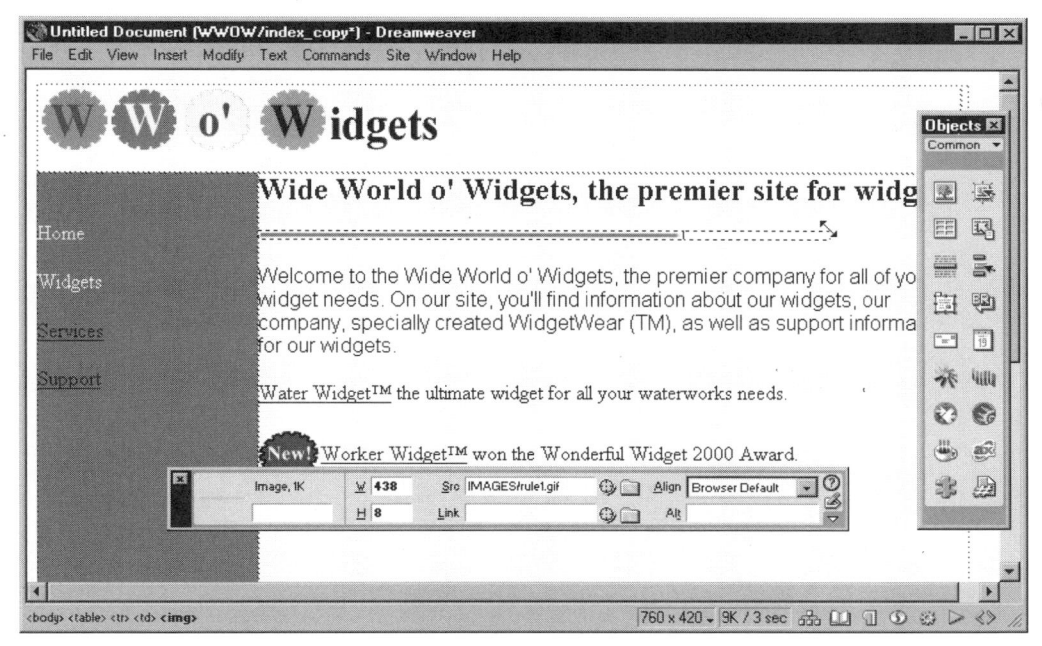

Figure 6-31   Resizing an image.

3. Optionally, resize the image precisely.

To precisely resize an image, select the image, and then enter a new size in the W and H (Width and Height) boxes of the Property inspector. The default unit is pixels—to make the image size relative to the size of the browser window (a good idea for horizontal rules and other simple, repeating graphics), enter the size in percentage by adding a percent sign after the size you enter. Clear the Keep Aspect Ratio check box if it's okay to distort the image by adjusting the height and width nonproportionally.

NOTE   *In general, images shouldn't be sized by percent because they'll end up strangely distorted, the wrong size, or pixilated. Some exceptions are images used as horizontal lines and images used as visual dividers.*

Adjusting Image Layout

To adjust how text is laid out with an image—for example, how it's aligned with the image and how much spacing is in between the image and the text, follow these steps:

1. **Select the image.**

2. **Specify the alignment.**

    To specify how you want to align text adjacent to your image, choose an option from the Align drop-down list box on the Property inspector, as shown in Figure 6-32. Figure 6-33 shows a list of the alignment options.

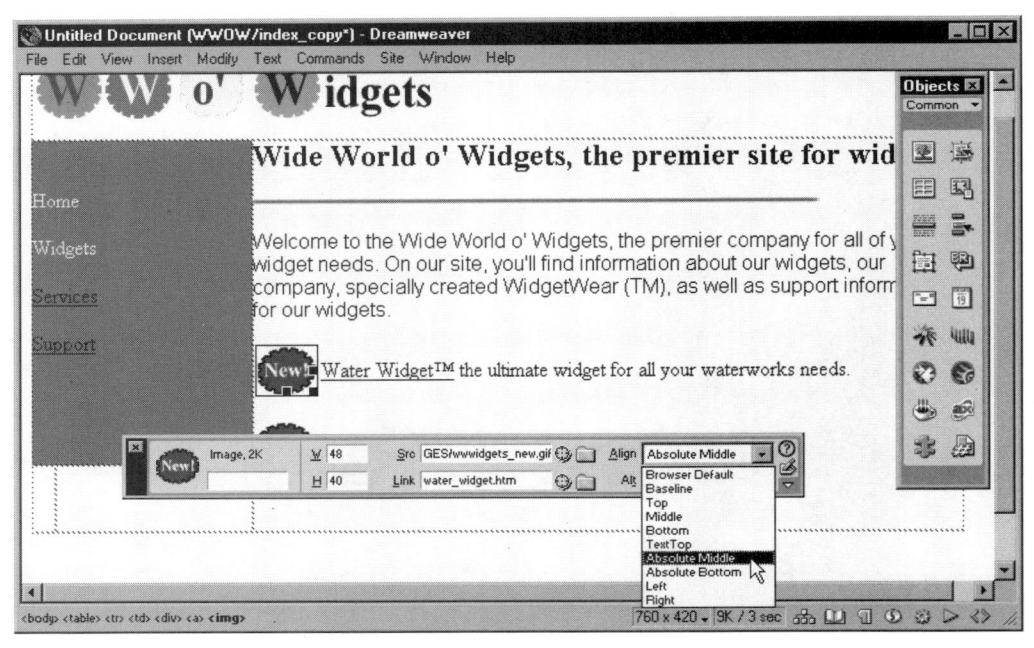

Figure 6-32   Specifying how text next to an image should be aligned.

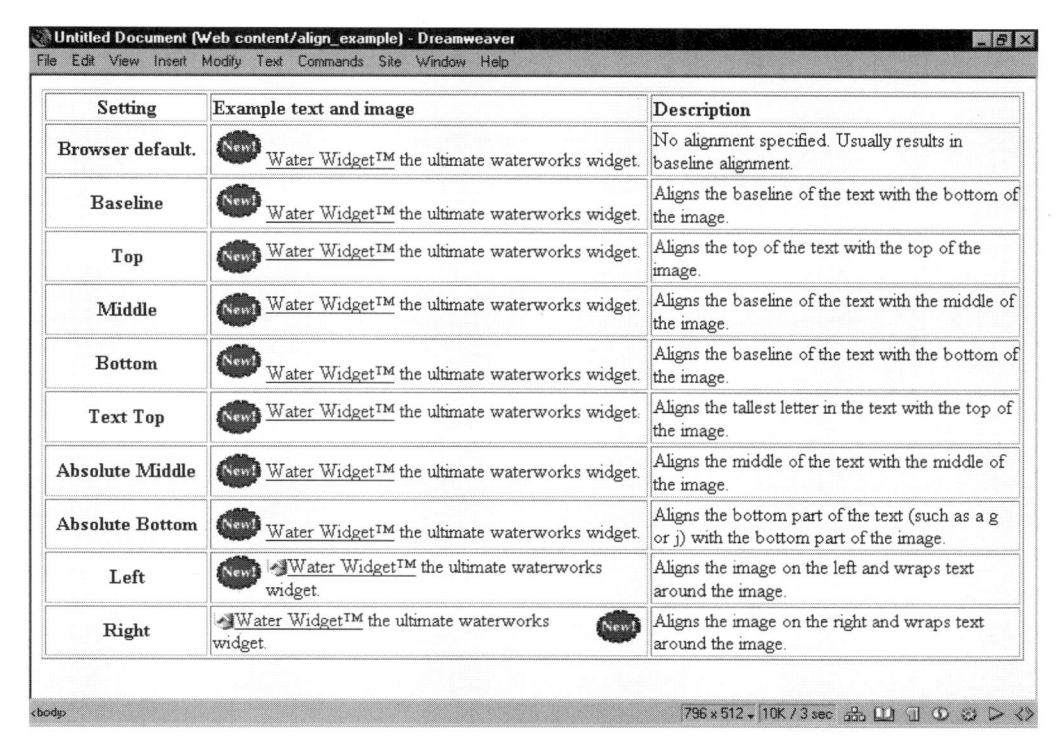

Setting	Example text and image	Description
Browser default.	Water Widget™ the ultimate waterworks widget.	No alignment specified. Usually results in baseline alignment.
Baseline	Water Widget™ the ultimate waterworks widget.	Aligns the baseline of the text with the bottom of the image.
Top	Water Widget™ the ultimate waterworks widget.	Aligns the top of the text with the top of the image.
Middle	Water Widget™ the ultimate waterworks widget.	Aligns the baseline of the text with the middle of the image.
Bottom	Water Widget™ the ultimate waterworks widget.	Aligns the baseline of the text with the bottom of the image.
Text Top	Water Widget™ the ultimate waterworks widget.	Aligns the tallest letter in the text with the top of the image.
Absolute Middle	Water Widget™ the ultimate waterworks widget.	Aligns the middle of the text with the middle of the image.
Absolute Bottom	Water Widget™ the ultimate waterworks widget.	Aligns the bottom part of the text (such as a g or j) with the bottom part of the image.
Left	Water Widget™ the ultimate waterworks widget.	Aligns the image on the left and wraps text around the image.
Right	Water Widget™ the ultimate waterworks widget.	Aligns the image on the right and wraps text around the image.

Figure 6-33 The different alignment options available.

3. **Set the image spacing.**

   To control how much space there is between the image and whatever it's next to, click the down arrow in the lower right corner of the Property inspector to display the advanced image properties. Use the V Space and H Space boxes to control the amount of spacing (in pixels) on all sides of the image, as shown in Figure 6-34.

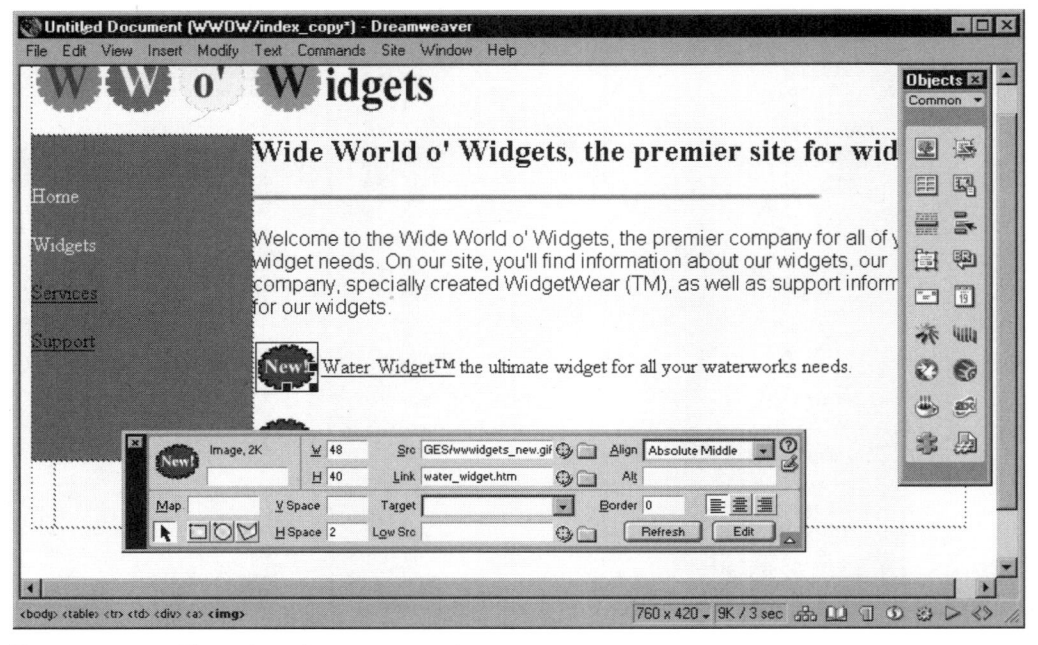

Figure 6-34 Changing the image spacing.

4. Set the border thickness.

To add a border around the image, in the Border box enter a border thickness in pixels.

Setting Alternative Image Representations

One way you can make a Web page more effective is to provide alternative text-based descriptions of your images. These descriptions are displayed while the images are loading (which on slow Internet connections can often take a while), or they display in browsers that have images disabled, and can help make your Web site usable for a wider audience.

> TIP *Setting alternatives is a good practice, but it is no substitute for creating pages that load quickly. In general, your Web pages should load in less than 30 seconds over a 28.8 connection. (See the page size and download time display on the lower right part of Dreamweaver's Status Bar for an estimate of how long the current page will take to load.) See "Step 7: Polish Your Pages" for more help on optimizing your Web pages.*

To specify what your alternative text should be, select the image and then enter the text you want visitors to see when they cannot see your image in the Alt box on the Property inspector, as shown in Figure 6-35.

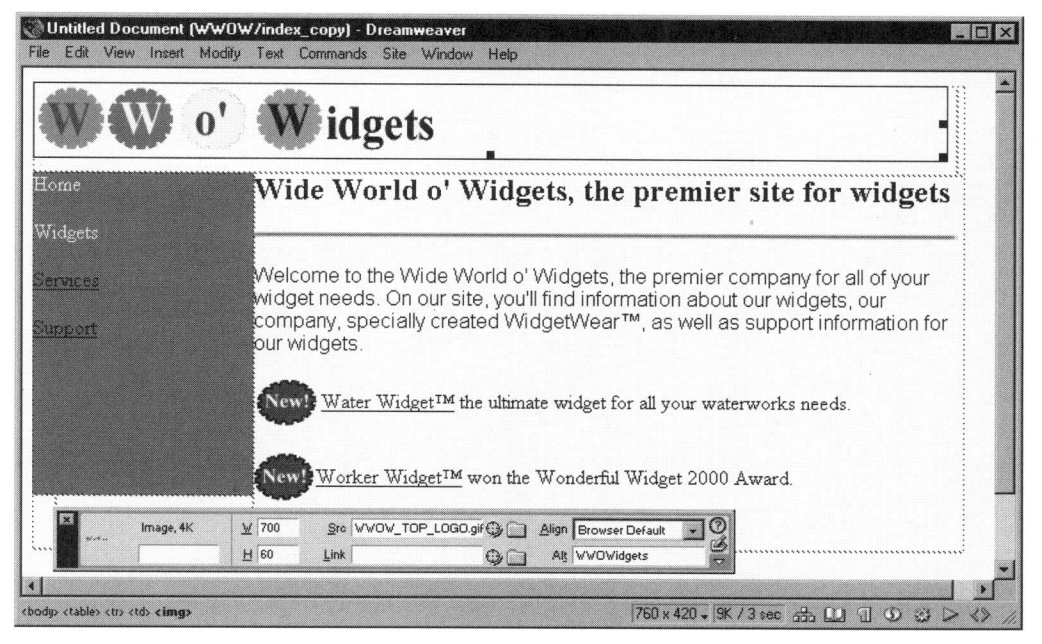

Figure 6-35 Setting alternative representations for an image.

To specify a low-resolution image to display while the full-size image is loading, click the down arrow in the lower right corner of the Property inspector to display the advanced image properties, click the folder icon next to the Low-Src text box, select the image you want to display, and then click OK.

> **TIP** *In general, don't worry about providing a low-resolution version of an image unless you have a very large image on a Web page. If this is the case, consider reducing the image size (create a thumbnail) and linking it to the full-size version for visitors who want to see the larger image.*

Creating Image Maps

Image maps are an occasionally useful tool when creating a Web site. They allow you to create multiple hyperlinks within a single image—with each hyperlink assigned to a different region of the image. To create an image map, follow these steps:

1. **Select the image.**

2. **Open the advanced properties.**

   Click the down arrow in the lower right corner of the Property inspector to display the advanced image properties.

3. **Draw a hotspot.**

   Click either the Square Hotspot, Oval Hotspot, or Polygonal Hotspot button on the Property inspector, and then click and drag inside the image to create a region that users can click on to activate a hyperlink, as shown in Figure 6-36.

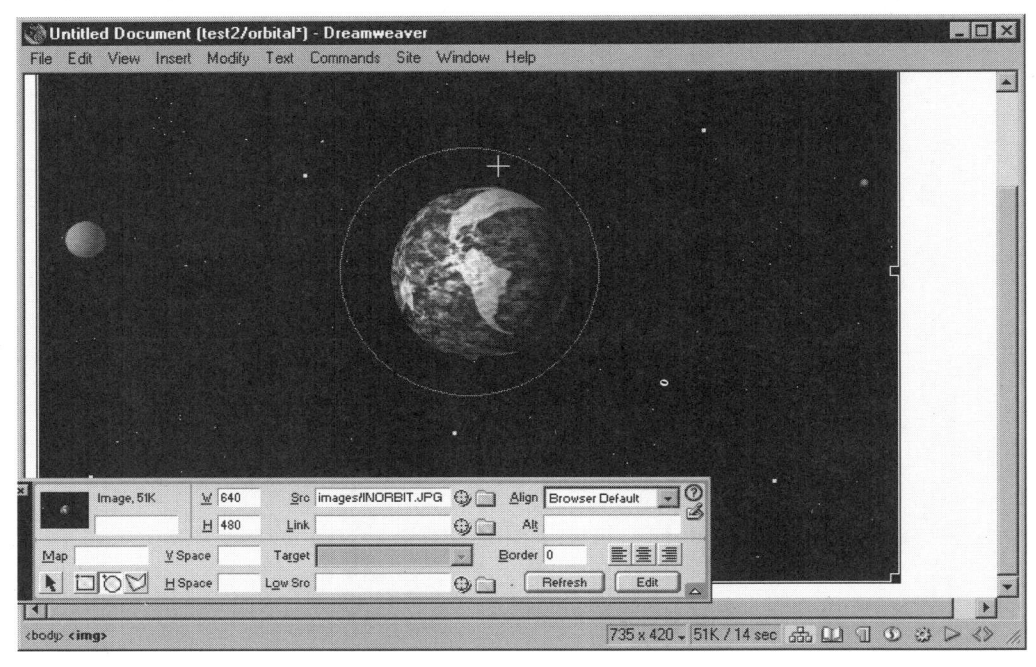

Figure 6-36 Creating the outline for a hotspot.

4. **Create the hyperlink.**

   Click the folder icon next to the Link box in the Property inspector to locate a Web page or file to which you can link the hotspot.

5. **Set the alternate text.**

   Enter a short but descriptive name for the hotspot in the Alt box of the Property inspector, as shown in Figure 6-37. This name will be used for browsers that don't support images, as well as those browsers that display the Alt information in a small ToolTip when the cursor is moved over the hotspot.

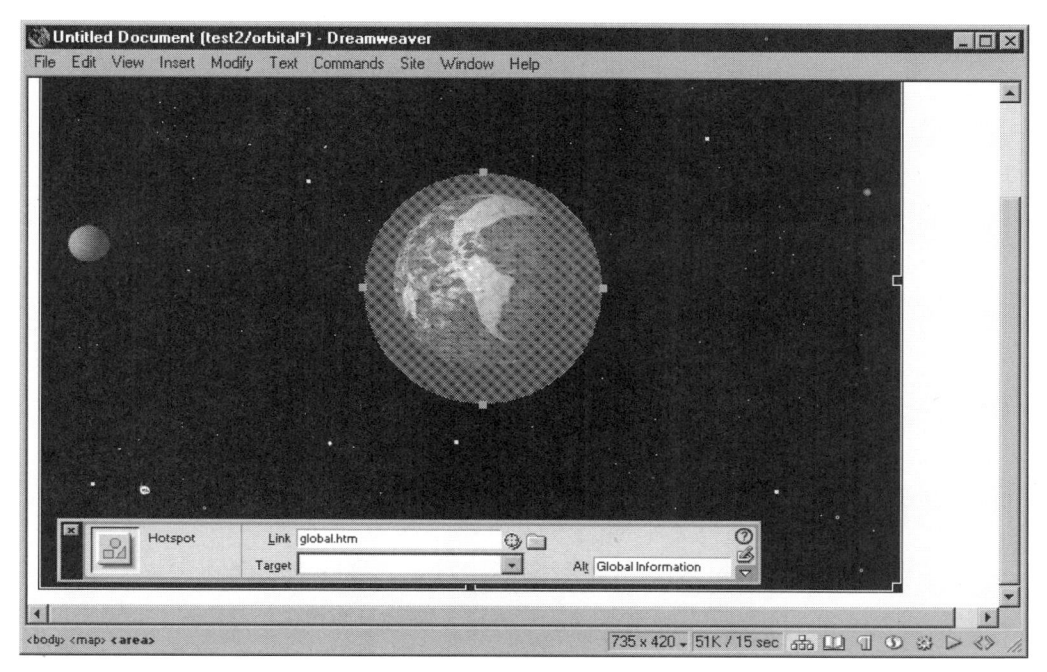

Figure 6-37 Creating the outline for a hotspot.

Adjusting Page Properties

Besides adding content to a Web page, you may need to modify the properties of the page itself—to change the Web page title, add a background image, to change the page margins, or to specify a background image.

In general, when you need to make the colors consistent across multiple pages, this information should be edited on a template or a style sheet should be created and linked to all relevant documents. However, there are times when page colors and background information will need to be adjusted manually (for example, to create the template), so it's handy to learn how to change these elements.

To manually change page colors and background information, follow these steps:

1. **Choose the Modify menu's Page Properties command.**
2. **Title your page.**

    In the Title box, enter a descriptive title for the page.

3. **Specify the background, text, and link colors.**

   To change the color of the page's background, text, or hyperlinks, select the box corresponding to the element you want to change and pick a color from the pop-up color picker, as shown in Figure 6-38. You can also move the cursor (which is now an eyedropper) over any element in Dreamweaver to select that color. To restore the default color, click the Default button (the middle button in the lower right corner of the pop-up window).

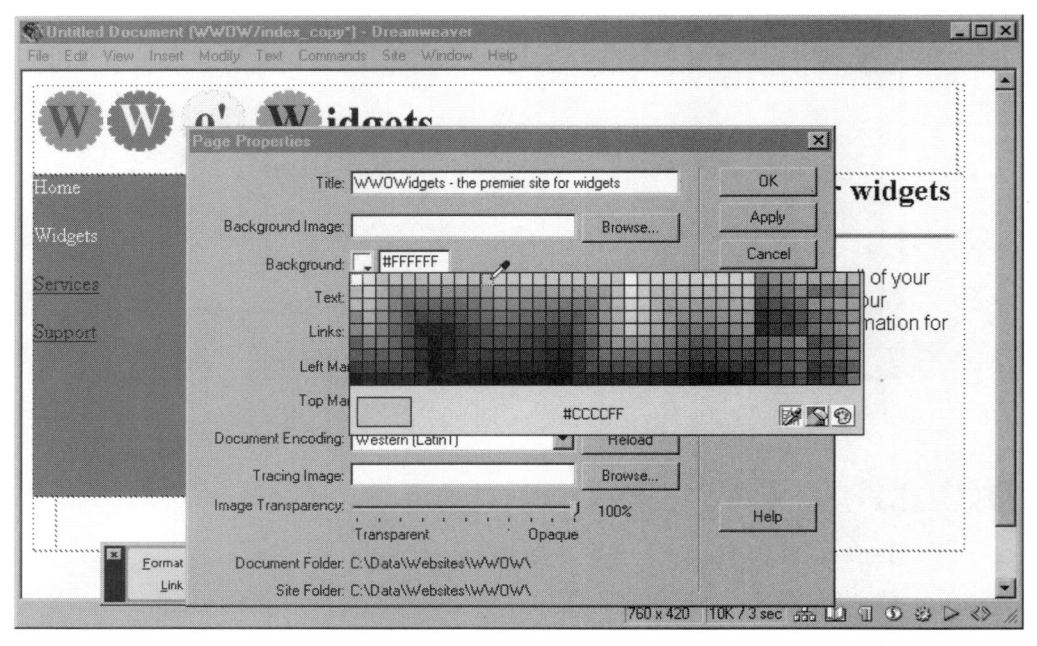

   Figure 6-38 Changing the Web page colors.

4. **Set the page margins.**

   To create margins for your page, in the Margin text boxes enter a size for your margins in pixels.

   > **WARNING** *In order for the margins to appear in both Internet Explorer and Netscape Navigator, you need to enter the side margin value in **both** the Left Margin and Margin Width boxes and the top margin value in **both** the Top Margin and the Margin Height boxes.*

A more elegant way of adjusting the colors on your Web page is to use a color scheme. Dreamweaver provides a Set Color Scheme command that contains a large number of predesigned color schemes for your Web pages.

To use a color scheme, follow these steps:

1. **Choose the Commands menu's Set Color Scheme command.**

   This opens the Set Color Scheme Command dialog box, as shown in Figure 6-39.

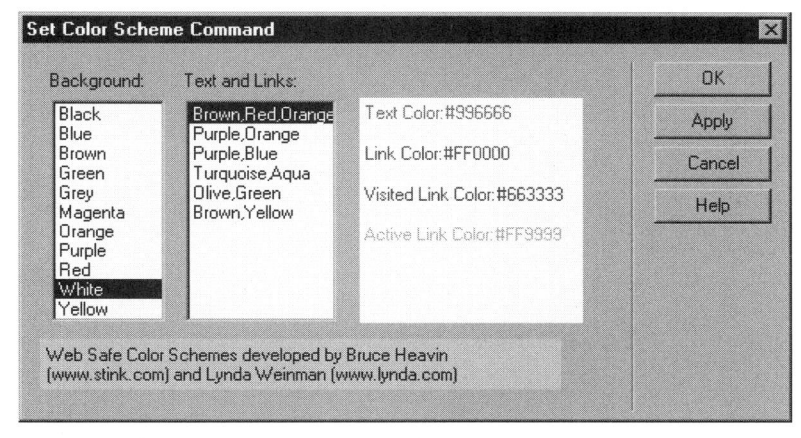

Figure 6-39 Picking a coordinated color scheme.

2. **Select the background color.**

   In the Background box, choose the background color you want to use for your page.

3. **Select the color scheme for the text and links.**

   In the Text And Links box, select a color scheme. The colors used for normal text, hyperlinks, visited hyperlinks, and hyperlinks currently clicked on are displayed in the Preview box. Click OK when you're satisfied with your color scheme.

Summary

This step showed you how to accomplish all the basic Web-page-creation tasks. These tasks include working with text and images, creating hyperlinks, formatting text, and changing the properties of your Web pages.

Step 7

POLISH YOUR PAGES

Featuring:
- Creating an Effective Home Page
- Making Your Pages Look Consistent
- Advanced Web Page Layout
- Ensuring Proper Display of Your Pages

To turn your basic pages into pages that will hold the interest of your visitors, you'll need to learn how to make an effective home page, how to make your pages look consistent, and how to create advanced Web page layouts using layers and tables. To help any visitors who may have trouble finding your site, you also need to know how to prepare your home page for search engines. This step explains how to do these tasks.

Creating an Effective Home Page

The home page (index.htm or index.html) is the first page visitors see. It acts as a summary of the entire Web site, serves as a navigational aid, and is used by search engines to determine how to catalog your Web site. As such, an effective home page should meet the following goals:

- Summarize the content of the Web site.
- Attract visitors' interest and attention.
- Show up prominently in search engines.

The following sections address these topics to make sure that your home page accomplishes all these goals.

Choosing the Best Content for Your Home Page

Because the home page is the first page visitors see when they come to your Web site, it's important to adequately summarize the contents of your site on the home page (this also helps your Web site place well in search engines). This doesn't mean putting a table of contents on the home page, but it does mean including hyperlinks to your major content categories. One good way to provide a content summary is to create a navigation bar, or set of hyperlinks, which also helps visitors easily navigate your site.

Along with summarizing the content of your Web site, the home page should also catch the interest of visitors. One way effective Web sites do this is by having a part of the home page that tells visitors what's new or of particular interest on the site.

Keep the content on your home page short. Each featured section should contain only a couple of lines of text with one or two small images. A good example of a site that provides effective, brief content on its home page is the Fortune Web site *(www.fortune.com)*, shown in Figure 7-1. It highlights key articles and then links to other content of interest. In addition, the site is clean, quick to load, and easy to understand.

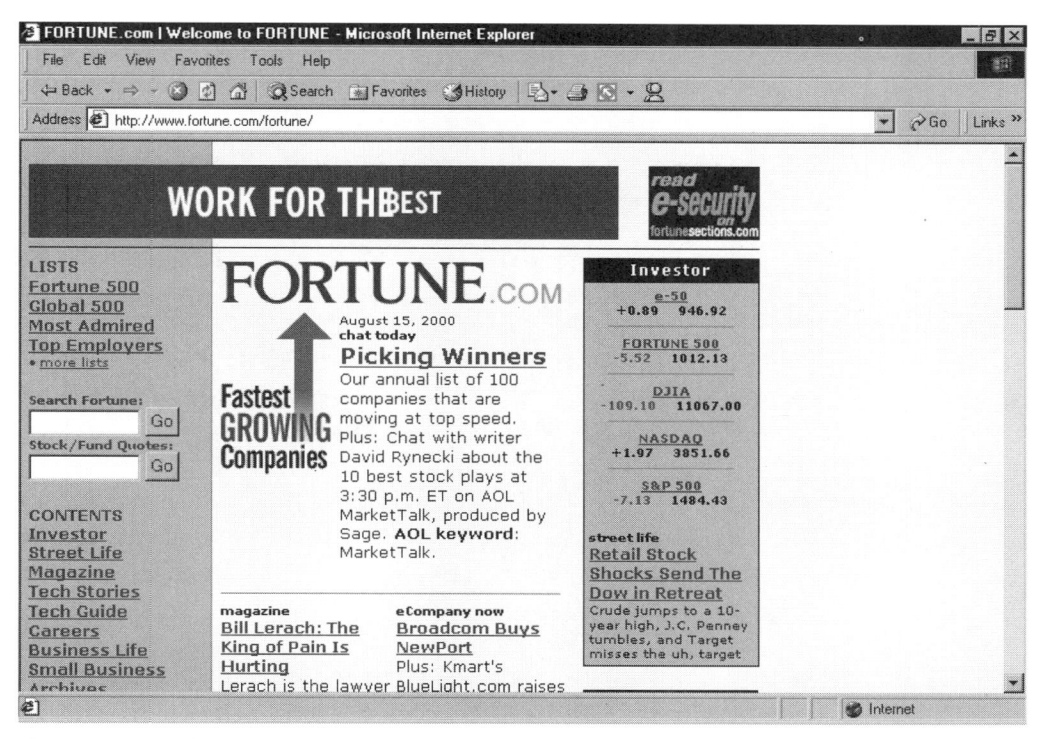

Figure 7-1   A home page with well-chosen content.

Working with Navigation Bars

Navigation bars are a series of buttons that help visitors quickly access the most important pages on a Web site. Although no more functional than a simple list of hyperlinks, navigation bars look more polished and have become the standard navigational aid for Web sites.

To make a navigation bar, follow these steps:

1. **Create a series of image buttons.**

   Using a program such as Macromedia Fireworks or Microsoft PhotoDraw, create a button image for each link you'd like to include in your navigation bar.

2. **Place the buttons in your navigation bar.**

   Insert the images in a table along one side of the page, at the top or bottom of the page, or in a frame (a separate section of a page that can contain a completely different Web page; see "Appendix C: Using Frames" for more information).

3. **Assign hyperlinks to the buttons.**

   Link the images to the pages you want to include in your navigation bar. (See "Step 6: Create Your Pages" for help with creating hyperlinks.)

TIP *Frames can make good navigation aids. By placing a navigation bar in a navigation frame and placing your home page in the main frame, the navigation bar will be available from any page on your Web site without any additional work.*

This method is simple, easy, and compatible with all Web browsers. (Make sure to assign alternate text to the images so that visitors can navigate without images if they want to.) However, it does lack pizzazz.

TIP *A technique that was pioneered on news Web sites that can be put to use on other Web sites is the related links section, usually found at the bottom of a Web page. These links enable visitors to get to other pages that feature similar content.*

Dreamweaver provides a special Navigation Bar object that you can use to insert a navigation bar with rollover buttons—buttons that change appearance when you move the mouse over them or click them. This type of navigation bar quickly increases the visual appeal of your site, and since the images are small, the extra time involved to download them is usually a worthwhile trade-off.

NOTE *The rollover effect won't appear in Web browsers that don't support Javascript (such as version 2 browsers).*

To create a navigation bar with rollover buttons, follow these steps:

1. **Create a series of image buttons.**

   Using a program such as Macromedia Fireworks or Microsoft PhotoDraw, create a button image for each link you'd like to include in your navigation bar. Create a different version of each button for each image state you want to use. The four states are shown in Table 7-1.

BUTTON STATE	DESCRIPTION
Up	Default—no user action required.
Over	When the user moves the mouse over the image.
Down	When the user clicks the image.
Over While Down	When the user clicks the image and then moves the mouse over it.

Table 7-1   The different image states for a rollover button.

Typically, two or three image states are adequate (Up, Down, and Over). Usually the Over image has some sort of glowing effect to it (or brighter text), and the Down image looks depressed or the text is drawn lighter.

2. Insert a Navigation Bar object.

Either click the Insert Navigation Bar object on the Objects palette or choose the Insert menu's Navigation Bar command. This displays the Insert Navigation Bar dialog box, as shown in Figure 7-2.

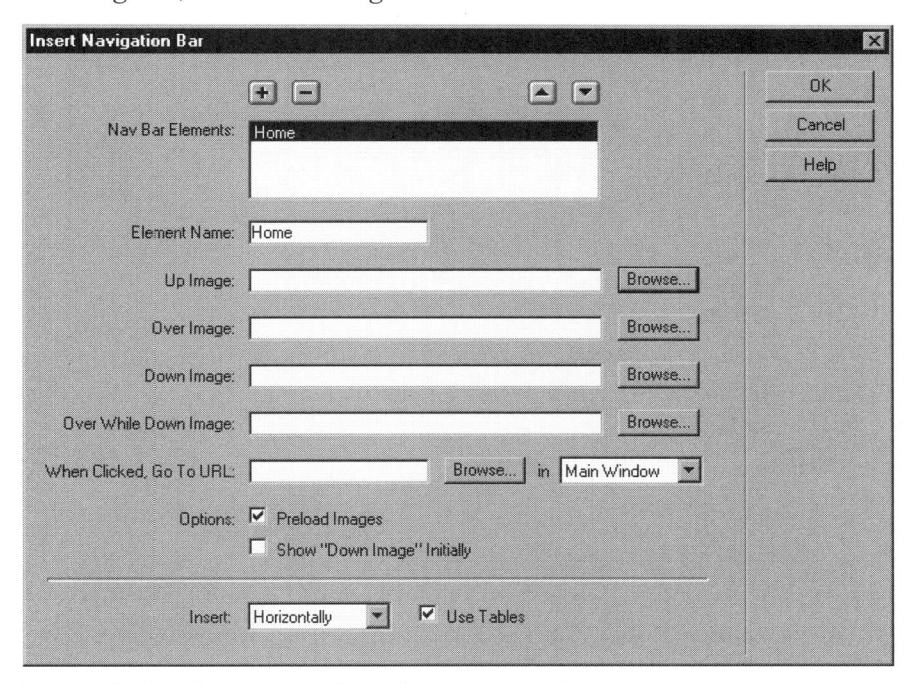

Figure 7-2   Creating a rollover button navigation bar.

Step 7 *Polish Your Pages*   **173**

3. **Name the first button.**

   In the Element Name box, enter the name for the first navigation button (probably Home). This button name is also shown in the Nav Bar Elements list, which shows the buttons in your navigation bar.

4. **Specify the images.**

   Click the Browse button next to each image state you want to specify (Up Image, Over Image, Down Image, and Over While Down Image). Use the Select Image Source dialog box, shown in Figure 7-3, to select the images.

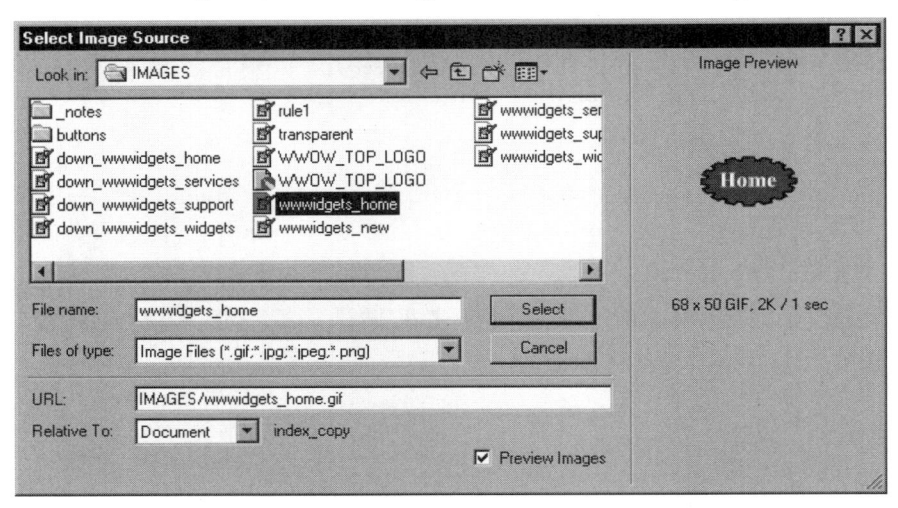

Figure 7-3 Selecting images for the navigation bar.

5. **Assign hyperlinks to the button.**

   Link the button to the page you want by clicking the Browse button next to the When Clicked, Go To URL box and selecting the page. If your page uses frames, select the frame in which your page should open from the Main Window drop-down list box next to the URL field.

6. **Add more buttons.**

   To create additional buttons, click the plus sign (+) at the top of the dialog box and then repeat steps 3 through 5. To remove a button, select it in the Nav Bar Elements list and click the minus sign (-). To rearrange the buttons, use the up and down arrows above the Nav Bar Elements list.

7. Specify options.

To preload the images for hidden button states so that there isn't a delay when a visitor moves his or her mouse over the button, leave the Preload Images option selected. Select the Show "Down Image" Initially check box to have the button appear depressed initially. (Select this option for the Home button so that when a visitor initially loads the home page, your navigation bar indicates that he or she is viewing the home page.) Use the Insert drop-down list box at the bottom of the dialog box to specify whether the navigation bar should be created horizontally (all buttons in a row) or vertically (all buttons in a column). Select the Use Tables check box to create the navigation bar in a table. Click OK when you're finished.

> **TIP** *Determining which pages to include on your navigation bar(s) may initially involve a bit of head scratching. Users should be able to easily figure out where they are, where in the Web site they should go next, and how to get back to where they were. This is often accomplished by selecting the Home check box, but in deep sites it may be handy to use the Child Level option in addition to selecting the Home Page and Parent Page check boxes. Regardless, you'll probably want to fiddle with these settings and test the results.*

To modify the navigation bar, select an image in the navigation bar and then choose the Modify menu's Navigation Bar command, as shown in Figure 7-4. Alternatively, click the Navigation Bar object on the Objects palette. Dreamweaver alerts you that it can insert only one navigation bar per page and asks whether you'd like to modify the existing one. Click OK to do so.

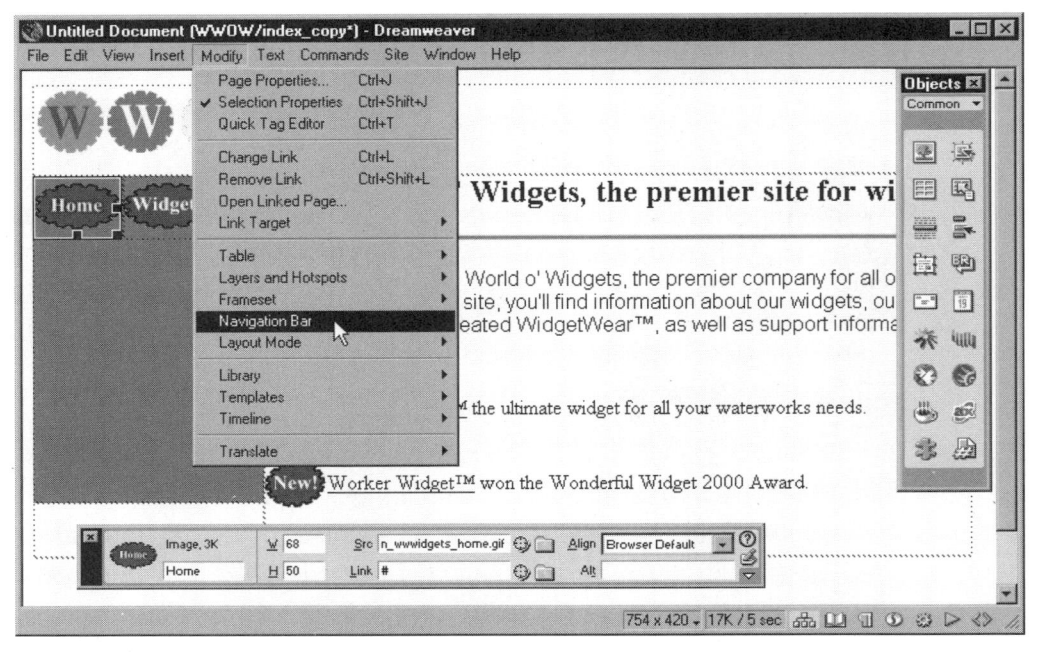

Figure 7-4 Modifying an existing navigation bar.

> TIP *Besides using navigation bars, it's often helpful to create smaller navigational aids for certain sections of your Web site. For example, multiple-page stories can benefit from a mini Table of Contents with links to all pages in the story. Long pages can benefit from using named anchors (hyperlinks to a different part of the same page) to improve the ability to quickly get to part of the page.*

Making Your Home Page Visually Appealing

The same techniques that make a visually appealing home page apply to all Web pages in general. However, here are some recommendations specifically to improve the attractiveness of your home page:

- Use your company logo. Convert it to a GIF file and place it on your home page, perhaps in a template or in Dreamweaver's Library (discussed later in the section "Using the Library"). Keep the logo small, place it in a consistent location with a consistent size, and consider saving it as a transparent GIF using a stand-alone image editor so that the logo isn't outlined with a solid color. If you don't have a company logo (or don't have one in computer-readable format), consider hiring a graphics professional to create one.

- Use an attractive set of colors. Dreamweaver ships with a wide selection of color schemes that you can use to give your Web site a more professional look. See "Step 6: Create Your Pages" for more information on using color schemes.

- Don't overload your home page with too much content. Overloading your home page makes it difficult for visitors to find the most important links and information, so choose some key elements to display and leave the rest of the page blank.

- Have good visual flow. Design your pages to attract the eye to the entire page, not just a single part of it. Be careful not to overload your page though; otherwise, the eye won't be able to settle comfortably on anything.

- Make sure that your home page doesn't take too long to load. In general, all pages should take less than 30 seconds to download over a 28.8Kbps modem. Dreamweaver's Status Bar gives an estimate of how long it will take to download any open page.

TIP *Preview your Web pages in a Web browser. To do so, choose the File menu's Preview In Browser command and then select a browser from the submenu.*

Preparing Your Home Page for Search Engines

One crucial part of Web site design that you shouldn't overlook is preparing your site for search engines. This includes more than just submitting your site to the most popular search engines. It also means adding some special HTML codes to your home page that tell search engines how to deal with your Web site.

These special codes are called meta tags, and they store information about your Web site, such as a description and keywords, that search engines use to determine when to display your site in a list of search results, as well as how to display it. While not all search engines look for these tags, enough are out there to justify including the tags on your home page. (Many search engines that don't index pages based on meta tags will display the description you enter in your home page's Description meta tag in the search results they generate.) To insert meta tags into a Web page using Dreamweaver, follow these steps:

1. **Insert a keywords object.**

    Open your home page, and then click the Insert Keywords object in the Head grouping of the Objects palette. (Click Common on the Object palette to select a different group.)

2. **Create the Keywords meta tag for your site.**

   In the Keywords box, enter all the keywords you want search engines to use to identify your site, separated only by commas, as shown in Figure 7-5. Click OK when you're finished.

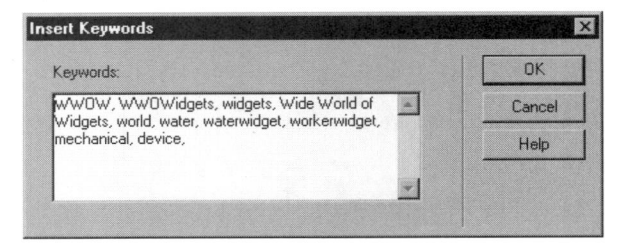

   Figure 7-5   Creating the Keywords meta tag to help search engines find your site.

   TIP   *Enter any common misspellings of your company or organization's name along with the rest of the keywords to enable visitors to find your site even with a spelling mistake.*

3. **Insert a description object.**

   Click the Description object in the Head grouping of the Objects palette. (Click Common on the Object palette to select a different group.)

4. **Create the Description meta tag for your site.**

   In the Insert Description box, enter a concise (25 words or less) but attractive description of your Web site, as shown in Figure 7-6. Avoid repeating your site's name or claiming absolutes, such as "the best widgets on the Web."

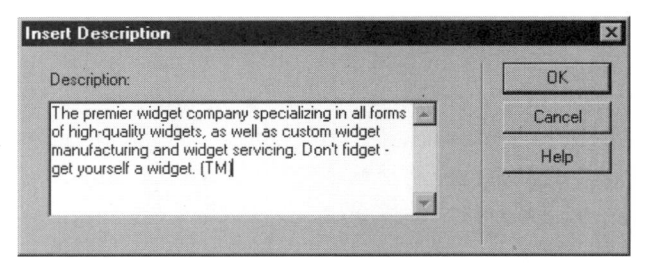

   Figure 7-6   Creating the Description meta tag to describe your site for search engines.

   TIP   *For more information on how search engines find pages and how to make your Web site more effective with search engines, check out* www.searchengine.com.

Making Your Pages Look Consistent

A Web site appears coherent and well integrated when the pages in the site are consistent in look and feel. This doesn't mean they all have to be identical. It's good to have some variation, and depending on the size of the site, you may want to have a couple different looks for your pages. However, your site has a better overall impact if your pages use consistent colors, graphics, and page designs.

The following sections tell you how to create templates to use for quickly creating new pages that already have the same look and feel as an existing page, create Library items for images and text that you want to reuse across your Web site, and standardize the text and color formatting for your Web pages using style sheets.

> **TIP** *One way to make your pages look consistent is to reuse images on different pages by creating Library objects from them and inserting these Library objects into your pages. (This technique also decreases the load time for pages and the amount of time required to make changes to the image on each page.)*

Creating Templates for Pages

Creating templates is a great way to streamline the page-creation process as well as to help give the pages on your site a consistent look.

A template is a Web page that you can use as a sort of cookie cutter to rapidly construct other pages based on the template. Dreamweaver's templates vary somewhat from normal templates—they contain editable regions, which you can modify like any typical Web page, and uneditable regions, which are locked to ensure that these regions look the same on all pages using the template. In addition, when you make changes to a locked region of a template, the locked, or uneditable, regions of all pages that were created using that Dreamweaver template are automatically updated. This feature makes it easy to revise multiple pages on your Web site, and it is ideal for a page header containing the company logo or a sidebar with navigation hyperlinks.

To create a template, follow these steps:

1. **Create a Web page exactly how you want the template to appear.**

   Create a new page or open an existing one, and enter any text and images you want to appear in the template. Format the text and colors as appropriate (or better yet, link the page to an external CSS style sheet). You may want to insert placeholder text and graphics in the regions you will make editable so that it's easy to see how content should be placed in the new pages.

2. **Save the page as a template.**

   Choose the File menu's Save As Template command, select the site in which you want to save the template from the Site drop-down list box, enter the name for the template in the Save As box, and then click Save, as shown in Figure 7-7.

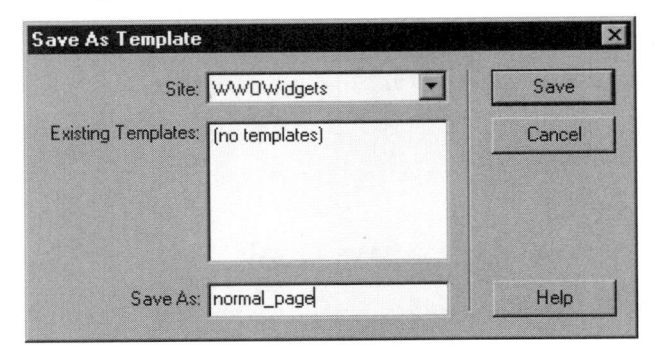

   Figure 7-7   Saving a page as a template.

   TIP   *Place all meta tags directly in the template, and the tags will then be applied to all pages that are created using the template. To individually modify meta tags on a page-by-page basis, you need to manually edit the tags in the HTML code.*

3. **Mark regions as editable.**

   All regions in a Dreamweaver template start out locked so that users can't edit them in the pages that are created using the template. To "unlock" regions and make them editable, select a block of text, an image, a table, or a layer; choose the Modify menu's Templates command; and choose Mark Selection As Editable from the submenu.

4. **Name the editable region.**

   In the New Editable Region dialog box, shown in Figure 7-8, enter a name for this editable region. The name can't contain single or double quotation marks (' "), angle brackets (< >), or an ampersand (&). Click OK when you're finished. The editable region shows up selected in a different color.

Figure 7-8   The Save As Template dialog box.

TIP   *Creating new layers in template-created pages is a challenge if you don't want overlapping layers. To work around this difficulty, create all necessary layers as editable regions in the template file itself. For a discussion of layers, see the section "Using Layers."*

To create a page using the template, follow these steps:

1. Create the page.

Choose the File menu's New From Template command, and then select the site and template you want to use as a basis for your new page, as shown in Figure 7-9. Click Select to create the page. You can also apply a template to an existing page by displaying the Templates palette, selecting the desired palette, and clicking Apply, although this may create an unpredictable and undesirable page layout.

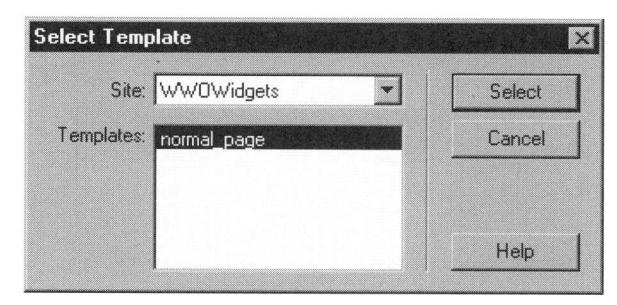

Figure 7-9   Creating a page from a template.

2. Add content to the editable regions.

Enter content and modify it in the editable regions as if they were normal Web pages. To select an editable region, click in the region and then click the <mm:editable> tag in the Tag selector. You can also choose the Modify menu's Templates command and choose the region you want to edit from the submenu, as shown in Figure 7-10.

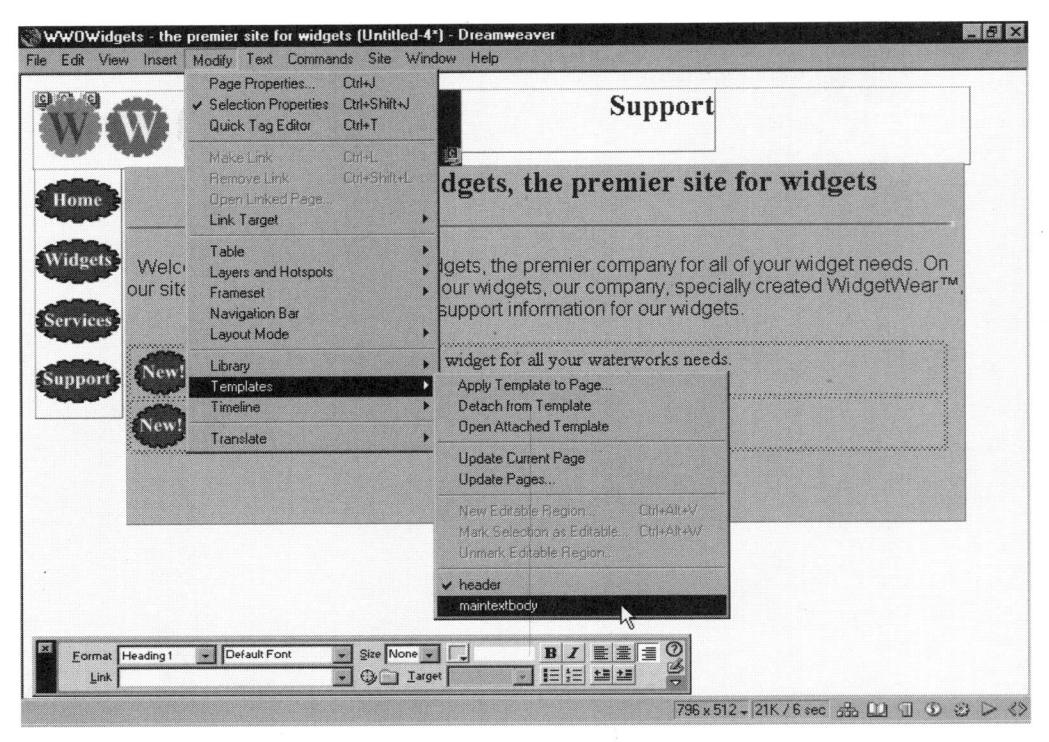

Figure 7-10 Selecting an editable region in a page created with a template.

To modify a template after creating it, open the template from the Templates folder located in the local folder of the site in which you saved the template. Dreamweaver templates have the .dwt file extension.

Using the Library

The Library is another invaluable tool that you can use to quickly create consistent-looking Web pages that can be easily modified en masse from a central location. The Library tool works similarly to Dreamweaver templates.

Any object on a Web page can be easily placed in the Library and then inserted into any page in your Web site. Objects taken from the Library can't be edited directly in the Web page in which they were inserted—instead, they are edited centrally from the Library. So, just as with Dreamweaver templates, to make a change all you need to do is edit the object once in the Library and all the pages containing the object are automatically updated. This is an incredible time-saver when changing objects such as a company logo, legal text, navigation links, or any other object that you need to use in multiple pages.

To use the Library, follow these steps:

1. **Create a Library object.**

   Display the Library, if it's not already visible, and then drag any text, image, or object into the Library palette to turn it into a Library object. Enter a name for the object in the Untitled object that is created in the Library, as shown in Figure 7-11. Don't rename any Library objects after creating them, since doing so will break all links to the objects.

   Figure 7-11 Creating a new Library object.

2. **Insert the new Library object into a page.**

   Display the Library, and then drag the object you want into the Web page. The object appears in the page highlighted in yellow to indicate that it's a Library object.

3. **Edit the Library object.**

   Select a Library object in a Web page, and click the Open button in the Property inspector. You can also open the Library palette, select the object, and click the Open Library Item button at the lower right of the palette. To delete a Library object, select the object in the Library and click the Delete button in the palette (the trash can icon).

   TIP   *To disconnect a Library object in a Web page from the Library—preventing it from being centrally updated and permitting direct editing in the Web page—select the object and click the Detach From Original button in the Property inspector.*

Advanced Web Page Layout

When you're designing Web pages, it doesn't take long to get frustrated with HTML's limited positioning abilities. It's hard to indent text, it's difficult to wrap text around images, and it's really hard to make columns or line up items on a Web page.

There are a couple techniques you can use in Dreamweaver to create better Web page layouts. The first technique is to use layers—or more precisely, CSS layers. You can use layers to position anything in a Web page, anywhere onscreen. The main drawback to layers is their incompatibility with Web browsers that don't support Cascading Style Sheets (CSS), such as Internet Explorer or Netscape Navigator versions 3.x and older.

If compatibility with older Web browsers is important to you, create your layouts using tables, which are built and modified much like tables in a word processor. Tables allow you to create layout effects similar to those of layers, and they can be made invisible so as not to reveal the tool used to position the objects on the Web page. Of course, tables are also useful for presenting data or items in a list, so even if you use layers for your layouts, tables are still an invaluable tool for creating Web pages.

Layers and tables are discussed in the following sections.

TIP *Another tool that professional Web developers use when creating advanced layouts is transparent GIF images. Create a small, completely transparent GIF image, and then use it to fill the space that you want to appear blank. If the image isn't quite the right size, resize it using the Image Properties dialog box.*

Using Layers

Dreamweaver makes positioning text and images in layers very easy. Using layers, you can place objects pixel perfectly anywhere on your Web page. However, if you want to maintain resolution independence so that visitors can properly view your Web pages at a variety of screen resolutions and window sizes, special caution needs to be taken.

You can also use layers to graphically create tables. Create layers for the text and objects you want to place in a table, and then use the Convert Layers To Table command to create a table out of your layers. Many users find this a faster method of creating complex tables than actually creating and modifying layers from scratch.

TIP   *Making text wrap around images is easy—you don't even have to use layers. Just select the image you want to wrap text around and select Left or Right from the Align drop-down list box in the Property inspector.*

Creating Layers

You can create layers in a couple of ways. If you already have your page laid out using tables, you can convert this layout to layers by following these steps:

1. Use the Convert Tables To Layers command.

Choose the Modify menu's Layout Mode command, and then choose Convert Tables To Layers from the submenu.

2. Choose your options.

In the Convert Tables To Layers dialog box, shown in Figure 7-12, select Prevent Layer Overlaps if you think you might at some point want to convert your layout back into tables. Select Show Layer Palette if you want to display the Layer palette, which is useful for selecting layers. Select Show Grid to display a grid that Dreamweaver uses to position layers, and select Snap To Grid to force layers to be aligned on this grid. Click OK when you're finished.

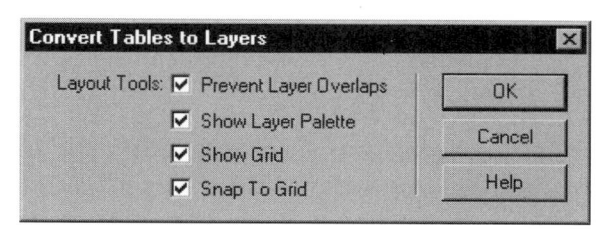

Figure 7-12   Converting a page using tables into a page using layers.

To create layers from scratch, most likely on an empty page, follow these steps:

1. Draw a layer.

To draw a layer, click the Draw Layer object in the Objects palette, and then draw your layer by clicking and dragging the layer outline to the size you want, as shown in Figure 7-13. When you release the mouse button, the layer appears in your page, as well as in the Layer palette, if you have that displayed. The layer is anchored by its <div> tag, which is placed in the top left of the page, resulting in an absolutely positioned layer that won't move onscreen regardless of the window size.

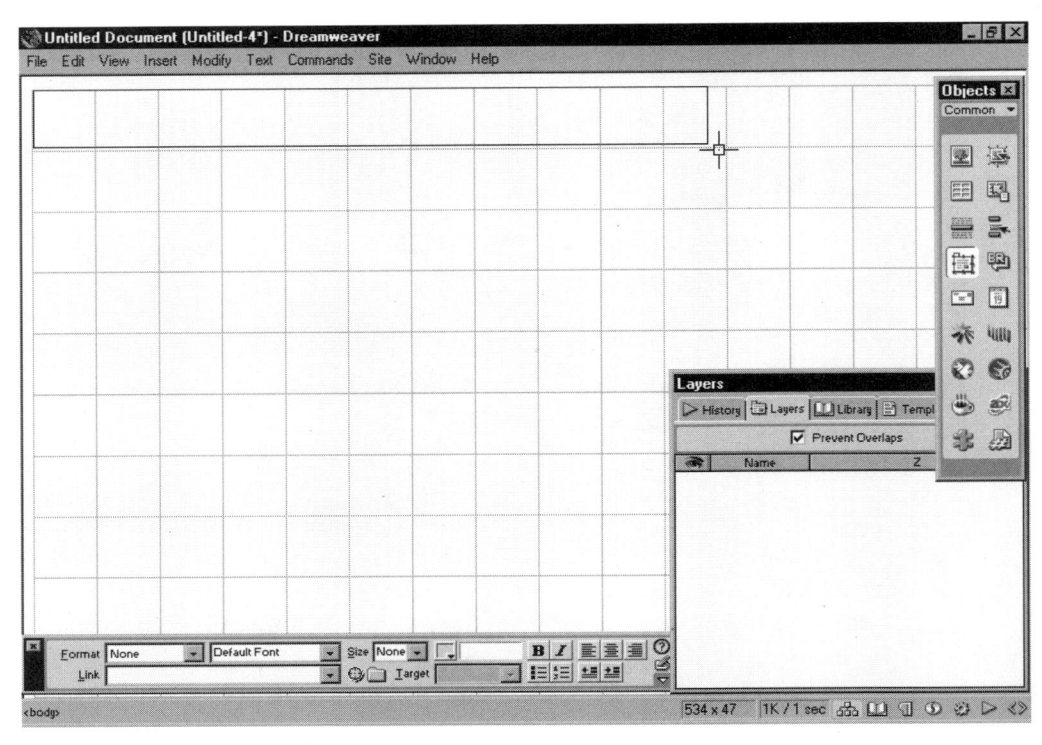

Figure 7-13   Drawing a layer.

2. Insert a layer.

To insert a relatively positioned layer at a particular cursor location onscreen, drag the Draw Layer object from the Objects palette to the location where you want the layer to appear. When you release the mouse button, the layer appears in your page, as well as in the Layer palette, if you have that displayed. The layer is anchored by its <div> tag, which is placed where you dropped the layer, resulting in a relatively positioned layer that will move around to compensate for changing window sizes. A relatively positioned layer is shown in Figure 7-14.

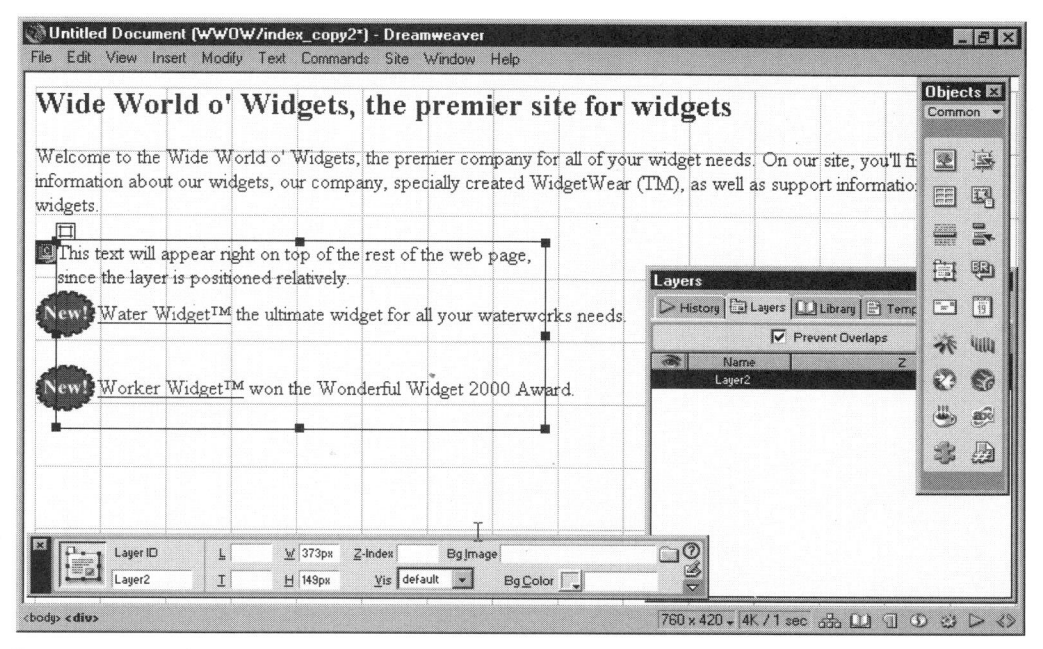

Figure 7-14 A relatively positioned layer.

WARNING *Netscape 4 has a bug in the way it displays layers. If you resize a window with layers, the layers lose their positioning information. You can fix this bug in Dreamweaver by choosing the Commands menu's Add/Remove Netscape Resize Fix command or by choosing the Edit menu's Preferences command, selecting Layers in the Category list, and then selecting the Netscape 4 Compatibility check box to automatically insert this fix when creating layers.*

How Dreamweaver Positions Layers

Layers are anchored by a <div> tag, which appears graphically in Dreamweaver as a yellow "C" usually placed at the top left of the page. Most layers you create are positioned absolutely onscreen in pixels, measured from the top left of the page (and controlled by the T and L boxes in the Property inspector).

If you drag a Draw Layer object onto your Web page and drop the object into your page, a relatively positioned layer is created at the location where you dropped the object. This layer will move depending on the window size and how the text or images surrounding its <div> tag adjust to the changing window size. Needless to say, relatively positioned layers move around rather unpredictably depending on the window size of the browser displaying the Web page. To avoid this dilemma, test the page at different resolutions or stick to absolutely positioned layers.

All layers are displayed by default on top of any Web page content not placed in a layer. If you don't want content in layers displayed on top of other content, adjust the Z-Index of the layers you want to appear behind Web page content so the layer has a negative Z-Index. (For more information, see the following section, "Positioning Layers.")

Positioning Layers

To position a layer, follow these steps:

1. **Select the layer.**

   To select a layer, either click its positioning handle (the box attached to the top left of the layer), click inside the layer and then click the <div> tag in the Tag selector to select the entire layer, or select the layer from the Layer palette.

2. **Resize the layer.**

   Move the mouse over one of the positioning handles on the layer's outline until the cursor turns into a double-sided arrow, and then click and drag the layer's outline to the desired size. You can also enter the layer's width and height in the W and H boxes of the Property inspector. To size a layer relatively, enter the size in percentage. For example, the layer shown in Figure 7-15 is sized at 85% width; its height is left blank so that it can adjust the height to compensate for a changing width.

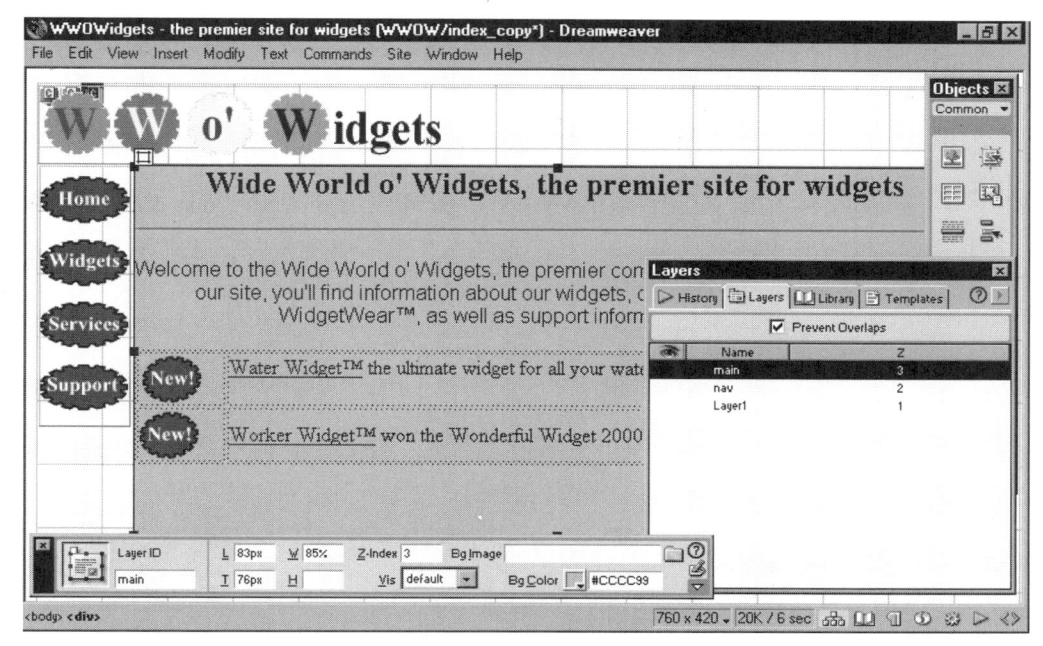

Figure 7-15 A relatively sized layer.

TIP   *To maintain resolution independence, size your main body layer relatively in at least one dimension. To do so, enter the width or height in percent. To ensure that all content fits inside the layer, size one dimension relatively and leave the other dimension left unspecified.*

3. Reposition the layer.

To move a layer, either click the layer's positioning handle and drag the layer where you want it, or enter the coordinates relative to the top of the screen and the left edge of the screen in the T and L boxes of the Property inspector. If you want to position a layer relatively based on where the layer's <div> tag is located (the yellow "C" tag in your page), delete the coordinates in the T and L boxes.

TIP   *To change the size of the positioning grid, choose the View menu's Grid command and then choose Settings from the submenu.*

Adjusting Layer Visibility

In addition to having a position relative to the top left of the Web page (the Y and X axes), all layers also have a position on the vertical, or Z, axis. This allows layers to overlap each other (unless you have the Prevent Layer Overlaps option selected in the View menu). You can hide layers too, although in general you should do this only temporarily in order to edit an overlapping layer, since even hidden layers take time to download. To adjust layers, follow these steps:

1. **Adjust the layer's visibility.**

   To specify whether you want to display or hide a layer, click in the eye column of the Layers palette, as shown in Figure 7-16. Click the eye above the column to mark all layers explicitly visible. You also adjust a layer's visibility using the Vis drop-down list box of the Property inspector (when a layer is selected).

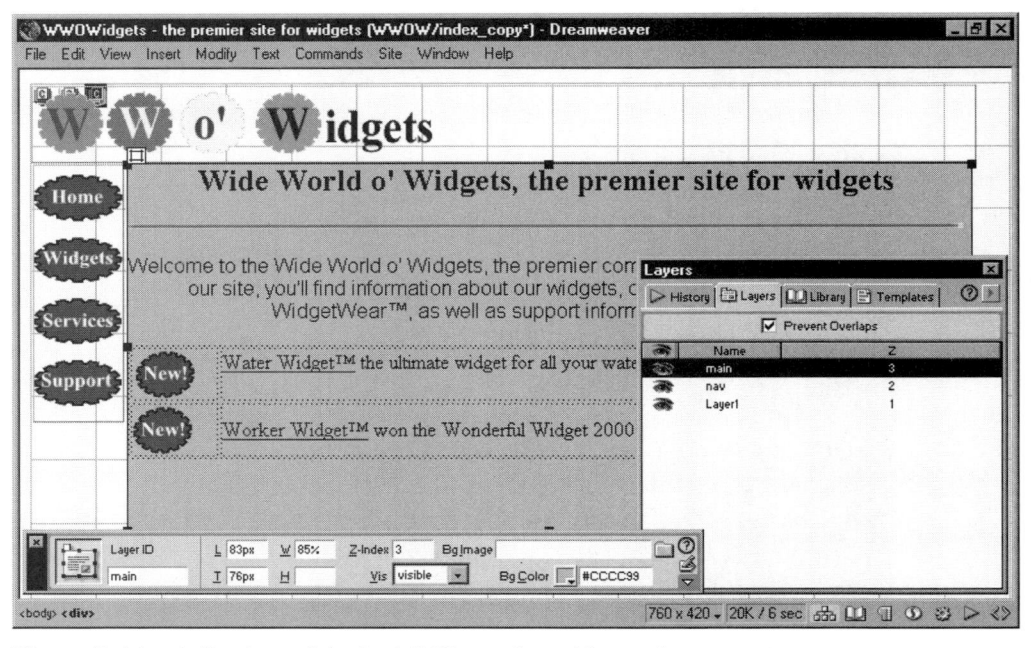

Figure 7-16   Adjusting a layer's visibility and stacking order.

2. **Adjust the layer's Z-Index.**

   To control how layers stack on top of each other, select a layer and then enter a stacking order in the Z-Index box of the Property inspector, as shown in Figure 7-16. Layers with higher numbers are displayed on top of layers with lower numbers, and any objects not placed in a layer are considered having a Z-Index of zero.

Working with Tables

Tables are incredibly useful for creating advanced layouts in a Web page and are used much more often than you might realize. Besides their obvious use for creating tables of text and graphics, tables are often used to make more precise text and graphic layouts than can be accomplished simply with standard techniques. They are also compatible with older Web browsers.

Creating Tables

To create a table using the Insert Table toolbar button, follow these steps:

1. **Position the cursor where you want to insert the table.**

2. **Use the Insert Table object.**

    Either click the Insert Table object on the Objects palette to insert the table at the cursor location or drag the Insert Table object to the location you want.

3. **Specify the number of rows and columns.**

    In the Insert Table dialog box, shown in Figure 7-17, enter the number of rows and columns for the table in the Rows and Columns boxes.

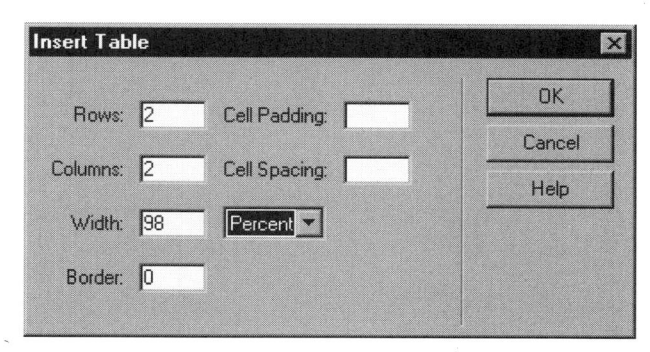

Figure 7-17 Creating a table.

4. **Specify the table size.**

    Enter a width for the table in the Width box. Use the drop-down list box to specify whether the table should be sized relatively (in percent, so the table changes in size with window size) or absolutely (in pixels, so the table never changes size).

5. **Modify the border size.**

   In the Border box, enter a border width for the table in pixels. To make the table boundaries invisible, enter a border width of zero.

6. **Add content to the table.**

   Add content to the table by entering text or inserting images, or select a block of text or an image and drag it into a table cell to move the text or image into the new table.

   TIP   *You can sort the contents of a table by selecting the table and choosing the Commands menu's Sort Table command.*

Modifying Table Properties

The tables that Dreamweaver creates usually require a little tweaking before they can be put to use on a Web site. For example, if you're using a table to position text more precisely, you'll want to make the table invisible by eliminating the table borders. Or you may need to adjust the sizing of the table, how it's aligned on the page, or the colors or background image that's used. To do these tasks, follow these steps:

1. **Select the table.**

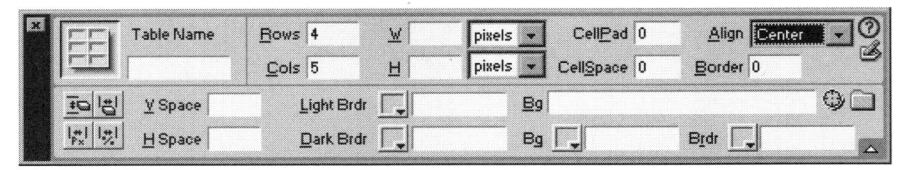

   Click anywhere in the table and then click the <table> tag in the Tag selector to select the entire table.

2. **Specify how the table should be aligned on the page.**

   Select an entry from the Align drop-down list box in the Property inspector, as shown in Figure 7-18, to specify how the table should be aligned on the page.

   Figure 7-18   Using the Property inspector to change a table's appearance.

3. **Specify the cell padding and spacing.**

   In the CellPad box, specify how many pixels you want between the contents of a cell and the cell wall. In the CellSpace box, enter the width in pixels of the cell wall. Note that this is different from the width of the border. You can have a CellSpace value higher than zero and still have the border be invisible.

4. **Optionally, add extra rows or columns.**

   You can add rows or columns to a table either by changing the number of columns or rows specified in the Rows and Cols boxes of the Property inspector or by pressing Tab in the bottom right cell of a table (to add a new row). You can also choose the Modify menu's Table command and choose Insert Rows Or Columns from the submenu. In the dialog box, as shown in Figure 7-19, select either Rows or Columns, specify how many to insert, and indicate whether to insert them above or below the current selection.

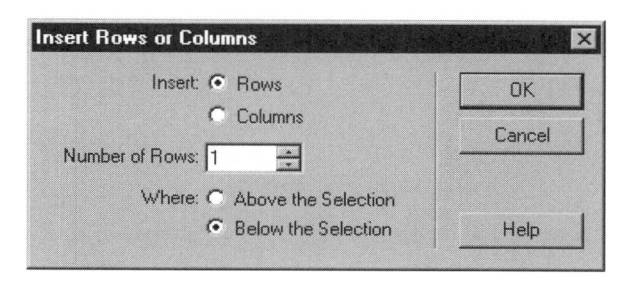

   Figure 7-19   Inserting extra rows or columns using the Insert Rows Or Columns command.

5. **Manually specify the width and height of the table.**

   To manually control the width and height of the table, enter the width or height of the table in the W (width) and H (height) boxes. Specify whether the sizes are in percent or in pixels by selecting % or Pixels from the drop-down list boxes. You can also change the widths of the table's rows and columns in the Advanced Properties section of the Property inspector. (Click the small triangle in the bottom right corner of the palette to display this section.)

   - Use the Clear Column Widths and Clear Row Heights buttons to allow columns and rows to fit the content exactly.

   - Use the Convert Table Widths To Pixels button to make all cell and columns widths sized absolutely, or use the Convert Table Widths To Percent button to quickly make your column sized relatively so that it can resize with the browser window.

6. **Specify the thickness of the table's lines.**

   In the Border box, enter a thickness for the table's dividing lines in pixels. You can also use the Brdr, Light Brdr, and Dark Brdr boxes in the Advanced Properties section of the Property inspector to change the colors used to draw the dividing lines.

TIP *To hide all lines in a table so that only the contents show, set the border thickness to zero.*

7. **Optionally, select a background color or image for the table.**

   Select a background color for your table from the Color drop-down list box in the Background section, or select the Use Background Picture check box and type the name of the image you want to use in the text box provided. Click OK when you're finished.

NOTE *Only Internet Explorer 3.0 and newer versions support using background pictures in a table. Currently Netscape Navigator and WebTV don't support this feature.*

8. **Specify how much space to leave around the table.**

   In the V Space and H Space boxes, enter the amount of space, in pixels, to leave around the table.

Specifying Cell Properties

You can change the properties of individual cells or a group of cells, such as a column or row, separately from the rest of the table. This is useful if you want the contents of particular cells to be aligned differently, or perhaps if you want to visually set some cells apart by giving them a different colored background. (This feature can also be used with invisible tables to create a visual divider in a page, without the actual table showing up.)

To change the appearance of an individual cell, follow these steps:

1. **Select the cell(s) you want to modify, and open the cell properties.**

   Select the cells you want to modify by clicking inside one and clicking the <td> tag in the Tag selector to select the cell or clicking the <tr> tag to select the row. Alternatively, hold down the Ctrl key while clicking inside individual cells to select them, or move the mouse over the top of a column or to the left of a row until the cursor turns into either a vertical or horizontal arrow, and then click to select the whole column or row.

2. **Modify the cell properties.**

   Cell properties are the same as those for a table, except for a couple of advanced options that are accessible by clicking the up arrow in the bottom right corner of the Property inspector, as shown in Figure 7-20.

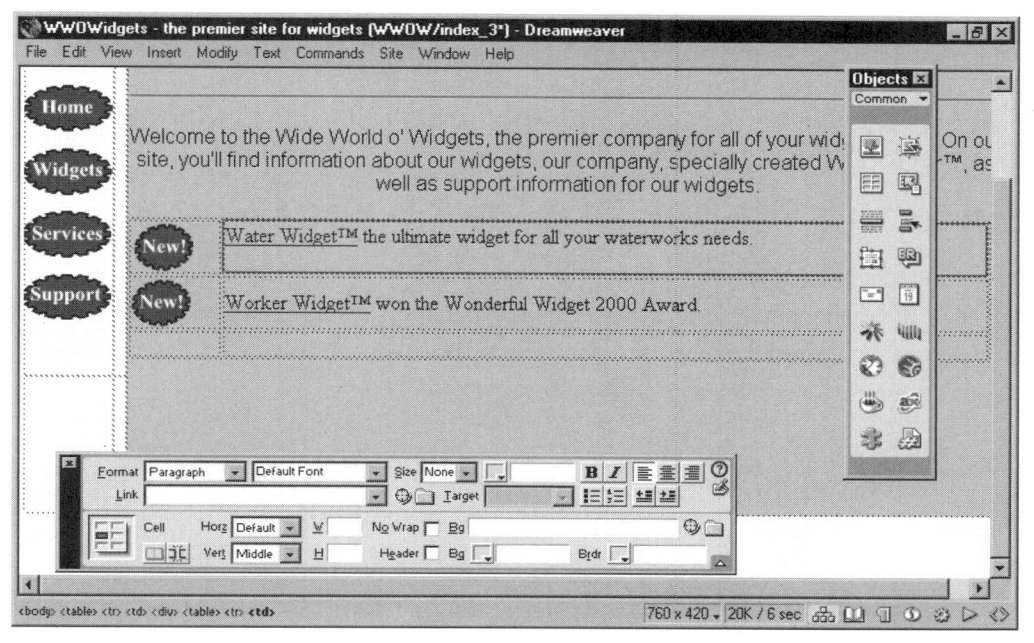

   Figure 7-20   Modifying the properties of a table cell.

   To modify cell properties, select from the following options:

   - Select the Header Cell check box if the cell is a header for the table. (This makes the cell's contents boldface and centered.)

   - Select the No Wrap check box to force all the text inside a cell to remain on one line, no matter how small the window size gets. (This is useful for text that absolutely cannot wrap; use it sparingly.)

   - Click the Merges Selected Cells Using Spans button to merge selected cells into one cell.

   - Click the Splits Cells Into Rows Or Columns button to split the selected cell into two cells. Use the Split Cell dialog box, as shown in Figure 7-21, to specify whether to split the cell into rows or columns and how many cells to split it into.

Step 7 Polish Your Pages   **195**

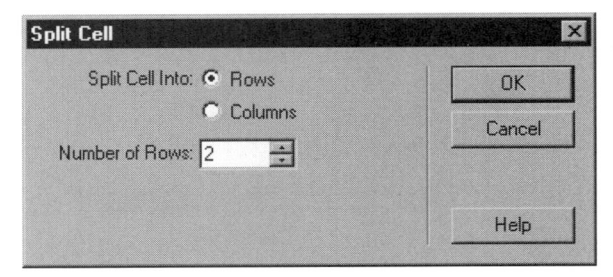

Figure 7-21   Splitting a cell into multiple cells.

Ensuring Proper Display of Your Pages

It's important that your Web pages display properly in your visitors' Web browsers, regardless of the browser type and version they're using, and what screen resolution they're running. The following sections help you tailor your pages to display properly in a wide range of environments.

Making Your Pages Compatible with Multiple Browsers

Your home page (and other pages) need to be accessible to your audience, no matter what type of Web browsers they're using. If your site doesn't work properly in visitors' browsers, they'll move on to some other company's Web site.

Dreamweaver can test your pages for potential Web browser compatibility problems, redirect visitors with a particular browser version to an alternate version of your home page, and convert any pages that use layers into pages that are compatible with version 3 browsers.

Testing Pages for Browser Compatibility

To test a Web page for compatibility problems, follow these steps:

1. **Open the Site window.**

    You can test for page compatibility in the Document window, but only one page at a time. To test multiple pages, use the Site window.

2. **Select the pages you want to check for compatibility problems.**

    Select the pages that you want to check by holding down the Ctrl key and clicking each page, as shown in Figure 7-22. Alternatively, hold down the Shift key, click the first file in a list, and then click the last file to select every file in between. (You can also press Ctrl-A to select all files.)

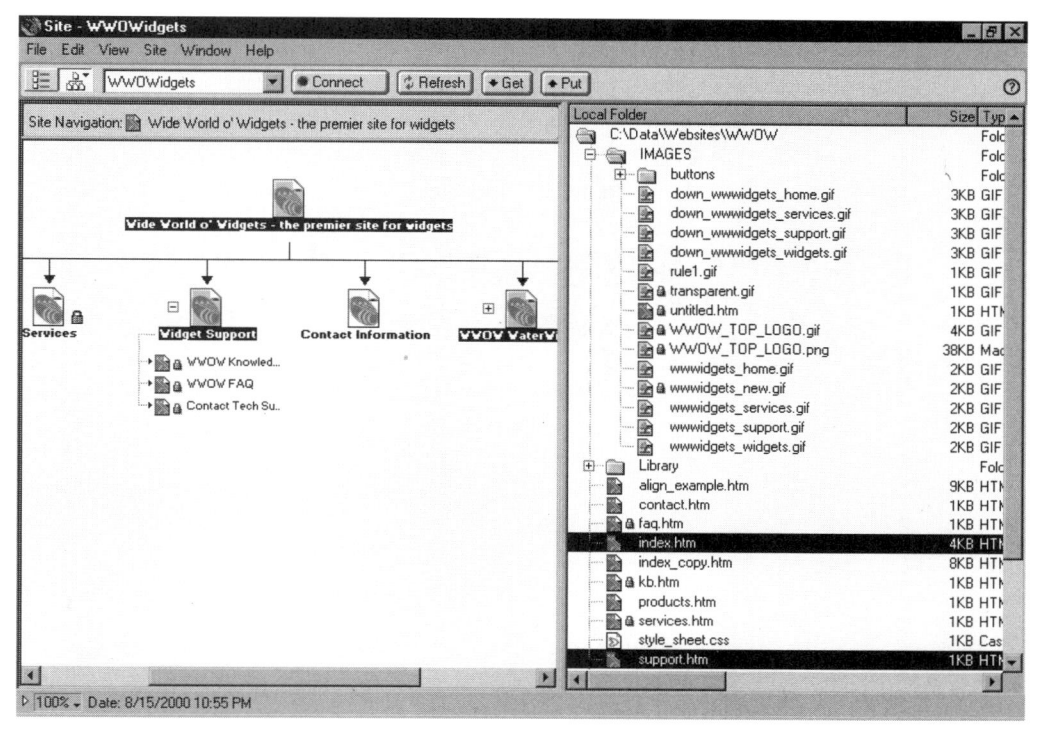

Figure 7-22   Selecting pages to check for compatibility problems.

3. **Choose the File menu's Check Target Browsers command.**
4. **Choose the browser versions you want to support.**

   In the Check Target Browsers dialog box, shown in Figure 7-23, select the browser versions you want to check for compatibility problems. To make multiple selections, hold down the Ctrl key when clicking on browser versions. Click the Check button to perform the compatibility test.

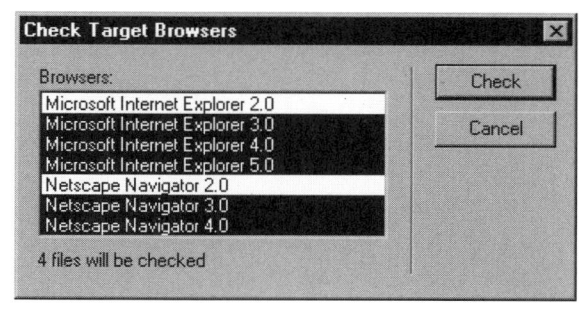

Figure 7-23   The Check Target Browsers dialog box.

Step 7 Polish Your Pages   **197**

5. **Review the compatibility report.**

   Dreamweaver examines your selected files and issues a report, as shown in Figure 7-24. At the top of the report is a listing of how many errors and warnings were found for each browser version. Scroll down to view each error, the line number on which it's found (in the actual HTML), and the tag containing the error.

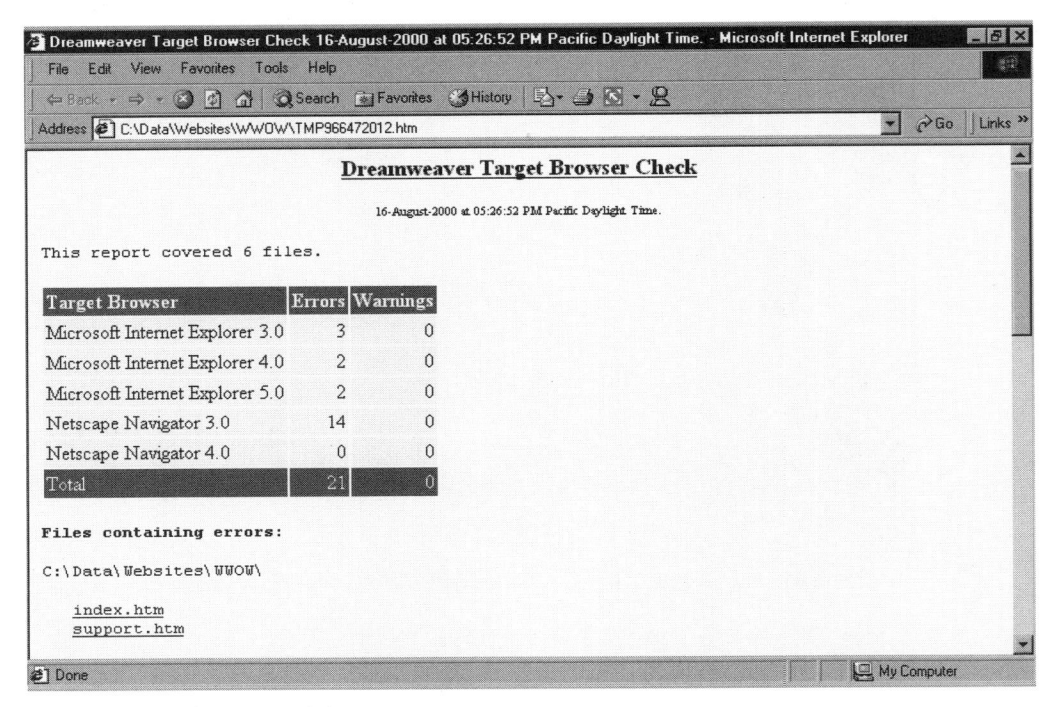

   Figure 7-24 A compatibility report.

6. **If necessary, edit your pages.**

   If you want to view or change the line of your Web page with an error or warning, open the page, click the Show HTML Source button on the Mini-Launcher, select the Show Line Numbers check box, and then scroll to the appropriate line. Select the offending line to see the object highlighted in the Document window, as shown in Figure 7-25.

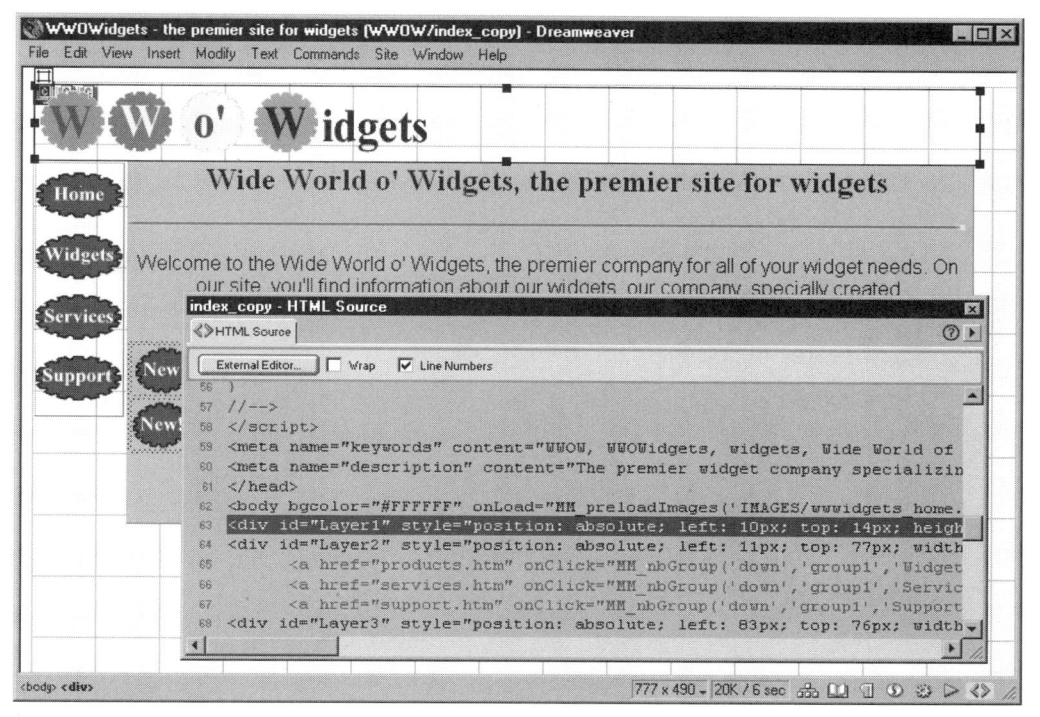

Figure 7-25 Viewing an incompatible object in HTML view and the Document window command.

Redirecting Visitors with Old Browsers

Dreamweaver allows you to redirect visitors with older browsers to a version of your Web page that supports their browser. This is done by inserting a special behavior for the Web page that detects the visitor's browser version.

Although Dreamweaver makes this task easy to do, you should carefully consider whether this makes sense for your company or organization. The advantage of redirecting visitors with old browser versions is that you can make Web pages that optimally target newer browsers without worrying about the pages displaying improperly in older browsers. The disadvantage is that redirecting visitors can double the number of pages that you need to create and keep updated. An alternative to this situation is to make multiple versions only of your home page.

The best way to redirect visitors is to create a blank home page that detects a visitor's browser version and redirects the visitor to the appropriate version of your home page. This saves visitors from having to wait while your home page loads, only to be redirected to your alternate home page and having to wait again while this page loads. You'll also have to redirect visitors from each home page version in case they got to the home page via a different route.

To create your alternate home page that redirects visitors based on the browser version they're using, follow these steps:

1. **Create and save a blank page.**

   Create a new blank page, making sure that the page background is the same color as your main home page. You'll also want to title this page and insert the same Keywords and Description meta tags so that search engines can still properly locate your page, as discussed earlier in the section "Preparing Your Home Page for Search Engines."

2. **Select the entire page.**

   Click the <body> tag on the Tag selector to select the body of the page.

3. **Add the Check Browser behavior.**

   Display the Behaviors palette, if not already visible, click the plus sign, and choose Check Browser from the pop-up menu, as shown in Figure 7-26.

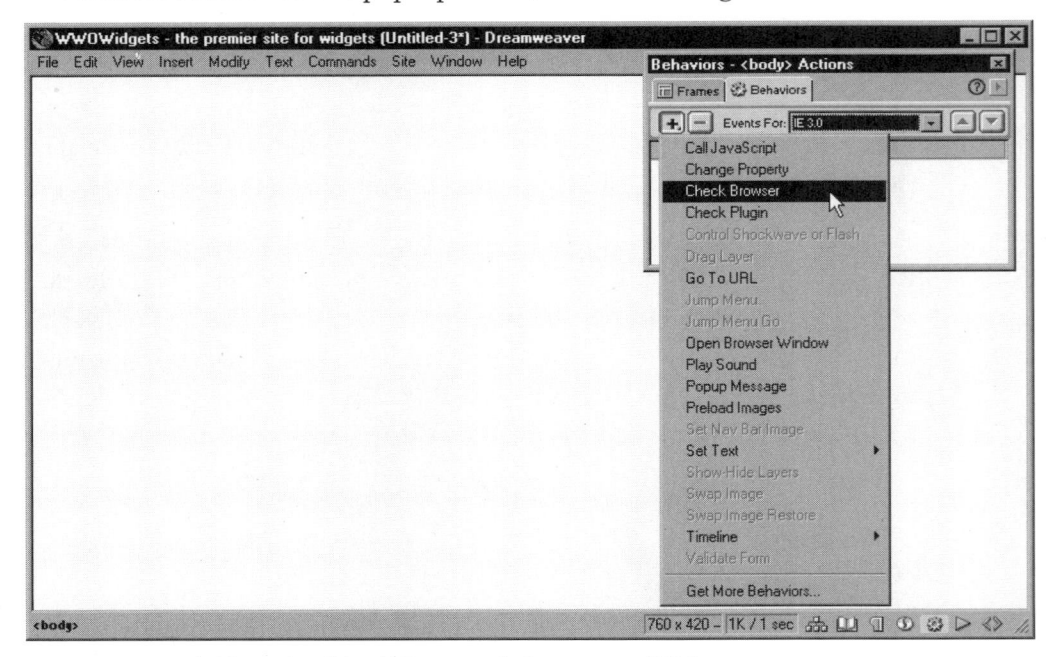

Figure 7-26 Adding the Check Browser behavior to a Web page.

4. **Specify where to send new browsers.**

   In the Check Browser dialog box, shown in Figure 7-27, click the Browse button next to the URL box to specify the main home page to which you want to redirect visitors with new browsers. Use the Select File dialog box to select the appropriate page.

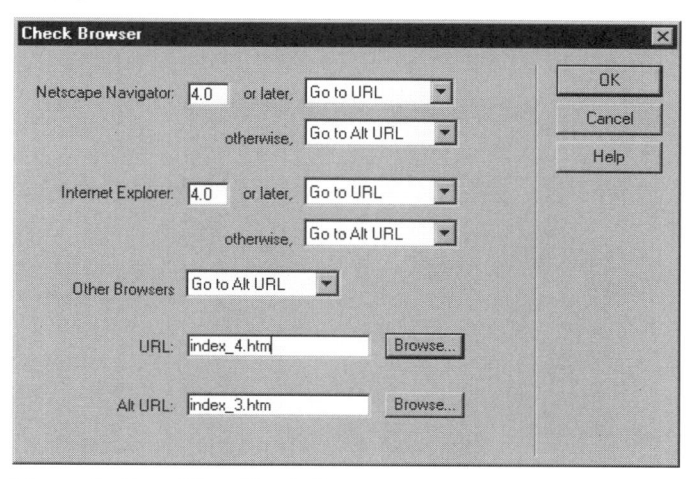

   Figure 7-27   The Check Browser dialog box.

5. **Specify where to send old browsers.**

   In the Check Browser dialog box, click the Browse button next to the Alt URL box to specify the alternate home page to which you want to redirect visitors with old browsers. Use the Select File dialog box, shown in Figure 7-28, to select the appropriate page.

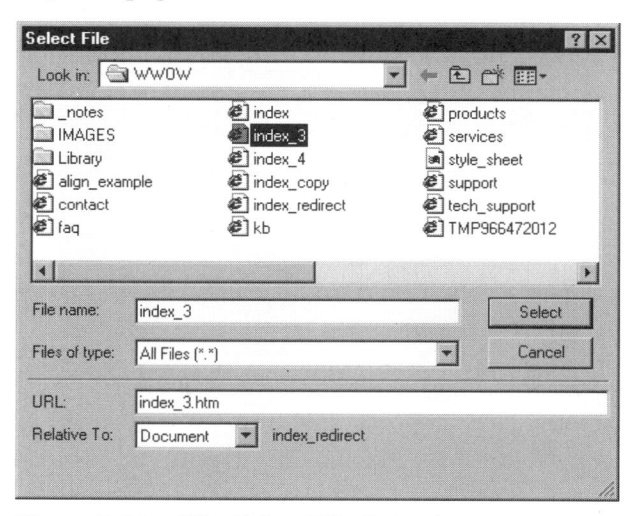

   Figure 7-28   The Select File dialog box.

6. **Set up redirection in the two pages.**

   As mentioned earlier, you should set up each alternative home page to redirect visitors with the incorrect browser version to the other version of the home page. To do so, repeat steps 2 through 5 for each page, except that in the Check Browser dialog box, select Stay On This Page for the browser version for which the page is designed. For example, if the page was designed for version 4 browsers, select Stay On This Page from the Or Later drop-down list boxes, as shown in Figure 7-29.

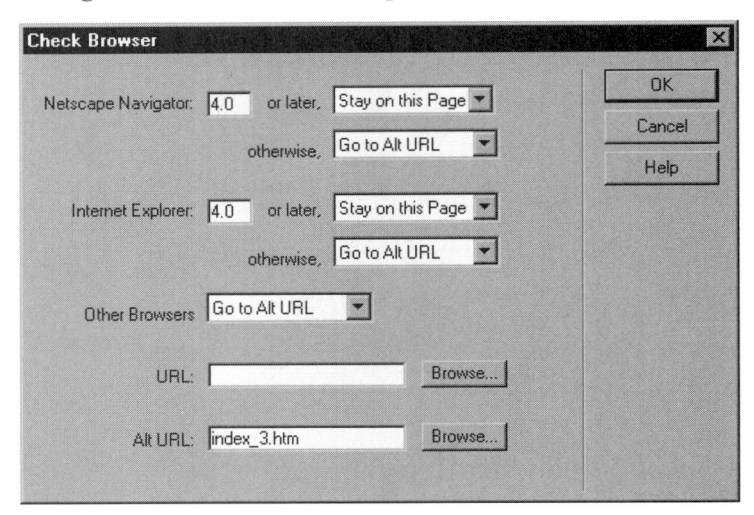

Figure 7-29 The redirection settings for the main home page.

Converting Layers and Tables

Layers are a powerful and elegant way of creating advanced layouts on your Web pages. (For more information on layers, see the section "Using Layers" earlier in this step.) However, layers are only compatible with browsers that support Cascading Style Sheets (CSS), such as Internet Explorer and Netscape Navigator versions 4 and newer. To help you deal with this, Dreamweaver can convert pages that use layers into new pages that use tables to achieve a similar layout. (For more information on tables, see the section "Working with Tables" earlier in this step.) Dreamweaver also lets you go the other way—you can convert pages that use tables into pages that use layers so that you can then more easily customize the layout.

Figure 7-30 shows a page created using layers. Figure 7-31 shows the same page, converted to a page layout using tables that is compatible with version 3 browsers. As you can see, Dreamweaver generally does an excellent job with the conversion. If you decide to use layers to create your tables, do all the layout using layers and then convert the layers to a table when it's time to publish the page.

Effective Executive's Guide to Dreamweaver Web Sites

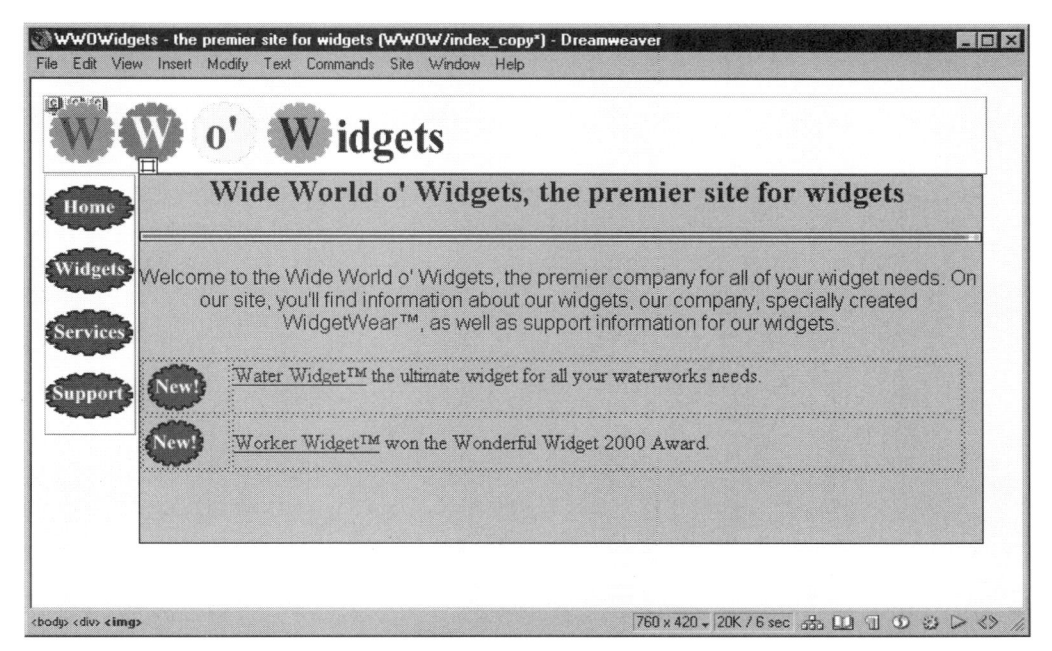

Figure 7-30 A Web page designed in Dreamweaver with layers.

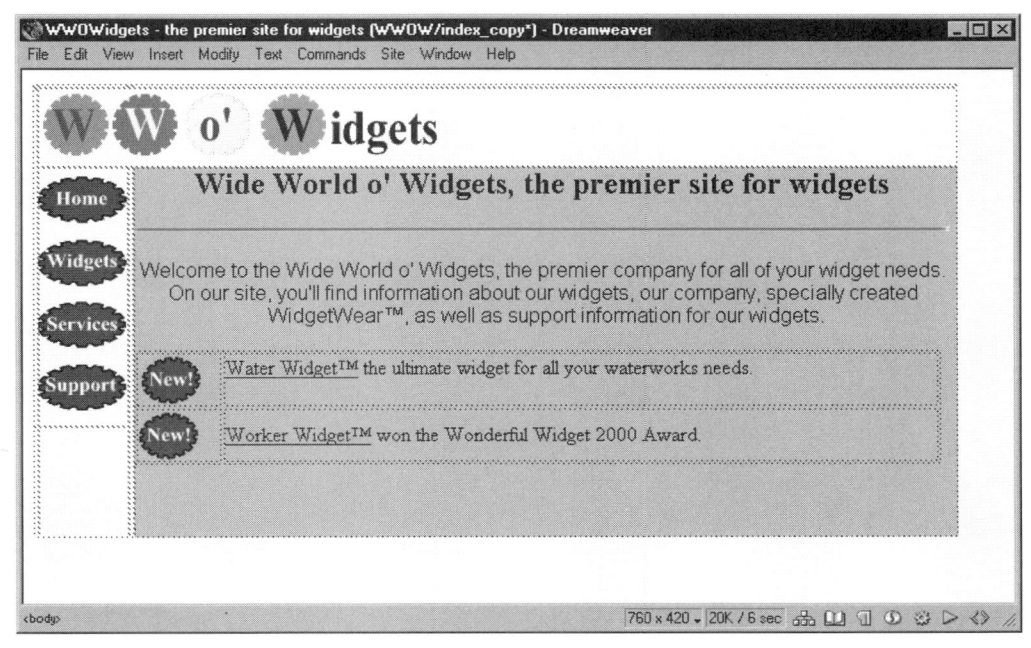

Figure 7-31 This same page, converted by Dreamweaver to a layout that uses tables.

TIP   *If you are using CSS Styles in the page you want to make compatible with version 3 Web browsers, choose the File menu's Convert command and choose 3.0 Browser Compatible from the submenu. This command converts any CSS Styles you have in the page into standard HTML, in addition to converting layers to tables. If you don't have any CSS Styles in the page, using the procedure below provides additional control over the conversion process.*

To convert a page that uses layers into a page that uses tables to achieve a similar effect, follow these steps:

1. **Convert all content to layers.**

    All content must be in a layer in order to be converted to a page using tables. To quickly move all content into a layer, choose the Modify menu's Layout Mode command and then select Convert Tables To Layers. Make sure Prevent Layer Overlaps is selected, as shown in Figure 7-32, and click OK.

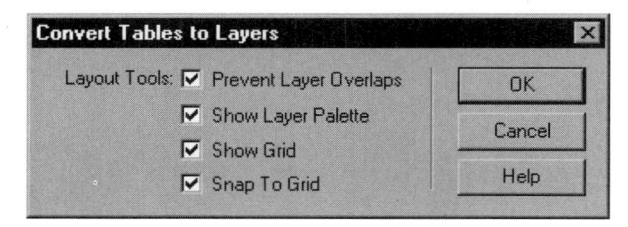

    Figure 7-32   Converting all content into layers.

2. **Make sure no layers overlap.**

    Choose the View menu's Prevent Layer Overlap command to prohibit layers from overlapping when you position them. Move any currently overlapping layers away from each other so they don't overlap.

3. **Eliminate any nested layers.**

    You can't place a layer within a layer and still convert the page, so make sure that you don't have any nested layers.

4. **Save the page with a different filename.**

    It's a good idea to save the page to a different filename before you convert it to preserve the formatting of the existing page. If you're creating two versions of the page and redirecting visitors to the version compatible with their browser, you need to save the page with a different filename.

5. **Convert the page.**

   Choose the Modify menu's Layout Mode command, and then choose Convert Layers To Table from the submenu to open the Convert Layers To Table dialog box, as shown in Figure 7-33.

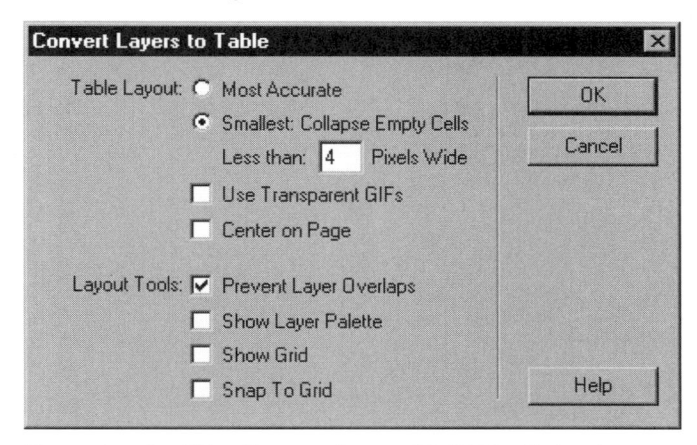

   Figure 7-33 The Convert Layers To Table dialog box.

6. **Specify the conversion options.**

   In the Convert Layers To Table dialog box, select from the following options, and click OK:

   - Select Most Accurate to create a table that most closely mimics the layout you created using layers. This option creates extra table cells that are empty to preserve the spacing between layers. Don't select this option if you're trying to achieve resolution independence for your Web page.

   - Select Smallest: Collapse Empty Cells to create a table that doesn't have extra empty cells and that is easier to resize. Select this option if you want to make your page resolution independent (as discussed in the following section).

   - Clear the Use Transparent GIFs check box if you want to be able to resize the table that is created. Clear this option if page resolution independence is important to you

Dreamweaver converts the page into a page using tables for layout. Modify the resulting table as you would any other table. If there are any errors (such as overlapping layers), Dreamweaver won't make the conversion and will instead display an error message, as shown in Figure 7-34.

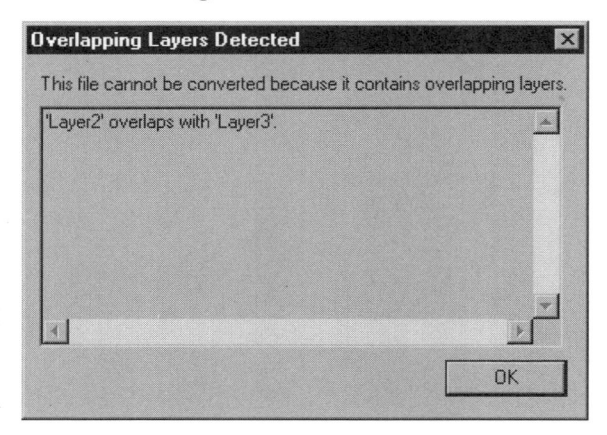

Figure 7-34 The error message for overlapping layers.

Making Your Home Page Resolution-Independent

Visitors will view your Web site at many different screen resolutions and window sizes, so it's important that your home page (and entire site) look good at the widest possible range of sizes. Some visitors will be browsing with old computers running their display at 640x480, some will be using huge monitors at 1600x1280 resolution, and some will even be using a TV-based Web appliance, possibly running at 544x372 resolution. Figure 7-35 shows a resolution-independent Web page at 640x480 resolution; Figure 7-36 shows the same page at a typical 1024x768 resolution.

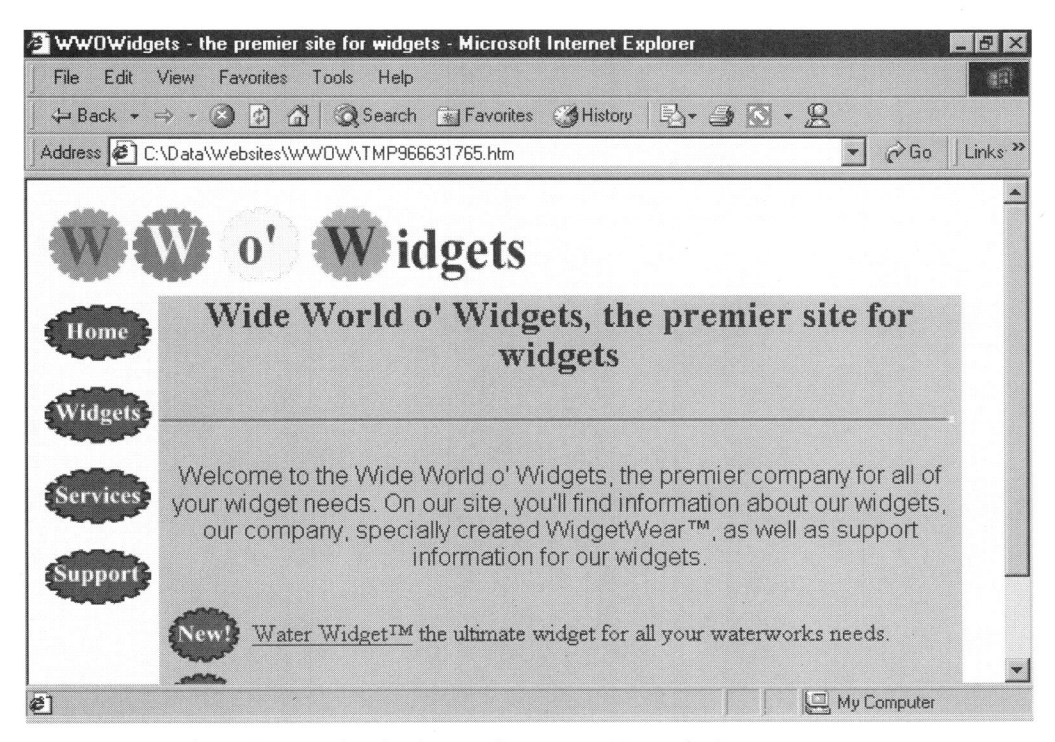

Figure 7-35 A Web page that looks good at 640x480 resolution.

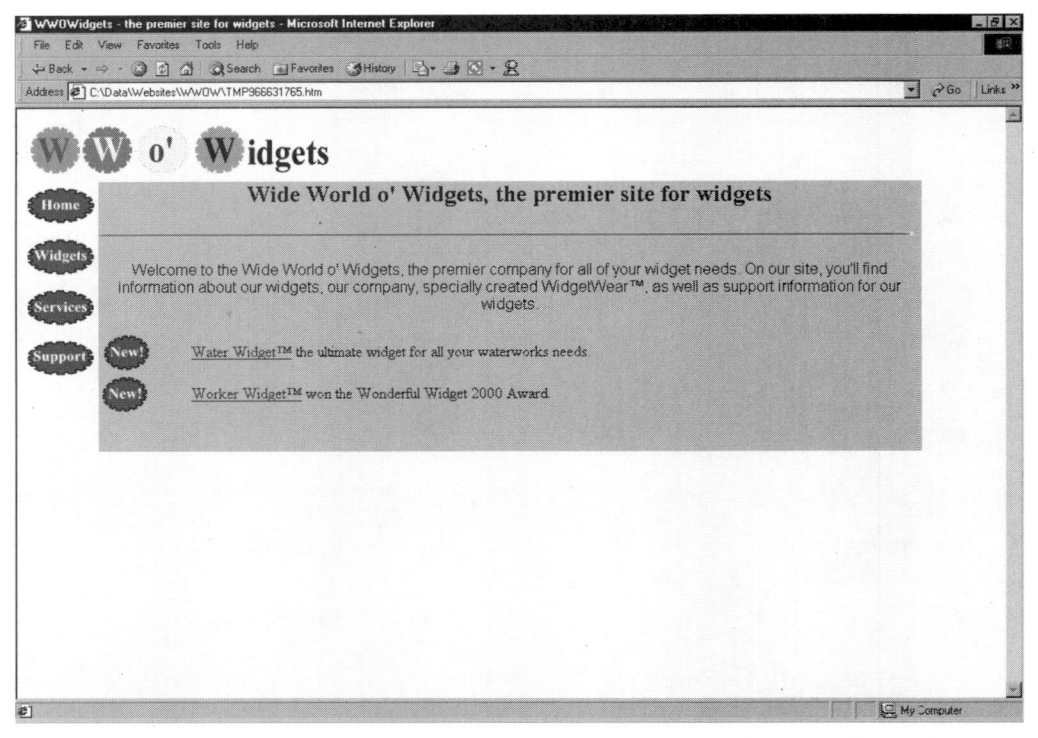

Figure 7-36 The same page, scaling well to a higher resolution (1024x768).

Dreamweaver makes it easy to preview how your Web pages will look at different resolutions. Simply click the Window Size display on the Status Bar and select a resolution from the pop-up menu. Dreamweaver adjusts its window size to match the typical viewable area that visitors will have in their Web browsers when viewing your page. Thus, if a visitor has her or his monitor set to 800x600 resolution and has his or her Web browser window maximized (filling the screen), typically only 760x420 resolution will be available for viewing pages, after accounting for the Web browser's menu bar, status bar, and toolbars.

Here are some recommendations for making your site look good at all these resolutions:

- Don't overload your home page and other pages with so much content that the pages are wider than a 640x480 screen. It's okay to have long pages so that users have to scroll down, but users should never have to scroll from side to side.

- Make sure that your graphics aren't too wide to fit in a 640x480 screen (or 544x372 for WebTV support).

- Don't press the Enter key at the end of each line of text. Dreamweaver automatically wraps lines as appropriate for a given window size. Allowing Dreamweaver to wrap the lines makes your pages adapt well to both higher and lower resolutions.

- If you need to force a line break, but don't want to create a new paragraph, press Shift-Enter to insert a line-break tag (<br>).

- When creating tables, specify the table size in percentage, not in pixels. This allows the table to grow in size to fill large-size windows.

- When creating layers, try to size your main body text layer relatively by using a percentage, for example, 85% width. You'll have to tinker a bit, since other layers will be sized absolutely, but using percentage allows the main part of your page to grow and shrink with window size.

- Size horizontal lines in percentage, not in pixels.

- Test your pages at high and low resolutions and with a variety of different window sizes. You can use the Window Size feature of the Status Bar to resize the Dreamweaver window to reflect different screen resolutions, but you should also preview your pages in a Web browser.

Summary

In this step, we showed you some specific techniques you can use to make your Web pages more effective. This included ways to sharpen up your home page by improving site navigation and increasing visual appeal, as well as how to make all the pages in your Web site consistent in appearance and how to create advanced page layouts using layers and tables.

Step 8

DEPLOY YOUR WEB SITE

Featuring:

- Testing Your Web Site
- Publishing Your Web Site
- Publicizing Your Web Site
- Monitoring Your Web Site

After you create your Web site, it's prudent to perform some testing to make sure the site works properly before it's published to the Internet. Then when your Web site is up and running, you'll need to promote it by taking advantage of both Internet and offline advertising opportunities to generate traffic. Ongoing monitoring is a necessary part of maintaining an effective Web site, and keeping track of the number and type of visitors who come to your site as well as collecting the results of any forms are a part of this maintenance. This step demonstrates some procedures your company or organization can use to accomplish these tasks.

Testing Your Web Site

Testing before publishing your Web site can result in fewer complaints from visitors as well as a more effective site.

Here are some recommendations for Web site tests:

- Check your site for broken hyperlinks.
- Test your site with different Web browsers.
- Perform usability testing with users who haven't yet seen your site.

> **TIP** *You should also make sure that none of your pages require too much time to download. Unfortunately, Dreamweaver provides no centralized method of doing this, so you'll have to open each page manually and check the download time indicator on the Status Bar.*

Testing and Fixing Hyperlinks

Broken hyperlinks, the scourge of Webmasters everywhere, can be easily vanquished using a couple of tools provided by Dreamweaver. The first is the Check Links Sitewide feature that allows you to check the status of all hyperlinks in your site. The second is the Change Link Sitewide command, which you can use to change all occurrences of a hyperlink to a new address.

Checking Hyperlinks

Although Dreamweaver generally does an admirable job of maintaining valid hyperlinks as you move and rename filenames, it's not perfect, and inevitably broken hyperlinks creep into your Web site. You can use Dreamweaver to check individual Web pages for broken hyperlinks, or you can check your entire site all at once. To check your hyperlinks, follow these steps:

1. **Open the Site window.**

   Click the Show Site button on the Mini-Launcher (located on the right side of the status bar). This displays the Site window.

2. **Choose the Site menu's Check Links Sitewide command.**

   Choose the Check Links Sitewide command to check hyperlinks on all the pages in your site, as shown in Figure 8-1. Alternatively, select one or more pages in the Local Folder pane or Site Map and choose the File menu's Check Links command to test hyperlinks only in the selected pages.

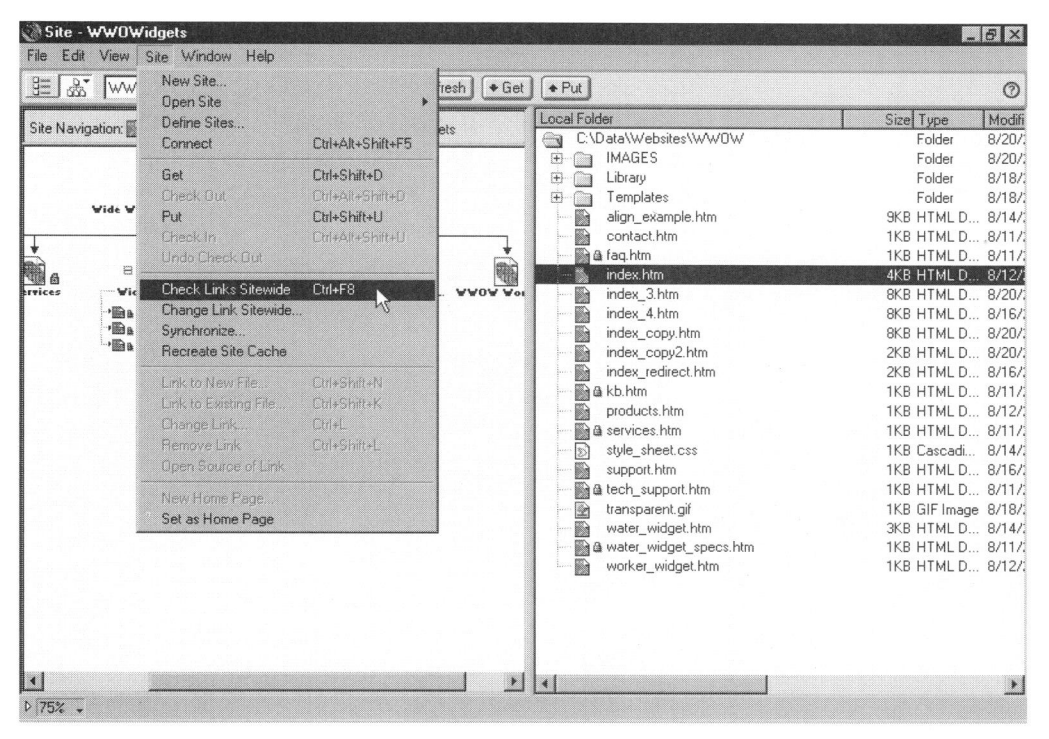

Figure 8-1 Using the Check Links Sitewide command.

3. Review the broken links.

In the Link Checker dialog box, shown in Figure 8-2, review the list of broken hyperlinks. The Files heading shows which files contain broken hyperlinks, and the Broken Links heading displays the incorrect hyperlinks.

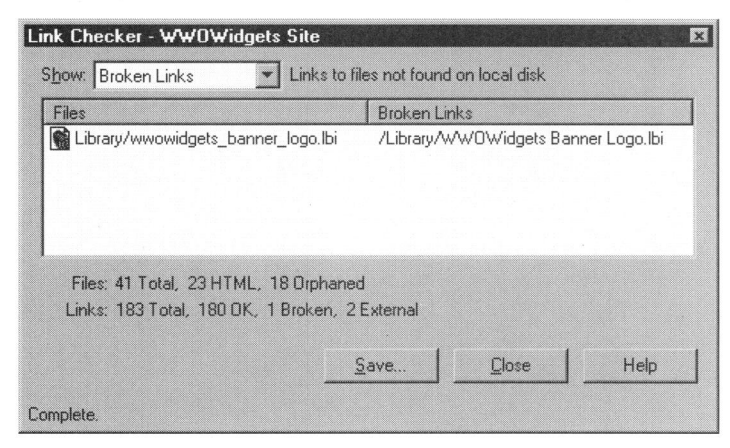

Figure 8-2 The Link Checker dialog box.

Step 8 Deploy Your Web Site   **213**

4. **Fix broken links.**

   To change the links, double-click the file in the Files column to open it and edit it directly. You can also select the file, click the broken link next to it, and type in the correct link or click the small folder icon that appears to the right of the broken link to locate the correct file. Alternatively, you can also use the Change Link Sitewide command, discussed in the following section, to change a broken link that appears multiple times on your pages.

5. **View orphaned files.**

   Choose Orphaned Files from the Show drop-down list box in the Link Checker to display a list of files that haven't been linked to on your site. Although orphaned files don't affect visitors, they can take up extra server space. If you are running out of space on your Web server, look for orphaned files to delete.

6. **View external links.**

   External links, or hyperlinks to locations outside of your own Web site, frequently break as Web sites you link to reorganize their sites or go out of business. To view a list of external hyperlinks so that you can check their validity, choose External Hyperlinks from the Show drop-down list box in the Link Checker. Unfortunately, you'll have to test the links manually by entering them in a Web browser.

7. **Optionally, save the report.**

   To save the link check report as a tab-delimited text file that you can import into a spreadsheet program such as Microsoft Excel, click Save, enter a name in the File Name box, and click Save, as shown in Figure 8-3.

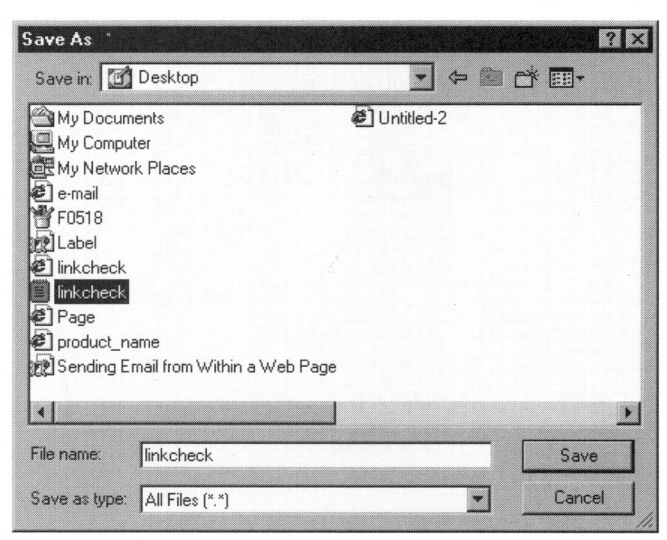

Figure 8-3   Saving a link check report as a tab-delimited text file.

Changing Hyperlinks

Dreamweaver lets you easily change all instances of a hyperlink in your Web site, which can be particularly valuable for fixing broken hyperlinks. It can also be handy when you want to update a link to point to new content. For example, if you have a monthly column, you could easily change all "Current Month" hyperlinks to point to the new month's column instead of the previous month's column.

To use this feature, follow these steps:

1. **Open the Site window.**

   Click the Show Site button on the Mini-Launcher (located on the right side of the Status Bar). This displays the Site window.

2. **Select the link you want to change.**

   Optionally, select a file from the Site Map or the Local Folder pane from which you want to divert hyperlinks.

3. **Choose the Site menu's Change Link Sitewide command.**

4. **Select the hyperlink to change.**

   In the Change All Links To box of the Change Link Sitewide dialog box, shown in Figure 8-4, enter the link you want to change, or click the folder icon to select the file from which you want to divert links.

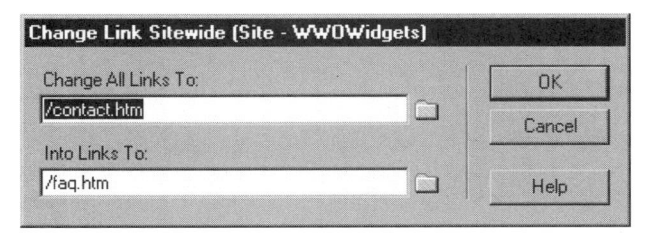

Figure 8-4   The Change Link Sitewide dialog box.

5. **Enter the new hyperlink.**

   Enter the new hyperlink in the Into Links To box, or click the folder icon to select the file to which you want to make all new links, as shown in Figure 8-5.

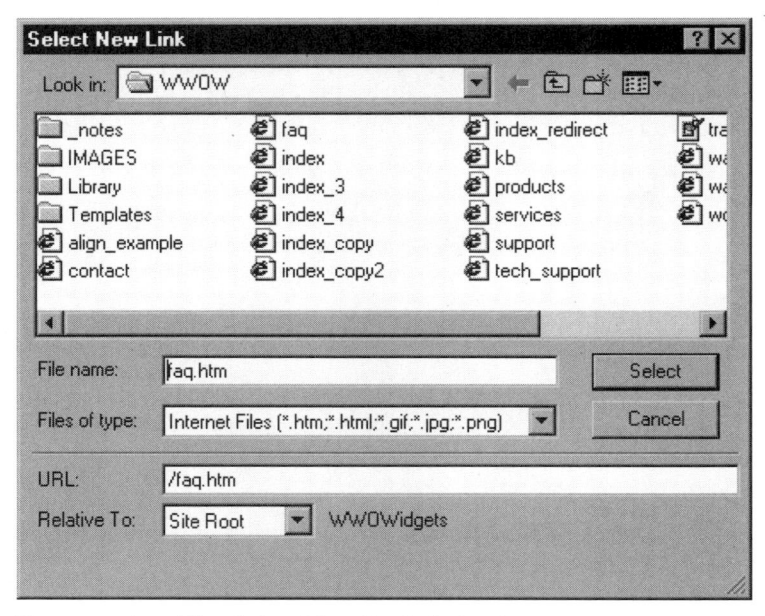

Figure 8-5   The Select New Link dialog box.

6. Click OK, and select the pages to update.

Dreamweaver displays the Update Files dialog box, as shown in Figure 8-6. Select the pages you want to update (hold down the Ctrl key while clicking to select multiple pages), and then click Update. Dreamweaver processes the selected files, changing each hyperlink.

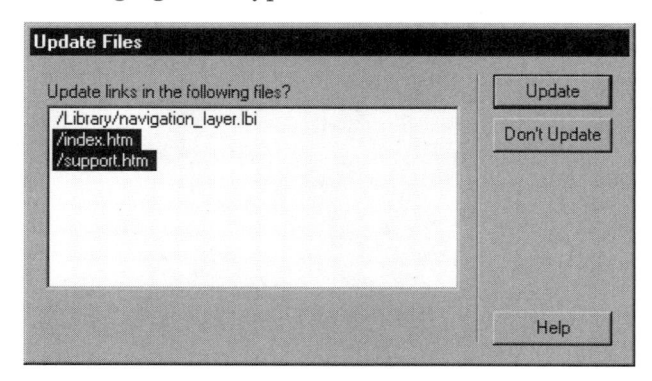

Figure 8-6   The Update Files dialog box.

NOTE   *When replacing hyperlinks, Dreamweaver uses the addressing format used by the hyperlink it replaces, on a page-by-page basis. Thus, if your index.htm links to your contact.htm page using a document relative address, this format will be maintained, as will the site-root relative address used by a different page. The Relative To drop-down list box shown in Figure 8-5 has no effect on the links replaced using the Change Link Sitewide command.*

Testing Your Site in Different Browsers

Dreamweaver does a pretty accurate job of portraying your Web pages as they will appear in a Web browser. However, your Web site might look drastically different when displayed in another company's Web browser or on a non-PC platform, such as WebTV. In order to confirm that your Web site is functional and effective for all your visitors, you need to test your site using several different browsers.

The easiest way to test your site in several browsers is to open each Web browser using Dreamweaver's Preview In Browser command. If you have Web browsers installed on your computer that don't appear in the Preview In Browser list, you should add them to this list. The following sections show you how to do these tasks.

TIP   *In addition to previewing your Web pages in a number of browsers, you should also run a browser compatibility check using Dreamweaver's Check Target Browsers feature, as discussed in "Step 7: Polish Your Pages."*

Previewing Web Pages

To Preview a Web page you've created in Dreamweaver, open the page, choose Preview In Browser from the File menu, and then choose a browser from the submenu. Figures 8-7, 8-8, and 8-9 show a Web page created in Dreamweaver, as displayed in Microsoft Internet Explorer 5.5, Netscape Navigator 4.75, and Opera 4.02.

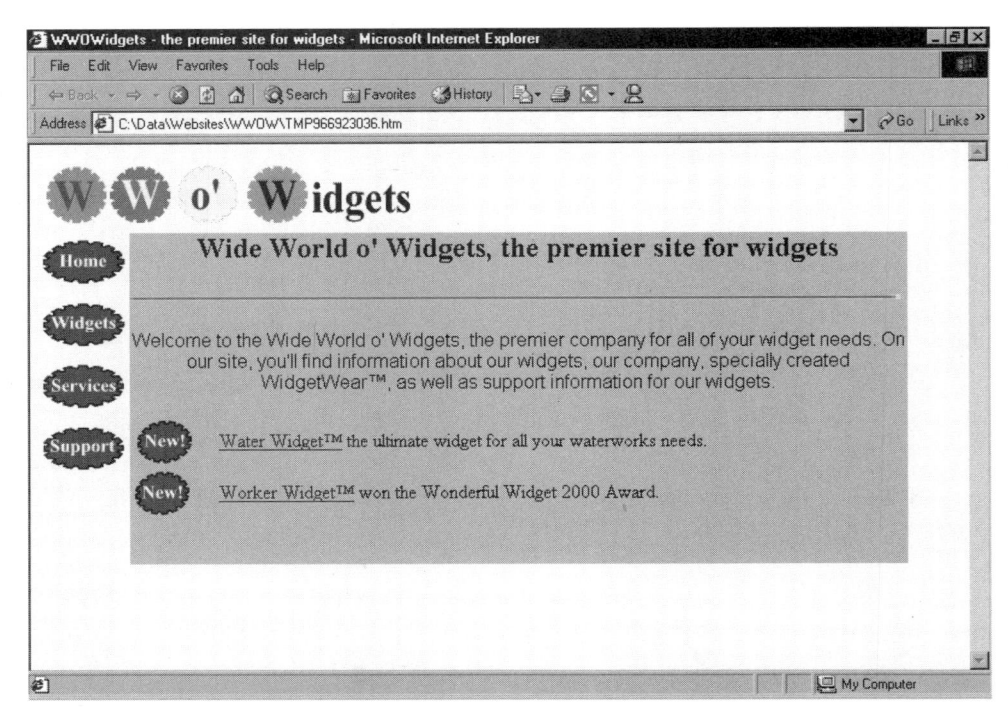

Figure 8-7 A Web site as it appears (properly) in Internet Explorer 5.5.

NOTE *Test your Web site with the latest versions of Internet Explorer and Netscape Navigator. If you have access to computers running older versions of the browsers or a different browser, such as Opera, consider testing your site in these browsers, too. Testing on Macintosh and information appliances (such as WebTV) is usually easiest to do after your site has been published to the Internet.*

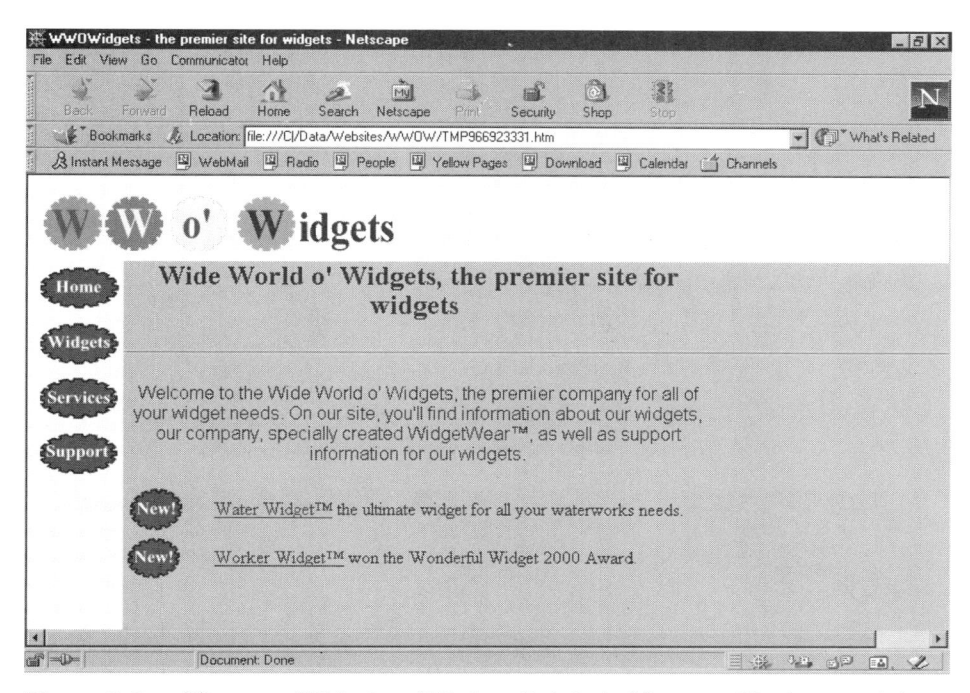

Figure 8-8 The same Web site, differing slightly in Netscape Navigator 4.75.

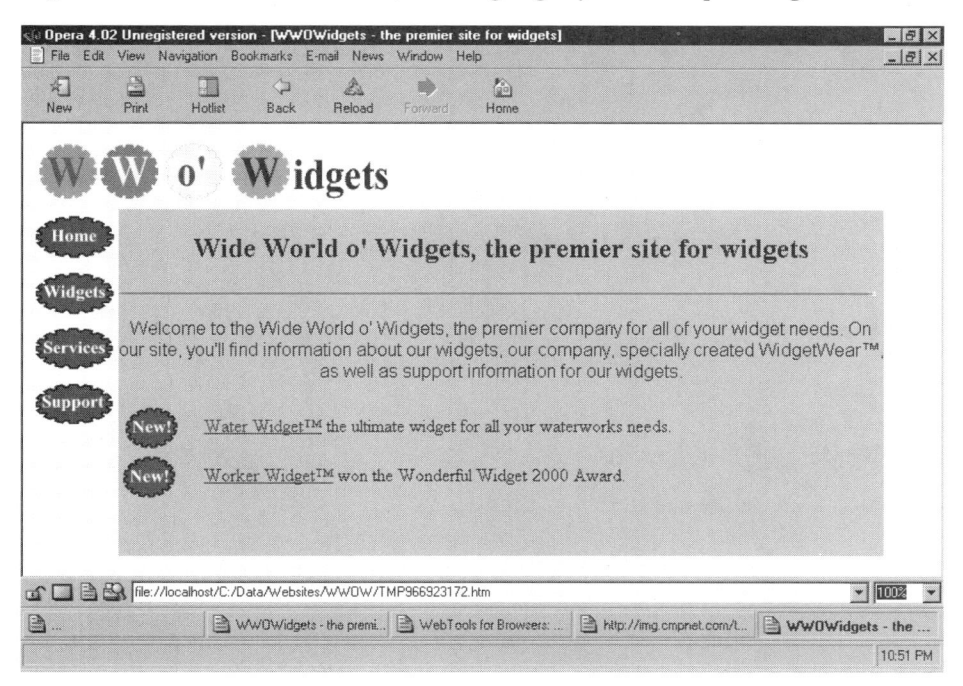

Figure 8-9 The same Web site in Opera 4.02.

Step 8 Deploy Your Web Site

After opening your Web site in a couple of browsers, spend a few minutes testing all the links and examining each page. Is the layout consistent on all the browsers? Do all the features work as expected? Make notes on which pages have problems, and then go back into Dreamweaver and see whether you can fix them.

Adding Browsers to the Preview In Browser List

If your Web browsers aren't set up to work with Dreamweaver's Preview In Browser command, then follow these steps:

1. Open the Preferences dialog box.

Choose the File menu's Preview In Browser command, and then choose Edit Browser List from the submenu, as shown in Figure 8-10.

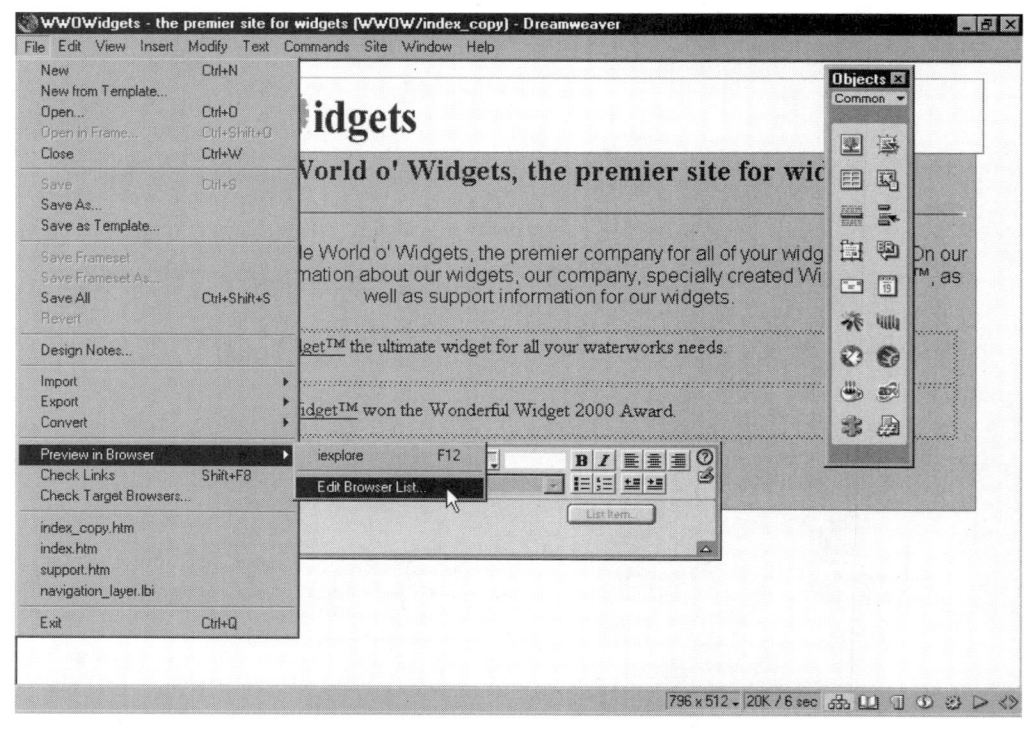

Figure 8-10 Choosing the Edit Browser List command.

2. **Add your browser.**

   Click the plus sign in the Preview In Browser section of the Preferences dialog box, as shown in Figure 8-11.

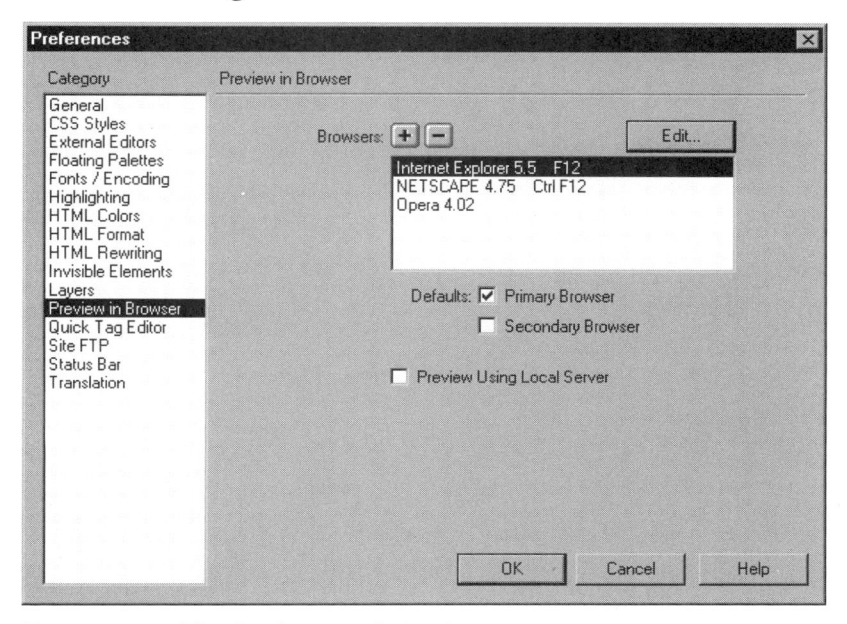

   Figure 8-11   The Preferences dialog box.

3. **Specify your browser settings.**

   In the Add Browser dialog box, shown in Figure 8-12, enter the name of the browser, and then click the Browse button to locate the program file for your browser. Select the Primary Browser check box to make this your default browser in Dreamweaver, or select the Secondary Browser check box to make the browser your secondary browser. (The primary and secondary browsers have their own hotkeys you can press to quickly preview your page in the browser.)

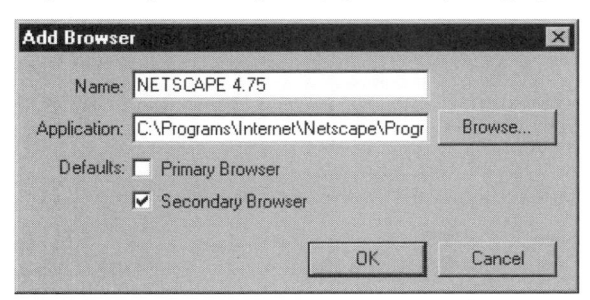

   Figure 8-12   Adding a browser to the Preview In Browser list.

Step 8 Deploy Your Web Site   **221**

4. **Modify the browser list.**

   In the list of browsers (see Figure 8-11), select a browser and click Edit to change the browser's display name. To delete a browser from the list, select it and click the minus sign. To preview Web pages using your computer's Web server (if you have a Web server such as Internet Information Server installed on your computer), select the Preview Using Local Server check box.

   NOTE *Using the Preview Using Local Server check box will enable some Web pages to preview more accurately (images and links that might not work otherwise often do when previewed this way); however, some things don't work as well, such as site-root relative hyperlinks. The best way to test a Web site is to publish it to a Web server—either on the company network or on the Internet—and then test the pages there.*

Usability Testing

In addition to testing for broken links and browser incompatibilities, your company or organization will find it informative to perform some usability testing. Here are some recommendations for simple usability tests:

- Recruit people who aren't involved in the Web site project to test your site. The feedback of your customers or other people in your target audience can be invaluable in evaluating the effectiveness of your site. For very small organizations, even recruiting family and friends to test your site can provide valuable feedback.

- Develop some purposeful tasks for your testers to perform, and then watch how they accomplish them. You might use tasks such as "Find the company contact information" or "Find the product information for product x." If you need to help the testers, your site might need more work.

- Pay special attention to the navigational structure of your Web site. How well can users locate information using your site? See "Step 4: Collect and Organize Your Content" and "Step 7: Polish Your Pages" for more information on creating an effective navigational structure.

- Test your Web site at a variety of resolutions. (See "Step 7: Polish Your Pages" for more information on creating resolution-independent Web pages.) We recommend that you test your site at 640x480 (a low resolution) and at 1024x768 (a typical high resolution).

- If you decide to publish your site immediately, perform the testing after it is published. A short user survey on your site can also be a good way to gather feedback.

> **NOTE** *If your site contains online ordering capabilities, it is very important to thoroughly test your system no matter what the size of your company or Web site. For more information about online ordering, see "Appendix B: Creating Web Stores."*

Publishing Your Web Site

When you're ready to make your Web site available to the general public on the World Wide Web, you need to publish it to the Internet. Publishing your site to your Web hosting company's Web server is easy. To do this, follow these steps:

1. Open the Site window.

Click the Show Site button on the Mini-Launcher (located on the right side of the Status Bar). This displays the Site window, as shown in Figure 8-13.

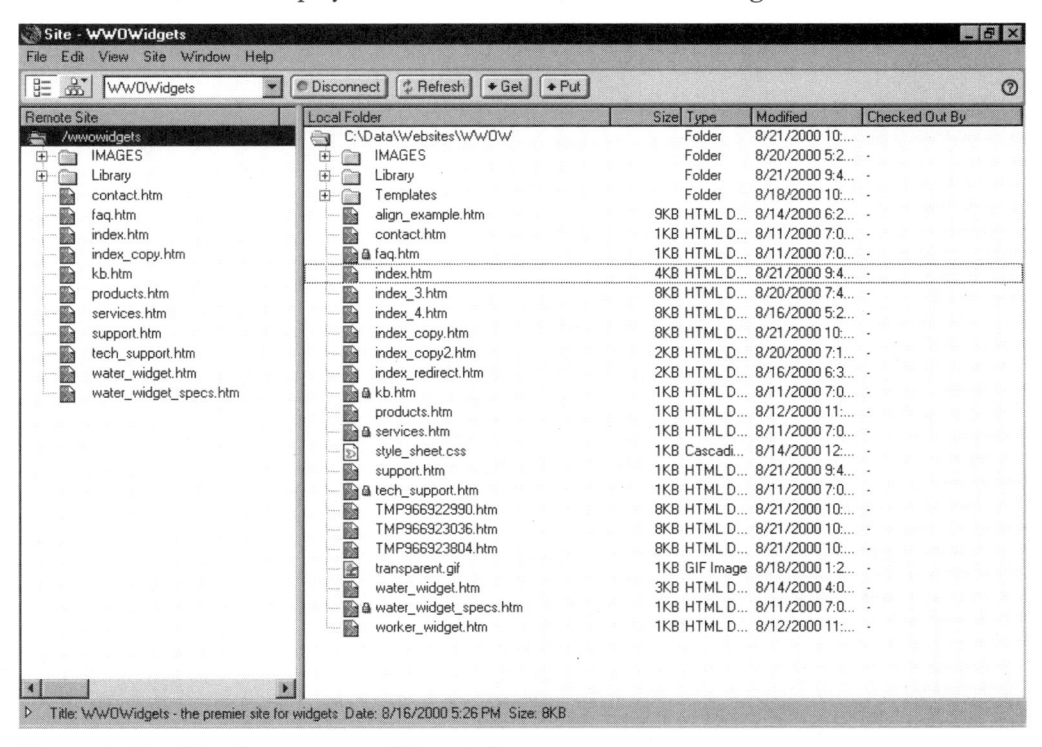

Figure 8-13   The Dreamweaver Site window.

2. **Connect to your remote site.**

   Click the Connect toolbar button to connect to your remote site. (You might need to connect to the Internet first.) The contents of the remote site are displayed in the Remote Site pane.

3. **Choose the Site menu's Synchronize command.**

   To synchronize all changed files, use the Synchronize command. To publish a few files manually, select the files and click the Put toolbar button. To retrieve a few files from the remote site, select them and click the Get toolbar button.

4. **Specify how many files to synchronize.**

   In the Synchronize drop-down list box, select Entire Site to synchronize all files in the site or select Selected Files Only to synchronize only the currently selected files in the local folder or remote site, as shown in Figure 8-14.

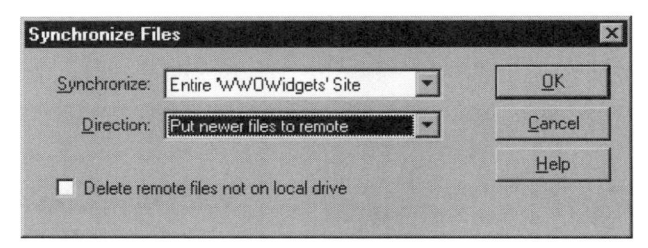

Figure 8-14   The Synchronize Files dialog box.

5. **Specify a direction in which to transfer files.**

   In the Direction drop-down list box, select Put Newer Files To Remote to publish only new files from the local folder to the remote site. Alternatively, select Get Newer Files From Remote to retrieve only new files from the remote site, or choose Get And Put Newer Files to synchronize the remote site and local folder with each other, downloading and uploading the newest files. Select Delete Remote Files Not On Local Drive if you want to remove orphaned files from the remote site, freeing up some server space.

6. **Click OK.**

   Dreamweaver checks the remote site and local folder to see which files are newest, and then displays the Site dialog box, as shown in Figure 8-15. Note that if you get an error message, you may need to reconnect to your remote site, as many FTP servers will timeout if you take too long after connecting to do something.

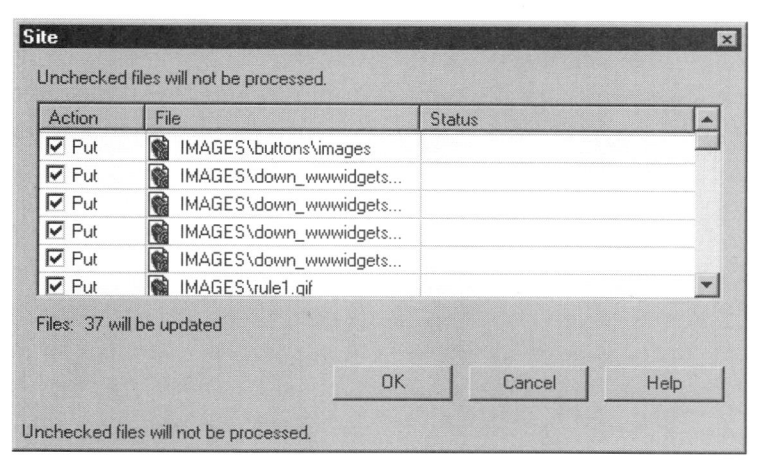

Figure 8-15 Selecting which files to synchronize.

7. **Select the files to synchronize.**

   In the Site dialog box, shown in Figure 8-15, clear the check boxes for any files you don't want to synchronize, and then click OK. Dreamweaver synchronizes the files and displays the results in the Site dialog box.

   > **WARNING** *All the users who work on your Web site should make sure that their computer clocks are synchronized; otherwise, it's possible that one user could overwrite changes made by another.*

Publicizing Your Web Site

In order for your Web site to succeed, you need to publicize it. There are numerous ways to publicize your site, both on and off the Internet. Online methods include search engines, online advertising, newsgroups, and mailing lists. Offline methods include placing links on all print material that your company or organization creates, Yellow Pages ads, and newspaper ads. These methods are discussed in greater detail in the sections that follow.

> **TIP** *One form of publicity that we don't cover here is word of mouth. This is not a method to underestimate. The best way to stimulate positive publicity via word of mouth is to have high-quality, timely content on your Web site.*

Submitting Your Site to Search Engines

Since most people locate a Web site using a search engine, the most important step you can take to publicize your Web site is to submit it to the top search engines. Although this process takes some time, it pays off in the end.

> **TIP** *Avoid using a search engine submission service. These services usually offer to submit your site to hundreds of search engines for a sum of money—sometimes with recurring fees. Since the vast majority of searches are conducted on only a handful of search engines, this level of submission is superfluous. In addition, submission firms usually don't submit your site to directory-based search engines, or if they do, they do an inadequate job of it. Take the time to submit to search engines yourself—it's worth it.*

Before you start submitting to search engines, it helps to understand them. There are three types of search engines: crawler-based search engines, directories, and the hybrid search engine, which is a combination of the first two. Crawler-based search engines automatically crawl (explore) the Web, examining Web sites and adding the relevant information from each site into its search database. Directories such as Yahoo! take descriptions submitted by Web site authors and use human editors to review the submissions. The editors then create a hierarchical, topic-based directory out of the Web sites submitted that visitors can either browse by topic or perform a search on. Hybrid search engines are usually search engines that also contain a human-created directory. Editors create the directory by looking at the search engine's results, the actual Web sites, and sometimes sites that are submitted by site authors to the hybrid directory.

> **NOTE** *A few search services don't fit neatly into the crawler-based, directory, or hybrid categories. For example, Ask Jeeves (www.askjeeves.com) uses a natural-language-processing search engine that searches a human-created database of Web sites. Mamma.com is a meta-search engine—a search engine that performs searches on a number of other search engines.*

The type of search engine determines how you'll submit your site. Crawler-based search engines generally request only your Web site's URL, as shown in Figure 8-16. The search engine then automatically visits your site, examines the title and text on your home page, reviews your site's Keywords and Description meta tags, and then adds your site to the search engine's database.

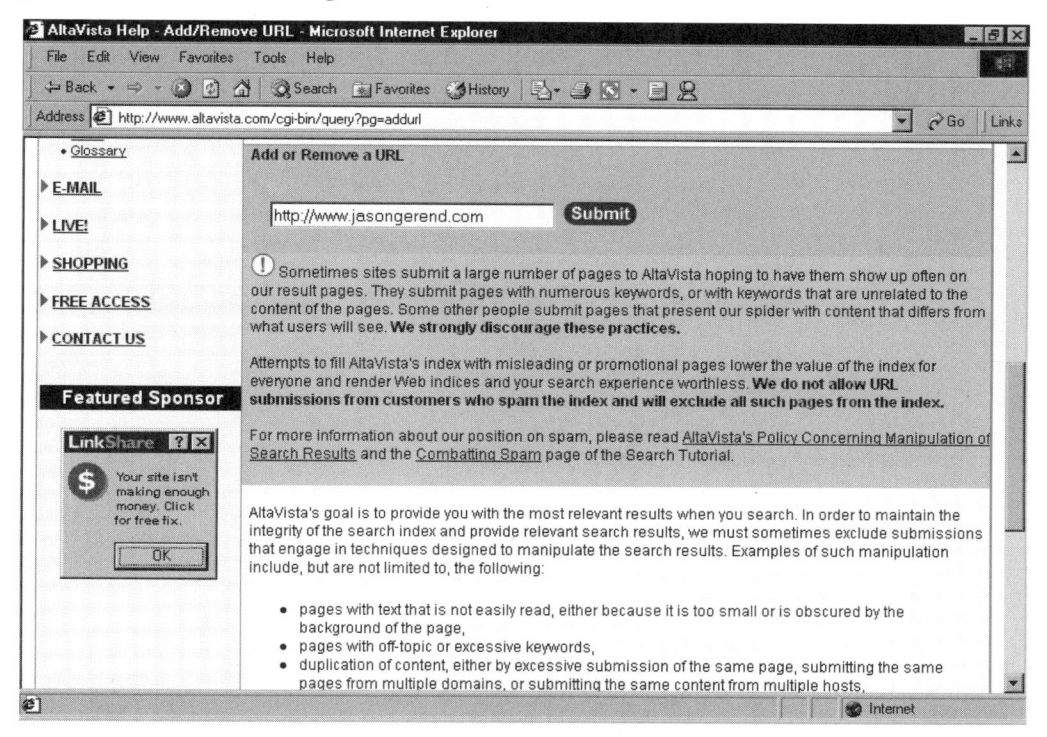

Figure 8-16 Submitting to a crawler-based search engine.

TIP   *Although search engines generally look into your Web site for content on pages other than your home page, you can't always count on this, so it's a good idea to submit your two or three most important pages separately to each search engine. (Make sure each of these pages has Description and Keywords meta tags inserted and a good title.) But limit yourself to two or three pages; submitting too many pages to the same search engine can actually hurt your site.*

Directory-style search engines require a greater amount of effort for submission. First, visit the directory (such as Yahoo!) and perform some searches for content similar to that of your Web site. Second, take note of the kinds of sites that are returned in the search results and the categories under which they're listed. It's very important with directories to find the most specific and appropriate category for your site, so do some exploring. (Your site may belong in multiple categories. If this is the case, note each one.) Third, read the directory's Site Submission Tips or the equivalent page for the procedure the directory wants you to follow when submitting your site. Most require that you navigate to the category under which you want to list your site, and then click the Suggest A Site link. Fourth, in the actual submission form, as shown in Figure 8-17, submit the title of your Web site (generally your official business or company name), your site's URL, and a 25-word-or-less description of your site.

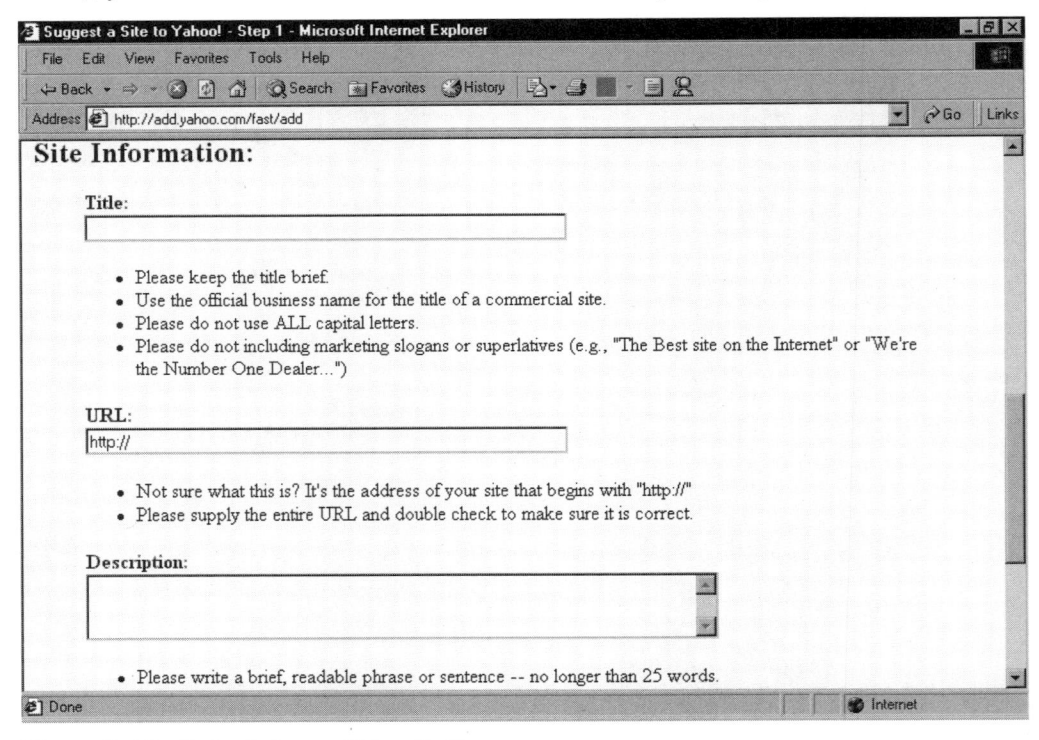

Figure 8-17 Submitting to Yahoo!'s directory.

TIP   *Make your site description more than just a series of keywords. It should be a succinct, well-written summary of what visitors will find on your site.*

Table 8-1 lists search engines that we recommend you submit your site to, their URLs, and their type.

SEARCH ENGINE	URL	SEARCH ENGINE TYPE
AOL Search	search.aol.com	Hybrid using Open Directory
AltaVista	www.altavista.com	Hybrid using Open Directory and LookSmart
Direct Hit	www.directhit.com	Crawler-based, modified by popularity
Excite	www.excite.com	Crawler-based
Go/Infoseek	www.go.com	Hybrid
Google	www.google.com	Crawler-based, modified by popularity
HotBot	www.hotbot.com	Hybrid, with results from Direct Hit and Open Directory
LookSmart	www.looksmart.com	Directory
Lycos	www.lycos.com	Hybrid, using Open Directory
MSN Search	search.msn.com	Hybrid, using LookSmart
Netscape Search	search.netscape.com	Hybrid, using Open Directory
Northern Light	www.northernlight.com	Crawler-based
Open Directory	dmoz.org	Directory
Snap	www.snap.com	Directory
WebCrawler	www.webcrawler.com	Crawler-based
Yahoo!	www.yahoo.com	Directory

Table 8-1   The major search engines.

Online Advertising

In addition to submitting your Web site to search engines, a number of other methods are available for advertising on the Web. Some of these are effective in increasing the number of visitors to your site, and some are probably a waste of time and money. In the following sections we offer recommendations on which methods to consider and which to ignore.

Purchasing Banner Ads

The most obvious method of online advertising is the banner ad. Banner ads are the ubiquitous (and often disregarded) rectangular ad boxes that adorn most Web sites.

In general, we recommend that you avoid paying for banner ads. They require too much time and effort to create, cost money, and are limited in their ability to draw visitors to your site. However, if there are any prominent Web sites that draw your target audience (for example, sites that cover topics related to your company or organization), it may be advantageous to purchase a banner ad.

Using Link Exchanges

One of the best methods of advertising online is to get other Web sites to link to your site, creating what's known as a link exchange. This method is cost-effective (free) and can also increase your ranking in search engines that pay attention to the number of links to a particular Web site.

There are three ways that you can establish links to your company or organization's site. First, use a Link Exchange service that allows you to exchange links with other random Web sites; second, join a Web ring of sites that are similar to your own; and third, contact Web sites personally and inquire about exchanging links.

Link Exchange services often don't work well for most companies and organizations. This is because the site that ends up linking to yours frequently doesn't have anything to do with your site's purpose, so it is unlikely to generate visitors who are interested in viewing your site.

Web rings devoted to a topic covered by your Web site are an effective means of attracting traffic to your site. The way a Web ring works is that Web sites with a common topic contact each other, decide to set up a Web ring, and then pay to place a banner ad for the Web ring on their home pages, as shown in Figure 8-18. This banner ad is usually configured with automatically updated links to other sites in the Web ring. By joining the Web ring, your site becomes accessible through these links and is also listed in the Web ring's directory. The site *www.webring.com* is a good place to look if you are interested in joining a Web ring.

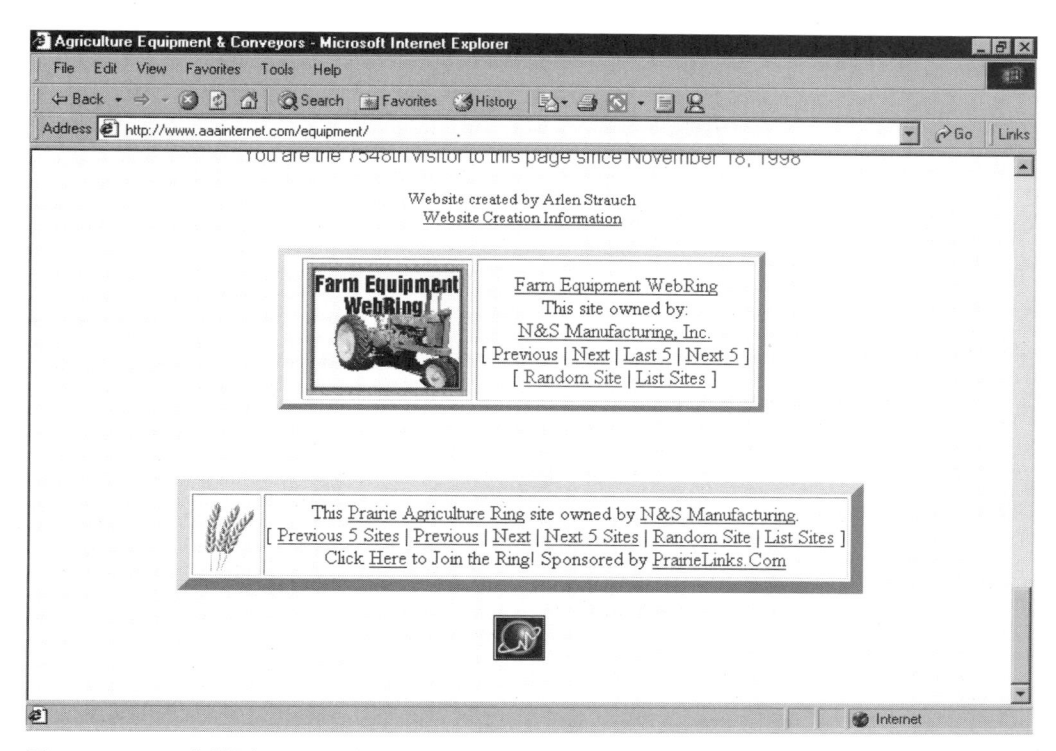

Figure 8-18 A Web site with a couple of Web ring ads.

Contacting Web sites personally by manually identifying sites that are complementary to your target audience's interests is an effective way of advertising online. Once you've identified Web sites that cover similar or related topics, contact the sites' Webmasters about setting up a link exchange.

TIP   *One way to convince a Web site to exchange links is to place a link to their site on your Web site, send them an e-mail informing them of this, and then suggest that they link to your site as well.*

Using Newsgroups to Gain Exposure

Newsgroups in general aren't the best place to publicize a Web site. Newsgroup participants usually react negatively to ads placed on newsgroups, and their dynamic nature ensures that anything your company or organization posts will stay up for only a couple of weeks before getting deleted.

Having said this, you can use newsgroups to publicize your Web site if you're careful about how you do it. Start by locating a newsgroup that deals with issues related to your company or organization's line of business and then posting some legitimate articles, such as tips or responses to questions other newsgroup members have. Along with the articles you post, make sure to include your Web site's URL, as well as a short summary of your site to entice people to visit it. Being an active and positive participant in a newsgroup can reflect well on your company or organization and also bring additional visitors to your site—just be careful to avoid posting ads.

> **TIP** *To find a suitable newsgroup, conduct a search on Deja.com at* www.deja.com/usenet.

Creating a Mailing List

Mailing lists are a voluntary form of bulk e-mailing that allows a company or organization to easily send out mail, such as a newsletter or update, to a large number of people. Sending regular e-mails about your Web site or company to visitors who have joined your mailing list is an effective way of reminding them about your company and also featuring new or changed parts of your Web site. This increases the chances that they will visit your site again.

> **NOTE** *Make sure that what you send via your mailing list is valuable content to subscribers. Otherwise, your subscribers will delete the message or unsubscribe from your list. This content can include tips, how-to sections, product specials, and new additions to your site. Always include instructions for unsubscribing to the list with every message you send.*

You can handle mailing lists using three different types of mailing programs: a standard mail program, a stand-alone bulk mail program, or a server-based mailing list program.

TIP *Whichever method you use to send your messages to mailing list members, consider creating a form on your Web site that visitors can use to subscribe to your mailing list. To do so, either insert the code provided to you by your mailing list provider or create a simple form with a text box for e-mail address input and a Submit button. Configure the form to send the results to your e-mail address (or if you've hired a professional to create your forms, a form results file on your Web server).*

You can use a standard e-mail program, such as Microsoft Outlook or Outlook Express, to send mail to everyone on your list, provided the number of subscribers is small. To use Outlook or Outlook Express, create a separate folder in your Contacts folder or Address Book for the mailing list subscribers, create a contact for each subscriber, and then add each user to the BCC field of a new mail message. This method is inconvenient and slow, but it is simple to set up and it can work well for a beginning mailing list. Most companies and organizations quickly outgrow it, however.

Another method is to use a stand-alone bulk mailer program, such as Aureate Group Mail *(www.group-mail.com)*. Bulk mail programs are specially designed for sending out an e-mail message to a large number of mailing list subscribers. These programs are generally inexpensive ($50 is a typical price) and are an appropriate option for companies or organizations that don't require the complexity of a server-based mailing list solution (as described below).

The most sophisticated and complicated method of creating a mailing list is to use a server-based mailing list program, such as L-Soft's Listserv *(www.lsoft.com)* or Majordomo. Both of these programs are typically available to you from your Web hosting company for an additional monthly fee—starting at roughly $15 per month for a small number of subscribers. One advantage of using a server-based solution is the ability to allow users to subscribe and unsubscribe from the mailing list themselves, although this advantage is partially offset by the difficulty of configuring and maintaining the mailing list. If your company or organization finds itself outgrowing bulk mail programs though, a server-based mail program can be an excellent solution.

TIP *Many companies and organizations will find that Web-based mailing list providers such as eGroups.com and Listbot (www.listbot.com) are a better solution than the traditional Listserv and Majordomo programs. Additionally, many of these Web-based list servers can be used for free, provided you don't mind having ads inserted in your messages.*

Offline Publicizing

Your company or organization can get so caught up in publicizing your Web site online that you forget about the more traditional channels of publicity, such as company publications, phone books, and newspaper ads, and traditional marketing methods, such as speaking engagements.

Any time that you draw attention to your business or organization, you can also increase the number of visitors to your Web site—provided that you make it clear to your audience how to find your site. Generally, you publicize your Web site in the same way that you publicize your company, but in addition to (or possibly instead of) providing a phone number as a contact method, list your URL. Many people consider the Web their preferred source of information, so whenever you provide people with a way of obtaining information about your company or organization, list your URL.

Here are some recommendations for offline channels that you may want to consider for publicizing your Web site:

- Company letterhead and business cards
- Coffee mugs, magnets, stickers, and any other ephemera your company prints
- Newsletters, program guides, brochures, sell sheets, or other printed documents
- Phone books and newspaper ads
- Answering machine or voice mail
- Press releases
- Speaking engagements and broadcast media

Monitoring Your Web Site

After you publish and publicize your Web site, you may want to monitor it to determine the number of visitors who come to your site and the type of browsers they are using. This can give you a better feel for whether or not your Web site is achieving its desired results, demonstrate the effectiveness of your Web site publicity efforts, and perhaps reveal whether or not you need to rethink the browser compatibility of your site.

To obtain useful statistics on your Web site's usage patterns, such as the number of visitors coming to your site or what browsers they're using, you need to use a third- party monitoring solution. Typically, your Web hosting company will provide usage statistics for your site as a part of your Web hosting package, as shown in Figure 8-19. However, if this service isn't included with your hosting plan, or if the statistics provided are inadequate, you can use a third party to collect statistics on your Web site traffic. Sites for some companies that offer Web site statistics collection include *www.counter.com*, *www.sitegauge.com*, and *www.fxweb.com/tracker*.

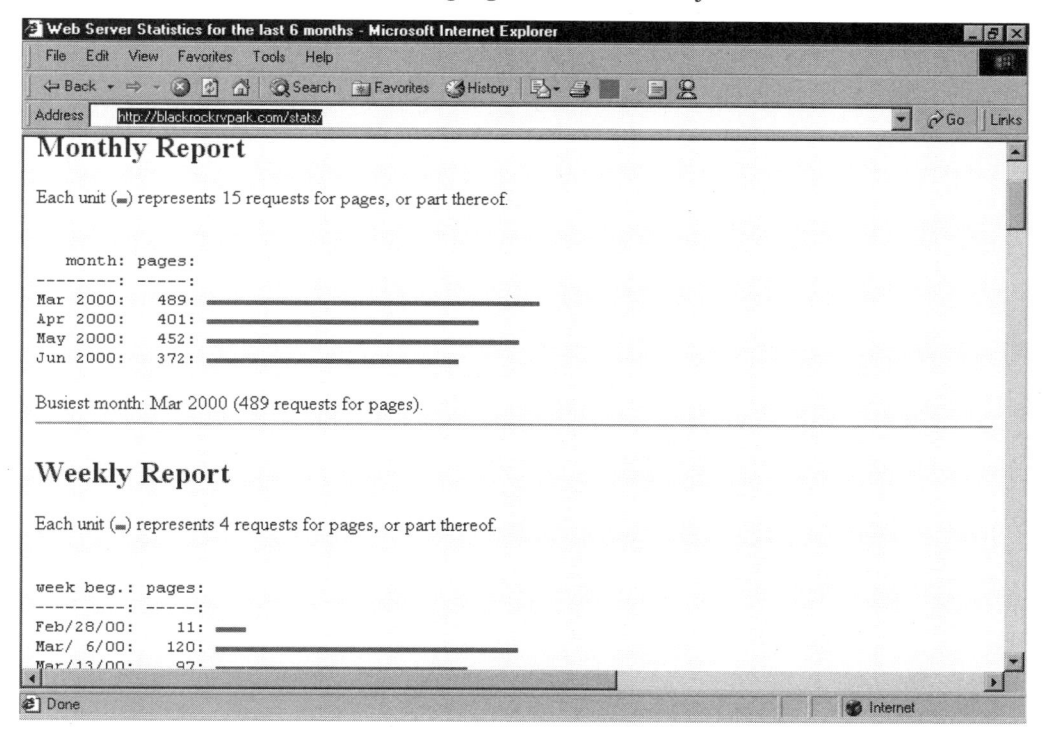

Figure 8-19 The traffic statistics for a Web site.

Here are some recommendations about what to look for when reading the statistics on your Web site:

- Total number of visits and average hits per day. This number tells you how many people are visiting your site, although it may include multiple visits by the same person.
- How visitors are finding your site. Some usage statistics show which Web sites referred visitors to your site. This data can help you determine your most important referral sources.
- What type of Web browsers visitors are using to view your site. Seeing the breakdown of which browsers and browser versions are being used to view your site helps you better tailor your site to your visitors.
- What type of operating systems are being used to view your site. This information can help identify the platforms on which you should be testing your Web site, as well as show you how up-to-date your visitors are.

Summary

In this last step, we showed you how to test your site for errors or design problems, as well as how to publish the site to your Web hosting company's Internet Web server. We also gave you some strategies and suggestions for publicizing your site, both online and offline, as well as briefly discussing components to monitor on your Web site after it's been published.

Appendix A

SETTING UP YOUR WEB SITE ON A LOCAL SERVER

In addition to creating a central content folder (as discussed in "Step 4: Collect and Organize Your Content"), you may want to set up a remote site that's located on a local Web server (one on your company network) so that multiple users can coordinate their work on the Web site using Dreamweaver's Check In/Out feature, without performing all work on your live Web site (as discussed in "Step 5: Set Up Your Site").

You can use any Web server software; however, if you don't already have a Web server set up on your network, you'll probably find it's easiest to set up a Windows 2000 computer you have on your network with Internet Information Server (IIS)—the built-in Web server software for Windows 2000.

Setting up a Web server and creating a new directory on it for your Web site can be a little daunting. If you have someone in your company or organization who configures your computers, have that person do this for you. However, the process itself isn't really that difficult, especially if you're running Windows 2000.

> **NOTE** *IIS doesn't run on Windows 98 or Windows Me, although you can use Personal Web Server, a limited Web server that is available for use on Windows 98. If more than about a half a dozen people will be working on the Web site at the same time, you should use a computer using Windows 2000 Server, because Windows 2000 Pro can only allow 10 simultaneous connections to the server, as is also the case with other versions of Windows and Windows NT.*

If you don't have a Web server configured, use the brief description that follows. (The following procedure describes the setup for Windows 2000; it will be slightly different for Windows NT 4.) To configure a server, follow these steps:

1. **Make sure IIS is installed.**

   If any computers on your local network are running Windows 2000 with IIS installed, use one of those computers. Otherwise, on a Windows 2000 computer, click the Start button, choose Settings and then click Control Panel. Double-click Add/Remove Programs, click Add/Remove Windows Components, and then select Internet Information Services (IIS). Click Next to perform the installation.

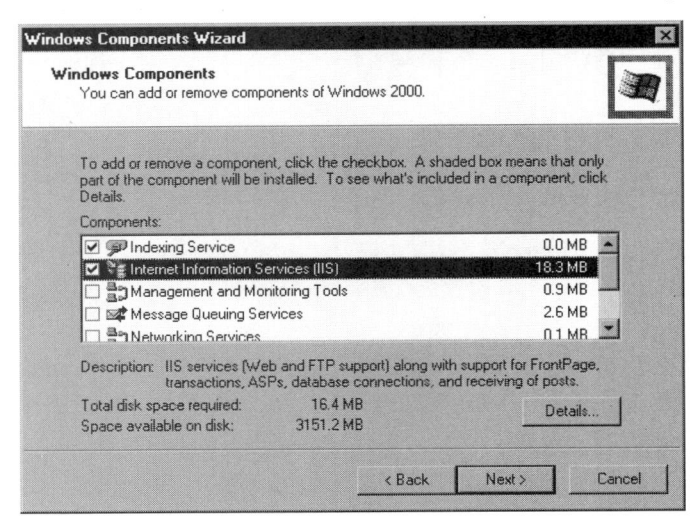

Figure A-1   Installing IIS and Indexing Service in Windows 2000.

2. **Create a new folder for your Web site.**

Your Dreamweaver Web site needs to be stored somewhere. You can use any directory to store the local version of your Web site, although it's usually placed either in the \Inetpub folder on your local Web server in a subdirectory named after your Web site (for example, \Inetpub\mycompany) or in a folder near your central content folder. This folder doesn't have to be located on the local Web server; it can be on any accessible computer on your local network, as long as you create a virtual directory for it, as described below. In any case, create the folder using the same procedure described in the "Creating a Central Content Location" section in "Step 4: Collect and Organize Your Content."

NOTE   *The \Inetpub folder is the default location for Web sites in IIS, and it is usually located on the drive on which Windows 2000 or Windows NT is stored.*

TIP *If you want to control who in your company or organization can access and edit pages on your Web site, it's best to create the folder on a drive using the NTFS file system, which provides advanced security features.*

3. **Open the Computer Management tool.**

   From the Control Panel folder of your local Web server, double-click the Administrative Tools folder, and then double-click the Computer Management tool to open it. Click the plus sign next to Services And Applications, and then click the plus sign next to Internet Information Services to view your local Web server's properties.

4. **Start the Virtual Directory Creation Wizard.**

   Right-click Default Web Site listed under Internet Information Services, as shown in Figure A-2. Choose New from the shortcut menu, and choose Virtual Directory from the submenu to start the Virtual Directory Creation Wizard.

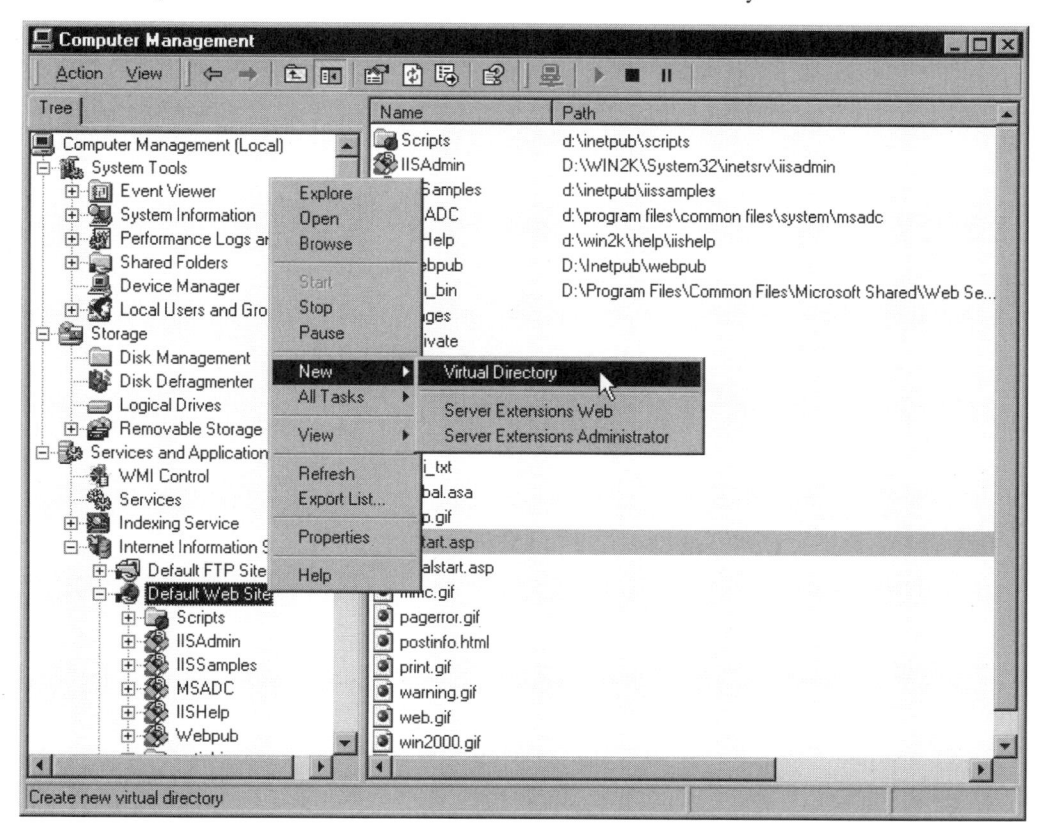

Figure A-2 Starting IIS's Virtual Directory Creation Wizard in Windows 2000.

Appendix A Setting Up Your Web Site on a Local Server

5. **Enter an alias for your local Web site.**

   Click Next in the first screen of the wizard, and then enter in the Alias box the name you want to use to access your Web site locally. For example, if the domain name for your Web site is *www.mycompany.com,* consider using *mycompany* as the alias. Click Next.

6. **Specify in which directory your Web site will be located.**

   In the Directory box, enter the path to the folder where your Web site will be stored. Click Browse to visually locate the directory, if that's easier, and then click Next.

7. **Enter the username and password required for the folder.**

   If the folder that will store your Dreamweaver Web site is located on a network disk instead of locally on the Web server, enter the username and password of a user with Administrator privileges for that network disk. Click Next.

8. **Specify the permissions for the folder.**

   Select the Read, Run Scripts, Write, and Browse permissions to allow you to properly create, administer, and test your Web site locally before publishing it to your Internet Web server. Click Next, and then click Finish to complete the wizard. Your Dreamweaver Web site can now be created, accessed, and tested on your local Web server.

Appendix B

CREATING WEB STORES

Featuring:

- How Web Stores Work
- E-Commerce Options for Your Company

Web-based storefronts are very enticing to many companies and organizations. Unfortunately, Dreamweaver 3 doesn't provide a way for you to collect information from visitors, and to operate a Web store, you've got to be able to take in orders from customers.

Of course, there are other ways in which small or medium-size businesses or organizations can set up Web stores, and the following sections describe some of these options. A brief primer outlines what's involved in creating a Web store and steps through the online transaction process.

NOTE *Your company or organization may not require interactivity on its Web site. We recommend that you postpone adding such advanced features until after you have a simple Web site up and running.*

How Web Stores Work

There are many ways to create a Web-based store—from providing a simple product catalog and order form that visitors can print out and mail in to the full-fledged e-commerce solutions that companies such as Amazon.com and Buy.com have made everyday sights on the Web. These fully integrated online stores are what most businesses and companies think of when contemplating e-commerce, so it's useful to understand what is involved in these stores and why they are so complex and expensive to set up and maintain. The following two sections detail a typical Web-based order from the perspective of the shopper and then from the perspective of the Web server, describing what technologies are used.

What the Shopper Sees

To begin with, a visitor is presented with an online catalog of products and services that he or she can look through, such as the one shown in Figure B1.

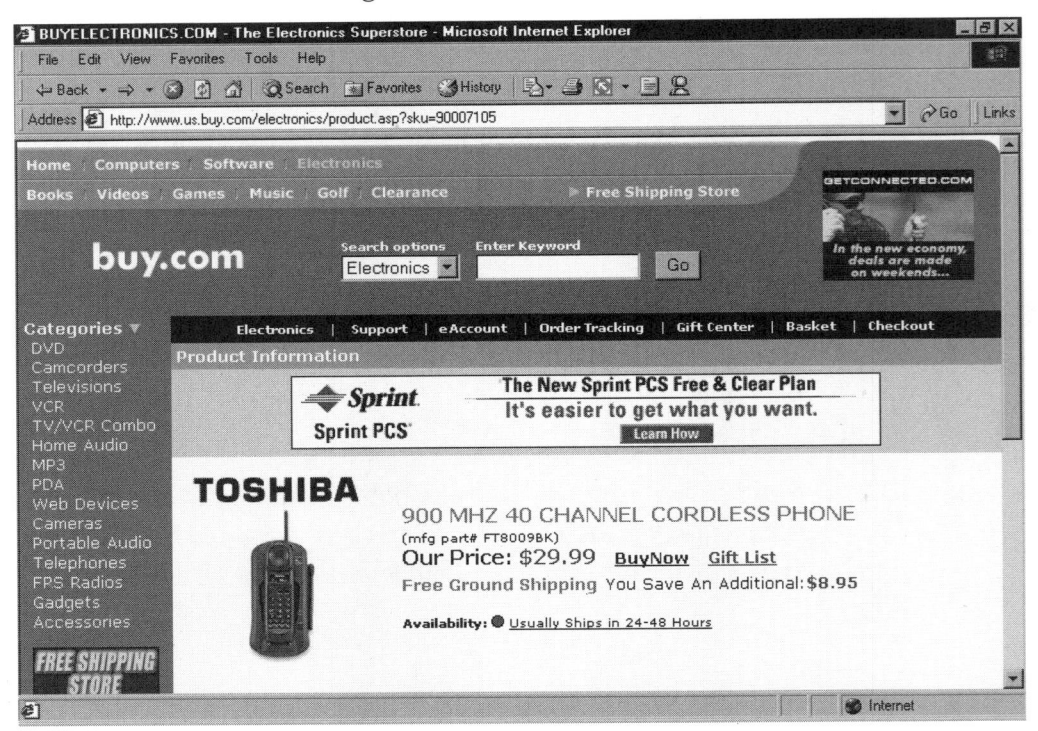

Figure B-1   Buy.com's online product catalog.

Effective Executive's Guide to Dreamweaver Web Sites

When the visitor finds a product to purchase, he or she clicks an Add To Shopping Cart or similarly named link, which adds the product to a virtual shopping cart, as shown in Figure B-2. The shopping cart displays all the products that the visitor has picked out, the prices, and a total price, usually with shipping and tax included. Ideally, the shopping cart also displays whether or not the products are in stock.

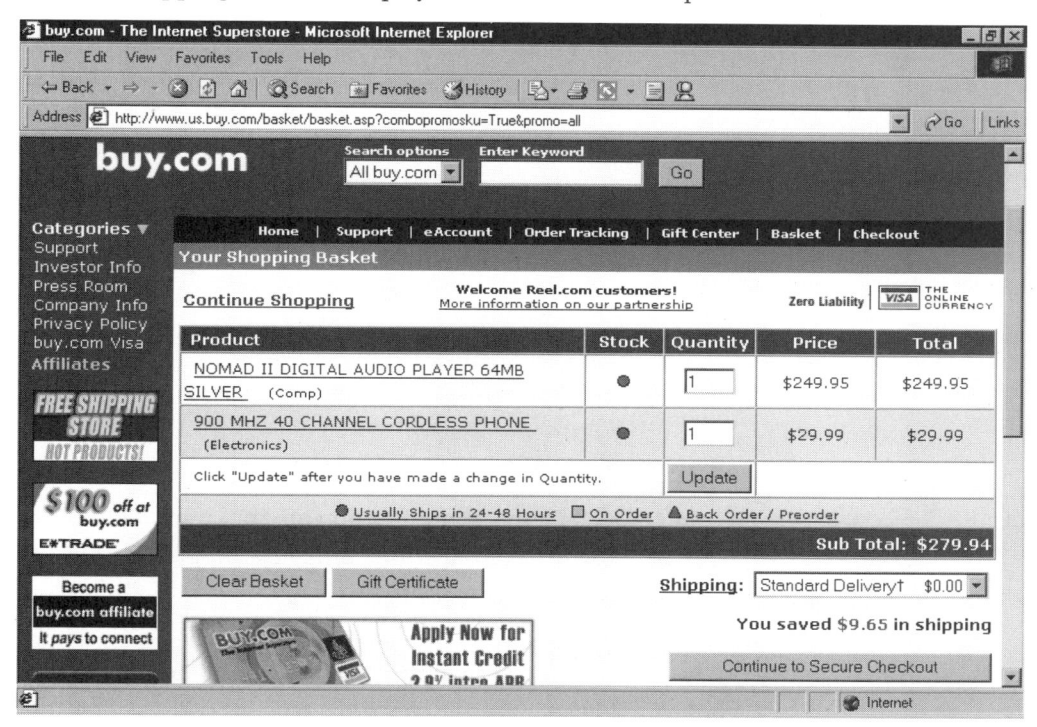

Figure B-2 Buy.com's online shopping cart.

After the shopper has reviewed the items, he or she may then purchase the items by clicking the Continue To Secure Checkout or a similarly named link. At this point, a secure Web page is displayed prompting the shopper for billing and shipping information, including a credit card number. When the shopper is finished completing the form, he or she clicks a Submit Order button that then processes the order and displays an order confirmation showing that the order was placed.

What the Web Server Does

Behind the scenes of the above-described order process a sequence of events unfolds involving several different Web site technologies and techniques.

The online catalog is the simplest part. It can consist of a series of standard Web pages, such as those you create in Dreamweaver. However, the process gets more complicated as soon as the visitor wants to add items to a shopping cart.

To handle a shopping cart, the Web site needs to keep track of each visitor and what items he or she is placing in the shopping cart. This can be done a number of ways, but it usually involves maintaining a database that exists solely to keep track of what items are placed in the shopping cart. Since Dreamweaver 3 doesn't provide any shopping cart component, you need to use a third-party shopping cart system in order to do this. (This is discussed in greater detail in the "Using a Shopping Cart System" section later in this appendix.)

In order for the shopping cart to display the current stocking information of the products, it must be tied to your business's inventory database. This takes a significant amount of database programming and a substantial amount of configuration.

To collect the shopper's billing and shipping information, a simple form is used on a secure Web server (which your Web hosting company can provide for an additional cost or as part of your Web hosting plan). This form takes the order information (which is encrypted for security) and passes along the payment information, such as the credit card number and how much to charge to the account, to a credit card processing company or bank. The bank then charges the shopper's account and credits your company's Internet Merchant account for the amount of the purchase, minus a transaction percentage and fee. The form also enters the information into your ordering database (which is ideally the same as your inventory database), which your company then queries to see what orders it needs to fill and how to fill them.

E-Commerce Options for Your Company

Now that you have an idea of what is involved with a full e-commerce solution, let's take a look at the options that are available to you and the ones that might make the most sense for your company.

Your company can set up a Web-based store using one of three methods: the non-interactive method, which is no different from a print catalog; the basic online order form method; and the full-fledged shopping cart method, with or without credit card processing.

Creating a Non-Interactive Catalog

The easiest way to allow visitors to order products from your company is to create an online version of your print catalog and include your phone number or an order form that visitors can print out and then mail or fax to your company. This is very simple to do. You can use Dreamweaver to create your online product catalog just as you would any other page, making sure to include each product's price as well as your company's telephone number. To allow visitors to mail or fax orders to your company, you can take an existing order form and convert it into a Web page (or create it from scratch) or optionally, an Adobe Acrobat file. You can then place this order form on your Web site for visitors to print out and return to you via mail or fax.

Using a Secure Form to Collect Orders

A more sophisticated approach to online stores is to create an order form hosted on a secure Web site to collect customer orders. In this way, you can safely accept orders with credit card information. Unfortunately, this approach quickly presents challenges for the average user because you need to know how to set up CGI scripts on your Web server in order to allow Dreamweaver to collect form data from visitors.

> **TIP** *If your ISP supports FrontPage Server Extensions, you'll have better luck using Microsoft FrontPage 2000 rather than Dreamweaver for this scenario. You could create a FrontPage web that consists of a single form page for placing orders and then link your Dreamweaver-created Web site to this FrontPage web.*

Credit card information is collected using the order form you create; orders are processed by manually downloading them from your Web site and then using a standard credit card reader to process the transaction. For small businesses, this method is much more cost-effective than dealing with online credit card processing, which universally costs more than processing credit card transactions offline using a standard credit card reader.

> **TIP** *Some Web hosting companies include a free shopping cart system with Web hosting plans that provide secure connections. If this is the case with your Web hosting company, you'll probably want to use it instead of the method described below.*

To create a secure online order form, follow these steps:

1. **Create your online catalog.**

   Create a catalog of products or services in Dreamweaver as you would any other Web site or series of pages, making sure to include pricing information.

2. **Create an order form.**

   Create an order form using Dreamweaver, or optionally, using FrontPage.

3. **Configure the form properties.**

   Select the form, and in the Property inspector's Action box, specify the proper string for posting form data to your secure Web server. (You'll need help from your ISP or a consultant to get this set up.)

   If you're using FrontPage 2000, right-click inside a form in FrontPage that you've created and choose Form Properties from the shortcut menu to modify the properties of the order form. Make sure that the form results are stored in the _private/ directory, as shown in Figure B-3, so that only you can view orders that have been placed.

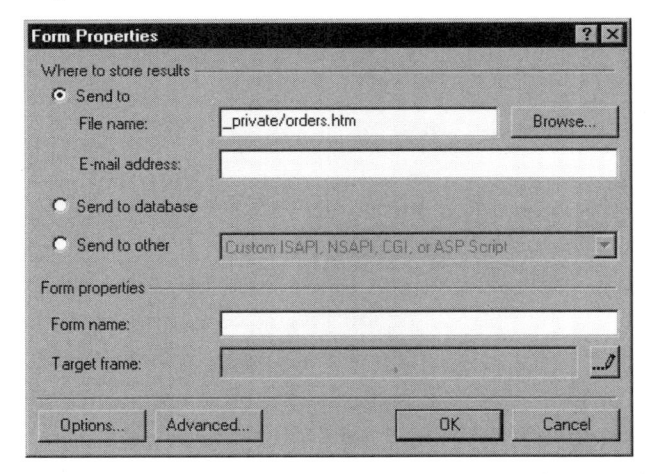

Figure B-3 Changing the location in which form results are stored, using FrontPage 2000.

WARNING *Do not send form results to an e-mail address if your form is collecting credit card information. Non-encrypted e-mail is not a secure medium and should never be used for sending credit card information.*

4. **Link your catalog to your order form.**

   Create a hyperlink in your catalog to your new order form using the secure Web site alias provided by your Web hosting company. Usually this will be in the form of *https://www.myhostingcompany.com/mycompany/order_form.htm*.

   NOTE *Web hosting companies usually configure a secure alias to your Web site, for example, https://www.myhostingcompany.com/mycompany/anypage.htm. The alias allows you to securely access any page on your site. For specifics, contact your Web hosting company.*

5. **Retrieve orders.**

   If you're using FrontPage 2000 to create your forms, open your FrontPage ordering web directly by using the secure alias. To do this, in FrontPage 2000, choose the File menu's Open Web command and then enter the secure URL provided by your Web hosting company, as shown in Figure B-4; for example, *https://www.myhostingcompany.com/mycompany*. After your Web site is open in Dreamweaver, go to the _private/ directory and open your form results page to retrieve the list of orders placed since you last emptied the form results file.

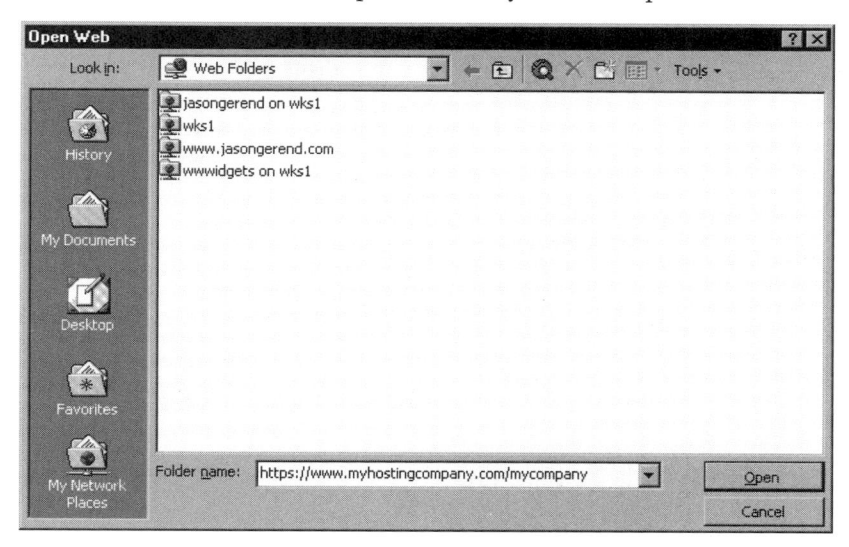

Figure B-4 Opening your Web site using a secure connection.

NOTE *Because it's unwise to send form results containing credit card information over e-mail, you'll need to check your form results regularly to see whether orders have been placed.*

6. **Process the orders.**

   Use your credit card reader to process any credit card orders, and fill your orders.

TIP *One way of processing the orders that are contained in your form results page is to save the page onto your hard drive and take the order information from this file instead of from the form results page on your Web site. You can then safely delete the contents of the form results page on your Web site to reduce the risk of processing an order twice (since the orders will exist only in the file on your hard drive).*

Using a Shopping Cart System

The most elegant and sophisticated way of setting up an online Web store is to use a shopping cart, ideally with online credit card processing. Dreamweaver has no built-in support for creating online shopping carts, so if this is a service you need, you'll have to look elsewhere. In general, you can take three routes.

The first route is to use one of the e-commerce companies that provide a full e-commerce solution, including all Web hosting, a shopping cart system, and credit card processing. This is definitely the easiest way to set up an online Web store, since the entire Web site is created using templates provided for you. (See Figure B-5 for an example of a Web site created by using one of these companies.) It's also not too expensive. Web sites are often provided for free, and credit card processing starts at about $25 per month, with a charge of 2.35 percent plus 20 cents per transaction. The biggest downside is the inability to create or edit your Web pages with Dreamweaver, or any other Web page editor for that matter. This can make it difficult to implement the features and layouts you want for your site, and it can also result in your site appearing less than unique. BigStep.com, FreeMerchant.com, Store.Yahoo.com, and JumboStore.com are four companies that provide these services.

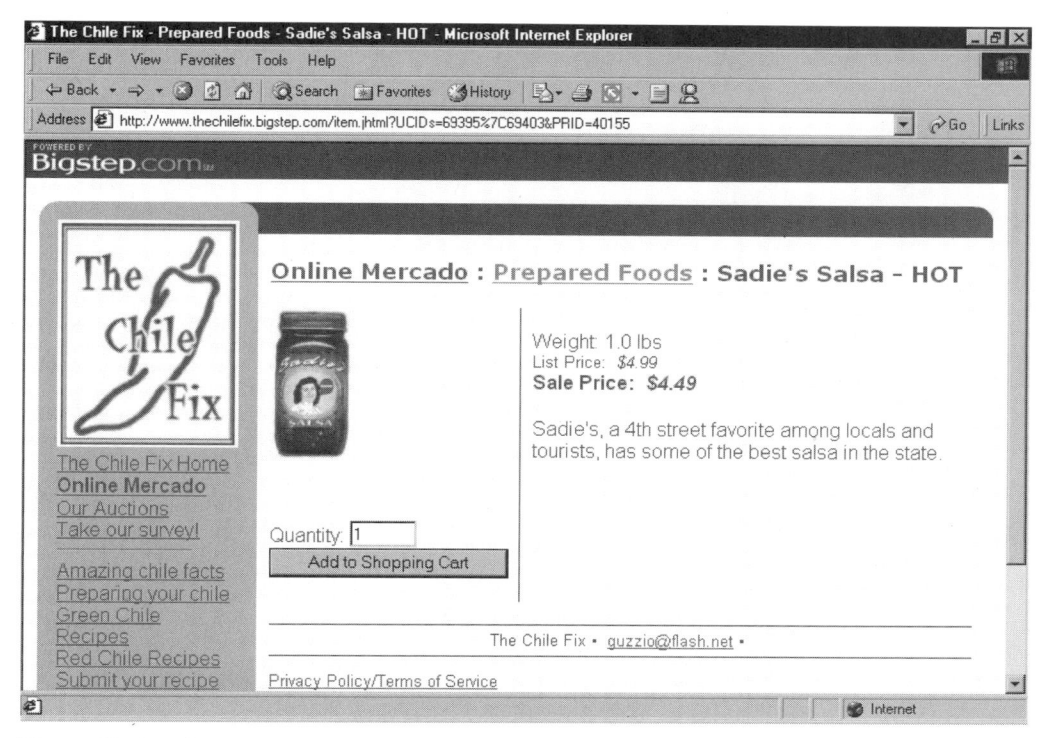

Figure B-5 An e-commerce site created on *www.bigstep.com*.

TIP   *Many e-commerce companies offer free hosting provided that you don't require online credit card processing. If this route is appropriate for your company, consider signing up with one of the services and experimenting with their software and hosting to see whether the service is adequate for you.*

The second route that many companies take when creating an online Web store is to sign up with a Web hosting plan that includes an online shopping cart in the monthly fee. Prices vary widely, but "commerce" hosting plans (or similarly named plans that provide a secure shopping cart for your Web site) can be had for as little as $30 per month. Plans often include many more features than free hosting sites, such as including support for Dreamweaver, more server space, and additional e-mail accounts. A Web site created using this approach is shown in Figure B-6.

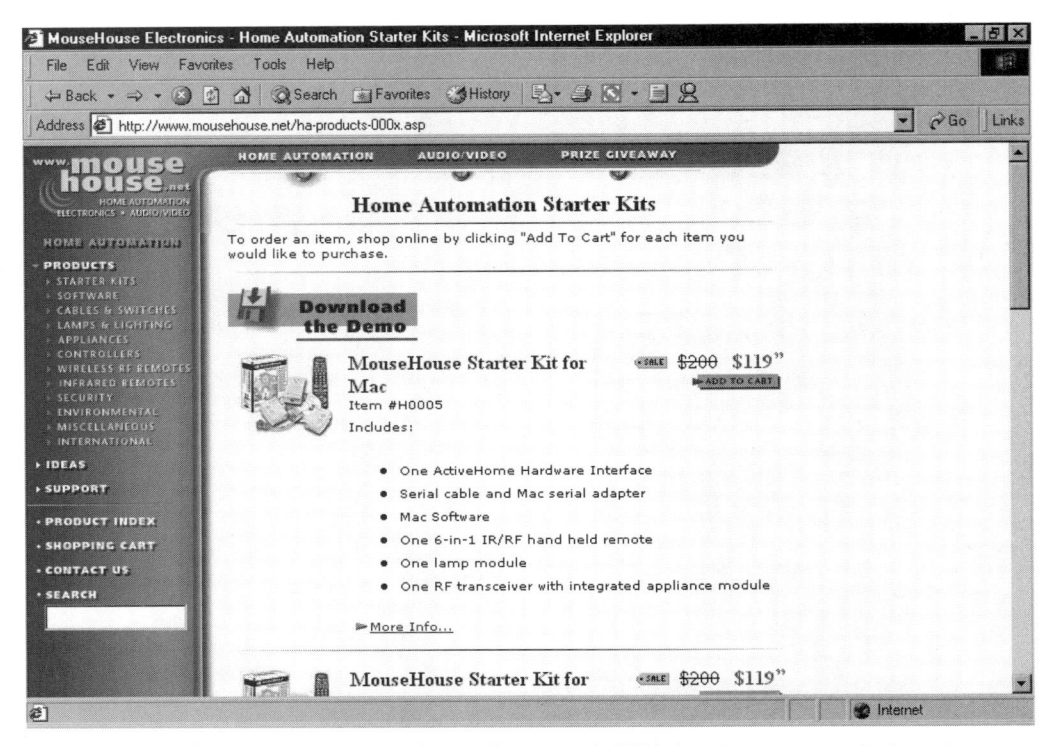

Figure B-6 An e-commerce site that makes use of a Web hosting company's shopping cart.

This approach can be ideal for many businesses, because it allows you to set up an online Web store—complete with online ordering for a low initial cost—and you still have the flexibility to create the site using Dreamweaver. If you want to add online credit card processing at a later time, your Web hosting company will often provide credit card processing for free, but with a large transaction fee (5 percent is typical); or you can get your own Internet Merchant account. However, most businesses will find it more economical to use the shopping cart to collect orders, securely connect to the Web site to view the orders that have been placed (see the previous section), and then process the orders offline using a traditional credit card reader. Forgoing online credit card processing and instead processing credit card orders using a traditional card reader usually results in lower transaction fees as well as lower monthly costs. If your online business grows enough to justify getting an Internet Merchant account, you can do so at a later time.

NOTE *Internet Merchant accounts vary in cost, but 2.39 percent plus 30 cents per transaction, with a $10-per-month bank statement fee and a $25-per-month monthly minimum, is an example of what to expect.*

The last method is to hire a contractor to set up your e-commerce site from scratch. This method usually yields the best results, but it is also typically very expensive. It can cost $10,000 or more depending on what features your company requires. In general, we recommend trying a more cost-effective strategy. If your needs become more sophisticated, you can always hire a contractor later, but it can be ruinous to a small company's financial state to make this kind of an expenditure on a Web site that turns out to be not as profitable as projected.

Appendix C

USING FRAMES

Featuring:

- Creating Frames
- Saving Frames
- Splitting and Deleting Frames
- Hyperlinks and Frames
- Creating a NoFrames Page

Frames are a popular tool for many Webmasters. As is often the case with popular tools, they have been abused and misused enough to earn them a place on more than one list of Web page technologies to avoid. However, when used correctly and sparingly, frames can be an invaluable tool on your Web site.

Frames are a handy way to create independent sections in a Web browser, with each section containing its own page. You can easily use frames to create a navigation page that is always available to visitors at the same location onscreen, as shown in Figure C-1, or to make headers and footers that do not move while visitors scroll and change pages.

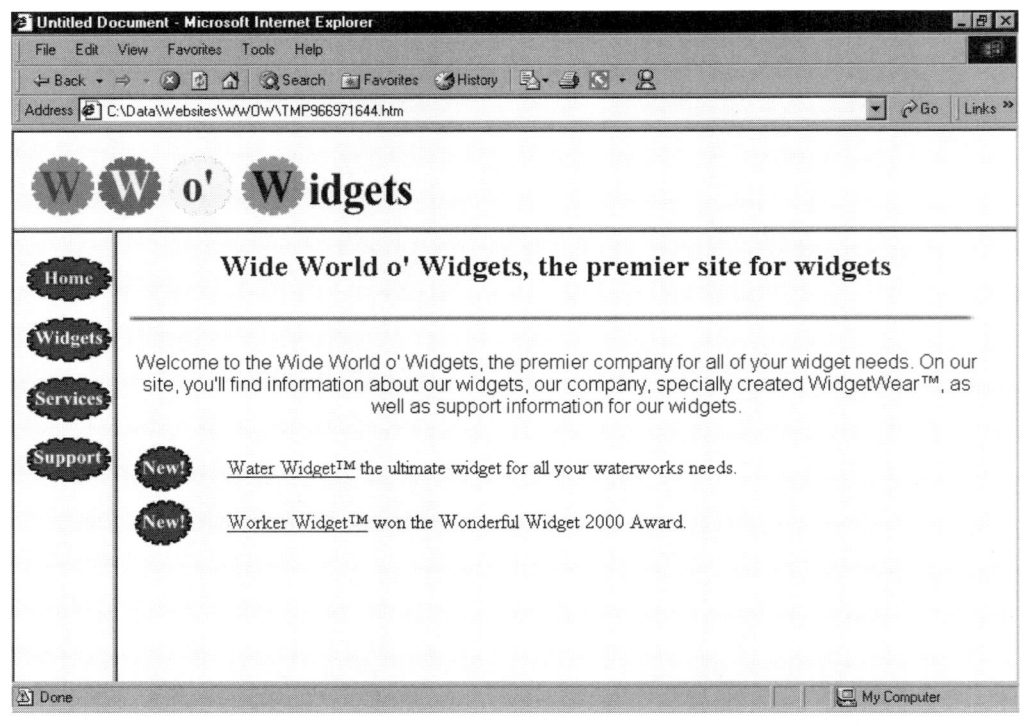

Figure C-1 A Web site using frames.

When you create a frames page, you are actually creating a page that simply points to other pages and contains nothing itself. This page is called the frameset. In this appendix we discuss how to create frames, save pages within frames, split and delete frames, and how to edit a frames page's properties.

Creating Frames

To create a new frames page, follow these steps:

1. Create or open a new page.

Open an existing page you would like to use as the body of your frames page, or create a new page in Dreamweaver.

2. **Insert a frames object.**

   Switch the Objects palette to the Frames category (by clicking the Common heading and choosing Frames from the list), and then click the frame page layout you want to use, as shown in Figure C-2. Note that the blue-colored frame is the frame that will hold the current Web page.

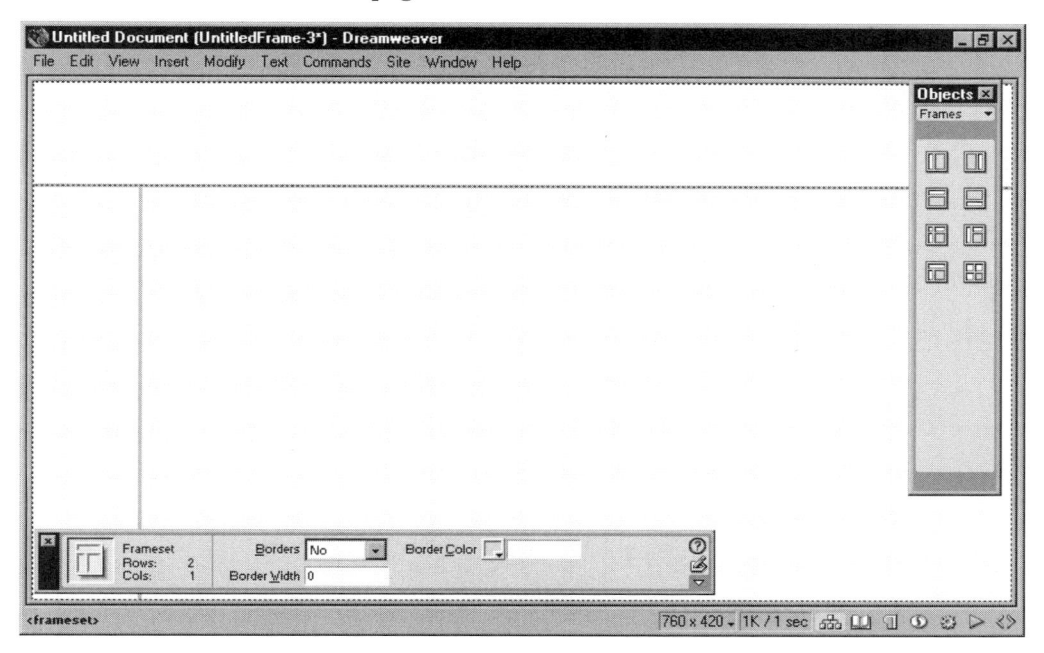

   Figure C-2   Choosing a frame page layout object.

3. **Modify the frameset's borders.**

   When you insert a new frame, the frameset (the page containing each frame) is selected automatically. (If it's not, you can select it by clicking the border around the Web page in Dreamweaver.) In the Property inspector, choose whether to display borders between the frames by selecting No, Yes, or Default from the Borders drop-down list box (choosing Default almost always enables borders). Choose a border color using the Border Color box, and specify the thickness of the border in the Border Width box. (Enter zero to hide the border.)

4. **Specify a page title.**

   The frameset page, despite being only a container for frames, is the page that has its page title displayed in Web browsers. Therefore, you should specify a title by choosing the Modify menu's Page Properties command and entering your page title in the Title box.

5. **Save the frameset.**

   Before you modify your frameset page further, you should save the frameset. To do so, choose the File menu's Save Frameset command, enter a name for the frameset page (the holder of each frame), and click Save.

6. **Select a frame to modify.**

   To modify a particular frame's properties, select it by clicking the frame you want in the Frames palette, as shown in Figure C-3. (You can edit frames as you would a normal Web page, but you need to select a frame to modify the frame's properties.)

   Figure C-3   Selecting a frame.

7. **Create or specify frame pages.**

   Each frame needs to display a different Web page, and you can either modify the blank Web pages inserted when you create the frameset or you can specify an existing page to use. To specify an existing page, select the frame you want to modify and click the folder icon next to the Src box in the Property inspector to locate the Web page, as shown in Figure C-4.

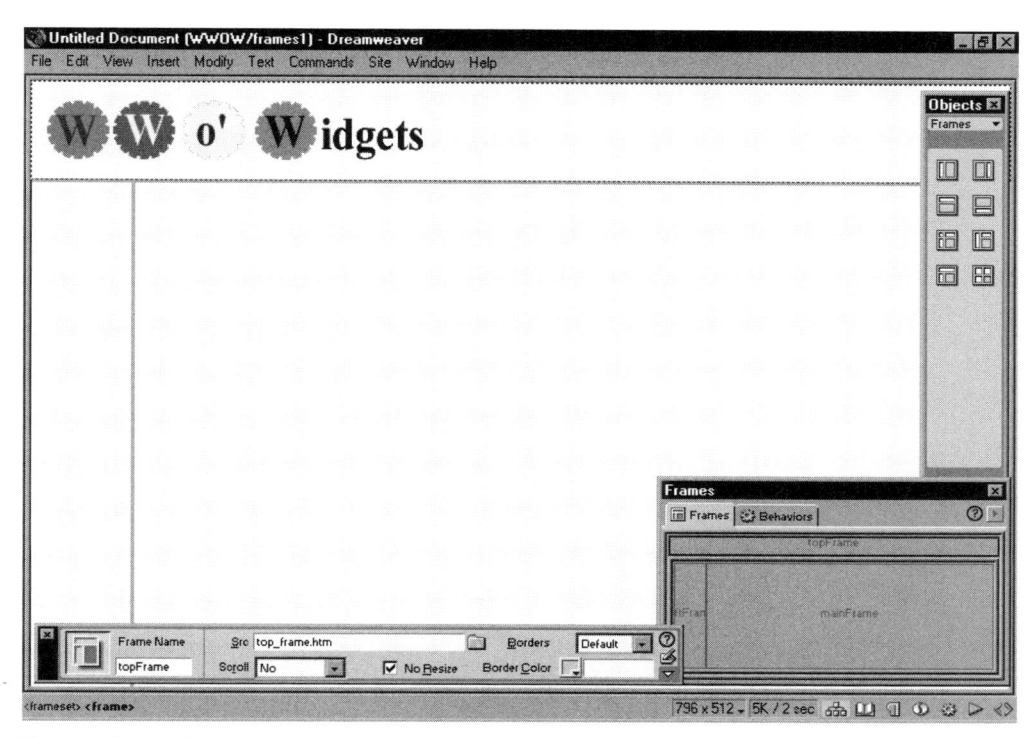

Figure C-4 Specifying what page to use in a frame.

8. **Edit the frame's name.**

   Each frame needs to have its own name so that hyperlinks can target each frame properly. To modify a frame's name, select the frame and then change the name specified in the Frame Name box of the Property inspector.

9. **Adjust the frame size.**

   To change the size of a frame, click and drag the frame border to the size you want, or select the frameset and use the Advanced Properties section of the Property inspector (accessible by clicking the down arrow in the lower right corner of the palette).

   TIP *If you specify frame sizes using the Property inspector, always use absolute (pixel) sizes for navigation frames, headers, and footers. Use the Relative setting for the other frames so that you fill the entire window and maintain resolution independence.*

Appendix C Using Frames **257**

10. **Adjust frame margins.**

    Specify the size of the margins between the frame's contents and the frame border by using the Margin Width and Margin Height sections of the Property inspector (hidden in the Advanced Properties section), as shown in Figure C-5.

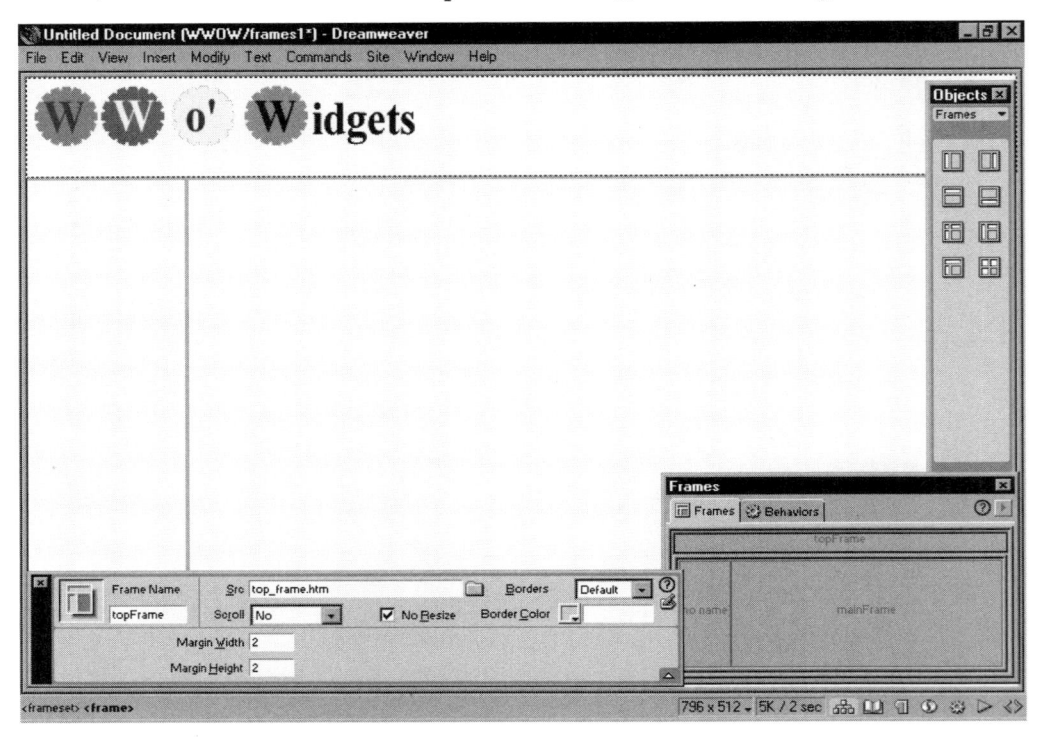

Figure C-5   Modifying the properties of an individual frame.

11. **Specify whether the frame should be resizable.**

    Clear the No Resize check box in the Property inspector if you want to enable visitors to be able to resize the selected frame.

12. **Choose whether to display scrollbars.**

    To always display scrollbars in the selected frame, choose Yes from the Scroll drop-down list box in the Property inspector. To have scrollbars inserted as needed, choose Auto. To never display scrollbars, choose No.

13. **Optionally, modify individual frame borders.**

    You can modify the borders within individual frames by selecting the frame and then using the Borders and Border Color boxes in the Property inspector to override the frameset's border settings. This permits each frame within a frameset (Web page using frames) to have its own unique borders.

Effective Executive's Guide to Dreamweaver Web Sites

Saving Frames

When you use the File menu's Save Frameset command on a frames page, you are saving the frames page only, not the pages contained in your frames. To save a page you have inside of a frame, click inside the frame you want to save and then choose the File menu's Save or Save As command. To save all frames and the frameset at the same time, choose the File menu's Save All command.

Splitting and Deleting Frames

To split a frame into two smaller frames, click in the frame you want to split, choose the Modify menu's Frameset command, and choose Split Frame from the submenu. Alternatively, hold down the Alt key and drag a frame border to the desired size of the new frame—Dreamweaver automatically creates a new frame with the desired dimensions.

To delete a frame, drag the frame's border into the border of its parent frame, or the side of the window such that the frame doesn't have any width or height. Dreamweaver automatically removes the frame from your page.

Hyperlinks and Frames

One of the biggest reasons frames have a bad name in some circles is the improper use of hyperlinks and frames. Without a little care and some testing, hyperlinks in frames can turn your Web site into an unusable mess.

All hyperlinks open by default in the same frame containing the hyperlink. This works well for hyperlinks contained in your main frame, but if you have a navigation bar, pages linked to from the navigation bar end up opening in the navigation bar frame, which certainly isn't ideal. You need to create the hyperlinks to specifically target a different frame—most likely mainFrame.

To create a hyperlink that targets a specific frame, follow these steps:

1. **Select the object from which you want to create a hyperlink.**
2. **Specify the hyperlink.**

    In the Link box of the Property inspector, enter the page to which you want to link, or click the folder icon to browse to the page.

3. **Specify the target frame.**

   Display the Advanced Properties section by clicking the down arrow in the lower right corner of the Property inspector, and then select a frame from the Target drop-down list box, as shown in Figure C-6.

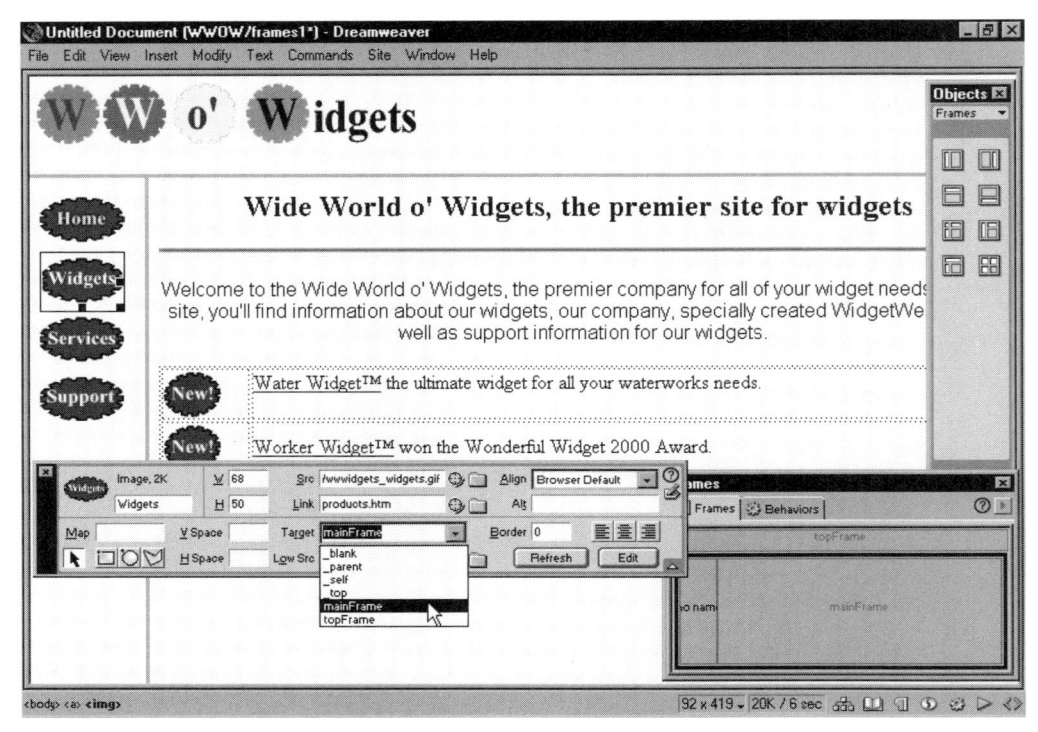

Figure C-6   Targeting a particular frame with a hyperlink.

Table C-1 provides a description of each generic target frame.

TARGET FRAME	WHAT IT DOES
_blank	Opens the link in a new window.
_parent	Opens the link in the parent frameset (if you have nested frames).
_self	Opens the link in the same frame.
_top	Opens the link in the full browser window, eliminating any frames.
_mainFrame	Opens the link in the frame named "mainFrame" (this can be any frame).

Table C-1   The targeting options available for hyperlinks.

TIP *In general, you should always use the _top target for external hyperlinks—hyperlinks to Web sites outside of your own site. You should also be careful not to have links to your frameset page from a navigation bar—instead, link to the main page you're using as your home page.*

Creating a NoFrames Page

Although almost every modern browser supports frames (Netscape Navigator 2 and Microsoft Internet Explorer 3 were the first browsers to support frames), you should still create a page for browsers that don't support frames. There are a couple reasons to do this:

- It makes your site accessible to visitors with really old browsers.
- It makes your site accessible to visitors with text-based browsers or Internet appliances.
- It helps search engines catalog your Web site.

Dreamweaver makes it easy to create a page for frames-incapable browsers—in fact, it does it for you. All you need to do is edit the page, as described in the following steps:

1. **Open the NoFrames page.**

   Choose the Modify menu's Frameset command, and choose Edit NoFrames Content from the submenu. Dreamweaver displays the NoFrames page.

2. **Modify the page.**

   Create your NoFrames page as you would any other Web page, as shown in Figure C-7. We suggest that you limit the page to only text and hyperlinks, to add all important links to it as well as a good description of your Web site. You should also add Keywords and Description meta tags to this page so that search engines can properly index your site (as discussed in "Step 7: Polish Your Pages").

Figure C-7 An example of a simple NoFrames page.

3. Switch back to your frames.

To switch back to editing your frames, choose the Modify menu's Frameset command and deselect Edit NoFrames Content in the submenu. Dreamweaver redisplays your frames.

TIP   *State clearly on the NoFrames page that your Web site requires frames and that this is the frameless/text-only version.*

GLOSSARY

Active Server Pages
Abbreviated ASP. Dynamically created pages from a Microsoft Access or SQL database.

banner ad
A rectangular-shaped advertisement on a Web page.

bookmark
A placeholder within a Web page that allows **hyperlinks** to refer to this location within the Web page. Also known as a **named anchor.**

cable modem
A device that allows computers to access the **Internet** using a cable TV connection. The local cable TV company must enable cable modem access to a home or business in order for a cable **modem** to work.

Cascading Style Sheets
Abbreviated CSS. A standard for applying formatting and positioning information to a Web page. CSS information can be used within a Web page or placed in an external style sheet file. Web pages that are linked to external style sheets obtain text-formatting information from the style sheet.

CGI scripts
A standard for running small programs on a **Web server.** Typically used on Unix Web servers.

chat
A form of real-time communication that typically involves two or more users typing messages to each other.

content folder
A separate folder in which to store content before it is added to a **Web site.**

crawler-based search engine
A **search engine** that automatically "crawls" the Web searching for **Web sites** to examine and include in the search engine's database of Web sites.

discussion group
A part of a **Web site** that emulates **newsgroups,** allowing visitors to post messages and read and reply to other visitors' messages.

DNS
An abbreviation for Domain Name Service. Translates numerical **IP addresses** into user-friendly **domain names,** and vice versa.

domain
A group of computers on a network that all use a central server to handle users and security policies. The server must run either Windows NT Server or Windows 2000 Server.

domain name
The main part of a Web address. Domain names usually represent companies, organizations, or individuals and must be registered with an accredited domain name **registrar.**

DSL
An abbreviation for Digital Subscriber Line. A persistent (always on) high-speed form of **Internet** access that works over standard telephone lines that qualify for DSL service.

e-mail

A form of communication that involves sending mail-like messages across a network (typically the **Internet**).

e-mail account

An **e-mail** address that has its own mailbox, that is, mail isn't forwarded to another account as is the case with **E-mail aliases.**

e-mail alias

An e-mail alias works like a sort of virtual **e-mail** address that forwards received mail to another address.

encryption

The process of scrambling data to prevent unauthorized users from viewing the data.

firewall

A server or device on a network that acts as a barrier between the **Internet** and the local network, protecting the local network from hacking attempts.

floating palette

A small, repositionable window in Dreamweaver containing frequently used tools or settings.

form handler

The software that gathers data from a form. Form handlers are either a part of **FrontPage Server Extensions, CGI Scripts,** or **Active Server Pages**.

frames

An **HTML** feature that permits splitting a Web page into multiple areas (frames) within which separate Web pages are displayed. Not supported by all **Web browsers.**

FrontPage Server Extensions

A set of extensions to **Web servers** that enables Microsoft FrontPage to easily accomplish advanced server-based tasks, such as handling submitted form data.

Glossary

GIF

An abbreviation for Graphics Interchange Format. A file format used most commonly for small graphics on Web pages. Contains a maximum of 256 colors and can be made partially transparent or into a short animation.

home page

Also called a front page. The first page that is displayed on a **Web site,** typically named index.html, index.htm, or Default.htm.

host name

The name of an individual computer on the **Internet** or an **intranet.** It is the leftmost part of a Web address. For example, for the address *wks1.microsoft.com,* the host name is *wks1*.

hotspot

A single region within an **image map** that contains a **hyperlink.**

HTML

An abbreviation for Hypertext Markup Language. The coding language used to create Web pages.

hyperlink

A piece of text or image that when clicked takes the visitor to another page, image, or file.

IIS

An abbreviation for Internet Information Server. A Microsoft **Web server** program that comes with Windows NT and Windows 2000.

image map

An image that contains multiple hyperlinks—each corresponding to a different region or **hotspot** of the image.

Instant Messaging

A form of communication that is roughly a cross between **chat** and telephone. Users run an Instant Messaging program that notifies them when people they know are online. Users can then conduct a text-based "conversation."

Internet

A worldwide computer network running the TCP/IP protocol suite and consisting of hundreds of millions of computers.

Internet Merchant account

An account with a bank or financial institution for the purpose of processing online credit card transactions.

Internet service provider

Abbreviated ISP. A company that provides access to the **Internet** via dial-up connections, **DSL**, leased lines, or other connection methods.

intranet

A private network that uses **Internet** technology—the TCP/IP protocol suite and **Web servers**.

IP address

The unique address for a single network card on a network using TCP/IP. All computers (hosts) on the Internet or an **intranet** must have an IP address to communicate.

ISDN

An abbreviation for Integrated Services Digital Network. A form of moderately high-speed **Internet** connection, ISDN uses one or two telephone lines that are configured for ISDN service and provides a typical maximum of 128Kbps when both lines are used.

JPEG

An abbreviation for Joint Photographic Experts Group. A file format used for photos and other high-quality images on Web pages. Uses image compression to reduce file size.

keyword

A word placed in a Web page using a **meta tag** to allow **search engines** to recognize that the Web page contains content related to the keyword.

local area network
Abbreviated LAN. A group of computers that are all located within the same local area (typically one building) and that can communicate with each other.

mailing list
A list to which users can subscribe that allows them to receive **e-mail** messages on a particular topic sent by a company or organization.

meta tags
Also known as meta variables. Meta tags store information about a **Web site,** such as a description and **keywords. Crawler-based search engines** often use these tags to determine when to display a site in a list of search results, as well as what description to display.

modem
An analog device that allows a computer to communicate with other computers over standard telephone lines. Capable of a maximum of 53Kbps download rate.

multiprocessing
Using more than one processor in a single computer. Each processor can work independently, making multiprocessing-aware applications faster.

named anchor
A tag that you can place in a specific location within a Web page that serves as the destination for in-page **hyperlinks.** Creating a hyperlink to a named anchor allows a user to quickly scroll a long page to a particular location.

navigation bars
A series of buttons or **hyperlinks** that help visitors quickly access the most important pages on a **Web site.**

newsgroups
Electronic bulletin boards on the **Internet** where people can post messages, read other users' posts, and reply to them.

page banner
An automatically created heading that displays the title of the Web page.

permissions
The level of access given to a user or group for a particular file or folder.

pixel
A single dot on a computer screen. Everything displayed on a computer monitor is made up of pixels. Common screen resolutions are 640x480 or 800x600—800 pixels wide and 600 pixels high.

PNG
An abbreviation for Portable Network Graphic. A newer file format designed for high-quality images with optional transparency. Not supported by all **Web browsers**.

Property inspector
A Dreamweaver **floating palette** that displays the properties for the selected object.

proxy server
A network server that sits in between the local network and the Internet, protecting the local network from attacks as well as caching Web pages to improve Web-browsing performance for local clients. A type of **firewall**.

RAID
An abbreviation for Redundant Array of Independent Disks. A collection of hard drives that is treated as one drive by the operating system and usually provides extra speed and reliability.

registrar
A company that is permitted to sell Internet **domain names**.

search engine
A program contained on a **Web site** that allows visitors to search for Web pages on the **Internet**.

Glossary

shortcut menu

The menu that is displayed when you right-click an item on the screen. Also called a context-sensitive menu.

SSL

An abbreviation for Secure Sockets Layer. A way of **encrypting** data that is transferred to and from a **Web site** and is typically used for **Web stores** that process credit card transactions.

status bar

The bar that runs across the bottom of a window displaying the status of the current selection. In Dreamweaver, the status bar also contains useful tools such as the Tag selector and the Mini-Launcher.

subdomain

A **domain** that is a child of another domain. For example, *support.microsoft.com* is a subdomain of *microsoft.com*.

table

A formatting tool that enables text and images to be placed in a grid. Tables are extremely useful for creating advanced layouts on Web pages.

tag

The building block of an **HTML** document. It begins with a right angle bracket (<) and ends with a left angle bracket (>).

Tag selector

The leftmost part of Dreamweaver's **status bar.** Clicking a **tag** in the Tag selector selects the portion of the Web page within that particular tag.

template

A Web page that acts as a starting point for new Web pages. Any content or formatting information on a template is automatically applied to new pages created with the template, streamlining the process of making pages.

thumbnail image
A small version of an image that is **hyperlinked** to the full-size version.

top-level domain
The highest level (rightmost) part of a **domain name,** for example, .com, .net, or .org.

underscore
The "_" character. It is often used to represent a space in filenames on the **Internet** because it is compatible with both the Windows naming scheme and the Unix naming scheme.

UPS
An abbreviation for Uninterruptible Power Supply. A battery backup for a computer, or occasionally, a backup generator that ensures that a computer can continue operating, or at least shut down properly, in the event of a power failure.

URL
An abbreviation for Uniform Resource Locator. An address for a file, usually on the **Internet**.

virtual domains
The ability to make a single computer host multiple **domain names.** When discussing **Web hosting** plans, virtual domain support means that you can use your own **domain name.**

Web browser
A program used to display Web pages.

Web hosting
To store a **Web site** and make it available for others to view on the **Internet.**

Web ring
A collection of **Web sites** that all cover the same topic and that post a Web ring **banner ad** on their sites, allowing visitors to easily view other sites in the Web ring.

Index

A

absolute hyperlink addresses, 16
Active Server Pages, 56, 263
ActiveX, 18
Add Browser dialog box, 221
addresses, hyperlink, 15–17
Adobe Photoshop, 86
advertising
    affiliated, 34
    banner-type, 33, 230
    carrying for others, 33–34
    by companies and organizations, 26–28
    generating revenue from, 33–34
    offline, 234
    online, 229–31
    as reason to have Web site, 19, 26
    to sell products and services, 29–31
    using link exchanges, 230–31
    the Web site itself, 28, 229–31, 234
    what content to include, 26–28
aesthetics of Web sites, 23, 176–77
affiliated advertising, 34
aliases, 57, 240, 247, 265
aligning
    tables, 192
    text adjacent to images, 160–62, 185
AltaVista, 229
alternative home pages, 199–202
Amazon.com Web site, 21
angle brackets (<>), in HTML code, 11
AOL Instant Messenger, 9
AOL Search, 229
appliances, information, 218
ArtToday Web site, 36–37
Ask Jeeves, 226
.asp files, 83
Asus's Web site, 29–30
<a> tag, 13

B

background, Web page, changing, 165–66, 194
banner ads, 33, 230, 263
Barnes and Noble Web site, 51
BigStep.com, 248, 249
.bmp files, 83
<body> tag, 13, 14
bookmarks, 26. *See also* named anchors
borders
    adding to Web page images, 162
    specifying thickness in tables, 193–94
broken hyperlinks, 212–17
browsers. *See* Web browsers

 tag, 14, 149
bulletin board analogy, 45–46
buttons. *See* navigation bars

C

cable modems, 4, 5, 263
cameras, digital, 89–90
cascading style sheets (CSS), 18, 44, 145, 150, 263. *See also* layers, CSS
catalogs, online, 29–31, 242, 244, 245
CDs, pictures on, 91–93
cells, table, specifying properties, 194–96
CGI scripts, 18, 56, 245, 264
Change Link Sitewide dialog box, 215
chat, 9, 264
chat-based customer support, 40–41
Check Browser dialog box, 201, 202
checking. *See* testing
checking files in and out, 122–25, 237
Check Target Browsers dialog box, 197
closing
    floating palettes, 133
    Web pages in Dreamweaver, 139
code. *See* HTML code
colors, Web page, changing, 165–66, 167
columns, table, adding, 193
Commands menu, 138
comments. *See* Design Notes
company logos, 176
compatibility, Web browser, 196–99
Computer Management tool, 239
.com top-level domain, 52
content, Web site. *See also* digital content; images; text
    advertising-related, 26–31
    charging visitors for access, 35–37
    choosing home page content, 170–71
    collecting what exists, 77–82
    contact information, 28, 39
    converting to other file formats, 83–87
    creating new documents, 96
    creating site plan for, 98–99
    creating staging area location for files, 73–76
    current activities, 27
    curriculum-related information, 41–43
    developing a strategy, 25–46
    digital, 77–99
    for disseminating information, 31–33
    financial information, 27–28
    frequently asked question (FAQ) lists, 38
    importance of, 21–22
    importing, 83–87, 142–48
    location and direction information, 27
    methodologies for developing, 45–46
    offering subscriptions to, 36–37
    online catalogs, 29–31, 242, 244, 245
    online discussion groups, 39–40
    organizing, 97–98
    planning, 25–46, 72
    printed documents, 95–96
    product support information, 31, 37–41
    school-related information, 41–43
    selling content online, 35–37
    showcasing companies and organizations, 26–28
    showcasing products and services, 29–31
    static vs. dynamic, 21–22
content folder, 73, 80, 82, 264
converting
    layers to tables, 202–6
    tables to layers, 185, 202
    Web content to other file formats, 83–87
copying files between folders, 80, 82, 118
crawler-based search engines, 226, 227, 264
credit cards, 245, 246, 250
.css files, 83. *See also* cascading style sheets (CSS)

D

databases, 56
deleting
    frames, 259
    Web pages, 119–20
description objects, 178, 227
Design Notes, 120–22
digital cameras, 89–90
digital content
    charging for, 35–37
    collecting, 77–82

converting to other file formats, 83–87
creating, 88–96
searching for files, 80–82
types of, 77–78
digital images
    creating, 88–95
    dots per inch, 88–89
    overview, 88–89
    printing, 88–89
    resolution issues, 88–89
Digital Subscriber Line (DSL) service, 3–4, 5, 264
Direct Hit, 229
discussion groups, online. *See also* mailing lists
    chat-based, 40–41
    glossary definition, 264
    overview, 39–40
disseminating information. *See also* content, Web site
    charging for content, 35–37
    reasons to share, 31–33
<div> tag, 14, 185, 186, 188
DN Resources Web site, 63
DNS (Domain Name Service), 48–49, 264
document-relative hyperlink addresses, 16–17
Document window
    defined, 101
    floating palettes feature, 132–33
    overview, 128–29
    resizing, 130–31
    status bar, 129–32
    Tag selector, 13, 14, 129–30
    Window Size pop-up menu, 130–31
domain hosting, defined, 56. *See also* Web hosting services
domain names
    aftermarket, 53
    background information, 48–50
    checking for availability, 52–53
    disputes over, 54
    glossary definition, 264
    hierarchy of, 49–50
    importance of, 50–51
    multiple, 52
    purchasing, 53, 55
    registering, 55, 65–66
    rules for, 53–54
    selecting, 51–54
    transferring, 67–69
    and Web hosting services, 55, 65–66
Domain Name Service (DNS), 48–49, 264
domains, 49, 50, 52, 264
downloading Web pages, 131–32
Draw Layer objects, 185, 186, 188
Dreamweaver
    adjusting Web page properties, 165–67
    checking files in and out, 122–25, 237
    closing Web pages, 139
    configuring to work with firewalls, 105–7
    creating image maps, 163–65
    creating new Web pages using New command, 140
    defining new local sites, 102–5
    Document window overview, 101, 128–29
    entering local site information, 102–3
    and forms, 20, 134, 245–48
    importing Web content, 83–87, 142–48
    interface overview, 127–38
    menus, 129, 138
    opening browser from, 141
    opening local sites, 107
    opening Web pages, 139
    optimizing images in, 86–87
    previewing Web pages, 141, 217–20
    reasons for using, 2
    saving Web pages, 140–41
    Site window overview, 101, 107, 108–9
    specifying Web server type, 103–4
    starting, 102
    status bars, 108, 113, 129–32
    Tag selector, 13–14
    using digital content in, 83–87
    and Web hosting, 56
DSL. *See* Digital Subscriber Line (DSL) service
Dynamic HTML (DHTML), 18, 44
dynamic Web site content, 21–22

Index   **275**

E

e-commerce. *See* Web stores
Edit menu, 138
eGroups, 233
e-mail
    alias availability, 57, 265
    glossary definition, 265
    overview, 6–7
    setting up accounts, 69, 265
    ways to access accounts, 58
    Web hosting service accounts, 57–58
encryption, 246, 265
entering text, 149–50. *See also* importing
Excite, 229

F

favorites rule, 26
Federal Express Web site, 31
file formats, converting, 83–87
File menu, 138
files. *See also* Web pages
    adding Design Notes, 120–22
    checking in and out, 122–25, 237
    copying between folders, 80, 82, 118
    deleting from Web sites, 119–20
    managing in Site window, 108–9
    opening using Site window, 109
    rules for naming, 76–77
    searching for, 80–82
    sorting in Site window, 109
    viewing list in Site window, 107
finding files, 80–82
firewalls, 105–7, 265
Fireworks program, 86
Flash program, 18, 44
floating palettes. *See also* Property inspector
    closing, 133
    displaying, 132
    glossary definition, 265
    History palette, 136–37
    Library palette, 136
    and Mini-Launcher, 132
    moving, 132–33
    Objects palette, 133–35
    overview, 132–33
    resizing, 133
    tabbed, 133
    vs. toolbars, 129
folders
    content, 73, 80, 82, 264
    copying files between, 80, 82, 118
    creating, 75–76
    deleting from Web sites, 119–20
formatting text, 149–50
form handlers, 265
forms
    adding to Web pages, 134
    for collecting orders, 245–48
    and Dreamweaver, 20
Frame relay, 5
frames
    adding to Web pages, 134
    creating, 254–58
    creating NoFrames alternative, 261–62
    deleting, 259
    glossary definition, 265
    and hyperlinks, 259–61
    relative merit, 44
    saving, 256, 259
    splitting, 259
    when to use, 253–54
FreeMerchant.com, 248
frequently asked question (FAQ) lists, offering online, 38
FrontPage 2000, 245, 246, 247
FrontPage Server Extensions, 56–57, 61, 245, 265
FTP (File Transfer Protocol), 103, 104, 106, 107, 224

G

.gif files, 85, 86, 176, 184, 266
goal-setting, for Web site development, 43–44
Go/Infoseek, 229
Google, 229
graphic images. *See* images

H

Help menu, 138
hidden data, adding to Web pages, 134
History palette, 136–37
home pages
    alternative, 199–202
    choosing content, 170–71
    creating, 170–83
    glossary definition, 266
    preparing for search engines, 177–78
    specifying in Site Definition dialog box, 104
    for visitors with older browsers, 199–202
    visual appeal, 176–77
horizontal rules, 157
hosting. *See* Web hosting services
host names, 49–50, 266
HotBot, 229
hotspots, 164, 266
.htm files, 83
HTML code
    exporting documents, 84
    glossary definition, 266
    importing documents from Word, 143–45
    importing HTML files, 142–45
    meta tags, 13, 177–78
    newer technologies, 18
    overview, 11–13
    relative merit, 44
.html files, 83
<html> tag, 11
.htx files, 83
hyperlinks
    absolute addresses, 16
    changing in Site Map, 116–17
    changing using Site menu, 215–17
    checking, 212–14
    creating for image maps, 164
    creating in Site Map, 115–16
    creating links to Web pages, 151–52
    creating to e-mail addresses, 152
    creating within Web pages, 153–54
    document-relative addresses, 16–17
    and frames, 259–61
    glossary definition, 266
    how URLs work, 7, 12–13
    opening links in different window, 154–55
    replacing, 215–17
    site-root relative addresses, 17
    types of addresses, 15–17
    viewing in Site Map, 114–18
Hypertext Markup Language (HTML). *See* HTML code

I

ICQ, 9
IIS. *See* Internet Information Server (IIS)
image buttons, creating, 171–72
image editors, 86
image maps, 163–65, 266
images. *See also* photos
    adding borders to, 162
    adding to Web pages, 133, 134, 155–58
    adjusting layout, 160–62
    adjusting spacing, 161–62
    aligning adjacent text, 160–62, 185
    avoiding large sizes, 87, 163
    digital, 88–95
    importing, 85–87
    low-resolution, 163
    printing, 88–89
    for products and services, 30
    representing with text, 162–63
    resizing, 158–60
    resolution issues, 88–89, 163
    scanning, 88, 89, 90–91
    text-based descriptions, 162–63
    transmission times, 5–6
    transparent, 86
    when to use thumbnails, 87, 163
IMAP, 58
<img> tag, 12, 15

importing
    HTML files, 142–45
    images, 85–87
    plain text, 145–47
    spreadsheets, 85, 147–48
    tables, 85, 147–48
    Web content, 83–87
    Word documents, 143–45
index.htm, as home page name, 104, 170
\Inetpub folder, 238
information, disseminating. *See also* content, Web site
    charging for content, 35–37
    reasons to share, 31–33
information appliances, 218
information collection, as reason to have Web site, 19–20
Insert menu, 138
instant messaging, 9–10, 266
Integrated Services Digital Network (ISDN), 4, 5, 267
Internal Revenue Service Web site, 31–32
Internet. *See also* World Wide Web
    connecting from Site window, 109
    defined, 3, 267
    methods of communication, 6–10
    telephone software packages, 10
    ways to connect to, 3–5
Internet Explorer. *See also* Web browsers
    opening from Dreamweaver, 141, 217, 218
Internet Information Server (IIS), 237, 238, 266
Internet Merchant accounts, 250–51, 267
Internet service providers (ISPs), 3, 267
intranets, 103, 267
IP addresses, 48, 267
IRS Web site, 31–32
ISDN. *See* Integrated Services Digital Network (ISDN)

J

Java, 18, 44
Javascript, 18, 44
JPEG file format, 86, 267

.jpeg files, 85
.jpg files, 85
JumboStore.com, 248

K

KB (kilobytes), 3
Kbps (kilobits), 3
keywords, 177–78, 227, 267
knowledge bases, creating, 38–39
Kodak Picture CD, 91, 92–93

L

Launcher palette, 132
Layer palette, 185
layers, CSS
    absolutely positioned, 185, 188
    adjusting visibility, 190
    converting tables to, 185, 202
    converting to tables, 202–6
    creating, 185–87
    drawing, 185–86
    how they work, 188
    how to position, 188–89
    inserting, 186
    moving, 189
    nested, 204
    overlapping, 190, 204
    overview, 184
    relatively positioned, 186–87
    relative merit, 44
    resizing, 188–89
    uses for, 184–85
leased lines, 5
Library, 136, 182–83
line breaks, 149
lines. *See* borders
link exchanges, 230–31
links. *See* hyperlinks
Listbot, 233
list servers, 58, 233
local area networks, 268

local root folder, 73, 102. *See also* content folder
local sites
    creating, 102–5
    defined, 102
    opening, 107
    placing on local servers, 237–40
    switching between, 107
Locate A Web Presence Provider Web site, 63–64
logos, 176
LookSmart, 229
low-resolution images, 163
Lycos, 229

M

Macintosh, 218
Macromedia Dreamweaver. *See* Dreamweaver
Macromedia Fireworks, 86
Macromedia Flash, 18, 44
mailing lists
    creating, 232–33
    as form of advertising, 232–33
    glossary definition, 268
    Web host support for, 58
majordomos, 58, 233
Mamma.com, 226
mapping. *See* Site Map
margins, Web page, 166
MB (megabytes), 3
menu bar, Site window, 108
menus, Dreamweaver, 129, 138
meta-search engines, 226
meta tags, 13, 177–78, 227, 268
Microsoft FrontPage 2000, 245, 246, 247
Microsoft FrontPage Server Extensions, 56–57, 61, 245, 265
Microsoft Knowledge Base, 38
Microsoft Locate A Web Presence Provider Web site, 63–64
Microsoft PhotoDraw, 86
Microsoft Product Support Services Web site, 38, 39

Microsoft Word files, importing into Dreamweaver, 143–45
Mini-Launcher, 132
modems, 3, 4, 5, 268
Modify menu, 138
moving
    floating palettes, 132–33
    Web pages, 118
MSN Messenger, 9, 10
MSN Search, 229
multiprocessing, 268

N

named anchors, 153–54, 268
naming files, 76–77
navigating Web sites, 22
navigation bars
    defined, 171, 268
    image buttons for, 171–72
    inserting objects, 172, 173–74
    modifying, 175–76
    rollover buttons for, 172–75
Netscape Navigator, 26, 187, 217, 218, 219. *See also* Web browsers
Netscape Search, 229
.net top-level domain, 52
Network Solutions, 55, 66
new folders, creating, 75–76
newsgroups, 8–9, 232, 268
NoFrames pages, 261–62
Northern Light, 229
notes. *See* Design Notes
NTFS file system, 239

O

objects
    adding to Library, 136
    adding to Web pages, 133–35
Objects palette, 133–35
OCR programs, 95, 96
offline advertising, 234

Index   **279**

older Web browsers
    alternative home pages for, 199–202
    converting layers to tables for, 202–6
    testing Web sites in, 218
online advertising, 229–31
online catalogs, 29–31, 242, 244, 245
online discussion groups. *See* discussion groups, online; mailing lists
online photo services, 94–95
online shopping. *See* Web stores
Open Directory, 229
opening
    floating palettes, 132
    Site window, 223
    Web pages in Dreamweaver, 139
Opera (Web browser), 217, 218, 219
order forms, 245–48
ordering information, 30–31
.org top-level domain, 52
.otm files, 83

P

\<p\> tag, 11, 15
page banners, 269
pages. *See* Web pages
palettes. *See* floating palettes
passwords, 66, 240
permissions, 240, 269
Personal Web Server, 237
PhotoDraw, 86
photos. *See also* images
    from digital cameras, 89–90
    and online photo services, 94–95
    and picture CDs, 91–93
    scanning, 88, 89, 90–91
    transmission times, 5–6
Photoshop, 86
PhotoWorks.com Web site, 94
picture CDs, 91–93
pictures. *See* images; photos
pixels, 88, 89, 269

plain text, importing, 145–47
.png files, 85, 269
POP servers, 58
PowerPoint, exporting presentations to Web pages, 83–84
Preferences dialog box, 105–6, 221
Preview In Browser list, 220–22
previewing
    screen resolution, 208
    Web pages, 141, 217–20
print documents, 95–96
product manuals, 41
products
    advertising on Web sites, 29–31
    offering support online, 31, 37–41
properties, adjusting for Web pages, 165–67
Property inspector, 135, 149–50, 192, 193, 269
proxy servers, 105, 106, 269
publicizing Web sites, 225–34
publishing, as reason to have Web site, 19
publishing Web sites to Web hosting services, 223–25

R

RAID (Redundant Array of Independent Disks), 74, 269
redoing actions, 136–37
registrars, domain name, 55, 269
removing. *See* deleting
renaming Web pages, 119
repeating actions, 136–37
resizing
    Document window, 130–31
    floating palettes, 133
    images, 158–60
resolution-independent Web pages, 206–9. *See also* screen resolution
rollover buttons, creating, 172–75
root, viewing in Site Map, 113–14
root folder, 73, 102. *See also* content folder
rows, table, adding, 193
rules, creating for naming files, 76–77

280   *Effective Executive's Guide to Dreamweaver Web Sites*

S

saving
   frames, 256, 259
   Site Map views, 117–18
   Web pages in Dreamweaver, 140–41
scanning images, 88, 89, 90–91
screen resolution
   and Document window size, 130–31
   and dots per inch, 88–89
   making Web pages resolution-independent, 206–9
   previewing, 208
   tips for effective Web pages, 209
search engines
   crawler-based, 226, 227
   directory-style, 226, 228
   glossary definition, 269
   list of sites, 229
   overview, 226–27
   preparing home pages for, 177–78
   submitting Web sites, 226–29
   types of, 226
searching for files, 80–82
Secure Sockets Layer (SSL) security, 59
security issues
   NTFS file system, 239
   and online orders, 245–48
   passwords, 66
Select File dialog box, 201
Select New Link dialog box, 215–16
services, advertising on Web sites, 29–31
Shockwave, 18, 44
shopping carts, online, 243, 244, 248–51. *See also* Web stores
shortcut menus, 129, 270
.shtm files, 83
.shtml files, 83
Site Definition dialog box, 102–5, 106
Site Map
   changing existing links, 116–17
   creating new links, 115–16
   creating new pages linked to existing pages, 110–12
   displaying, 111
   overview, 113–14
   saving as graphic, 117–18
   switching to Site Files view, 109
   uses for, 114
   viewing links, 113–14
Site menu, 138
site-root relative hyperlink addresses, 17
Site window
   copying Web pages, 118
   defined, 101
   deleting Web pages, 119–20
   vs. Document window, 101
   hiding left pane, 108
   moving Web pages, 118
   opening, 223
   overview, 108–9
   renaming Web pages, 119
   switching sites in, 107
   uses for, 109
sizing Document window, 130–31
Snap, 229
sorting files in Site window, 109
Space Imaging Web site, 35
special characters, adding to Web pages, 133, 134, 137
spreadsheets, importing content, 85, 147–48
SSL security, 59, 270
static Web site content, 22
statistics, monitoring, 234–36
status bars
   Document window, 129–32
   glossary definition, 270
   Site Map view, 113
   Site window, 108
.stm files, 83
stores. *See* Web stores
Store.Yahoo.com, 248
subdomain names, 49–50
subdomains, 58, 270
support, product, 31, 37–41
synchronizing files, 224–25

Index   **281**

T

T1 connections, 60
tabbed palettes, 133
tables
   adding background color, 194
   adding rows and columns, 193
   adding to Web pages using Objects palette, 133, 134
   aligning, 192
   cell padding and spacing, 192
   converting layers to, 202–6
   converting to layers, 185, 202
   creating, 191–92
   glossary definition, 270
   importing, 85, 147–48
   modifying properties, 192–94
   overview, 191
   relative merit, 44
   specifying border thickness, 193–94
   specifying cell properties, 194–96
   specifying width and height, 193
tags, HTML
   glossary definition, 270
   list of, 14–15
   overview, 11–13
Tag selector, 13, 14, 129–30, 270
telephones, communicating via Internet, 10
templates
   creating, 179–81
   creating Web pages from, 181–82
   defined, 179
   glossary definition, 270
   modifying, 182
testing Web sites
   checking hyperlinks, 212–14
   in different browsers, 217–22
   overview, 212
   for usability, 222–23
text
   entering, 149–50
   formatting, 149–50
   importing HTML files, 142–45
   importing Word documents, 143–45
   plain, importing, 145–47
text files, importing, 145–47
Text menu, 138
thumbnail images, 87, 163, 271
<title> tag, 13
toolbar, Site window, 108. *See also* floating palettes
top-level domains, 49–50, 52–53, 271
traffic statistics, 234–36
transaction processing, as reason to have Web site, 20
transferring files, 224–25
transparent images, 86, 184
.txt files, 83

U

underscore character, 271
undoing actions, 136–37
Update Files dialog box, 216
UPS (Uninterruptible Power Supply), 271
UPS (United Parcel Service) Web site, 31
URLs (Uniform Resource Locators)
   glossary definition, 271
   how they work, 7, 12–13
U.S. Internal Revenue Service Web site, 31–32
usability testing, 222–23

V

View menu, 138
Virtual Directory Creation Wizard, 239–40
virtual domains, 56, 271

W

Web browsers
   adding to Preview In Browser list, 220–22
   compatibility of Web pages, 196–206
   deleting from Preview in Browser list, 222
   glossary definition, 271
   older, 199–206, 218
   opening from Dreamweaver, 141
   role of, 7
   testing Web sites, 217–22

WebCrawler, 229
Web hosting services
   Active Server Pages support, 56
   assessing Web server reliability, 61
   assessing Web server speed, 60–61
   choosing, 55–64
   comparing features, 56–61
   database support, 56
   data transfer limitations, 59
   disk space allotment, 57
   domain hosting support, 56
   and domain names, 55, 65–66
   e-mail accounts, 57–58
   glossary definition, 271
   local vs. national, 62
   mailing list support, 58
   and online stores, 245, 248, 249–50
   publishing Web sites to, 223–25
   signing up for service, 64–69
   and SSL security, 59
   subdomain support, 58
   support for FrontPage 2000 Server Extensions, 56–57, 61
   technical support, 59
   virtual domain support, 56
   where to find, 62–64
Web pages. *See also* content, Web site; home pages; Web sites
   adding Design Notes to, 120–22
   adding hyperlinks to, 151–55
   adding images to, 155–60
   adding objects to, 133–35
   adding text to, 141–50
   adding to Web sites, 110–12
   adjusting page properties, 165–67
   and browser compatibility, 196–206
   changing colors and backgrounds, 165–66, 167
   changing margins, 166
   checking in and out, 122–25
   closing in Dreamweaver, 139
   copying, 118
   creating home pages, 170–83
   creating image maps for, 163–65
   creating in Dreamweaver using New command, 140
   creating site plan for, 98–99
   creating templates for, 179–82
   defined, 7
   deleting, 119–20
   different versions for older browsers, 199–202
   ensuring proper display, 196–206
   how they work, 10–11
   moving, 118
   opening in Dreamweaver, 139
   previewing from Dreamweaver, 141, 217–20
   renaming, 119
   saving in Dreamweaver, 140–41
   and screen resolution, 206–9
   time to download, 131–32
Web rings, 230–31, 271
Web servers. *See also* Web hosting services
   assessing reliability, 61
   assessing speed, 60–61
   making Web sites available on, 237–40
   role in how Web works, 7
   role in Web stores, 244
   specifying type in Dreamweaver, 103–4
Web sites. *See also* content, Web site; Web pages
   adding Web pages, 110–12
   advertising of, 28, 229–31, 234
   changing address, 51
   copying Web pages, 118
   creating plans for, 98–99
   creating structure in Dreamweaver, 110–14
   creating templates for pages, 179–82
   critiquing, 21–23
   defined, 7
   deleting Web pages, 119–20
   determining goals, 43–44
   effectiveness of, 21–23
   importance of useful content, 21–22
   making available on local servers, 237–40

Web sites *continued*
   methodologies for developing content, 45–46
   monitoring, 234–36
   moving Web pages, 118
   navigating, 22
   obtaining traffic statistics, 234–36
   organizing content, 97–98
   publicizing, 225–34
   publishing, 223–25
   reasons for having, 19–21
   renaming Web pages, 119
   role of aesthetic appeal, 23, 176–77
   submitting to search engines, 226–29
   testing, 212–23
Web stores
   how they work, 241–44
   non-interactive catalogs, 244, 245
   overview, 241
   role of Web servers, 244
   shopping cart setup options, 248–51
   types of setups, 244
   using order forms to collect orders, 245–48
WebTV, 218
Window menu, 138
Windows 2000 Server, 61, 237
Window Size pop-up menu, 130–31
Windows NT, 61
wireless Internet access, 5
wizards. *See* Virtual Directory Creation Wizard
World Book Web site, 36
World Wide Web, 7–8. *See also* Web sites

X

XML (Extended Markup Language), 18

Y

Yahoo!, 33–34, 226, 228, 229, 248

Z

Z-Index, 188, 190

The manuscript for this book was prepared and submitted to Redmond Technology Press in electronic form. Text files were prepared using Microsoft Word 2000. Pages were composed using PageMaker 6.5 for Windows, with text in Frutiger and Caslon. Composed files were delivered to the printer as electronic prepress files.

Interior Design

Stefan Knorr

Project Editor

Paula Thurman

Indexer

Julie Kawabata

Layout

Minh-Tam S. Le

ARE YOU A BUSINESS USER OF EXCEL 2000 OR EXCEL 97?

MBA's Guide to Microsoft Excel 2000: The essential Excel reference for business professionals is the only book that specifically describes how you can more easily, more productively, and more powerfully use Microsoft® Excel 2000 in business.

QuickPrimers™ move you to professional proficiency in all Excel skill categories. The *MBA's Guide to Microsoft Excel 2000* begins at the beginning. If you need it, you first get friendly help on all the basics, including building simple worksheets and creating charts you can use for both analysis and presentation. If you don't need this help, you can easily skip it.

Step-by-step approach makes even Excel's most powerful tools easy to use. Once you've become comfortable with Excel, *MBA's Guide to Microsoft Excel 2000* moves you beyond the basics. You get easy-to-understand, jargon-free help on using all of Excel's business tools, including PivotTables, PivotCharts, Solver, BackSolver, and Small Business Manager.

EasyRefreshers™ let you build and maintain your business skills. As you advance, *MBA's Guide to Microsoft Excel 2000* moves on and describes how to use Excel's often poorly documented tools for statistical analysis, financial calculations, sharing corporate data, and optimization modeling. Discussions usually start with *EasyRefreshers™* that let you update old skills or acquire new core business skills.

Works for all business users. Written for anyone who wants to use Excel as a business tool for powering better business decisions, *MBA's Guide to Microsoft Excel 2000* works for MBA students, MBA graduates, Excel users with undergraduate degrees in business or a related field—and for anyone else who's serious about using Excel as a tool for making better business decisions.

Companion CD supplies starter and sample workbooks. The *MBA's Guide to Microsoft Excel 2000* companion CD supplies starter Excel workbooks for business planning, profit-volume-cost analysis, break-even calculations, capital investment budgeting, asset depreciation, and debt amortization so you get a head start on creating your own workbooks. The CD also supplies samples of all the workbooks discussed in the book.

496 pages, paperback, $39.95   Available at bookstores everywhere and at all online bookstores.
ISBN 0-9672981-0-5

DO YOU NEED TO GET YOUR PROJECT STARTED QUICKLY?

Written specifically for busy executives and project managers, *Effective Executives—Guide to Project 2000* walks you through the eight steps of organizing, managing and finishing your project using Microsoft® Project 2000:

Step 1: Learn the Language. Start here with a refresher on the language of project management, and Project 2000.

Step 2: Describe the Project. Describe your project in general terms, including start date, end date, and calendar of workdays.

Step 3: Schedule Project Tasks. Break your project down into component tasks, specifying task order and relationships.

Step 4: Identify and Assign Project Resources. Identify and then allocate project resources, such as people and equipment.

Step 5: Review Project Organization. Review your project for structural soundness and reasonableness.

Step 6: Present Project to Stakeholders. Present your plan to project team members and management.

Step 7: Manage Project Progress. Monitor progress and costs, assuring your project stays on course.

Step 8: Communicate Project Status. As the project progresses, keep project team members and other stakeholders apprised of the project's status and communicate important project information and changes.

ABOUT THE AUTHORS:

With more than 3,000,000 books sold in English, **Stephen L. Nelson** is arguably the best-selling author writing about using computers in business. Nelson's project management experience includes work in software development, commercial real estate development, and book publishing.

Pat Coleman is a technical editor and author who writes about intranets, the Internet, Windows, and Windows applications. The co-author of *Mastering Intranets, Mastering Internet Explorer 4*, and *Windows 2000 Professional: In Record Time* (all published by SYBEX), Coleman has worked as the editorial director of Microsoft Press, deputy editor at World Almanac and as a project analyst at Encyclopaedia Britannica.

Kaarin Dolliver is the managing editor of Redmond Technology Press and has been a contributing editor to a series of bestselling books.

304 pages, paperback, $24.95   Available at bookstores everywhere and at all online bookstores
ISBN: 0-9672981-1-3

ARE YOU AN EXECUTIVE USER OF THE INTERNET WHO NEEDS TO GET STARTED QUICKLY?

Written specifically for busy executives, managers, and other professionals, ***Effective Executive's Guide to the Internet*** provides a fast-paced, executive summary of the seven core skills you need to know to use the Internet at work, on the road, or at home:

Skill 1: Understanding the Environment. This skill gives you an overview of the Internet: what it is, how it works, and how it came to be.

Skill 2: Making Internet Connections. This skill provides step-by-step instructions for connecting your computer or network to the Internet.

Skill 3: Browsing the Web. This skill focuses on the Internet Explorer Web browser included with all the latest versions of Windows. We explain how a Web browser works and how to customize Internet Explorer.

Skill 4: Communicating with Electronic Mail. In this skill, we describe how to use Outlook Express, the mail and news reader included with Windows.

Skill 5: Using Search Services. This skill describes in detail how search services work and how you can best use them. A special topic at the end of this skill gives you some ways to get started gathering business information.

Skill 6: Understanding Other Internet Services. In this skill, we look at FTP, Telnet, Mailing lists, and using your computer as a fax machine and telephone.

Skill 7: Publishing on the Web. Learn how Web pages work, how to develop a Web strategy, how to set up your domain and your server, how to collect and create digital content, and how to create your Web pages.

ABOUT THE AUTHORS:

Pat Coleman writes about intranets, the Internet, and Microsoft Windows 2000. Formerly the editorial director of Microsoft Press, Coleman is also the co-author of the best-selling ***Effective Executive's Guide to Project 2000*** and ***Effective Executive's Guide to Windows 2000,*** both published by Redmond Technology Press.

Stephen L. Nelson: With more than 3 million books sold in English, Nelson is arguably the best-selling author writing about using computers in business. Formerly a senior consultant with Arthur Andersen & Co., he is also the co-author of ***Effective Executive's Guide to Project 2000*** and ***Effective Executive's Guide to PowerPoint 2000.***

288 pages, paperback, $24.95   Available at bookstores everywhere and at all online bookstores.
ISBN 0-9672981-7-2

ARE YOU AN EXECUTIVE USER OF WINDOWS 2000 PROFESSIONAL?

Written specifically for busy executives, managers, and other professionals, *Effective Executive's Guide to Windows 2000* provides a fast-paced, filtered executive summary of the seven core skills you need to know to use Microsoft Windows 2000 Professional at work, on the road, or even at home:

Skill 1: Understanding the Desktop. This skill explains logging on, using the Start menu, using the Taskbar, working with the desktop icons, and creating shortcuts.

Skill 2: Managing Files and Folders. This skill explains the Windows 2000 Professional file systems, including how to organize and protect your documents.

Skill 3: Printing. This skill shows you how to install and manage a local printer, how to print documents, how to customize the printing process, and how to install and use fonts.

Skill 4: Working on a Network. This skill gives you step-by-step instructions for setting up a small network, installing a network printer, setting up users and groups, and installing network applications.

Skill 5: Customizing Windows 2000 Professional. This skill suggests ways to customize everything from the display to the hardware.

Skill 6: Using the Internet. This skill tells you how to connect to the Internet and how to use Internet Explorer and Outlook Express.

Skill 7: Preventive Maintenance and Troubleshooting. This skill gives you guidelines for protecting the health of your computer, maintaining the system, and troubleshooting when a problem arises.

In addition, *Effective Executive's Guide to Windows 2000* also includes two appendixes that review the Windows 2000 Professional Accessories (including Address Book, NetMeeting, Notepad, WordPad, Fax Service, and Calculator) and explain how to use Windows 2000 Professional on a portable computer.

ABOUT THE AUTHOR:
Pat Coleman is a technical editor and author who writes about intranets, the Internet, and Microsoft Windows 2000. Coleman is also the co-author of the best-selling *Effective Executive's Guide to Project 2000* and *Effective Executive's Guide to the Internet,* both published by Redmond Technology Press.

304 pages, paperback, $24.95   Available at bookstores everywhere and at all online bookstores
ISBN: 0-9672981-8-0

ARE YOU AN EXECUTIVE POWERPOINT USER WHO NEEDS TO GET STARTED QUICKLY?

Written specifically for busy executives, managers, and other professionals, **Effective Executive's Guide to PowerPoint 2000** walks you through the seven steps of creating high-value, high-impact presentations:

> **Step 1: Learn the Logic.** Start here with an overview of what PowerPoint is and how it helps you make better presentations.
>
> **Step 2: Outline Your Content.** Create a textual list, or *outline*, of the messages and points you want to share.
>
> **Step 3: Add Objects.** Use tables, charts, and pictures to augment the information in your outline.
>
> **Step 4: Design Your Look.** Move past the substance of your presentation and address its appearance and "look" to create a professional presentation.
>
> **Step 5: Add Special Effects.** Use transitions, animation, sound, and video to enhance your presentation's impact.
>
> **Step 6: Prepare Your Presentation.** Prepare by creating speaker's notes, rehearsing, producing any handouts, and tailoring your presentation's slides for the presentation method.
>
> **Step 7: Deliver Your Presentation.** Deliver a successful, memorable presentation to your audience by comfortably using the appropriate PowerPoint tools.

More than just a book about Microsoft PowerPoint 2000, **Effective Executive's Guide to PowerPoint 2000** explains how to make effective, compelling presentations that audiences understand and remember.

ABOUT THE AUTHORS:

Stephen L. Nelson: With more than 3 million books sold in English, Nelson is arguably the best-selling author writing about using computers in business. Formerly a senior consultant with Arthur Andersen & Co., he is also the co-author of **Effective Executive's Guide to Project 2000**.

Michael Buschmohle: The President of APPLAUSE! Associates, Buschmohle has more than 40 years' experience delivering presentations to Fortune 500 companies and government agencies. He coaches CEOs, executives of high-tech firms, attorneys, U.S. mayors, and government officials on presentation and media skills. His clients have appeared on *Oprah, Good Morning America,* and the *Today Show.*

272 pages, paperback, $24.95   Available at bookstores everywhere and at all online bookstores
ISBN: 0-9672981-4-8

DO YOU WANT TO GET A FRONTPAGE WEB SITE UP AND RUNNING QUICKLY?

Written specifically for busy executives, managers, and other professionals, **Effective Executive's Guide to FrontPage Web Sites** walks you through the eight steps of designing, building, and managing Microsoft FrontPage 2000 Web sites:

> **Step 1: Learn the Logic.** Start here with a discussion about how the Web works, why Web sites make sense, and what makes a site effective.
>
> **Step 2: Develop a Content Strategy.** Identify the purpose of the Web site and the required content.
>
> **Step 3: Lay a Foundation.** Prepare the foundation of your Web site by getting a domain name and locating a company to host your Web site.
>
> **Step 4: Collect and Organize Your Content.** Collect existing content or develop new content—then create a central warehouse to store and organize this material.
>
> **Step 5: Create Your Web Site.** Set up your Web pages and other Web site components using FrontPage.
>
> **Step 6: Polish Your Pages.** Refine your Web pages to make them more effective and professional.
>
> **Step 7: Add Interactivity to Your Web Site.** Enhance your Web site through the addition of interactive features.
>
> **Step 8: Deploy Your Web Site.** Test and publish your Web site and then draw attention to it by submitting your site to search engines, sharing links, using newsgroups and list servers, and generating offline publicity.

More than just a book about FrontPage, **Effective Executive's Guide to FrontPage Web Sites** explains how to create business and nonprofit organization Web sites that really work.

ABOUT THE AUTHORS:

Stephen L. Nelson: With more than 3 million books sold in English, Nelson is arguably the best-selling author writing about using computers in business. Formerly a senior consultant with Arthur Andersen & Co., he is also the co-author of **Effective Executive's Guide to Project 2000** (Redmond Technology Press 2000).

Jason Gerend: Gerend, a freelance technical writer, has contributed to or co-authored a series of acclaimed and best-selling computer books, including **Effective Executive's Guide to Dreamweaver Web Sites** (Redmond Technology Press 2000).

304 pages, paperback, $24.95   Available at bookstores everywhere and at all online bookstores
ISBN: 0-9672981-3-X